Communications
in Computer and Information Science 2338

Series Editors

Gang Li , *School of Information Technology, Deakin University, Burwood, VIC, Australia*

Joaquim Filipe ⓘ, *Polytechnic Institute of Setúbal, Setúbal, Portugal*

Zhiwei Xu, *Chinese Academy of Sciences, Beijing, China*

Rationale

The CCIS series is devoted to the publication of proceedings of computer science conferences. Its aim is to efficiently disseminate original research results in informatics in printed and electronic form. While the focus is on publication of peer-reviewed full papers presenting mature work, inclusion of reviewed short papers reporting on work in progress is welcome, too. Besides globally relevant meetings with internationally representative program committees guaranteeing a strict peer-reviewing and paper selection process, conferences run by societies or of high regional or national relevance are also considered for publication.

Topics

The topical scope of CCIS spans the entire spectrum of informatics ranging from foundational topics in the theory of computing to information and communications science and technology and a broad variety of interdisciplinary application fields.

Information for Volume Editors and Authors

Publication in CCIS is free of charge. No royalties are paid, however, we offer registered conference participants temporary free access to the online version of the conference proceedings on SpringerLink (http://link.springer.com) by means of an http referrer from the conference website and/or a number of complimentary printed copies, as specified in the official acceptance email of the event.

CCIS proceedings can be published in time for distribution at conferences or as post-proceedings, and delivered in the form of printed books and/or electronically as USBs and/or e-content licenses for accessing proceedings at SpringerLink. Furthermore, CCIS proceedings are included in the CCIS electronic book series hosted in the SpringerLink digital library at http://link.springer.com/bookseries/7899. Conferences publishing in CCIS are allowed to use Online Conference Service (OCS) for managing the whole proceedings lifecycle (from submission and reviewing to preparing for publication) free of charge.

Publication process

The language of publication is exclusively English. Authors publishing in CCIS have to sign the Springer CCIS copyright transfer form, however, they are free to use their material published in CCIS for substantially changed, more elaborate subsequent publications elsewhere. For the preparation of the camera-ready papers/files, authors have to strictly adhere to the Springer CCIS Authors' Instructions and are strongly encouraged to use the CCIS LaTeX style files or templates.

Abstracting/Indexing

CCIS is abstracted/indexed in DBLP, Google Scholar, EI-Compendex, Mathematical Reviews, SCImago, Scopus. CCIS volumes are also submitted for the inclusion in ISI Proceedings.

How to start

To start the evaluation of your proposal for inclusion in the CCIS series, please send an e-mail to ccis@springer.com.

Nimmi Rangaswamy · Gavin Robert Sim ·
Pranjal Protim Borah
Editors

Human-Computer Interaction

Design and Research

15th Indian Conference, IndiaHCI 2024
Mumbai, India, November 7–9, 2024
Proceedings, Part II

 Springer

Editors
Nimmi Rangaswamy
IIIT Hyderabad
Hyderabad, Telangana, India

Gavin Robert Sim
University of Central Lancashire
Preston, UK

Pranjal Protim Borah 🆔
IIT Jodhpur
Jodhpur, Rajasthan, India

ISSN 1865-0929   ISSN 1865-0937 (electronic)
Communications in Computer and Information Science
ISBN 978-3-031-80831-9   ISBN 978-3-031-80832-6 (eBook)
https://doi.org/10.1007/978-3-031-80832-6

Preface

The IndiaHCI conference series is a premier platform for Human-Computer Interaction (HCI) in India. First organized in 2004, it has been held annually since 2010. Initially, groups of volunteers managed the conferences. HCI Professionals Association of India was formed as a not-for-profit organization in 2013, and it has since taken over the financial responsibility for the conference. Previous conferences were held in different cities in India, namely Mumbai, Bangalore, Pune, Delhi, Guwahati and Hyderabad.

IndiaHCI 2024 was the 15th edition of the conference. This year's conference featured multiple tracks, each undergoing a rigorous review process, as outlined below.

(I)Track - Papers:

The **Papers Track** offered a platform for researchers to showcase their work across diverse areas of HCI and design. It offered an opportunity to share pioneering and cutting-edge research, engage in meaningful scholarly discussions, and contribute to advancing these fields.

Each paper underwent a rigorous review process overseen by the two Paper Chairs (Program Committee Chairs). Each submission was assigned two Associate Chairs and two external reviewers, all of whom were experts in the field of HCI. The second Associate Chair (2AC) and the external reviewers provided blind reviews, while the first Associate Chair (1AC) contributed a meta-review. Each reviewer was tasked with evaluating approximately 3 to 4 papers. Authors of selected papers received the initial reviews and were given the opportunity to submit a 500-word rebuttal to address questions or clarify any misunderstandings raised by the reviewers. The final decision on whether to accept or reject a paper was made during a virtual Program Committee (PC) meeting, where the Paper Chairs, 1AC and 2AC discussed each submission, managing any conflicts. High-quality papers were accepted directly, while promising papers requiring revisions were shepherded and accepted only if the shepherd approved the changes.

All acceptances were conditional, contingent on potential changes suggested by the Papers Committee for the final camera-ready draft. The primary author of each accepted paper received detailed instructions on how to submit a final, publication-ready version of the paper. Formal acceptance into IndiaHCI was granted once authors revised their submissions and submitted a final draft for approval by the Program Committee.

There were 84 submissions for the Papers Track, of which 15 were accepted as full papers.

(2) Other Tracks - Game Design, Student Research Consortium, Posters and Demo, Artworks and Installations:

In addition to the Papers Track, the conference included other tracks such as Game Design, Student Research Consortium, Posters and Demos, and Artworks and Installations.

- The **Game Design Track** provided a platform for individuals passionate about games, game design, applied games, gamification, play and related areas to engage in the conference. This Track offered opportunities for participants to share insights, explore emerging trends and contribute to the evolving field of game design and play.

- The **Student Research Consortium Track** offered undergraduate, postgraduate and doctoral students unique opportunities to present their research efforts. This Track facilitated connections with peers, helped expand professional networks and provided valuable feedback and guidance from experts, supporting students in refining their research.
- The **Posters and Demos Track** provided students and professionals from diverse disciplines a platform to collaborate in advancing HCI for positive social impact. It offered an opportunity to present innovative ideas, connect with peers, expand networks and gain insights from domain experts, fostering cross-disciplinary engagement.
- The **Artworks and Installations Track** offered a space for artists and researchers exploring the intersection of art, design, technology and HCI. This Track aimed to build a community of creative professionals and researchers, encouraging exploration of how these fields converge and inspiring thought-provoking discussions on the role of art and technology in shaping human experiences.

The Game Design Track featured two categories: short papers and demos. The review process for short papers followed a double-blind format, while demos underwent a single-blind review. Each submission in both categories received three reviews—two individual reviews and one meta-review—by domain experts.

The Student Research Consortium and Posters and Demos Tracks followed a double-blind review process. Each submission received three reviews (two individual reviews and one meta-review) from domain experts. For the Student Research Consortium, the chairs also ensured that selected papers were shepherded, with final acceptance granted only upon the shepherd's approval.

Submissions for the Artworks and Installations Track were reviewed by the Track Chairs and a panel of domain experts through a single-blind peer-review process. Each paper in this track received three reviews—two individual reviews and one meta-review.

The final decision on accepting or rejecting papers in all these tracks was made during a virtual meeting where the track chairs discussed each submission. All acceptances were conditional, pending revisions suggested by the reviewers. The primary authors of accepted papers were provided with detailed instructions on submitting a final, camera-ready version. Formal acceptance into IndiaHCI was confirmed after authors revised their submissions and received approval from the track chairs.

- There were 48 submissions in the Game Design Track, of which three were accepted as full-length papers and six as short papers.
- There were 54 submissions in the Student Research Consortium (SRC) Track, of which seven were accepted as full-length papers and one as a short paper.
- There were 36 submissions in the Posters and Demos Track, of which four were accepted as full-length papers and two as short papers.
- There were 13 submissions in the Artworks and Installations Track, of which three were accepted as short papers.

October 2024

Nimmi Rangaswamy
Gavin Robert Sim
Pranjal Protim Borah

Organization

General Chairs

Pallavi Rao Gadahad	IIT Bombay, India
Bhakti Khandekar	eQ Technologic, India

Program Chairs

Khyati Priya	IIT Bombay, India
Pallavi Rao Gadahad	IIT Bombay, India

Paper Chairs

Gavin Sim	University of Central Lancashire, UK
Nimmi Rangaswamy	IIIT Hyderabad, India

Associate Chairs

Aakash Johry	IIT Delhi, India
Abhishek Shrivastava	IIT Guwahati, India
Anirudha Joshi	IIT Bombay, India
Ayushi Tandon	Mahindra University, India
Devanuj Balkrishan	JK Lakshmipat University, India
Dipanjan Chakraborty	BITS Pilani, India
Gautami Tripathi	Jamia Hamdard, India
Girish Dalvi	IIT Bombay, India
Jyoti Kumar	IIT Delhi, India
Khyati Priya	IIT Bombay, India
Malay Dhamelia	IIT Bombay, India
Mamata Rao	NID Ahmedabad, India
Manjiri Joshi	Swansea University, UK
Manohar Swaminathan	Microsoft Research, India
Naveen Bagalkot	Srishti Manipal Institute, India
Pallavi Rao	IIT Bombay, India
Pradipta Biswas	Indian Institute of Science, India

Pranjal Borah	IIT Jodhpur, India
Pratiti Sarkar	Paytm, India
Pushpendra Singh	IIIT Delhi, India
Ravi Mahamuni	TCS Research, India
Sandeep Athavale	TCS Research, India
Saurabh Tewari	IIT Delhi, India
Sayan Sarcar	Birmingham City University, UK
Seema Krishnakumar	IIT Hyderabad, India
Shrikant Ekbote	MIT Institute of Design, India
Siddharth Gulati	University of Manchester, UK
Wricha Mishra	MIT ADT University, India

Game Design Chairs

Malay Dhamelia	IIT Bombay, India
Sandeep Athavale	TCS, India
Aakash Johry	IIT Delhi, India

Student Research Consortium Chairs

Pranjal Borah	IIT Jodhpur, India
Saurabh Tewari	IIT Delhi, India

Posters and Demos Chairs

Sajan Pillai	DP World, India
Amaltas Khan	NID Vijayawada, India

Artworks and Installations Chairs

Jayesh S. Pillai	IIT Bombay, India
Harshit Agarwal	Adobe, India

Proceedings Team

Proceedings Chair

Pranjal Borah   IIT Jodhpur, India

Proceedings Coordinators

Sayali Tharali   IIT Bombay, India
Nimmi Thomas   IIT Bombay, India

Contents – Part II

Student Research Consortium

Posters and Demos

Artworks and Installations

Contents – Part I

Game Design

Dichotomy of Game Design and Gaming Practice: Examining Gaming Toxicity and Online Gaming Communities in India

Rahul Garg[1]([✉])[ID], Aditya Deshbandhu[2][ID], and Nimmi Rangaswamy[1][ID]

[1] International Institute of Information Technology, Hyderabad, India
`rahul.garg@research.iiit.ac.in, nimmi.rangaswamy@iiit.ac.in`
[2] University of Exeter, Exeter, UK
`A.Deshbandhu@exeter.ac.uk`

Abstract. This paper contributes to the expanding research on toxicity in online games, exploring the relationship between game design and player behaviours in India. Using an ethnographic approach and in-depth interviews with gamers, we capture firsthand accounts of toxic gaming experiences, delving into game design, game mechanics, and player interactions intersecting to shape player behaviours. While previous research on toxicity in gaming environments has largely focused on the role of game design, aspects of gender and, to a lesser extent, race, primarily within the context of the Global North, our study shifts the focus to India and, by extension, the Global South. We seek to uncover broader dimensions of gaming toxicity that go beyond design and gender. Our analysis examines the underlying factors contributing to the prevalence and persistence of toxic behaviours in Indian gaming environments by highlighting the influence of cultural and contextual elements in producing toxic behaviours. Expanding the scope of research to include these overlooked aspects, our study aims to provide a more comprehensive understanding of the complexities of toxicity in online gaming spaces within the Indian context.

Keywords: Online gaming · India · Toxicity · Qualitative Study · Player Behaviour

1 Introduction

The jury is still out in defining what toxic play in the online gaming world is - even if a player follows game rules, s/he could be considered toxic. The vagueness of defining and responding to toxicity in gaming propels us to search for new ways to understand toxic behaviour. Our study seeks to understand toxicity in Indian online gaming spaces, offering an ethnographic focus on players in gaming environments. We extend our analyses to broader aspects of game design and player interaction by examining factors that contribute to the performance and endurance of toxic acts and behaviours in gaming environments. We begin this

N. Rangaswamy et al. (Eds.): IndiaHCI 2024, CCIS 2338, pp. 3–22, 2025.
https://doi.org/10.1007/978-3-031-80832-6_1

by exploring the normalisation [6, 7] of toxicity in competitive gaming, moving on to examining design elements galvanising hostile behaviours often rationalised as part of the mediums competitive spirit. Through a qualitative study of players in India, we go beyond a plethora of existing research underscoring the relationship between game design and toxic gaming environments [6, 7, 18, 31, 36, 41]. To obtain a comprehensive view of toxic playing from thick interview data, we adopt a grounded, bottom-up approach to push the boundaries of exploring embedded gaming and social dynamics in online multiplayer gaming. From an in-depth analysis of data, we ask the following questions about game design influencing the intensity of toxic behaviours among gamers. 1. Understand the role of game design in aspects of gaming toxicity 2. Going beyond game design to explore the role of key actors in gaming [external influencers like streamers, game-based content creators, and YouTubers] in shaping behavioural norms and prevalent practices towards toxicity 3. Identify practices of in-game toxicity influenced by societal contexts. We begin by examining how game mechanics and design choices can be manipulated to hinder player progress, turning interactions into disruptions that intensify toxic behaviour. This highlights the challenge for game designers in balancing the reduction of toxicity while maintaining an engaging gaming experience. We elaborate game formats, particularly symmetric and asymmetric game design, shaping or directing toxicity through the intra-player dynamic of skilled players expressing hostility towards lesser-skilled teammates. An integral part of our findings is about going beyond game design to explore game dynamics wherein actors like broadcasters and streamers constitute what can be termed 'external entities' commanding vast audiences, setting trends in gameplay styles and communication behaviours, as well as defining norms that influence attitudes and behaviours of followers and levels of toxicity in the gaming community. Prominent streamers with substantial followings can dominate community spaces, overshadowing the voices and contributions of smaller, less powerful groups. Lastly, through interview and observational data, we attempt to re-frame the existing global understanding of toxicity in online game environments by specifically charting Indian online game spaces as economically and socially diverse, characterised by distinctions beyond gender.

2 Literature Review

Toxicity in gaming is understood both as an outcome of game design and the interplay between player interactions with other players and the game. These behaviours range from using hate speech and aggressive language to employing unfair advantages such as scripts and hacks, as well as disrupting game integrity by not completing objectives or deliberately underperforming [29]. Toxic players can be classified as stable, radicalized, pacified, or fickle-minded, based on the consistency of their toxic behaviours over time, augmenting the challenges of deafening and addressing toxicity [35]. Initial toxic acts in multiplayer gaming often produce subjective experiences, potentially triggering a retaliatory cycle among players [28]. Our main focus in this review of prior literature is the relationship between game design and gaming toxicity, going beyond game design to explore gender dimensions in toxic behaviours and social dimensions in gameplay leading to toxicity.

2.1   Game Design and Toxicity

Initial frameworks suggest that toxicity in competitive eSports is often rationalized as inherent to the competitive nature of the game, leading to its reinforcement and normalization within gaming communities [6]. Game design elements, like chat logs, can normalize toxic behaviour while discouraging positive communication [41]. Muting chat to avoid negativity can unintentionally isolate players from positive interactions [41]. Ambiguities in role identification and game objectives further fuel toxic interactions [18], while anonymity lowers accountability, fostering both positive and negative behaviours [7]. Experienced players, familiar with community norms, often engage in subtler forms of toxicity [36]. Post-game interactions can vary based on emotional states between winning and losing teams, commonly expressed through gg (good game). The size of live-streaming chat communities also affects the nature of toxic communication [42]. Additionally, the gap between the intended and actual use of reporting tools highlights challenges in managing in-game behaviour [31].

2.2   Symmetry vs. Asymmetry in Game Design

Symmetric games provide players with identical roles, abilities, and goals, creating a competitive environment that can unintentionally foster toxic behaviour as players compete on equal terms. In contrast, asymmetric games offer varied roles and objectives, promoting collaboration and strategic interdependence, which can reduce toxicity by emphasizing teamwork over competition [39,52]. By focusing on collective goals, these games shift attention from individual rivalry to shared success [25]. Studies on asymmetric design suggest that it fosters meaningful interactions and collaboration across different social contexts, creating a more inclusive gaming environment regardless of players' familiarity with each other [24,26].

2.3   Dynamics of Gender Toxicity

The under-representation of women in competitive gaming underscores the challenges to achieving gender inclusivity within the gaming industry. Gender dynamics within the gaming community reflect significant barriers rooted in longstanding masculine cultures impacting the career paths of female professionals and implications for women's inclusion in gaming [4,11]. Further studies [34,40] have examined how stereotypical gender roles hinder female participation. A fresh perspective on identity fusion within gamer cultures [33] explores merging individual and group identities to normalize exclusionary and hostile behaviours. Negative gender-related experiences can discourage womens participation and career aspirations in gaming, while positive interactions can enhance their sense of belonging and perseverance [50]. In response to toxic environments, many female gamers seek adaptive strategies, such as concealing identities, avoiding voice chat, and reducing visibility in gaming spaces [12]. Many female gamers are deterred from esports due to anticipated toxicity and higher performance standards, compounded by stereotypical roles that often reduce women to supportive functions, overshadowing individual skills [48].

Toxicity in online gaming spaces is a complex, context-dependent phenomenon shaped by both player interactions and the technical design of games [1]. Women, LGBTQ players, and other marginalized groups frequently face harassment and exclusion, exacerbated by the masculine culture, leading many to withdraw due to the lack of safe spaces [14]. Persistent hostility in gaming environments reinforces exclusionary dynamics, further marginalizing players belonging to non-cis genders. Research highlights women players' coping strategies like 'ludic mithridatism' building resilience to toxic behaviour to remain engaged in gaming spaces [1]. However, these coping mechanisms do not address the root causes of toxicity, which remain ingrained in gaming cultures. On platforms like Twitch, female streamers face gendered harassment, exemplified by the derogatory term 'titty streamers' reflecting deeper anxieties around gender, legitimacy, and labour within gaming [47]. Feminist and queer game studies argue for a shift toward more inclusive representation in games to combat these toxic environments. They emphasize the need for diversity beyond tokenistic portrayals of marginalized identities, advocating for meaningful representation [51]. However, while LGBTQ content is present in games like Undertale, it is often "straight-washed" by players and the broader gaming community, revealing the limitations of representation in challenging ingrained biases [46].

The overwhelming focus on gendered toxicity overshadows the reporting of other forms of toxicity, such as race-based abuse in online gaming. Prejudice against racial and ethnic minority groups arises from the overrepresentation of majority groups-predominantly male and white-in gaming communities in the Global North. This imbalance in online gaming spaces often contributes to racial toxicity. Racism in gaming [20] is not just historical but is entrenched in the programming logic that constructs games and facilitates play. With regards to the programming of racial bias In games [53]in the context of Pokmon Go, research reveals the game's augmented and inherently mobile-driven gaming was dangerous to marginalized players due to the games inability to understand that people of racial and ethnic minorities were not welcome in several areas. Building on this argument of accessibility, there is a dire need to decolonize games to render them more democratic and accepting of players from minority communities. Existing literature also highlights how gamers of colour have been neglected in favour of a white masculine movement [9] and thus underrepresented in games while facing mental distress [27]. Similarly, a hegemonic social hierarchy in online gaming can be a source of racial prejudice against gamers of colour [22].

The Paradox of GamerGate. GamerGate emerged in August 2014 as a contentious movement within the gaming community, initially sparked by accusations against developer Zoe Quinn. It quickly shifted focus to alleged ethical issues in game journalism and resistance to diversity in gaming. While supporters claimed to advocate for transparency, the movement became notorious for harassment campaigns targeting women in the industry, including developers, journalists, and critics. This sparked broader debates on gender, race, and sexuality in games, impacting discussions on inclusivity and toxicity in gaming culture [13]. Despite lacking central leadership, GamerGate displayed organized behaviour, including communication strategies and social media promotion, yet its internal contradictions were evident [54]. The movement's documents advocated respectful discourse but normalized aggressive actions, such as death threats [37]. Vivian James, a character funded by GamerGate supporters, was intended to represent the 'average gamer'. However, her portrayal, featuring a neutral stance and a "shut up and play" attitude, subtly reinforced the silencing of women's voices in gaming. Her green and purple colour scheme referenced a controversial 4chan meme, normalizing misogynistic attitudes [10]. GamerGate's harassment included doxxing, threats, and targeted efforts to discredit perceived opponents, such as pressuring companies like Intel to withdraw advertising from sites promoting feminist critiques of online games and gaming arenas. [44]. The movement's actions highlighted the ongoing struggle over inclusivity and exclusion within gaming cultures. The release of "Hogwarts Legacy" and associated controversies over J.K. Rowlings tweets, perceived as transphobic, ignited calls for boycotts, spotlighting issues of diversity and toxicity in gaming [17, 19]. Despite the boycott, the games commercial success raises questions about the separation of art from its creators and the efficacy of boycotts in effecting cultural change [23].

2.4   Gaming Environments and Toxic Behaviours

Motivations behind gaming are complex and influenced by game design and the gaming environment. Research reveals that video gaming provides men with avenues for social support and connection, debunking the notion of gaming as solely isolating [55]. Studies indicate social interactions within games contribute to building relationships, trust, and social capital, which are crucial for emotional support in competitive gaming environments [8,15,21,32] impacting individuality and team cohesion [30,43]. In the MMO games, interpersonal dynamics reveal how mutual dependence and players passion can drive both toxic and prosocial behaviours [57]. Power dynamics within games influence player behaviours, fostering prosocial action from a sense of responsibility or leading to toxicity from a sense of power. Game mechanics can trigger a spectrum of responses, from stress relief to engagement in 'dark play, where players explore self-actualisation through negative activities [3,5,38,49]. Dark play challenges traditional views on gaming experiences and the psychological impacts of game design, like risk-reward structures that induce cognitive biases, including loss aversion [5]. Coping strategies for toxicity vary; some players choose to ignore or mute negative behaviours, a reflection of normalised toxicity or the belief that it 'does not' merit reporting. Others manage frustrations by switching to less competitive games [2,43]. The concept of moral disengagement in gaming discusses how players rationalise inaction or acceptance of negative behaviours, perpetuating toxicity within the gaming environment [7].

3 Methodology

3.1 Procedure

Our investigation into online gaming toxicity employed a qualitative research framework, utilising in-depth, open-ended interviews to delve into the player experiences within diverse online gaming communities. Conducted from August 2023 to February 2024, this study engaged 14 participants from a technology institute in Hyderabad and various locations across Bangalore, rapidly urbanising mega-cities and tech hubs in South India. The selection of these sites was strategic, reflecting their status as a microcosm of Indias technological advancement and cultural diversity, factors crucial for understanding the social dynamics in online gaming spaces. We adopted snowball sampling participants, beginning with initial contacts at the institute and expanding through their recommendations. This method facilitated access to a broader network of gamers, though it often led to male-centric recommendations, a reflection of the predominance of male gamers and their social networks - a phenomenon not unique to India. The gender distribution at the technology institute, with female students making up about 20% of the student population, resulted in a predominantly [male interviewee pool with one female participant, highlighting the challenges women face in the male-dominated gaming communities [16,45]. The participant pool represents diverse social backgrounds and is connected to various gaming community networks, playing a wide range of games (Table 1).

Interviews were structured to foster a comfortable and open dialogue, beginning with rapport-building questions that encouraged participants to share their personal gaming experiences and perspectives on toxicity. As discussions progressed, we explored how perceptions of toxicity varied among participants based on skill levels, gaming experience, and the gaming community they belonged to. We also examined the influence of game design on toxic behaviours, investigating both games with balanced dynamics, where toxicity often arose from communication challenges and team conflicts, and games with large skill disparities, which tended to exacerbate stress, isolation, and intimidation among less powerful players. In terms of methodology, we utilised a systematic approach in our qualitative data analysis, employing open, axial, and specific coding techniques to identify themes, organise data around identified themes, and explore unique instances, ensuring a comprehensive representation of diverse perspectives. To enhance the robustness of our analysis, the three authors of this paper independently verified coding consistency. The first and second authors also engaged in co-playing and observational methods with participants, immersing themselves in gaming environments to observe and participate in real-time player interactions. The latter helped identify triggers and responses to toxicity. This approach continued until data saturation was achieved, providing an understanding of the dynamics within various gaming environments and styles. Our research offers insights likely generalisable across urban and semi-urban centres in India, a valuable addition to studies about gaming in the Global South, and offers a research-based narrative on the meaning and production of toxicity in gaming and social interactions that contribute to it.

3.2   Participant Background

This study engaged with a group of college students from a technology institute in Hyderabad and various locations across Bangalore, South India, with some diversity-one of the 14 participants is under 18, two are working professionals,

Table 1. Social Profile of Players

Player	Age	Education	Games	Experience and Rank
P1	20-22	Undergrad	Valorant, Halo, Skyrim	Plays mostly unrated; Gold in Valorant; retaliates to toxicity
P2	18-20	Undergrad	Terraria, Minecraft, Valorant, Overwatch	Plat 2 in Valorant; increases toxicity with play
P3	20-22	Undergrad	League of Legends	Competitive and casual modes; engages in derogatory language
P4	24	Graduate & Working	L4D, DBD, The Forest	Prefers co-op; maintains calm, rarely faces toxicity
P5	17 (Minor)	Undergrad	Cruelty Squad, Bioshock, DBD, CS2	Extensive FPS experience; quits due to toxicity
P6	30 s	Graduate & Working	R6 Siege, DBD	Mid-tier, casual competitive; chooses teams to avoid toxicity
P7	20-22	Undergrad (Non-binary)	Valorant, Overwatch, Phasmophobia	Silver in Valorant, Platinum in OW; responds when provoked
P8	20-22	Undergrad	Valorant, Overwatch, Assassin's Creed	Casual in Valorant, Platinum in OW; uses mute function
P9	20-22	Undergrad	CS, Valorant, R6 Siege	Mid-tier competitive; retaliates to toxicity
P10	20-22	Undergrad	Valorant, CS, Rocket League	Gold in Valorant; uses toxicity strategically
P11	20-22	Undergrad	CS, Valorant	Plat in Valorant, MG in CS; "toxic for fun"
P12	20-22	Undergrad	Valorant, Osu	Plat 3 in Valorant; handles toxicity by proving others wrong
P13	20-22	Undergrad (Female)	Valorant	Plat in Valorant; faces gender-based toxicity
P14	20-22	Undergrad	Rocket League, PUBG Mobile	Competitive in Rocket League; engages in toxicity

one is female, one is non-binary, and all participants are part of various online gaming communities. The participants are identified here as P1 through P14 to preserve anonymity. None of the participants in this study are paid competitive players; their involvement in gaming ranges from casual to competitive levels within the online gaming community.

3.3   Research Ethics

We were deeply aware of the ethical considerations when engaging participants in discussions on sensitive topics and experiences with toxic behaviour. Ensuring a careful balance of power dynamics, we emphasised participants autonomy, allowing them to express their views without the influence of our preconceived notions or biases. This approach was vital in qualitative research to ensure the authenticity and depth of the data collected. Adhering to ethical guidelines, we implemented a participant-centred method, prioritizing comfort, privacy, and agency. Each participant was comprehensively briefed on the studys objectives, the interview questions, and the broader implications of their contributions. This briefing aimed to secure informed and explicit consent before their participation in the study. Aware of the emotional sensitivities around discussing gaming toxicity, we established protocols allowing participants to opt out of the interview at any stage, ensuring they could decline to answer particular questions if they needed to. To protect privacy and confidentiality, we anonymised all identifying information, using pseudonyms and omitting specific details that could reveal identities. All data was securely stored and accessed solely by the authors to prevent unauthorized exposure. Furthermore, our study included a minor, introducing additional ethical complexities. We obtained informed consent from both the minor and their legal guardian, fully informing them about the studys nature and the handling of the information provided. We took extra measures in our analysis and reporting to safeguard the minors privacy and ensure confidentiality.

4   Findings

We explore the dynamics of online gaming toxicity as a consequence of game design and game mechanics and go beyond design elements to suggest external and cultural sources of toxic gaming behaviours.

4.1   Toxicity and the Role of Game Design and Game Mechanics

A key dimension of our findings identifies elements of game design manifesting and reinforcing acts of toxicity during gameplay, culminating in their acceptance as a widespread practice. We explored the removal of anonymity as an element of game design with our participants in reducing toxicity, drawing resistance and mixed feelings. P11 noted, "anonymity is crucial... because you will face personalised toxicity otherwise," while accepting "anonymity also breeds toxicity because people think they can say anything [and] get away with it". The above quote underscores the delicate balance between protecting users from targeted harassment and preventing the shield of anonymity from encouraging harmful conduct. For example, P2 observed the more time he spent playing a game like Val [Valorant], the more toxic he became. In such cases, the role of anonymity seems superfluous if the entire in-game experience triggers toxicity amongst its players. However, it is important to consider toxic edicts among players, as P3 observed: "If someone plays badly, we ask them to kill themselves."

P6 introduces a comparison between gaming and real-world sports, claiming the formers lack of personal connection and accountability due to anonymity helps exacerbate toxicity. P7 and P8 touch upon the protective aspects of anonymity, with P7 noting anonymity can prevent personalised toxicity' and P8 stating, 'being anonymous... helps in reducing the severity of toxic interactions'. Anonymity for P10 is important to avoid recognition, prevent prejudgement by other players, and manage social dynamics, expectations and morale of the team.. P5 emphasises, "In DbD, an option allows you to go 'Anonymous basically', helping in obscuring ones game statistics from other players, thereby reducing the likelihood of being singled out or harassed". P5 goes on to explain rather elaborately, "Game mechanics are the core rules and structures that dictate how a video game operates. These include how players earn points, advance through levels, and the abilities their characters possess, which altogether shape the strategic depth and playability of the game For example, in a game like 'Super Mario Bros' the mechanics involve jumping over obstacles, collecting coins, and using power-ups to enhance Marios abilities. This set of rules not only guides how the game is played but also defines the interaction between the player and the game world. In some instances, these fundamental elements can be manipulated negatively, affecting a players experience". P 11 and 12 take this argument further, observing the potential for abuse inbuilt into game design, "...utility grenades and molotovs can do 'area damage', disrupting gameplay and is akin to troll behaviour, as players deliberately act to disrupt or sabotage the game for co-players" In-game communication as a necessary element for player coordination can turn into abusive interactions. P7, explains " gaming environments can lead to extreme emotional states when you are losing in a game toxic messages can go through the roofand anger fills the chat room". The testimonies of players like P6, who recall instances of 'teammates...destroying each other showcase the level of urgency in game mechanics leading to toxic gameplay.

In multiplayer online games, teams comprise various roles, including offensive, defensive, and support players. Offensive players focus on attacking and securing objectives, while defensive players protect key positions and counter enemy advances. Support players, crucial to team dynamics, provide healing, buffs, and other forms of assistance to enhance the teams overall performance. Each role is pivotal, contributing to the teams strategy and success, carrying different levels of prestige and responsibility within the team hierarchy [56]. P13 suggests "... support players are at the bottom of the player hierarchy and face implicit harassment due to extreme impositions by team players compelling these support players to play for the team sometimes even if the support player gets killed". As P13 notes: "Sage, a support role in a game often relegated to women players in a team, has a timer for the roles capabilities and is severely constrained in executing key game manoeuvres." Such perceptions exacerbate toxicity towards support players, who are berated for not fulfilling unrealistic expectations of constant availability and support.

Toxicity from Symmetric/Asymmetric Game Formats. P6 notes about symmetric formats like 5v5, "There is definite toxicity that can happen, especially if you are playing with random people...certain players who get paired with low-rank players...if they dont perform very well, then these guys, the ones who are experienced, will turn against their own team". This quote showcases intra-team dynamics of skilled players having a propensity to express hostility towards lower-skilled teammates, hence perpetuating toxicity. On the contrary, we have asymmetric games, such as DbD (Dead By Daylight), which has a 1 v 4 format, directing toxicity at a single individual. Toxicity in this game format four is to one team is often similar to what is expected from symmetric games. P6s experience in such games indicates that "Killers...are just frowned upon; they're just hated...just because they play a certain way that the survivors dont like". The solo player faces collective antagonism from the opposing team, intensifying the experience of targeted harassment. The interviewee elaborates, "In asymmetric games...everybody in the other team gangs up on you", highlighting the isolating nature of toxicity as the individual player is pitted against a team of players. This form of toxicity is distinct in its directness and intensity, differing from the intra-team conflicts observed in symmetric games. Building on manifestations of toxicity across game formats, P5 says, ".. in asymmetric scenarios, the solitary role, such as the Killer in DbD, bears a unique burden, where the killer has to...look for a lot of things...which puts too much responsibility, too much pressure leading to scenarios where the player either give up entirely or...end up becoming toxic". This encapsulates the compounded stress and isolation precipitating toxicity in roles a player assumes in solitude against a team. The Killer in DbD, as P5 notes, is "all on his own" with an immense burden, leading to a higher propensity for either disengagement or toxic behaviour. This solitary struggle, devoid of team support, starkly contrasts with the shared responsibilities in symmetric games like CS (Counter Strike) where "the job...the responsibility is split into five," diffusing the potential for individual-focused toxicity". Conversely, symmetric games like CS present a "slimmer of hope" due to the distributed responsibility among team members, which can mitigate the intensity of toxic exchanges. P5 points out, "in CS...once you die you can give away information so the other players can split the responsibility," highlighting the communal aspect of dealing with in-game adversity and its potential to dilute toxicity by sharing the burden. He points out the potential for self-blame among players, exacerbating the toxic environment. He articulates, "If you say 'sorry my bad', then...people may take advantage of that", illustrating how admissions of fault can fuel toxic interactions. This aspect of toxicity, rooted in blame and criticism, whether self-directed or cast by others, underscores the complex interplay of personal accountability and team dynamics in fostering a toxic atmosphere in symmetric games.

4.2 Beyond Design: External Entities and Toxicity

In the context of online gaming communities, broadcasters and streamers constitute what can be termed external entities due to their position outside the immediate gameplay environment. These individuals, through platforms like Twitch and YouTube, command vast audiences by sharing gaming experiences, strategies, and personal commentary. Their public personas, gameplay styles, and communication behaviours can set trends, define norms, and influence the attitudes and behaviours of followers. Broadcasters/streamers play a significant role in influencing the level of toxicity in the gaming community. As noted by P8 observing significant streamers like 'Speed' known for energetic, aggressive and childish demeanour, "...we realise that while their behaviour is for humour and entertainment, it can be misconstrued by younger audiences as acceptable behaviour. ..a lot of streamers actually start yelling in the games as a funny thing...but people, like the 9-year-old kids, 12-year-old kids who watch, they actually think its cool." This imitation by younger audiences can lead to amplification of toxicity, especially towards younger players. However, as noted by various interviewees, streamers often advocate for civility among their audience, preventing them from raiding or performing harmful actions towards a group. However, the juxtaposition of public condemnation and private endorsement is highlighted by an interviewee: "Its funny, so two-sided...when you see...someone tweets out hey, I got this guy getting really toxic in my game'...they are like 'so snowflakey...but when a streamer is toxic to someone in their streams...the entire chat is laughing at them along with the streamer." Furthermore, the interviewee pointed out a concerning trend among streamers who, despite their significant following, indulge in toxic behaviour, setting a negative example for impressionable audiences: "I find streamers forgetting responsibility...they get carried away, and they call racial slur ...."

This observation calls out the critical role streamers play in shaping the audiences behaviour, creating echo chambers where toxic attitudes are not only replicated but also amplified within the gaming community. P4 provides insights into the dynamics of online personas, particularly focusing on a YouTuber named Grasshopper, known for his toxic content. P4 observes, "he gets more views, and he uploads videos in which hes toxic to other people." This highlights the appeal of negative behaviour in content creation and its impact on viewer engagement. P4 further comments on the nature of online interactions and their real-life implications, "I think people might not be toxic in real life, but if toxic behaviour is accepted by a wider audience and getting views, the streamer just continues to be toxic." This suggests a disconnect between online personas and real-life behaviour, underlining the complexity of digital identities. The discussion with P4 also delves into the potential consequences of such toxic behaviour within the gaming community. P4 mentions, "A streamer is representing not just himself but the community for the particular game they are streaming and cannot demean the game or the players because the audience will despise the streamer and game developers might impose a ban forever." The above emphasises the broader implications of a content creators actions on their community and the possible repercussions from game developers. P4 adds, "... despite these self constraining measures there is much toxicity to combat..."

The phenomenon of echo chambers within streaming communities points to the power streamers wield, shaping viewer perceptions and the tendency to support the streamers viewpoint, often to the detriment of critical discussions. P5 further illustrates the negative consequences of echo chambers with the example of a streamer, Dowsey, who influenced his communitys opinion by suppressing dissenting voices, He [Dowsey] actually talked about changing gaming mechanics, a few perks, a few skill features of his community followers who might persuade others into thinking that he was actually right in saying toxic things when they are not actually right...."

The power dynamics within streaming communities can significantly sway a teams opinion towards the streamer to the detriment of the games balance and community harmony. P5 recounts an incident in "Hogwartss Legacy" where players were forced to quit due to harassment initiated by another streamers community. This not only illustrates the direct impact of streamer-led echo chambers on individuals but also highlights the potential for organised harassment campaigns, further exacerbating toxicity within the gaming ecosystem.

P5 introduces the concept of r/place, a collaborative online art project, as an analogy to highlight both the unity and division within the gaming community. In r/place, participants from around the world come together on a digital canvas, placing a pixel every few minutes, collectively creating vast, intricate artworks. This initiative demonstrates the remarkable potential for collaboration and unity among diverse groups. However, P5 notes a concerning trend where prominent streamers with substantial followings can dominate these communal spaces. He observes, "There are these big streamers with their big fan base...they can essentially just choose to disregard the community and make art of their own." This behaviour mirrors wider dynamics within online communities and streamers, with larger audiences overshadowing the voices and contributions of smaller, less powerful groups.

4.3   Beyond Design Culture and Toxicity

The distinction between player-driven toxicity and gaming behaviours suggests that social norms and players cultural upbringing significantly influence in-game behaviour. P5 points to servers in India are often characterised by the use of "classic Indian derogatory terms,". This specificity in language use within Indian servers showcases cultural and regional factors shaping expressions of toxicity in gaming environments. Moreover, P5 contrasts the linguistic diversity observed in Asian servers, with the limitations encountered in games like Dead by Daylight, which predominantly feature English underscoring the challenges in moderating and understanding toxic behaviour across language barriers. Regional servers might lead to a normalisation of certain behaviours if commonly exhibited and accepted among the group. For example, what might be considered aggressive or inappropriate behaviour in one cultural context might be perceived differently in another, affecting how toxicity is experienced and reported.

The concentration of players from a specific region may also lead to an echo chamber effect, where prevailing attitudes and behaviours are reinforced without exposure to alternative perspectives. This can intensify both positive and negative aspects of gaming culture, including the manifestation of toxicity. Regional servers often emphasise cultural homogeneity and shared language, potentially enhancing communication and cooperation. However, they can also magnify localised prejudices or stereotypes, reinforcing specific behaviours, including toxicity. Stereotypes based on age impacted younger gamers subjected to dismissive and condescending attitudes. P6s reflections on the treatment of younger players allude, "If I was a 12 or 13-year-old kid yeah, then I am very likely to be toxic towards other people, and I know that because people in my own age group are also toxic .. so for me, thats a very normal thing to do Revelations of child teammates often result in disgruntlement from a team due to high pitched sound, the expectation of aggravated emotions, and lesser team coordination. This affects the credibility and respectability of younger players, affecting gaming behaviour.

P6 also added a national dimension to the discourse by pinpointing nationalities perceived to have higher levels or instances of toxicity,".. if you really want to see toxic behaviour in the media, play against Russians or Chinese. This showcases the notorious reputation given to certain groups based on their geographic areas. P6 further elaborates on the behaviour of Russian and Chinese players, stating, "These guys are very, very infamous for using cheats and ruining the fun for everyone and being unsportsmanlike. pointing to stereotyping nationalities as engaging in unfair practices, breaching the games integrity and detracting from game enjoyment and fairness and contributing to an understanding of the intersection of culture and national identities with gaming behaviours.

5   Discussion

5.1   Toxicity Beyond Design

The normalization of toxicity in competitive gaming environments is a complex phenomenon shaped by both game design and the cultural aspects of the gaming community. Our study views toxicity as a byproduct of competitive behaviour and design choices. Motivations behind toxic acts often arise from the interplay between game mechanics and player responses. Game design can also help mitigate toxicity through features like muting and reporting. Many of our interviewees noted that while games are inherently competitive, toxicity can sometimes be perceived as enhancing the competitive experience. Factors such as game type, pace, and whether its player-vs-player (PVP) or player-vs-environment (PVE) can influence levels of toxicity. Different gaming genres also vary in their susceptibility to toxicity, especially those that require constant communication and teamwork. AI in gaming is seen as an 'actor' contributing to toxic gaming practices. Shooter games, which give players direct control over actions, often lead to personal attributions of success or failure.In contrast, strategy games involving AI can disperse responsibility, locating 'blame' and deeming the AI as contributing to toxic behaviour.

While toxicity is generally acknowledged as harmful, the gaming community often normalizes bad behaviour, reflecting a sense of resignation that ranges from rejection to acceptance, and sometimes even participation in toxic activities. The complexity of toxicity dynamics in gaming is further highlighted by social changes and increased awareness of the need for cultural sensitivity. Cultural biases against certain groups, such as younger players and racial minorities, can shape interactions in gaming spaces.

From both the GamerGate discourse and our interviews, the integration of woke culture into gaming is often seen as contentious. Many gamers view gaming as an escape from reality, and inclusivity and tolerance are not always prioritized or supported by game mechanics. As P6 notes, "Wokeness seems very force-fed to a lot of people and it is still a controversial thing...if being woke and cultural tolerance takes over gaming where people find refuge from real life, then its like invading into their private time." Despite this, the inclusion of "woke culture" themes in franchises like Assassins Creed demonstrates how cultural influences are gradually entering game narratives and user experiences. The legacy of GamerGate continues to contribute to discussions on identity, creativity, and the sociopolitical dimensions of digital gaming spaces. These instances underscore the complex dynamics of gaming culture, where progress towards inclusivity coexists with ongoing debates and challenges. The GamerGate controversy has driven HCI researchers to examine how online gaming platforms handle culturally sensitive issues, emphasizing the role of design in managing community engagement and response. The resistance within gaming communities to the infusion of "woke culture" underscores the tension between cultural shifts and preserving gaming as an escapist activity, illustrating the complex interplay between gaming culture and broader societal debates.

5.2   Underscoring Dichotomy in Game Studies

The exploration of player motivations and behaviours in gaming reveals a complex interplay among individual psychology, game design elements, and the broader cultural contexts in which gaming occurs. Our study finds that the influence of context on the gaming communitys perception of toxic behaviour is a "double-edged sword" for several reasons. For instance, anonymity-a key feature of game design-serves both as a shield from targeted harassment and as a facilitator of toxic behaviour. Remaining anonymous can encourage open and uninhibited communication, allowing players to interact without fear of personal judgment or reprisal, which can be particularly liberating for individuals facing discrimination or bias in real life. However, anonymity can also detach players from social norms and accountability, leading to a 'disinhibition effect' prompting behaviours without concern for identification or real-world consequences.

Fast-paced games also exhibit this duality, driving player engagement but sometimes escalating to excessive passion resulting in inappropriate behaviours.

Disrupting or hindering the achievement of in-game goals is one such example of toxic behaviour. As previously noted, the complex nature of GamerGate reflects a dichotomy where positive engagement coexists with the acceptance of gender-based toxicity. The character Vivian James, for example, becomes a paradoxical figure-promoting female participation while simultaneously silencing female voices within the community. Team dynamics have shown hostility from skilled players toward less-skilled teammates, fostering intra-team toxicity and performance disparities, ultimately leading to negative gaming environments. Our study also highlights a divide within the gaming community: a vocal minority advocating for a less toxic environment, while a silent majority allowing toxicity to spread through indifference. Our interviews and observations reveal that while inclusivity in online gaming spaces can enrich and engage players, communication tools can also become conduits for toxic behaviour. Addressing this duality in game design is crucial for a holistic understanding of the phenomenon and for initiatives aimed at detoxifying the gaming community.

Personal narratives from participants in our study, along with their varied perceptions and experiences of in-game toxicity, strongly suggest that toxicity in online gaming stems from factors beyond the gaming arena. Many of these factors lie at the intersections of online and offline domains. Our exploratory study highlights the need to examine toxicity in Indian gaming spaces with a deep understanding of game architectures, mechanics, and player identities, including their socio-economic profiles. This suggests that both the game and the player contribute to the manifestation and codification of toxic behaviours in gaming. Future research should explore the multidimensional aspect of toxic gaming to find solutions in the diverse and rapidly evolving landscape of the global gaming community.

References

1. Adams, P.R., Scholl, B., Sommers, M.: Gaming Platforms as Chaotic Neutral?: Toxic Performance, Community Resistance, and Agonistic Potential. https://doi.org/10.5210/spir.v2023i0.13388, https://spir.aoir.org/ojs/index.php/spir/article/view/13388
2. Adinolf, S., Türkay, S.: Toxic behaviors in esports games: Player perceptions and coping strategies. In: CHI PLAY '18 Extended Abstracts. ACM (28–31 2018). https://doi.org/10.1145/3270316.3271545
3. Agrawal, V., Naik, V., Duggirala, M., Athavale, S.: Calm a Mobile based Deep Breathing Game with Biofeedback. In: Extended Abstracts of the 2020 Annual Symposium on Computer-Human Interaction in Play, pp. 153–157. CHI PLAY '20, Association for Computing Machinery, New York, NY, USA (2020). https://doi.org/10.1145/3383668.3419876,
4. Ahmadi, M., Eilert, R., Weibert, A., Wulf, V., Marsden, N.: Hacking masculine cultures - career ambitions of female young professionals in a video game company. In: Proceedings of the Annual Symposium on Computer-Human Interaction in Play, pp. 413–426. CHI PLAY '19, Association for Computing Machinery, New York, NY, USA (Oct 2019). https://doi.org/10.1145/3311350.3347186,

5. Bandeira Romão Tomé, N., Klarkowski, M., Gutwin, C., Phillips, C., Mandryk, R.L., Cockburn, A.: Risking treasure: testing loss aversion in an adventure game. In: Proceedings of the Annual Symposium on Computer-Human Interaction in Play, pp. 306–320. CHI PLAY '20, Association for Computing Machinery, New York, NY, USA (Nov 2020). https://doi.org/10.1145/3410404.3414250
6. Beres, N.A., Frommel, J., Reid, E., Mandryk, R.L., Klarkowski, M.: Don't you know that you're toxic: normalization of toxicity in online gaming. In: Proceedings of the 2021 CHI Conference on Human Factors in Computing Systems. pp. 1–15. CHI '21, Association for Computing Machinery, New York, NY, USA (May 2021). https://doi.org/10.1145/3411764.3445157,
7. Beres, Frommel, R.M.K.: Don't you know that you're toxic: Normalization of toxicity in online gaming. In: CHI Conference on Human Factors in Computing Systems (CHI '21), May 8-13, 2021, Yokohama, Japan. ACM, p. 15 (May 2021). https://doi.org/10.1145/3411764.3445157
8. Boustani, K., Tally, A.C., Kim, Y.R., Nippert-Eng, C.: Gaming the Name: Player Strategies for Adapting to Name Constraints in Online Videogames. In: Proceedings of the Annual Symposium on Computer-Human Interaction in Play, pp. 120–131. CHI PLAY '20, Association for Computing Machinery, New York, NY, USA (Nov 2020). https://doi.org/10.1145/3410404.3414259,
9. Bulut, E.: White masculinity, creative desires, and production ideology in video game development **16**(3), 329–341. https://doi.org/10.1177/1555412020939873, publisher: SAGE Publications
10. Butt, M.A.R.: Shut up and play: Vivian james and the presence of women in gaming cultures. The University of Sydney Thomas Apperley, Deakin University, p. 12 (October 2015)
11. Butt, M.A.R.: Lifeworlds for player 2: affective networks, affordances, and gender dynamics in player-computer interaction. In: Extended Abstracts Publication of the Annual Symposium on Computer-Human Interaction in Play, pp. 687–690. CHI PLAY '17 Extended Abstracts, Association for Computing Machinery, New York, NY, USA (Oct 2017). https://doi.org/10.1145/3130859.3133230,
12. Butt, M.A.R.: "i never use headsets": Women, wariness, and hypervigilance for the inevitability of online harassment in gaming culture. The 20th Annual Conference of the Association of Internet Researchers, p. 4 (October 2019)
13. Chatzakou, Kourtellis, B.C.: Measuring #gamergate: A tale of hate, sexism, and bullying. ResearchGate p. 6 (April 2017). https://doi.org/10.1145/3041021.3053890
14. Cote, A.C.: THE PROS AND PERILS OF INTERDEPENDENCE: FEMINIST ORGANIZING IN ONLINE GAME FORUMS . https://doi.org/10.5210/spir.v2021i0.11890, https://spir.aoir.org/ojs/index.php/spir/article/view/11890
15. Depping, A.E., Johanson, C., Mandryk, R.L.: Designing for Friendship: Modeling Properties of Play, In-Game Social Capital, and Psychological Well-being. In: Proceedings of the 2018 Annual Symposium on Computer-Human Interaction in Play, pp. 87–100. CHI PLAY '18, Association for Computing Machinery, New York, NY, USA (Oct 2018). https://doi.org/10.1145/3242671.3242702,
16. Deshbandhu, A.: Gaming Culture(s) in India: Digital Play in Everyday Life. Taylor & Francis (May 2020), google-Books-ID: zOrkDwAAQBAJ
17. Deshbandhu, A.: Gender equality, gaming industry have miles to go. Telangana Today (2023)
18. Deslauriers, P., Lafrance St-Martin, L.I., Bonenfant, M.: Assessing Toxic Behaviour in Dead by Daylight Perceptions and Factors of Toxicity According to the Game's Official Subreddit Contributors. Game Studies **20** (Dec 2020)

19. DiPlacido, D.: The 'hogwarts legacy' debate explained. Forbes (January 2023). https://www.forbes.com/sites/danidiplacido/2023/01/12/the-hogwarts-legacy-debate-explained/?sh=381d74336a32
20. Fickle, T.: The Race Card: From Gaming Technologies to Model Minorities, vol. 22. NYU Press. https://www.jstor.org/stable/j.ctv1f885vr
21. Freeman, G., Wohn, D.Y.: Social support in esports: building emotional and esteem support from instrumental support interactions in a highly competitive environment. In: Proceedings of the Annual Symposium on Computer-Human Interaction in Play, pp. 435–447. CHI PLAY '17, Association for Computing Machinery, New York, NY, USA (Oct 2017). https://doi.org/10.1145/3116595.3116635,
22. Gandolfi, E., Ferdig, R.E.: Sharing dark sides on game service platforms: Disruptive behaviors and toxicity in DOTA2 through a platform lens 28(2), 468–487. https://doi.org/10.1177/13548565211028809, publisher: SAGE Publications Ltd
23. Gematsu: Hogwarts legacy sales top 1.5 million. Gematsu (May 2023). https://www.gematsu.com/2023/05/hogwarts-legacy-sales-top-15-million
24. Jung, S., Wu, Y., Lukosch, S., Lukosch, H., Mckee, R.D., Lindeman, R.W.: Cross-reality gaming: comparing competition and collaboration in an asymmetric gaming experience. In: Proceedings of the 29th ACM Symposium on Virtual Reality Software and Technology, pp. 1–10. VRST '23, Association for Computing Machinery, New York, NY, USA (Oct 2023). https://doi.org/10.1145/3611659.3615698,
25. Karaosmanoglu, S., Rogers, K., Wolf, D., Rukzio, E., Steinicke, F., Nacke, L.E.: Feels like team spirit: biometric and strategic interdependence in asymmetric multiplayer VR games. In: Proceedings of the 2021 CHI Conference on Human Factors in Computing Systems, pp. 1–15. CHI '21, Association for Computing Machinery, New York, NY, USA (May 2021). https://doi.org/10.1145/3411764.3445492
26. Karaosmanoglu, S., Schmolzi, T., Steinicke, F.: Playing with friends or strangers? the effects of familiarity between players in an asymmetric multiplayer virtual reality game. In: Companion Proceedings of the Annual Symposium on Computer-Human Interaction in Play, pp. 76–82. CHI PLAY Companion '23, Association for Computing Machinery, New York, NY, USA (Oct 2023). https://doi.org/10.1145/3573382.3616079,
27. Keum, B.T., Li, X.: Coping with online racism: patterns of online social support seeking and anti-racism advocacy associated with online racism, and correlates of ethnic-racial socialization, perceived health, and alcohol use severity 17(12), e0278763. https://doi.org/10.1371/journal.pone.0278763, https://journals.plos.org/plosone/article?id=10.1371/journal.pone.0278763, publisher: Public Library of Science
28. Kordyaka, B., Laato, S., Jahn, K., Hamari, J., Niehaves, B.: The cycle of toxicity: exploring relationships between personality and player roles in toxic behavior in multiplayer online battle arena games. Proc. ACM Human-Comput. Interact. 7(CHI PLAY), 611–641 (Sep 2023). https://doi.org/10.1145/3611043,
29. Kou, Y.: Toxic behaviors in team-based competitive gaming. In: Proceedings of the Annual Symposium on Computer-Human Interaction in Play (CHI PLAY'20). ACM, New York, NY, USA, p. 12 (November 2020). https://doi.org/10.1145/3410404.3414243
30. Kou, Y., Gui, X.: Playing with strangers: understanding temporary teams in league of legends. In: Proceedings of the first ACM SIGCHI annual symposium on Computer-human interaction in play, pp. 161–169. CHI PLAY '14, Association for Computing Machinery, New York, NY, USA (Oct 2014). https://doi.org/10.1145/2658537.2658538,

31. Kou, Y., Gui, X.: Flag and Flaggability in Automated Moderation: The Case of Reporting Toxic Behavior in an Online Game Community. In: Proceedings of the 2021 CHI Conference on Human Factors in Computing Systems, pp. 1–12. CHI '21, Association for Computing Machinery, New York, NY, USA (May 2021). https://doi.org/10.1145/3411764.3445279,

32. Kou, Y., Gui, X., Kow, Y.M.: Ranking Practices and Distinction in League of Legends. In: Proceedings of the 2016 Annual Symposium on Computer-Human Interaction in Play, pp. 4–9. CHI PLAY '16, Association for Computing Machinery, New York, NY, USA (Oct 2016). https://doi.org/10.1145/2967934.2968078,

33. Kowert, R., Martel, A., Swann, W.B.: You are what you play: the risks of identity fusion in toxic gamer cultures. Games: Res. Pract. 1(2), 17:1–17:3 (2023). https://doi.org/10.1145/3604402,

34. Madden, D., Liu, Y., Yu, H., Sonbudak, M.F., Troiano, G.M., Harteveld, C.: 'Why Are you playing games? you are a girl!: exploring gender biases in esports. In: Proceedings of the 2021 CHI Conference on Human Factors in Computing Systems, pp. 1–15. CHI '21, Association for Computing Machinery, New York, NY, USA (May 2021). https://doi.org/10.1145/3411764.3445248,

35. Mall, Nagpal, S.A.J.J.: Four types of toxic people: Characterizing online users' toxicity over time. Proceedings of the 11th Nordic Conference on Human-Computer Interaction: Shaping Experiences, Shaping Society (NordiCHI'20), October 25-29, 2020, Tallinn, Estonia, p. 11 (October 2020). https://doi.org/10.1145/3419249.3420142

36. Martens, Shen, I.K.: Toxicity detection in multiplayer online games. IEEE, p. 6 (2016). https://doi.org/10.5555/2984075.2984080

37. Massanari, A.: #gamergate and the fappening: How reddit's algorithm, governance, and culture support toxic technocultures. Sage Pub, p. 18 (2017). https://doi.org/10.1177/1461444815608807

38. Memeti, Z., Brühlmann, F., Perrig, S.A.C.: LoL, Why do you even play? validating the motives for online gaming questionnaire in the context of league of legends. In: Extended Abstracts of the 2022 Annual Symposium on Computer-Human Interaction in Play, pp. 81–86. CHI PLAY '22, Association for Computing Machinery, New York, NY, USA (2022). https://doi.org/10.1145/3505270.3558350, https://dl.acm.org/doi/10.1145/3505270.3558350

39. Moriarty, E.H., Perriman, N., Rutledge, J., Taylor, J., Graham, T.N.: Increasing player coupling in an asymmetric racing game. In: Companion Proceedings of the Annual Symposium on Computer-Human Interaction in Play, pp. 306–311. CHI PLAY Companion '23, Association for Computing Machinery, New York, NY, USA (Oct 2023). https://doi.org/10.1145/3573382.3616059,

40. O'Keeffe, E., Riordan, E., Loudoun, F., Boyle, B.: Understanding the Social Dividends and Risks for Female Gamers in Online Spaces. In: Extended Abstracts of the 2022 Annual Symposium on Computer-Human Interaction in Play, pp. 215–220. CHI PLAY '22, Association for Computing Machinery, New York, NY, USA (Nov 2022). https://doi.org/10.1145/3505270.3558347,

41. Poeller, S., Dechant, M.J., Klarkowski, M., Mandryk, R.L.: Suspecting sarcasm: how league of legends players dismiss positive communication in toxic environments. Proc. ACM Human-Comput. Interact. 7(CHI PLAY), 1–26 (2023). https://doi.org/10.1145/3611020

42. Poyane, R.: Toxic communication during streams on Twitch.tv. The case of Dota 2. In: Proceedings of the 22nd International Academic Mindtrek Conference, pp. 262–265. Mindtrek '18, Association for Computing Machinery, New York, NY, USA (2018). https://doi.org/10.1145/3275116.3275152

43. van Rhenen, J.W., Centeio Jorge, C., Matej Hrkalovic, T., Dudzik, B.: Effects of social behaviours in online video games on team trust. In: Extended Abstracts of the 2022 Annual Symposium on Computer-Human Interaction in Play, pp. 159–165. CHI PLAY '22, Association for Computing Machinery, New York, NY, USA (Nov 2022). https://doi.org/10.1145/3505270.3558316,

44. Romano, A.: What we still haven't learned from gamergate. https://www.vox.com/culture/2020/1/20/20808875/gamergate-lessons-cultural-impact-changes-harassment-laws

45. Roy, D., Deshbandhu, A.: Anxious postcolonial masculinity in online video games: race, gender and colonialism in Indian digital spaces. Gender, Place & Culture **29**(1), 104–129 (2022). https://doi.org/10.1080/0966369X.2020.1858030 publisher: Routledge

46. Ruberg, B.: Straight-washing "undertale": Video games and the limits of LGBTQ representation **28**. https://doi.org/10.3983/twc.2018.1516, https://journal.transformativeworks.org/index.php/twc/article/view/1516

47. Ruberg, B., Cullen, A.L.L., Brewster, K.: Nothing but a "titty streamer": legitimacy, labor, and the debate over women's breasts in video game live streaming **36**(5), 466–481. https://doi.org/10.1080/15295036.2019.1658886, publisher: NCA Website

48. Ruotsalainen, M., Friman, U.: "there are no women and they all play mercy": Understanding and explaining (the lack of) women's presence in esports and competitive gaming, p. 14 (2018). https://doi.org/10.7202/1084839ar

49. Seaborn, K., Iseya, S.: Meaningful play and malicious delight: exploring maldaimonic game UX. In: Companion Proceedings of the Annual Symposium on Computer-Human Interaction in Play, pp. 174–180. CHI PLAY Companion '23, Association for Computing Machinery, New York, NY, USA (2023). https://doi.org/10.1145/3573382.3616095, https://dl.acm.org/doi/10.1145/3573382.3616095

50. Shaer, O., Westendorf, L., Knouf, N.A., Pederson, C.: Understanding gaming perceptions and experiences in a women's college community. In: Proceedings of the 2017 CHI Conference on Human Factors in Computing Systems, pp. 1544–1557. CHI '17, Association for Computing Machinery, New York, NY, USA (May 2017). https://doi.org/10.1145/3025453.3025623,

51. Shaw, A.: Gaming at the edge - google books. https://www.google.co.in/books/edition/Gaming_at_the_Edge/GzB0DwAAQBAJ?hl=en&gbpv=0

52. Smilovitch, M., Lachman, R.: BirdQuestVR: A cross-platform asymmetric communication game. In: Extended Abstracts of the Annual Symposium on Computer-Human Interaction in Play Companion Extended Abstracts, pp. 307–313. CHI PLAY '19 Extended Abstracts, Association for Computing Machinery, New York, NY, USA (Oct 2019). https://doi.org/10.1145/3341215.3358246,

53. Trammell, A.: Decolonizing play **39**(3), 239–246. https://doi.org/10.1080/15295036.2022.2080844,, publisher: NCA Website

54. Trice, M.: Putting gamergate in context: How group documentation informs social media activity. ACM, p. 5 (2015). https://doi.org/10.1145/2775441.2775471

55. Vella, K., Johnson, D., Mitchell, J.: Playing support: social connectedness amongst male videogame players. In: Proceedings of the 2016 Annual Symposium on Computer-Human Interaction in Play Companion Extended Abstracts, pp. 343–350. CHI PLAY Companion '16, Association for Computing Machinery, New York, NY, USA (Oct 2016). https://doi.org/10.1145/2968120.2987734, https://dl.acm.org/doi/10.1145/2968120.2987734

56. Williams, J.P., Kirschner, D., Suhaimi-Broder, Z.: Structural roles in massively multiplayer online games: a case study of guild and raid leaders in world of warcraft. In: Symbolic Interaction and New Social Media, Studies in Symbolic Interaction, vol. 43, pp. 121–142. Emerald Group Publishing Limited (2014). https://doi.org/10.1108/S0163-239620140000043016, https://doi.org/10.1108/S0163-239620140000043016
57. Zhu, Z., Zhang, R., Qin, Y.: Toxicity and prosocial behaviors in massively multiplayer online games: The role of mutual dependence, power, and passion. J. Comput.-Mediated Commun. **27**(6), zmac017 (2022). https://doi.org/10.1093/jcmc/zmac017, https://academic.oup.com/jcmc/article/doi/10.1093/jcmc/zmac017/6700672

How Does Games User Research Measure and Guide Haptic Experience Design? A Critical Review

Saptarshi Samanta$^{(\boxtimes)}$ ⓘ, Sharmistha Banerjee ⓘ, and Pankaj Upadhyay ⓘ

Indian Institute of Technology Guwahati, Guwahati, India
saptarshi.samanta@iitg.ac.in

Abstract. Games User Research (GUR) is an established but relatively young field that explores and evaluates the interaction between players and digital games. Several elements in a digital game affect the player experience. Engagement of the sensory modalities is one such element that can affect the player experience. Digital game developers are moving beyond just engaging the visual and aural modalities. They are striving to provide players with a multimodal experience, such as engaging the sense of touch through haptics or, more recently, the sense of smell. It remains to be understood if the various methods in GUR can evaluate or guide the design of multimodal player experiences. In this paper, we critically review GUR methods and assess if these methods can determine the effect of the haptic modality on player experience. We reviewed literature from the Scopus database to identify the various GUR methods, the intent of those methods, key features, types of sensory modalities evaluated and if there is a scope to assess or guide the effects of the haptic modality on player experience. We observe that GUR has not significantly assessed the impact of the haptic modality on player experience. There is also a lack of haptic experience evaluation tools and methods in the context of digital games. For GUR, this presents an opportunity to utilize the insights from existing player experience evaluation toolkits and methods and expand the player experience evaluation process by developing new haptic experience evaluation tools or methods for digital games.

Keywords: Games User Research · GUR · haptic experience · game design

1 Introduction

Research to understand the relationship between player experience and game design has existed for almost as long as the game industry. Only in the last decade has Games User Research (GUR) gained formal recognition as a discipline (Zammitto, 2018). GUR is "an evidence-driven, powerful process that helps designers create better gameplay experiences by finding weaknesses in the design and structure of games across all phases of their life cycle, from early designs, through prototypes, and after launch" (Drachen et al., 2018). In the present day, the development of digital games is moving beyond engaging just the visual and aural modalities of the players. Researchers, game designers

© The Author(s), under exclusive license to Springer Nature Switzerland AG 2025
N. Rangaswamy et al. (Eds.): IndiaHCI 2024, CCIS 2338, pp. 23–38, 2025.
https://doi.org/10.1007/978-3-031-80832-6_2

and developers are striving to provide players with a multimodal sensory experience (Min et al., 2021). Adding the haptic modality to improve the player experience is one such method to enhance the multimodal experience of players. Research has established that the addition of haptic modalities enhances the player experience (Singhal et al., 2021), (Melo et al., 2022). Zyda (2005) emphasizes the importance of adding the haptic modality along with the visual and aural modalities and its positive impact on immersion. This necessitates having established haptic experience evaluation methods or processes to evaluate their effect on player experience and provide insights on improving the haptic experience design. However, amongst the various GUR methods available to researchers and game designers, there seemed to be a lack of clarity about which GUR methods would best suit haptic experience evaluation in different contexts. Our research question that emerged from this line of enquiry is:

Which GUR methods are suitable for evaluating the effects of the haptic modality on player experience?

Schneider et al. (2017), who first coined the term "HaXD" or haptic experience design, opined on the need to develop a haptic design language to improve communication among multidisciplinary team members and clients. The answer to the above research question will contribute to the haptic language design creation process by providing researchers and game designers with insights into the suitability of different GUR methods and processes in evaluating the haptic experience of players.

The rest of this paper will include five sections. In Sect. 2, we will be discussing about related work. Section 3 will cover the methodology adopted for the critical review. Sections 4 and 5 are for disclosing our results and discussing relevant insights. We conclude our paper in Sect. 6.

2 Related Work

Haptic modalities have been around for a considerable time (Shim et al., 2020a). We see the first introduction of haptic modality in a handheld controller as a "rumble pack" by Nintendo in 1997 (Söderström et al., 2022). Though GUR was not a well-known or established field at that time, it is imperative to know how the effects of various haptic modalities on users or players are evaluated in different contexts and what instrumentation and assessment techniques were used. Hamam et al. (2014) highlights the need to have measures for users' perception and psychological and physiological states to assess the user experience effectively in relation to haptic virtual environments. In the field of haptic experience design, haptic experience designers reported using a variety of psychological and human factor techniques like semantic differential scales, factor analysis and recording the meaning that users found in haptic sensations as a part of the haptic experience design process (Schneider et al., 2017). Using focus groups, surveys, and self-developed scales related to experiential themes are other ways haptic designers evaluate their designs' haptic experience (Kim et al., 2020).

In research related to developing and evaluating different types of haptic devices in the context of digital games, we observe various haptic modality evaluation methods similar to those used in GUR. However, these methods are context-specific and are challenging to generalize. In Table 1, we discuss the various haptic modality evaluation methods used for different types of haptic devices identified from the literature. We also identify the type of haptic modality present in the haptic devices and the analytical tools used to evaluate the user experience data related to the haptic modality and the associated apparatus.

Table 1. Haptic modality evaluation in haptic devices

Ref	Type of haptic feedback	Haptic modality evaluation method	Analytical method used	Instrumentation used
(Singhal et al., 2021)	*vibro-tactile*	*Subscales from Player experience inventory (PXI) for player experience Customized questionnaire to evaluate haptic experience*	*Friedman's test for significance testing Cohen's D test for effect size*	*Custom built ios App iphone 8 or newer*
(Ryu et al., 2021)	*Force-feedback*	*User feedback collected on a 7point Likert Scale*	*Wilcoxon Signed rank test*	*"Vive Pro HMD"*
(Shim et al., 2020b)	*Force-feedback*	*User interview*	–	*Prototype game pad (FS pad) Laptop with prototype game*
(Martínez et al., 2014)	*vibro-tactile*	*Olsen's utility assessment method*	–	*Prototype glove like device VITAKI -software for creating prototype vibration patterns*
(Honegger et al., 2021)	*vibro-tactile*	*Scalometer EZ Scale User interview*	*t-test for continuous variables chi-square for categorical variables Wilcoxon signed-rank test*	*Silent chamber - test room Projector for visuals Headphones for sound Vibration chair for vibration Fan to produce flowing air effect*

(continued)

Table 1. (*continued*)

Ref	Type of haptic feedback	Haptic modality evaluation method	Analytical method used	Instrumentation used
(Ahmed et al., 2017)	*vibro-tactile Force-feedback*	*Biosensors (ECG, EDA, ACC) Self-reported data FUGA Questionnaire (Social presence module)*	*RMANOVA*	*Leap Motion Occulus Rift VR HMD*
(Escobar-Castillejos et al., 2020)	*vibro-tactile Force-feedback*	*Perception Questionnaire and Likert Scale*	*Binomial Test T-test*	*Geo-magic touch Novint Falcon*
(Boldt et al., 2018)	*vibro-tactile*	*NASA TLX Intrinsic Motivation Inventory (interest-enjoyment and tension pressure subscales) PANAS*	*Mean and Standard Deviation*	*VR HMD*
(Söderström et al., 2022)	*vibro-tactile*	*MEC-Spatial Presence Questionnaire (altered)*	*2 sided T-test*	*Woojer vest edge (haptic vest) PS4 Controller*
(Qiu et al., 2022)	*vibro-tactile*	*Psychophysical tests*		*Soft stimulation actuator Motion sensors*
(Galofaro et al., 2022)	*Force-feedback*	*Performance evaluation*	*RANOVA Shapiro-Wilk Test Mauchly Test*	*Teslasuit Occulus Rift S*
(Tsai et al., 2022)	*Force-feedback (impact) vibro-tactile*	*Custom questionnaire User interview*	*RMANOVA Bonferroni correction*	*Impact Vest (prototype) Vive Pro HMD*
(Suzuki et al., 2021)	*Tactile*	*User study with custom questionnaire*	*Wilcoxon signed-rank test RMANOVA*	*HapticBots (prototype)*

(*continued*)

Table 1. (*continued*)

Ref	Type of haptic feedback	Haptic modality evaluation method	Analytical method used	Instrumentation used
(Su et al., 2021)	*Force-feedback*	*User study with custom questionnaire*	*One-way ANOVA Tukey's HSD test*	*Haptic gun (prototype) Blindfold Noise cancellation headphones Computer*

Though the list of haptic devices identified in the above table is not exhaustive, we can observe interesting patterns related to haptic modality evaluation. Table 1 shows that vibrio-tactile and force feedback are the two prevalent haptic modalities used in most haptic devices. No standard or common questionnaires are used in the haptic experience evaluation for the haptic devices. Custom questionnaires seem to be a common approach and are context dependent. Furthermore, most of the studied haptic devices have been developed and analyzed for use in relation to VR, and no relation to GUR evaluation methods has been observed.

Game development strives to provide players with a multimodal experience. GUR is essential in evaluating the player experience (Drachen et al., 2018) which makes it an integral component at every stage of the game development process. Medlock (2018a) has mapped some of the most common GUR methods to different stages of the game development process and has briefly defined these methods and their advantages and disadvantages. However, since the listed methods were inclined more towards the game development process, it was unclear how these methods could evaluate the effect of different sensory modalities on player experience. Several research publications associated with haptic device design, virtual reality and digital games have established that adding haptic modalities improves player experience (Lin et al., 2021; Melo et al., 2022; Singhal et al., 2021). However, the research literature shows that how the haptic modality affects the player experience is not clearly established. GUR can shed light on this aspect, but of the variety of GUR methods available, identifying which methods will be best to evaluate the effects of the haptic modality on player experience is a challenge. In this paper, we attempt to address this challenge in the following sections.

3 Methodology

We selected the Scopus database to identify the relevant literature related to GUR. We used two keyword search strings to determine the relevant literature. The first search string used was "Games User Research" OR GUR. We excluded research literature related to material science; biochemistry, genetics, and molecular biology; Agricultural and biological sciences; Veterinary; pharmacology, toxicology, and pharmaceuticals; earth and planetary sciences; energy; chemical engineering; chemistry; immunology and microbiology; economics, econometrics, and finance. The search string generated 696 results. The second search string used was game* AND user AND research AND haptic*, which generated 130 results. The results included articles, conference papers, book chapters, reviews, editorials, books, and short surveys as of August 2023. We used the following inclusion criteria to further sift through the search results generated from the two keyword search strings:

- Haptic experience in the context of digital games
- Player experience evaluation in the context of digital games
- Multimodal experiences in the context of digital games

We isolated 99 search results for an in-depth assessment using the above inclusion criteria. The shortlisted results included articles, conference papers, book chapters, reviews, editorials, and books in the English language. In the critical review, we attempted to identify the various GUR methods, the intent of those methods, key features, types of sensory modalities evaluated, and whether there is a scope to assess the effects of the haptic modality on player experience.

4 Results

This section will present our assessment of the different types of GUR methods identified for our critical review and the provisions for evaluating the effects of different sensory modalities on player experience. We are particularly interested in how the effects of the haptic modality on player experience are evaluated. Reviewing the selected research literature, we observed that the GUR methods can be broadly broken down into two groups: questionnaire-based and biometric.

We identified 15 GUR methods, which were questionnaire-based and are listed in Table 2.

Analyzing the research literature on biometric methods, we observed that these methods require very little manual intervention during data acquisition. The measurement methods primarily focused on measuring the emotional state and arousal state of players when engaged with a digital game. Players' emotional and arousal states are usually determined by observing changes in facial expressions, body posture, and physiological changes. Physiological data in GUR is usually gathered through electromyography (EMG), electrodermal activity (EDA), electrocardiography (EKG), and electroencephalography (EEG).

Table 2. Questionnaire-based GUR methods

GUR Method	Main purpose of method	Empirically validated	Key features	Types of Sensory Modalities evaluated	Scope to assess effects of haptic modality
Mini PXI toolkit (Haider et al., 2022)	*Short version of PXI method to make the player experience evaluation more efficient and easier*	Yes	*–Qualitative method* *–Supports efficient integration of the measure with existing GUR processes* *–Recommendations about when to use the miniPXI and when to use the longer PXI*	*Visual* *Aural*	*No*
HX Model (Kim et al., 2020)	*Identify different factors related to haptic modality that can influence the experience of players*	No	*–Theoretical model* *–Propose design parameters, usability requirements, and experiential factors as key factors for developing a haptic experience*	Haptic	Yes
Player Experience Inventory (PXI) (Abeele et al., 2020)	*Measures player experience at the level of functional consequences and psychosocial consequences*	Yes	*–Qualitative method* *–Evaluates how game design choices affect player action during gameplay*	*Visual* *Aural*	*No*
CORGIS (Denisova et al., 2020)	*Assess the extent of perceived challenge experienced by players*	Yes	*–Quantify and evaluate the challenge experience of players* *–Four subscales: Cognitive, Emotional, Performative, Decision-making*	*Visual*	*No*

(*continued*)

Table 2. (*continued*)

GUR Method	Main purpose of method	Empirically validated	Key features	Types of Sensory Modalities evaluated	Scope to assess effects of haptic modality
Ubisoft Perceived Experience Questionnaire (UPEQ) (Azadvar et al., 2018)	*Evaluate the satisfaction of different basic psychological needs by different digital games*	Yes	*–Has three subscales: autonomy, competence, relatedness* *–21-item questionnaire* *–Physical presence is an experimental scale*	*Not explicitly mentioned*	Yes
Game User Experience Satisfaction Scale (GUESS) (Phan et al., 2016)	*Comprehensive gaming scale suitable for playtesting and game assessment purposes*	Yes	*–55 item questionnaire with 9 subscales: usability/playability, narratives, play engrossment, enjoyment, creative freedom, audio aesthetics, personal gratification, social connectivity, visual aesthetics*	*Visual*	Yes
Contextual Gameplay Experience Model (Engl & Nacke, 2013)	*Measures player experience in a mobile context, also suitable for other digital game platforms*	Yes	*–Player experience is influenced by internal factors and external factors* *–Presents three layers affecting player experience: playability, player experience, contextual gameplay experience*	*Not explicitly mentioned*	Yes
Core Elements of the Gaming Experience Questionnaire (CEGEQ) (Calvillo-Gámez et al., 2010)	*Measures the player experience in relation to the presence of different core elements of gaming experience*	No	*–Can assess the player experience when using different interaction methods for the same game*	*Visual Aural*	Yes

(*continued*)

Table 2. (*continued*)

GUR Method	Main purpose of method	Empirically validated	Key features	Types of Sensory Modalities evaluated	Scope to assess effects of haptic modality
Game Engagement Questionnaire (GEQ) (Brockmyer et al., 2009)	*Measures levels of engagement while playing digital games*	*No*	*–Measures player level of engagement in 4 constructs, namely absorption, flow, presence, and immersion*	*Not explicitly mentioned*	*Yes*
Immersive Experience Questionnaire (IEQ) (Jennett et al., 2008)	*Evaluate a player's sense of immersion, flow, presence and cognitive absorption*	*Yes*	*–Measure Immersion subjectively as well as objectively* *–Provides an immersion score and more quantitative objective measures for immersion*	*Visual*	*No*
User Experience Questionnaire (UEQ) (Laugwitz et al., 2008)	*Quickly measure user experience simply and promptly and gather comprehensive user experience data*	*Yes*	*–26-item questionnaire Sub-scales are attractiveness, perspicuity, dependability, efficiency, novelty, and stimulation*	*Not explicitly mentioned*	*Yes*
Player Experience Need Satisfaction Questionnaire (PENS) (Ryan et al., 2006)	*Measures needs satisfaction for players*	*Yes*	*–26-item questionnaire Sub-scales are attractiveness, perspicuity, dependability, efficiency, novelty, and stimulation*	*Not explicitly mentioned*	*Yes*

(*continued*)

Table 2. (*continued*)

GUR Method	Main purpose of method	Empirically validated	Key features	Types of Sensory Modalities evaluated	Scope to assess effects of haptic modality
Positive and Negative Affect Schedule Extended (Watson & Clark, 1994)	*Evaluate specific emotional states or affects*	*Yes*	*–60 item schedule which measures 11 specific affects: Fear, Sadness, Guilt, Hostility, Shyness, Fatigue, Surprise, Joviality, Self-Assurance, Attentiveness, and serenity*	*Not explicitly mentioned*	*Yes*
Self-Assessment Manikin (SAM) (Bradley & Lang, 1994)	*Measures the players' pleasure, arousal, and dominance as an affective reaction to various stimuli generated*	*Yes*	*–Non-verbal pictorial assessment technique* *–Suitable for different contexts*	*Not explicitly mentioned*	*Yes*
Rapid Iterative Test and Evaluation Method (RITE) (Medlock, 2018b)	*Identify problems in an existing digital game and fix the problem as soon as it is detected and evaluate the solution*	*Yes*	*–Discount usability method performed in a rapid and collaborative manner* *–Focus on usability than experience* *–Intent of this method is to improve the product by observing and analyzing players playing a digital game*	*Not explicitly mentioned*	*No*

5 Discussion

In the previous section, we divided the different GUR methods into two groups: questionnaire-based and biometric. Amongst the questionnaire-based methods, we observe that PXI (Abeele et al., 2020), MiniPXI (Haider et al., 2022), GUESS ((Phan et al., 2016) and CEGEQ (Calvillo-Gámez et al., 2010) have provisions for evaluating the effects of the visual and aural modalities on the player experience. However, with respect to the haptic modality, there were no provisions to assess the effects of this modality on player experience. Hence, we can infer that these GUR methods must be modified to make them suitable for assessing the relation between haptic modality and player experience. In the case of CEGEQ, the theory on which it is based can be used to expand it to incorporate the effects of the haptic modality on player experience. The lack of empirical validation is its major shortcoming.

The CORGIS (Challenge Originating from Recent Gameplay Interaction Scale) (Denisova et al., 2020) and IEQ (Jennett et al., 2008) methods have provisions to evaluate the effects of the visual modality on player experience. There seems to be no scope to assess the effect of the haptic modality on player experience without modifying these methods. In the case of the IEQ, which focuses on evaluating the state of immersion of players, it can be argued that immersion is not affected just by the visual modality. Other sensory modalities, such as aural and haptic, also contribute to the sense of immersion of players, and it is necessary to expand the IEQ to incorporate the effects of these modalities on player immersion and experience. The effect of the haptic modality on the challenge experience of players is unknown. It can be reasoned that more research will be needed to understand how the haptic modality affects the challenge experience of players before the CORGIS model can be updated with haptic modality evaluation methods.

Of all the reviewed questionnaire-based GUR methods, the HX (Kim et al., 2020) model focuses on evaluating the effects of the haptic modality on player experience. This model is built on insights derived from the PXI model and can be considered as an extension of the PXI model in the context of haptic modality evaluation. This model is theoretical in nature and needs empirical validation before it can be deployed for widescale usage.

The UPEQ (Azadvar et al., 2018), Contextual Gameplay Experience Model (Engl & Nacke, 2013), GEQ (Brockmyer et al., 2009), UEQ (Laugwitz et al., 2008), PENS (Ryan et al., 2006), PANAS-X (Watson & Clark, 1994), SAM (Bradley & Lang, 1994), and RITE (Medlock, 2018.b) are generic and versatile questionnaire-based GUR methods. None of these methods have any specific provisions for evaluating the effects of different sensory modalities on player experience. However, the way these methods have been made makes them suitable for evaluating the effects of the haptic modality on player experience with minor modifications. Though the game industry and academia have used the GEQ method for quite some time, the model has not been empirically validated. Several research articles have highlighted this lack of empirical validation (Abeele et al., 2020; Medlock, 2018.b). The RITE method deals with usability and fixes problems as soon as they arise during game development. Assessing the effects of different modalities on player experience does not seem to be within the scope of the RITE method. However, it can be used to solve functional aspects of the game that affect the sensory modalities, which will eventually affect the player experience.

The biometric methods are versatile and can capture real-time player experience data. However, separate equipment and expertise are needed to gather and analyze data to derive insights related to player experience (Nacke, 2018). This might make the use of biometric methods expensive for GUR. Biometric methods capture data related to facial expressions, body posture, and physiological changes and relate them to the emotional and arousal states of the players. Biometric methods can be used to evaluate changes in the emotional and arousal states of the players when they are subjected to different types of haptic modalities in a digital game. This would require careful planning and designing of the experiment so that the relation between haptic modalities and player experience can be effectively evaluated using biometric methods.

From the above discussion, we can clearly identify which questionnaire-based GUR methods are best suited for evaluating the effects of the haptic modality on player experience. All of the generic type questionnaire-based GUR methods, apart from RITE, can be considered suitable for evaluating the effects of the haptic modality on player experience. The HX model will need empirical validation before it is ideal for extensive use. The other identified methods will need to be modified and validated to check their effectiveness in evaluating the effect of the haptic modality on player experience. This effectively answers our research question and can possibly provide suggestive directions to GUR researchers about the suitability of different GUR methods in evaluating the effects of the haptic modality on player experience. The use of biometric methods depends a lot on the context of use and the design of the experiment. Hence, we cannot suggest specific biometric methods for evaluating the effects of the haptic modality on player experience.

However, there are several challenges that one needs to be mindful of before extending existing GUR methods to evaluate the effects of the haptic modality on player experience. The first challenge arises from which part of the human body senses the haptic modality. Pacchierotti et al. (2017) highlights the possibility of delivering haptic feedback to different parts of the human body. Currently, haptic technology (Schneider et al., 2017) can be segregated into two broad categories based on the human sense modalities. These are tactile sensation-type technology perceived by the skin and proprioception-type technology, which deals with the sense of body location and force feedback. Since the entire human body can perceive different types of haptic sensations, the haptic technology used to deliver the haptic modality sensation and where on the human body that sensation is delivered will influence the player's experience. Hence, when developing GUR methods for haptic modality evaluation, there must be provisions to evaluate the player experience in the context of the haptic technology used and where the haptic sensation is delivered to the human body. The second challenge arises from the technology used to produce the haptic modality for players. At present, a wide variety of hardware platforms are available that are capable of generating the haptic modality for players. These platforms also have inherent inefficiencies, which affect the delivery of the haptic modality to players (Schneider et al., 2017). (Kim et al., 2020) and (Söderström et al., 2022) have also highlighted that the method or delivery system used to convey the haptic modality to the players affects the haptic experience of the players. Hence, GUR researchers need to be aware of the haptic technology used to evaluate the haptic experience of players. The variation in technology used to deliver the haptic experience also makes developing a uniform GUR method for assessing the effects of the haptic modality on player experience more complex. The third challenge arises from the paucity of evaluation tools and guidelines in the context of haptic experience evaluation (Kim et al., 2020; Schneider et al., 2017; Seifi et al., 2020). This scarcity could be related to the absence of a tactile language (Jansson-Boyd, 2011; Kim et al., 2020; Schneider et al., 2017). Hence, one can infer that the lack of GUR methods for evaluating the haptic modality on player experience may be related to the paucity mentioned above. The time frame associated with experiencing haptic modality presents the fourth challenge in integrating haptic modality evaluation in GUR methods. All the discussed GUR methods have been used mainly after the players have experienced the game or experimental game that is being developed. Using this approach, GUR researchers usually obtain reliable data related to player experience evaluation. However, in the case of the haptic modality, the experience greatly depends on the moment it is being experienced (Kim et al., 2020). The time frame involved in reasonably interpreting the perceived haptic modality is extremely short (Alsuradi & Eid, 2022). Hence, GUR researchers run the possibility of obtaining inaccurate data related to haptic experience evaluation if the existing GUR methods are used long after the haptic modality is experienced. The fifth challenge arises from the fact that the experience of haptic modality is very individual (Kim et al., 2020), and each user has their perception of haptic modalities (Jansson-Boyd, 2011; Schneider et al., 2017). Furthermore, players are unable to describe their haptic experience in simple language (Kim et al., 2020; Seifi et al., 2020). As a result, complications will arise when analyzing the data related to player experience and haptic modalities. The final challenge arises from the fact that the evaluation of the effect of haptic modalities on player experience is difficult to conduct remotely (Kim et al., 2020; Schneider et al., 2017). The reason can be associated with the fact that for haptic experience evaluation, the device used to create the haptic modality plays an important role. Hence, in the case of remote evaluation, the haptic device must be present at the testing site during the experimentation process. This will open up the experimentation process to the uncertainties related to the transportation of the device. Moreover, it might require the production of multiple haptic devices depending on the sample size. As a result, the time and cost of conducting the haptic experience evaluation will increase significantly, making remote evaluation unviable. There is also no way to ensure that the participants follow the experimentation criteria. The only way to ensure reliable data acquisition related to haptic experience evaluation is to conduct the experiments in the laboratory environment.

6 Conclusion

From the above critical review, we infer that GUR has not assessed the effects of the haptic modality on player experience significantly, which is made more evident by the paucity of haptic experience evaluation tools and methods in the context of digital games. This presents an opportunity to utilize the insights from existing player experience evaluation toolkits and techniques to expand the player experience evaluation process by adding methods to evaluate how different haptic modalities affect the player experience and what factors contribute to determining the quality of haptic experience in digital games or develop new haptic experience evaluation methods or tools.

The above list of questionnaire-based GUR methods in Table 1 is not an exhaustive list of all available methods in the field of GUR. We have focused on reviewing some well-known methods that appeared frequently in the shortlisted research literature. We must conduct a more comprehensive literature review to identify all relevant questionnaire-based GUR methods that might be capable of evaluating the effects of the haptic modality on player experience.

Disclosure of Interests. The authors have no competing interests to declare that are relevant to the content of this article.

References

Abeele, V.V., Spiel, K., Nacke, L., Johnson, D., Gerling, K.: Development and validation of the player experience inventory: a scale to measure player experiences at the level of functional and psychosocial consequences. Int. J. Hum. Comput. Stud. **135** (2020). https://doi.org/10.1016/j.ijhcs.2019.102370

Ahmed, I., Harjunen, V., Jacucci, G., Ravaja, N., Spapé, M.M.: Total Immersion: Designing for Affective Symbiosis in a Virtual Reality Game with Haptics, Biosensors, and Emotive Agents, pp. 23–37 (2017). https://doi.org/10.1007/978-3-319-57753-1_3

Alsuradi, H., Eid, M.: An ensemble deep learning approach to evaluate haptic delay from a single trial EEG data. Front. Robot. AI **9** (2022). https://doi.org/10.3389/frobt.2022.1013043

Azadvar, A., Canossa, A.: UPEQ: Ubisoft perceived experience questionnaire: A self-determination evaluation tool for video games. In: Deterding, S., et al. (eds.) 13th International Conference on the Foundations of Digital Games, FDG 2018. Association for Computing Machinery (2018). https://doi.org/10.1145/3235765.3235780

Boldt, M., et al.: You shall not pass: non-intrusive feedback for virtual walls in VR environments with room-scale mapping. In: Steinicke, F., Thomas, B., Kiyokawa, K., Welch, G. (eds.) 25th IEEE Conference on Virtual Reality and 3D User Interfaces, VR 2018, pp. 143–150. Institute of Electrical and Electronics Engineers Inc (2018). https://doi.org/10.1109/VR.2018.8446177

Bradley, M.M., Lang, P.J.: Measuring emotion: the self-assessment manikin and the semantic differential. J. Behav. Ther. Exp. Psychiatry **25**(1), 49–59 (1994). https://doi.org/10.1016/0005-7916(94)90063-9

Brockmyer, J.H., Fox, C.M., Curtiss, K.A., McBroom, E., Burkhart, K.M., Pidruzny, J.N.: The development of the Game Engagement Questionnaire: a measure of engagement in video game-playing. J. Exp. Soc. Psychol. **45**(4), 624–634 (2009). https://doi.org/10.1016/j.jesp.2009.02.016

Calvillo-Gámez, E.H., Cairns, P., Cox, A.L.: Assessing the Core Elements of the Gaming Experience, pp. 47–71 (2010). https://doi.org/10.1007/978-1-84882-963-3_4

Denisova, A., Cairns, P., Guckelsberger, C., Zendle, D.: Measuring perceived challenge in digital games: development & validation of the challenge originating from recent gameplay interaction scale (CORGIS). Int. J. Hum. Comput. Stud. **137** (2020). https://doi.org/10.1016/j.ijhcs.2019.102383

Drachen, A., Mirza-Babaei, P., Nacke, L.E.: Introduction to games user research. Games User Res., 1–11 (2018). https://doi.org/10.1093/oso/9780198794844.003.0001

Engl, S., Nacke, L.E.: Contextual influences on mobile player experience - A game user experience model. Entertain. Comput. **4**(1), 83–91 (2013). https://doi.org/10.1016/j.entcom.2012.06.001

Escobar-Castillejos, D., Noguez, J., Cárdenas-Ovando, R.A., Neri, L., Gonzalez-Nucamendi, A., Robledo-Rella, V.: Using game engines for visuo-haptic learning simulations. Appl. Sci. (Switzerland) **10**(13) (2020). https://doi.org/10.3390/app10134553

Galofaro, E., D'antonio, E., Lotti, N., Masia, L.: Rendering immersive haptic force feedback via neuromuscular electrical stimulation. Sensors **22**(14) (2022). https://doi.org/10.3390/s22145069

Haider, A., et al.: miniPXI: development and validation of an eleven-item measure of the player experience inventory. In: Proceedings of the ACM on Human-Computer Interaction, vol. 6 (2022). https://doi.org/10.1145/3549507

Hamam, A., El Saddik, A., Aljáam, J.: A quality of experience model for haptic virtual environments. ACM Trans. Multimedia Comput. Commun. Appl. **10**(3) (2014). https://doi.org/10.1145/2540991

Honegger, F., Feng, Y., Rauterberg, M.: Multimodality for passive experience: effects of visual, auditory, vibration and draught stimuli on sense of presence. J. Univ. Comput. Sci. **27**(6), 582–608 (2021). https://doi.org/10.3897/JUCS.68384

Jansson-Boyd, C.V.: Touch matters: exploring the relationship between consumption and tactile interaction. Soc. Semiot. **21**(4), 531–546 (2011). https://doi.org/10.1080/10350330.2011.591996

Jennett, C., et al.: Measuring and defining the experience of immersion in games. Int. J. Hum. Comput. Stud. **66**(9), 641–661 (2008). https://doi.org/10.1016/j.ijhcs.2008.04.004

Kim, E., Schneider, O., et al.: Defining haptic experience: foundations for understanding, communicating, and evaluating HX. In: 2020 ACM CHI Conference on Human Factors in Computing Systems, CHI 2020 (2020). https://doi.org/10.1145/3313831.3376280

Laugwitz, B., Held, T., Schrepp, M.: Construction and Evaluation of a User Experience Questionnaire, pp. 63–76 (2008). https://doi.org/10.1007/978-3-540-89350-9_6

Lin, Y.-H., et al.: HapticSeer: a multi-channel, black-box, platform-agnostic approach to detecting video game events for real-time haptic feedback. In: 10th International Conference on Materials Processing and Characterisation, ICMPC 2020 (2021). https://doi.org/10.1145/3411764.3445254

Martínez, J., García, A.S., Oliver, M., Molina, J.P., González, P.: VITAKI: a vibrotactile prototyping toolkit for virtual reality and video games. Int. J. Hum.-Comput. Interact. **30**(11), 855–871 (2014). https://doi.org/10.1080/10447318.2014.941272

Medlock, M.C.: An overview of GUR methods. In: Games User Research, pp. 99–116. Oxford University Press (2018a). https://doi.org/10.1093/oso/9780198794844.003.0007

Medlock, M.C.: The rapid iterative test and evaluation method (RITE). In: Games User Research, pp. 203–215. Oxford University Press (2018b). https://doi.org/10.1093/oso/9780198794844.003.0013

Melo, M., Goncalves, G., Monteiro, P., Coelho, H., Vasconcelos-Raposo, J., Bessa, M.: Do multisensory stimuli benefit the virtual reality experience? A systematic review. IEEE Trans. Visual Comput. Graphics **28**(2), 1428–1442 (2022). https://doi.org/10.1109/TVCG.2020.3010088

Min, W., et al.: Multimodal goal recognition in open-world digital games. In: Proceedings of the AAAI Conference on Artificial Intelligence and Interactive Digital Entertainment, vol. 13, no. 1, pp. 80–86 (2021). https://doi.org/10.1609/aiide.v13i1.12939

Nacke, L.E.: Introduction to biometric measures for Games User Research. In: Games User Research, pp. 281–299. Oxford University Press (2018). https://doi.org/10.1093/oso/9780198794844.003.0016

Pacchierotti, C., Sinclair, S., Solazzi, M., Frisoli, A., Hayward, V., Prattichizzo, D.: Wearable haptic systems for the fingertip and the hand: taxonomy, review, and perspectives. IEEE Trans. Haptics **10**(4), 580–600 (2017). https://doi.org/10.1109/TOH.2017.2689006

Phan, M.H., Keebler, J.R., Chaparro, B.S.: The development and validation of the game user experience satisfaction scale (GUESS). Hum. Factors **58**(8), 1217–1247 (2016). https://doi.org/10.1177/0018720816669646

Qiu, W., et al.: A moisture-resistant soft actuator with low driving voltages for haptic stimulations in virtual games. ACS Appl. Mater. Interfaces **14**(27), 31257–31266 (2022). https://doi.org/10.1021/acsami.2c06209

Ryan, R.M., Rigby, C.S., Przybylski, A.: The motivational pull of video games: a self-determination theory approach. Motiv. Emot. **30**(4), 344–360 (2006). https://doi.org/10.1007/s11031-006-9051-8

Ryu, N., Jo, H.-Y., Pahud, M.: GamesBond: bimanual haptic illusion of physically connected objects for immersive VR using grip deformation. In: 2021 CHI Conference on Human Factors in Computing Systems: Making Waves, Combining Strengths, CHI 2021 (2021). https://doi.org/10.1145/3411764.3445727

Schneider, O., MacLean, K., Swindells, C., Booth, K.: Haptic experience design: what hapticians do and where they need help. Int. J. Hum. Comput. Stud. **107**, 5–21 (2017). https://doi.org/10.1016/j.ijhcs.2017.04.004

Seifi, H., Chun, M., Gallacher, C., Schneider, O., MacLean, K.E.: How do novice hapticians design? A case study in creating haptic learning environments. IEEE Trans. Haptics **13**(4), 791–805 (2020). https://doi.org/10.1109/TOH.2020.2968903

Shim, Y.A., Park, K., Lee, S., Son, J., Woo, T., Lee, G.: FS-Pad: video game interactions using force feedback gamepad. In: 33rd Annual ACM Symposium on User Interface Software and Technology, UIST 2020, pp. 938–950 (2020a). https://doi.org/10.1145/3379337.3415850

Singhal, T., Schneider, O.: Juicy haptic design: vibrotactile embellishments can improve player experience in games. In: 2021 CHI Conference on Human Factors in Computing Systems: Making Waves, Combining Strengths, CHI 2021 (2021). https://doi.org/10.1145/3411764.3445463

Söderström, U., et al.: Haptic feedback in first person shooter video games. In: 33rd European Conference on Cognitive Ergonomics: Evaluating the Reality-Virtuality Continuum, ECCE 2022 (2022). https://doi.org/10.1145/3552327.3552333

Su, Y., et al.: Design and modeling of an ungrounded haptic gun that simulates recoil using asymmetric force. In: 2021 IEEE World Haptics Conference, WHC 2021, pp. 361–366 (2021). https://doi.org/10.1109/WHC49131.2021.9517202

Suzuki, R., Ofek, E., Sinclair, M., Leithinger, D., Gonzalez-Franco, M., et al.: HapticBots: distributed encountered-type haptics for VR with multiple shape-changing mobile robots. In: 34th Annual ACM Symposium on User Interface Software and Technology, UIST 2021, pp. 1269–1281 (2021). https://doi.org/10.1145/3472749.3474821

Tsai, H.-R., et al.: ImpactVest: rendering spatio-temporal multilevel impact force feedback on body in VR. In: 2022 CHI Conference on Human Factors in Computing Systems, CHI 2022 (2022). https://doi.org/10.1145/3491102.3501971

Watson, D., Clark, L.A.: The PANAS-X: manual for the positive and negative affect schedule - expanded form. In: Positive and Negative Affect Schedule - Expanded Form. University of Iowa (1994). https://doi.org/10.17077/48vt-m4t2

Zammitto, V.: Games User Research as part of the development process in the game industry: challenges and best practices. In: Games User Research, pp. 15–30. Oxford University Press (2018). https://doi.org/10.1093/oso/9780198794844.003.0002

Zyda, M.: From visual simulation to virtual reality to games. Computer **38**(9), 25–32 (2005). https://doi.org/10.1109/MC.2005.297

'Gamified Pathway'- A Framework for Enhancing User Journeys

Abirami Sankar[1]([✉]) [iD] and Sandeep Athavale[2] [iD]

[1] TCS iON GAMELab, Tata Consultancy Services Ltd, Thane, Maharashtra, India
abirami.sankar@tcs.com
[2] TCS iON GAMELab, Tata Consultancy Services Ltd, Pune, Maharashtra, India
athavale.sandeep@tcs.com

Abstract. Designing engagement features at several touchpoints across the user journey helps businesses enrol, excite, and retain its users. Gamification is an emerging popular approach to help enhance user engagement. There are several gamification frameworks that help designers to gamify their product/services effectively. However, most frameworks lack specific guidance and applicability across the length of user journey. In this paper we develop and propose, 'Gamified Pathway', a framework that enables quick gamification of every step of the user journey. It is a two-dimensional framework with a seven-stage user journey as the first and gamification elements as second dimension. The intersections of the dimensions provide specific guidance to designers for selecting actions of significance. We test the applicability of the framework through a case study approach. We observe that the 'Gamified Pathway' can help in designing compelling user journeys.

Keywords: User Engagement · User Journey · Gamification

1 Introduction

User engagement is a core part of any product/service in the field of human-computer interaction [14]. While it can be hard to quantify and measure, user engagement (assessed through clicks, page views, eye tracking etc.) is a key metric that businesses employ to define the success or failure of their ventures. In recent times, gamification has emerged as a popular approach to help enhance user engagement [18].

Gamification is popularly defined as "the use of game design elements in non-game contexts" [6] and as "the process of making activities more game like" [21]. Early gamification strategies involved the usage of rewards (points, badges, virtual currency) and competition (high scores and leader boards) to engage and motivate players [18]. Over-reliance of rewards to sustain user engagement can also become counterproductive since engagement is then based on external motivators which can overshadow any intrinsic motivation that the core content has to offer.

© The Author(s), under exclusive license to Springer Nature Switzerland AG 2025
N. Rangaswamy et al. (Eds.): IndiaHCI 2024, CCIS 2338, pp. 39–53, 2025.
https://doi.org/10.1007/978-3-031-80832-6_3

User engagement is not a single encounter phenomenon. Engagement can be understood as a process with separate phases that a user progresses through. For example, we have the point of engagement, sustained engagement, disengagement, and re-engagement [14]. To maintain user engagement and deal with the complete process, we need care and purposeful design at every step of the journey. A well-designed user journey thus becomes a crucial aspect of enhancing the overall user engagement. Therefore, it is essential to design for the entire user journey while using gamification in any product/service.

Designers have access to gamification frameworks but must make efforts in utilizing the different game elements across the steps in user journey. Game elements are just one component of gamification; the critical aspect is how these elements are chosen and implemented [21]. While expert designers can work that out, a novice might do piecemeal, incomplete deployment of elements or focus only on few steps in the journey. Present gamification frameworks often do not handhold designers while designing different stages of user journey.

Designers can do well to use a ready reference for gamification in every stage of user journey. In this paper we propose, 'Gamified Pathway', a two-dimensional framework that helps in designing a gamified experience at speed. We draw upon existing gamification frameworks and elements to then create its mapping over a seven-stage user journey. We demonstrate the application of the framework through a case study where we used it to create a gamified learning experience that helps users maintain consistency and change their attitude towards learning. We also evaluated the utility of the framework through the case study based on specific parameters and identified the main benefits of the framework and future scope.

2 Literature Review

In this Literature Review, we studied various gamification frameworks in use today (Sect. 2.1) and various models of a user journey (Sect. 2.2). For this study, we sought out frameworks and methods that aid designers in achieving effective gamification strategies and the materials that provide guidance about user journeys. We also looked for studies that analysed the utility of gamification frameworks as well as those focusing on gamification strategies across the entire user journey. We looked for well cited papers published in journals or conferences (accessed through ACM and ResearchGate) as well as reference books to get relevant details.

2.1 Gamification Frameworks

Gamification methods and frameworks have become an integral part of the UX design toolkit [17]. Some frameworks that are in use today are Octalysis Framework [4], the 6-D Framework [22], Hexad Framework [11], Motivational Design Lenses [5], PLEX Framework [1], RECIPE for meaningful gamification [13], Gameful design heuristics [17] etc.

One gamification methodology, called the Player Centred Design Methodology [9], outlines six essential steps for creating a gamified experience. Another, the PLEX framework [1] provides a systematic and structured way to look at several types of playful experiences by classifying the same into 22 distinct categories. However, the overlap between categories is not effectively handled by the framework [10]. The distinctions made can sometimes feel rigid. PLEX is accompanied by a toolkit with a 3-part story that the designer is prompted to create with different playful categories being the focus at different parts [1]. However, this does not deal with how some elements of playfulness are better suited in different parts. Robinson and Belloti's taxonomy of gamification [15] proposes 6 categories of gamification elements based on the various aspects of the user experience that they support. In Table 1, we summarize our findings from different frameworks:

Table 1. Analysis of Gamification frameworks

#	Name of the Framework	Author(s)	Definition	Summary of Findings
1	Player Centred Design Methodology	Janaki Kumar	8-step process that puts the focus on the player while providing guidance to designers at each step	Provides an overview of the different aspects that are needed to create a smooth experience for the players. It also provides different gamification mechanics that can be applied. However, it does not talk about applying it in the player/user journey
2	Playful Experiences Framework	Arrasvuori et al.	Providing a systematic classification of different types of playful experiences by classifying the same into 22 distinct categories	The toolkit comes with a 3-part story that designers are prompted to create. There isn't further elaboration on what categories are better suited for the different parts, certain combinations that might work/not work etc

(continued)

Table 1. (*continued*)

#	Name of the Framework	Author(s)	Definition	Summary of Findings
3	Octalysis Framework	Yukai Choi	The framework is built around eight core drives which can be used to design gamified experiences and evaluate existing products/services	The Framework is built on different levels where the core drives are used in different ways. In Level 2, we see the 8 drives used with a 4-stage user journey. In Level 3, the dimension of player archetype is also introduced. Level 2 offers a quick overview of the journey and doesn't elaborate on how the core drives behave differently in each stage
4	Hexad Framework	Andrzej Marczewski	Describes six types of players and their key motivators	The strength of this framework is its comprehensive review of player psychologies and player-player interactions. However, the framework doesn't offer any insight on crafting a user journey with different player types
5	Taxonomy of Gamification	Robinson and Belloti	Presents a categorization of gamification elements based on the various aspects of the experience that they support, and the level of commitment required from users	The taxonomy offers a comprehensive collection of gamification elements by compiling and considering various frameworks. The categories address different parts of the experience in terms of context, present in, designed for etc. The user journey within the overall experience does not find any mention here

(*continued*)

Table 1. (*continued*)

#	Name of the Framework	Author(s)	Definition	Summary of Findings
6	Gameful Design Heuristics	Tondello et al.	Presents a list of 28 heuristic elements mapped to 12 motivational dimensions to allow experts and amateurs to evaluate gamified experiences	The heuristics provides a comprehensive look at the different aspects important to an effective gamification strategy. It is intended to be used as a guide after the design is complete. However, we are looking for a guide that would help designers implement these different aspects while crafting the user journey

Observing Table 1, the lack of focus on the crafting gamification across the whole user journey can be noticed in these frameworks. Specifically, Mora et al. report that more than half of the reviewed frameworks failed to consider the onboarding and endgame actions [12], which represent the entry and exit points of the overall user journey. The Octalysis framework is an exception since in its Level 2, the framework is applied across the user journey.

The Octalysis Framework is a gamification framework designed by Yukai Choi. The framework is built around eight core drives [4] which can be used to design gamified experiences and evaluate existing products/services. Choi also presents the Octalysis level 2, where the eight core drives are applied to a four-stage user journey. While the level 1 of the framework, and the core drives have written about widely [20], we could not find studies that explored the usage of Octalysis level 2. Nonetheless, we noted two main drawbacks in this level.

The first drawback is that, at each stage of the user journey, a full Octalysis analysis is conducted, with only a brief guide provided on which core drives are more suitable for each stage. Secondly, applying the Octalysis level 2 necessitates a deep and complete understanding of level 1. While gamification experts might already be familiar with it, it requires significant effort and can especially challenging for novice designers.

2.2 User Journey

User journey refers to the steps that a user takes to achieve their goal within the product or service [7]. It encompasses significant changes in the user's needs, satisfaction levels with the product, or other usage metrics across various phases of their experience [8]. These details are captured and visualized through a journey map, which effectively communicates how the user engages with the experience.

A vital component of the journey map is the division of stages, each corresponding to different user actions during the experience. The exact stages within the journey may differ based on context, and designers and organizations may draft them differently to suit the requirements of the product/service. However, the journey map typically considers the stages that occur before, during, and after the user interacts with the product/service [19]. Some other examples of user journey stages for different contexts are provided by Nielson and Norman group, such as for e-commerce- discover, try, buy, use, seek support [7]. Octalysis level 2 consists of four user journey stages- discovery, onboarding, scaffolding, endgame [4]. However, apart from the Octalysis there weren't any examples that provided guidance on defining user journey stages for gamification.

In conclusion, it was found that many frameworks do not address gamification across the entire user journey. We investigated available structures of user journey amenable to gamification. While there is a lot of emphasis on customizing stages for different contexts with examples, there weren't any examples that focused on the division of journey stages for the gamification context. Among all the frameworks reviewed, the Octalysis Framework stands out as it presents a Level 2 Octalysis where the framework is applied across the user journey. However, even with this there are some difficulties such as the effort required, clarifying the relationship between core drives and user journey stages, and simplifying the overall process to make it more accessible to designers. We therefore propose a new framework that addresses these gaps and functions as a tool that helps designers craft a gamified user journey quickly.

3   Methodology

To reuse and build upon existing methods of developing new frameworks, we investigated the process by which some of the gamification frameworks were created.

The Gameful Design Heuristics framework is a collection of 28 heuristics organized within 12 motivational dimensions [17]. It was developed through a review of game design heuristics and gamification frameworks. The heuristics is built upon the motivational dimensions described by gamification frameworks, comparing them for overlaps and then categorizing them using the SDT (self-determination theory). The PLEX framework was developed by the authors as an extension and modification of the 13 dimensions of pleasure. The authors interviewed participants and analyzed the responses to create their framework with 22 categories of playful experiences [1]. The Octalysis framework's development is unclear, as the author refers to past experience and research but does not elaborate on the process of development.

Since the gamification frameworks did not offer all details about the process of creation, we looked further into other design frameworks. One study focused on the development of a gamification strategy for online learning [16]. Here, the authors employed a Design-Based Research (DBR) approach to gamification. Their approach involved first conducting a review of existing literature, a thorough examination of relevant theories, and the application of varied perspectives to gain a comprehensive understanding of the context. Another study we referred was the development of Endogen Framework for designing Educational Games [2]. The authors used the FBS (Function-Behaviour-Structure) ontology to guide their framework design.

The process we followed for the creation of the framework was aligned to the DBR approach since we used an iterative design and test approach. The guidelines drafted for the framework were derived from the FBS approach and are as follows.

The primary function of a framework is to serve as a valuable tool for decision making, control, communication, learning and transfer. To ensure effective utilization of the framework by designers, it must possess both prescriptive and descriptive qualities. This entails having a clearly defined process that designers can adhere to, consisting of specific steps and strategies. Design processes are amorphous and non-linear so the framework should allow designers to select and customize their approach accordingly.

The foundation of our framework revolves around segmentation of the user journey into seven stages. This allows for a systematic approach and facilitates clearer mapping of various gamification elements onto the user journey. In the subsequent section, we will delve into the main components of our framework in greater detail.

4   Synthesizing the Framework

The high-level structure of our framework consists of two dimensions – the first is the various stages of the user journey. The second dimension consists of gamification elements. The rationale for constructing these two dimensions was to create an intersection where we could provide ready-to-use reference that guides designers to determine gamification at every stage. Further, we also modified the stages of the user journey to adequately represent the needs of the gamification. The synthesis of the framework and the additions and modifications to user journey are explained in the following sections.

4.1   The User Journey Stages

In our framework, we have broken down the user journey into seven distinct stages- Discovery, Onboarding, First Interaction, Engagement, Progress Tracking, Delving Deeper, Community-Engagement. The first two stages, Discovery, and Onboarding, align with Octalysis level 2. The third stage in Octalysis is the scaffolding stage but it is too dense to use since all the major interactions happen in this stage. Therefore, we have further broken down these main interactions into three stages which are First Interaction, Engagement, Progress Tracking.

The fourth and final stage of Octalysis level 2 is the Endgame stage. Here, the platform no longer guides users through the experience. Users seek out new challenges, interaction modes, and become advocates who can influence new users to join. In our framework, this occurs in the final 2 stages – Continuous Engagement and Community Interaction. The stage is labelled 'continuous' to highlight that the platform offers additional opportunities for veteran users to re-engage, while the term 'endgame' implies the conclusion of engagement with the platform. Community Interaction is a fundamental aspect of gamification, being part of the eight core drives of Octalysis level 1 and being mentioned in other frameworks as well. We have included it as a separate stage in the user journey to to explicitly enhance engagement using community levers, having already exposed users to other basic levers.

We went through two iterations before finalising the seven stages (see Fig. 1), to understand and overcome shortcomings in the application. For example, in the second iteration, the first interaction stage was handled partly in the onboarding and engagement stages. By introducing a dedicated stage to this initial interaction, we can better control and optimize the user experience from the outset.

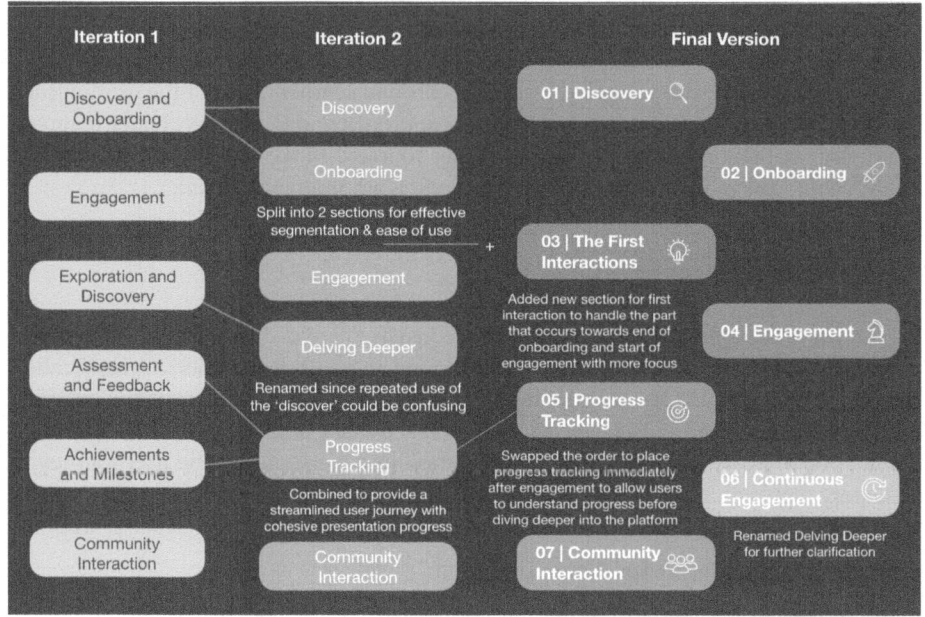

Fig. 1. Evolution of 7 stages of user journey

4.2   The Gamification Elements

Next, we compiled a comprehensive list of gamification elements that can be applied to the user journey. We intend to draw from the works of other researchers who compiled gamification elements for use by designers. We started with the Octalysis framework's 8 core drives, being the most popular framework. However, through literature survey we realised the limited consensus among various frameworks regarding the classification of game design elements [3]. For example, we have the inconsistent categorization of badges across different frameworks, with some considering them as a game interface design pattern, a game mechanic, a game dynamic, a motivational affordance, or a game component [3].

We therefore looked at frameworks that provide atomic classification. Two frameworks that stood out are briefly described here. Robinson and Belloti's taxonomy of gamification [15] identifies 42 common gamification elements, each categorized into 6 distinct categories and marked with the level of effort expected from the user. Finally, Gameful Design Heuristics draws upon frameworks like the Octalysis which are primarily built on motivational affordances and presents a list of 28 heuristic elements mapped to 12 motivational dimensions [17]. In addition to these, we found that The Empirical Analysis of Gamification Frameworks by Buckley et al. [3] uses Werbach and Hunter's 6D framework's 15 components [22] and presents a list of 22 gamification components and their usage across several gamified products/services available today.

Amongst the frameworks studied, we find the approach of the Gameful Design Heuristics [17], which focuses on motivational affordances, to be more suitable. This is because the Gameful Design Heuristics provides a concise list of gamification elements and is more aligned to Octalysis framework which has attracted attention and adoption by designers [20]. Though the intended use of heuristics framework is the evaluation of product/service experience that is already designed, it can be used as a guideline while crafting the user journey.

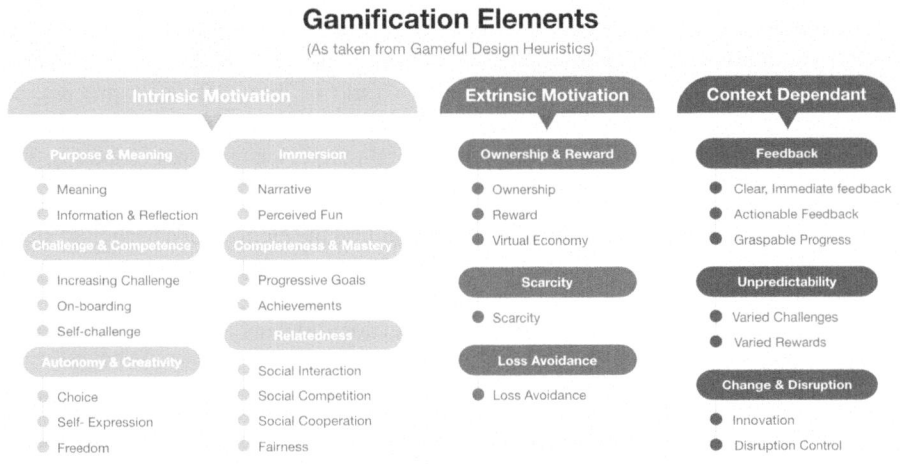

Fig. 2. Consolidated list of gamification elements – the 28 Gameful design heuristics [17]

We have adopted the entire list of heuristics for our framework. The heuristics are broadly divided into three categories – intrinsic motivation, extrinsic motivation, and context dependant. Most of the 28 heuristics fall under the intrinsic motivation category. This effectively ensures that designers can avoid over reliance on external motivators. The context dependant heuristics can cater to either intrinsic or extrinsic motivation based on the context. We found these to be very versatile and were applied across multiple stages in our user journey. The feedback elements focus on informing the users about their progress, performance, and way forward. The elements in Unpredictability encourage the platform to surprise the users in terms of challenges, rewards, narrative structure etc. Finally, with the Change and Disruption elements, designers are encouraged to set up avenues where users can actively participate and co-create aspects of the experience and set up checks in place to ensure that co-created aspects don't offer unfair advantages or create loopholes. The complete list of gamification elements used to create the final structure can be found in Fig. 2.

4.3 'Gamified Pathway' Framework

We started creating the final structure of the framework by drafting simple prompts that sets the tone for what is required to happen at each stage of the user journey. These are:

- Discovery - How are the users learning about the platform?
- Onboarding - How are the users entering into the platform?
- First Interactions - What is their first interaction with the platform?
- Engagement - Now that they are here and ready, what do they do?
- Progress Tracking - How do they know how well they are doing?
- Continuous Engagement - How do they know what else they can do and keep coming back?
- Community Interaction – Are they using the app just by themselves? How do they involve their social circles into the same?

To align gamification elements with the user journey, we used the descriptions provided by Tondello et al. [17] to evaluate the relevance and applicability of each element within the various stages of the user journey. To aid in this evaluation process, we implemented a straightforward traffic light system to categorize each element as either green (primary/must have), yellow (secondary/good to have), or red (not required). This classification was based on several factors, including:

- The potential significant positive impact of including the element at a particular stage.
- The noticeable frustration that may arise from the absence of a certain element, even if the positive effect may not be significant.
- Elements that may neither create a positive effect nor noticeably affect the user journey stage if absent.

Furthermore, we aimed to avoid overwhelming a single stage with an excessive number of gamification elements. However, some overlap is inevitable, e.g., Engagement and Continuous engagement stages had the highest number of elements mapped to them, with some degree of overlap. Using the intersection of the gamification elements and the journey stages, we can now define user actions to complete the gamified user journey. The final version of the framework (see Fig. 3) includes sample actions for each stage that can be used as a starting point by designers.

5   Explorative Evaluation

Any new framework that is developed needs to be adequately validated so that it can develop the credibility needed for its widespread usage [2]. We have currently developed the initial version of our framework and at this first stage an internal validation would be the most appropriate. Thus, we used a case study approach to validate the utility of the Gamified Pathway Framework. The authors attempted to use the Gamified Pathway framework to design a gamification strategy for a real use case that was presented to them at work.

We iteratively revised the framework by analyzing its utility based on the following parameters during the case study – a) clarity and comprehensibility, b) completeness, c) effectiveness and ease of use, and lastly d) flexibility. The test of clarity was necessary

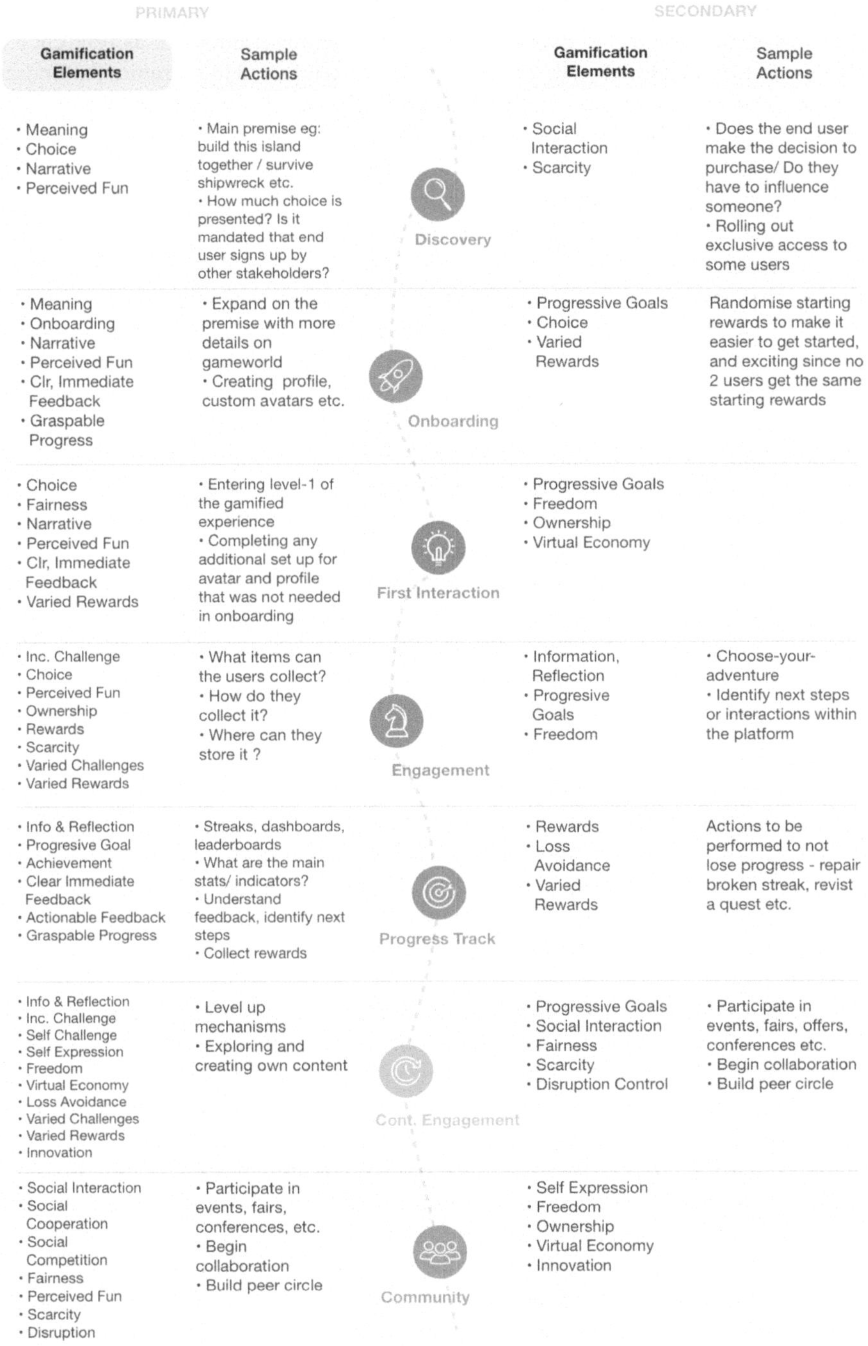

| PRIMARY | | | SECONDARY | |
Gamification Elements	Sample Actions		Gamification Elements	Sample Actions
• Meaning • Choice • Narrative • Perceived Fun	• Main premise eg: build this island together / survive shipwreck etc. • How much choice is presented? Is it mandated that end user signs up by other stakeholders?	**Discovery**	• Social Interaction • Scarcity	• Does the end user make the decision to purchase/ Do they have to influence someone? • Rolling out exclusive access to some users
• Meaning • Onboarding • Narrative • Perceived Fun • Clr, Immediate Feedback • Graspable Progress	• Expand on the premise with more details on gameworld • Creating profile, custom avatars etc.	**Onboarding**	• Progressive Goals • Choice • Varied Rewards	Randomise starting rewards to make it easier to get started, and exciting since no 2 users get the same starting rewards
• Choice • Fairness • Narrative • Perceived Fun • Clr, Immediate Feedback • Varied Rewards	• Entering level-1 of the gamified experience • Completing any additional set up for avatar and profile that was not needed in onboarding	**First Interaction**	• Progressive Goals • Freedom • Ownership • Virtual Economy	
• Inc. Challenge • Choice • Perceived Fun • Ownership • Rewards • Scarcity • Varied Challenges • Varied Rewards	• What items can the users collect? • How do they collect it? • Where can they store it ?	**Engagement**	• Information, Reflection • Progresive Goals • Freedom	• Choose-your-adventure • Identify next steps or interactions within the platform
• Info & Reflection • Progresive Goal • Achievement • Clear Immediate Feedback • Actionable Feedback • Graspable Progress	• Streaks, dashboards, leaderboards • What are the main stats/ indicators? • Understand feedback, identify next steps • Collect rewards	**Progress Track**	• Rewards • Loss Avoidance • Varied Rewards	Actions to be performed to not lose progress - repair broken streak, revist a quest etc.
• Info & Reflection • Inc. Challenge • Self Challenge • Self Expression • Freedom • Virtual Economy • Loss Avoidance • Varied Challenges • Varied Rewards • Innovation	• Level up mechanisms • Exploring and creating own content	**Cont. Engagement**	• Progressive Goals • Social Interaction • Fairness • Scarcity • Disruption Control	• Participate in events, fairs, offers, conferences etc. • Begin collaboration • Build peer circle
• Social Interaction • Social Cooperation • Social Competition • Fairness • Perceived Fun • Scarcity • Disruption	• Participate in events, fairs, conferences, etc. • Begin collaboration • Build peer circle	**Community**	• Self Expression • Freedom • Ownership • Virtual Economy • Innovation	

Fig. 3. Final version of Gamified Pathway

as the goal of our framework was to provide clearly defined steps and strategies. Test of flexibility was essential as we expect designers to use our framework as reference but suitably customize and modify their approach. We also referred to literature that indicate the qualities of a framework sought by designers. For example, we studied Weber et al.'s evaluation of the Octalysis framework [20] where they recruited novice designers and summarized the reflections and processes of using the framework. We used the findings from the study to frame remaining two parameters.

The case study is the application of the framework to design a learning and habit formation app that can positively influence learners into making effective use of their screentime to be engaged in learning. The final concept involved a phygital model with a physical habit tracker that reminds stay engaged with the learning platform, and a mobile platform where the learners can build their Gameworld as they progress and advance in their learning. The initial interactions with the phygital model were set up in such a way that the learners have enough choice in the mode of interaction. We took care to draft the onboarding stage in such a way that the 'build' aspect of the Gameworld provides the meaning and call to action gamification elements. The learning platform was also built around discovering and acquiring 'endogenous' collectibles through the learning content. The collectibles help in creating new engagement for learners and becomes a readily available feature for Progress Tracking. The collectibles were also extended into the Continuous Engagement stage where we added a maintenance aspect to the same to utilize the Loss Avoidance element. Finally, we completed the model by adding collaboration interactions and flows to connect learners to their community.

Using the evaluation parameters, we could understand how the framework performed during the case study.

- **Clarity and comprehensibility** – During our initial framework testing, the intersection of gamification elements and user journey stages contained blank cells for user actions. However, it was not giving any input to designers on what is the action to be taken. To make it clearer, we have provided sample user actions that could happen at each intersection. Also, the Engagement and Continuous engagement stages had a lot of overlap which made it hard to comprehend. We reduced the overlaps as much as possible.
- **Completeness** – The main strength of the framework is that it offers a quick, complete look at the user journey and the gamification elements that are applicable at each stage. We found the First Interactions and Progress Tracking stages to be quite useful. Incorporating progress tracking between engagement and continuous engagement allowed us to effectively examine the transition between these stages. In our final version of the user journey for the gamified learning experience, we also added an emotion graph to monitor expected and actual user reactions. These are some additional aspects that could be a part of future expansions.
- **Effectiveness and Ease of use**- The framework ensured that we did not have to keep going back to check for any missing or overlooked gamification elements. The predefined and organized user journey stages facilitated the process. To enhance ease of use, we could additionally provide quick reference cards describing how each gamification element adds value in the user journey stage.

- **Flexibility**- The framework helped us cater to different stakeholders of the platform and identify the interventions needed from them in each stage to ensure a smooth experience for the end user. While the framework was highly relevant to our online learning context, further validation is necessary to determine its ability to address a diverse range of contexts.

6   Conclusion and Future Work

Incorporating gamification into the user journey can benefit designers in creating designs that are both engaging and impactful. Our literature review provided an overview of multiple gamification frameworks and methodologies such as the PLEX framework, Octalysis framework etc. However, we discovered that many of these frameworks do not adequately address the integration of gamification throughout the entire user journey. It is this lack of guidance that motivated us to explore and attempt to fill this gap. In this paper, we proposed 'Gamified Pathway', a seven-stage journey model to facilitate the design of gamified experiences that span the entire user journey. Drawing inspiration from existing gamification frameworks and building upon the concepts presented in Nielsen and Norman's templates and the Octalysis framework, we have developed a comprehensive framework that addresses the limitations of existing models.

We illustrated the practical application of our framework by presenting a case study in which it was utilized to design a gamified online learning platform. Our evaluation of the framework was based its clarity and comprehensibility, completeness, effectiveness, and ease of use, and flexibility. The framework's main strengths lie in its clarity and completeness in terms of the seven stages and the various gamification elements. We also identified areas for improvement such as the addition of layers like the emotion graph and application to diverse contexts.

To advance our research, we would start by expanding the scope of validation to other applications and then introduce elements that may be missing or make necessary refinements. This can be achieved by conducting interactive sessions with designers from various backgrounds, where they can actively engage with and make use of the framework. Furthermore, it is important to not limit the validation process to a single domain, but to extend it to different contexts, such as healthcare and finance. By carrying out these comprehensive validation procedures, we aim to not only refine and improve our framework but also demonstrate its effectiveness and applicability across various domains. This will allow us to ensure that designers are able to create a smooth Gamified Pathway for their target users.

Acknowledgments. Authors like to acknowledge the opportunity provided by Rajesh Sundaresan, head of TCS iON GAMELab, to explore and develop a new gamification framework.

References

1. Arrasvuori, J., Boberg, M., Holopainen, J., et al.: Applying the PLEX framework in designing for playfulness. In: Proceedings of the 2011 Conference on Designing Pleasurable Products and Interfaces - DPPI 2011 (2011). https://doi.org/10.1145/2347504.2347531
2. Athavale, S., Dalvi, G.: Endogen: framework for designing endogenous educational games. In: Proceedings of DiGRA 2020 (2020)
3. Buckley, P., Noonan, S., Geary, C., et al.: An empirical study of gamification frameworks. In: Research Anthology on Game Design, Development, Usage, and Social Impact, pp. 1852–1869 (2022). https://doi.org/10.4018/978-1-6684-7589-8.ch090
4. Chou, Y-K.: Actionable Gamification: Beyond Points, Badges, and Leaderboards. Octalysis Group, United States (2014)
5. Deterding, S.: The lens of intrinsic skill atoms: a method for gameful design. Hum. Comput. Interact. **30**, 294–335 (2015). https://doi.org/10.1080/07370024.2014.993471
6. Deterding, S., Dixon, D., Khaled, R., Nacke, L.: From game design elements to gamefulness. In: Proceedings of the 15th International Academic MindTrek Conference on Envisioning Future Media Environments - MindTrek 2011, vol. 11, pp. 9–15 (2011). https://doi.org/10.1145/2181037.2181040
7. Gibbons, S.: Journey Mapping 101. Nielsen Norman Group (2018). https://www.nngroup.com/articles/journey-mapping-101/
8. Howard, T.: Journey mapping. Commun. Des. Q. Rev. **2**, 10–13 (2014). https://doi.org/10.1145/2644448.2644451
9. Kumar, J.: Gamification at Work: Designing Engaging Business Software. Design, User Experience, and Usability Health, Learning, Playing, Cultural, and Cross-Cultural User Experience, pp. 528–537 (2013). https://doi.org/10.1007/978-3-642-39241-2_58
10. Lucero, A., Holopainen, J., Ollila, E., et al.: The playful experiences (PLEX) framework as a guide for expert evaluation. In: Proceedings of the 6th International Conference on Designing Pleasurable Products and Interfaces - DPPI 2013 (2013). https://doi.org/10.1145/2513506.2513530
11. Marczewski, A.: User Types. Even Ninja Monkeys Like to Play: Gamification, Game Thinking and Motivational Design, 1st edn, pp. 65–80 (2015)
12. Mora, A., Riera, D., Gonzalez, C., Arnedo-Moreno, J.: A literature review of gamification design frameworks. In: 7th International Conference on Games and Virtual Worlds for Serious Applications (VS-Games), pp. 1–8. (2015). https://doi.org/10.1109/vs-games.2015.7295760
13. Nicholson, S.: A RECIPE for meaningful gamification. In: Wood, L., Reiners, T. (eds.) Gamification in Education and Business, pp. 1–20. Springer, New York (2014)
14. Peters, C., Castellano, G., de Freitas, S.: An exploration of user engagement in HCI. In: Proceedings of the International Workshop on Affective-Aware Virtual Agents and Social Robots - AFFINE 2009 (2009). https://doi.org/10.1145/1655260.1655269
15. Robinson, D., Belloti, V.: A preliminary taxonomy of gamification elements for varying anticipated commitment. In: Proceedings of the ACM CHI 2013 Workshop on Designing Gamification: Creating Gameful and Playful Experiences, Paris, France. ACM (2013)
16. Shrestha, S., Joshi, M., Bashyal, A., Timilsina, A.: User engagement in gamified online learning system. World J. Educ. Res. **8**, p46 (2021). https://doi.org/10.22158/wjer.v8n5p46
17. Tondello, G.F., Kappen, D.L., Ganaba, M., Nacke, L.E.: Gameful design heuristics: a gamification inspection tool. In: Human-Computer Interaction Perspectives on Design HCII 2019, vol. 11566, pp. 224–244 (2019). https://doi.org/10.1007/978-3-030-22646-6_16
18. Vaibhav, A., Gupta, P.: Gamification of MOOCs for increasing user engagement. In: IEEE International Conference on MOOC, Innovation and Technology in Education (MITE), Patiala, India, pp. 290–295. IEEE (2014)

19. Walter, S.: User Journey Mapping. SitePoint Pty, Limited, Sebastopol (2022)
20. Weber, P., Grönewald, L., Ludwig, T.: Reflection on the Octalysis framework as a design and evaluation tool. In: 6th International GamiFIN Conference 2022 (GamiFIN 2022), Finland (2022)
21. Werbach, K.: (Re)Defining gamification: a process approach. Persuasive Technol. PERSUA-SIVE **2014**(8462), 266–272 (2014). https://doi.org/10.1007/978-3-319-07127-5_23
22. Werbach, K., Hunter, D.: For the Win: How Game Thinking Can Revolutionize Your Business. Wharton Digital Press, Philadelphia (2012)

'Dhar-Pakad' Raising Awareness About Cleanliness and Sustainable Responsibilities Through Interactive Board Game Design

Shreyas Vernekar[✉] and Apoorv Anurag

Hyderabad, India
`shreyasver.5@gmail.com`

Abstract. With growing global emphasis on sustainability and eco-friendly practices by the UN and Indian government, there is a pressing need to cultivate awareness and responsibility towards cleanliness and environmental stewardship at an individual level. This paper details the development and evaluation of "Dhar-Pakad," a board game designed to address this need by enhancing awareness among Indian students, primarily, in classes 4 to 10 (aged 10–16 years). The game simulates a scenario where a Block Development Officer (BDO) conducts a surprise inspection in a village managed by a Pradhan. By immersing players in these roles, the game aims to deepen their understanding of personal responsibilities through interactive gameplay. Evaluation results demonstrate that the game effectively engages players, fosters discussions related to cleanliness, indicating towards information retention and it's potential as a valuable teaching supplementary tool.

Keywords: Roleplaying board game · Civic responsibilities · Sustainable development · Educational Game · Interactive Board Game

1 Research

1.1 Individual Civic Cleanliness and Sustainable Responsibilities

Global initiatives emphasize the need for individual participation in sustainability. United Nations' Sustainable Development Goals (SDGs) such as 'Ensure access to water and sanitation for all' (Goal 6) [1] and 'Ensure sustainable consumption and production patterns' (Goal 12) [2] address critical environmental issues including waste management, littering, and water conservation. In India, the Swachh Bharat Mission, launched in 2014, initially aimed to eliminate open defecation but has since broadened its scope to include solid and liquid waste management, as well as cleanliness in public spaces [3]. To foster individual

S. Vernekar and A. Anurag—Independent Designers

involvement, the government employs Information, Education, and Communication (IEC) [4] strategies through various media and activities. However, sustaining cleanliness and promoting environmental sensitivity ultimately depends on individual responsibility and active participation (Fig. 1).

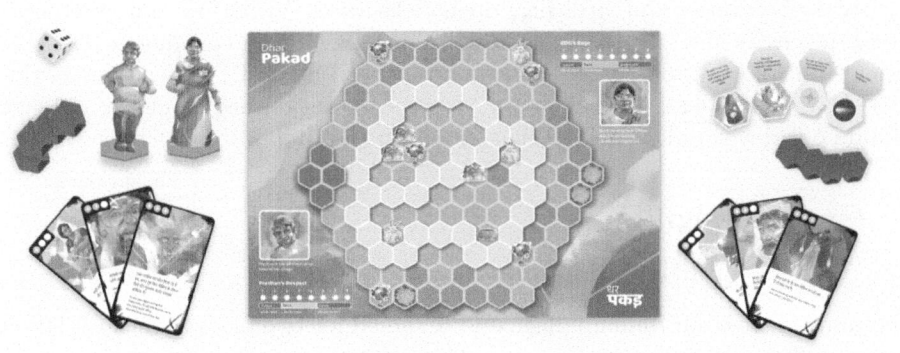

Fig. 1. The board game consists of a village map, conversation cards, character tokens, die and hex chips.

1.2 Efficacy of Games in Educating About Cleanliness and Sustainability

Games have proven to be a powerful educational tool as their engaging nature can make learning about cleanliness and sustainability both enjoyable and effective. By integrating sustainability themes into game design, players can immerse themselves in real-world scenarios through role-playing, decision-making, and collaboration. This hands-on approach enhances understanding and retention of environmental concepts more effectively than the traditional methods [5].

Several board games, such as Paved Paradise [5] and Blutube [6], address issues of sustainability and water conservation respectively. However for the Indian demographic, a game tailored to local contexts can further enhance eagerness to use the learning environment [7].

2   Objective

Our goal was to create a game that enhances awareness of social hygiene and environmental responsibility among Indian students, in class 4th to 10th, as they are familiar with these concepts in their curriculum [8]. The game can further deepen understanding and improve information retention, promoting responsible behavior through interactive scenarios, but that is currently out of the project's scope.

3   Ideation

Our ideation process drew from diverse sources. We analyzed board games like Paved Paradise and Blutube, and digital games such as Civic Sense [9], which focuses on garbage segregation. We were also inspired by Hide the Corpse [10], a VR game emphasizing urgency and strategy.

Local observations of littering, open defecation, urinating and spitting in public places pushed us to create a solution, promoting cleanliness and civic responsibility. Additionally, an episode from the Hindi OTT series 'Panchayat', by TVF Productions [11], featured a surprise sanitation inspection in a village, guiding our development of a game simulating the Indian bureaucracy system.

4   Game Design

4.1   Game Narrative and Roles

Our game is set in an Indian village and designed for two players: a Block Development Officer (BDO) and a Pradhan. The BDO oversees development programs and monitors regional progress, though they do not reside in the village. The Pradhan, the elected head of the Gram Panchayat, manages local governance and addresses community needs.

The scenario involves a surprise inspection by the BDO to assess the village's cleanliness and sustainability under the Swachh Bharat Mission. The BDO warns the Pradhan that identified issues could result in the Pradhan's expulsion, if not village could win the 'Swachha Gram' (Clean Village) award. The Pradhan must stay in the Panchayat office during the evaluation to avoid interference.

As the BDO inspects the village, the Pradhan moves secretly to alert residents and protect the village's reputation, creating a strategic contest between the two players. This dynamic inspired the game's name, 'Dhar-Pakad,' meaning 'to run after and catch.'

5   Game Mechanics

5.1   Overview

The game is set on a village map made up of hexagon tiles, each representing different positions. Players choose from BDO and Pradhan character tokens. They start by drawing five hexagonal (hex) chips from a shuffled pile of twenty. These hex chips contains a mix of *good and bad activities*, power-ups, and debuffs, with their contents hidden from the players (Fig. 2).

5.2   Gameplay

Players take turns placing their hex chips on the map strategically anywhere, except the main road and obstructions like ponds or houses. Once all the chips are placed, player role-playing the BDO rolls a die to determine their movement,

Fig. 2. Game area shows the map of the village, along with Panchayat office, obstructions, main road and sliders.

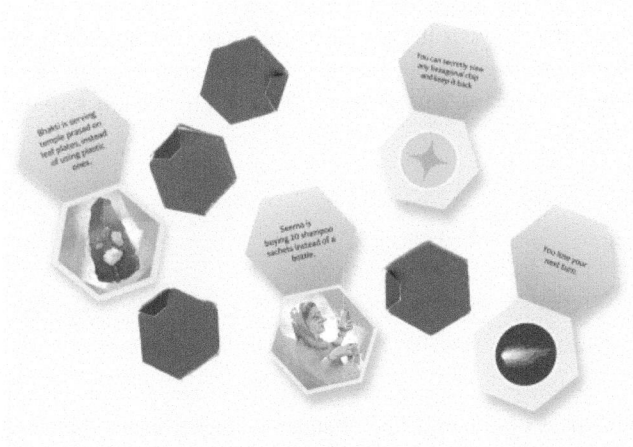

Fig. 3. Hex chips contains different characters performing good or bad activities. It can also have power-ups and de-buffs.

followed by the Pradhan. Both players aim to identify and address as many bad activity chips as possible. When an activity chip is revealed, The illustration and description provides clues to determine if the activity is sustainable or not. Players can consult a 'Guidelines to win Swaccha Gram Award' chart if necessary (Fig. 3).

5.3 Characters and Movement

BDO. Since BDO is new in the village, they can only move along the main road, with their path determined by a die roll. The vision expands with their rage level (Fig. 4). They can climb water tanks for an aerial view, revealing a hex chip within their line of sight. From this vantage point, Pradhan can be summoned to BDO's location for a meeting, unless the Pradhan is in the Panchayat office area, which is the designated safe zone.

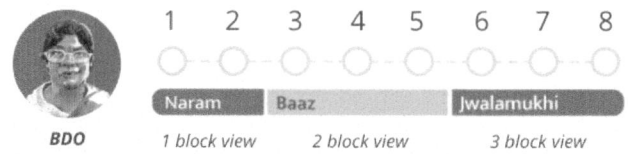

Fig. 4. Rage points and line of sight vision reference for BDO.

Pradhan. Pradhan can move on all tiles except obstacles, in a straight line based on die roll but can turn if they encounter an obstacle or boundary. When they address *bad activities*, their respect level increases, but harrassing ideal citizens would lead to losing one respect point. The vision expands with their respect level (Fig. 5).

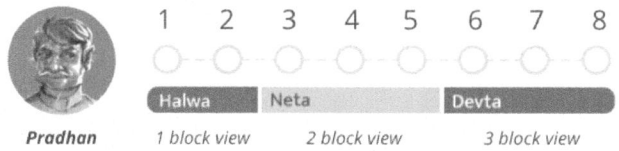

Fig. 5. Respect points and line of sight vision reference for Pradhan.

5.4 Components

Conversation Cards. Each player has nine conversation cards used during interactions when the BDO spots the Pradhan outside the Panchayat office. Each card has a power rating from 1 to 3. When caught, the Pradhan must move to the BDO's position. The BDO then draws a card from their set with varying severity of accusations and reads it aloud. The Pradhan responds by drawing a card from their set, which includes flattering or arrogant responses. The outcome is determined by the power of the cards played: the player with the higher power card wins. The difference in the power-cards gets added or deducted in the respective scales of winner and loser of that conversation round. If the Pradhan loses, Pradhan's token must return to the Panchayat office (Fig. 6).

Fig. 6. Conversation cards with varying power levels for BDO (left) and Pradhan (right).

Panic Token. The Panic token, usable once per game, allows a player to challenge their opponent for a conversation card giving them an opportunity to double their reward points. The losing player has their points deducted by the usual amount.

5.5   Winning Criteria

The game ends when all hexagonal chips on the board have been revealed. The player with the highest accumulated rage/respect points wins. In the event of a tie, the player who has caught the most bad activity chips is declared the winner. If a tie persists, players continue a battle of accusations using their remaining conversation cards until a winner is determined.

6   Designing for Relatability

While introducing the Pradhan and BDO characters, we focused on explaining their roles clearly and simply. Players from village backgrounds or those who have watched the popular web series 'Panchayat' may already be familiar with these roles. For those who aren't, we added brief descriptions of their responsibilities on the game board to encourage curiosity about village administration.

To humanize these characters, we introduced emotion scales of 'Respect' for the Pradhan and 'Rage' for the BDO, based on the cleanliness inspection event, allowing players to connect emotionally with the characters' actions. Adding a comical twist, we used playful, colloquial terms like "halwa," "neta," and "jwalamukhi," and incorporated culturally significant items such as the lota (water pot), paan (betel leaf), and charpai (cot). Events like distributing prasad and purchasing sachets from local shops further enhance this sense of familiarity. These elements ground the game in an accessible cultural context, helping players relate to the importance of practicing environmentally friendly and sustainable habits in their own surroundings.

7   Visual Design

The visual design of "Dhar-Pakad" integrates a whimsical and vibrant aesthetic to enhance player engagement. The characters are depicted with exaggerated comical facial features, bold dynamic strokes, drawing inspiration from games like 'Disco Elysium' [12] where character dynamics, statuses are highlighted through distinct visual annotations. The village is full of eccentric characters ranging from pious Bhakti to mischievous Brijesh, to accentuate this range of emotions we used dual lighting in the in-game illustrations and board design. This approach aims to make the characters appear larger than life, fostering a connection between players and their in-game personas (Fig. 7).

Fig. 7. Participants playing the game during evaluation.

8   Evaluation

Seven rounds of evaluation were conducted with young adults, including engineers, interaction designers, and board game enthusiasts aged 21–29, followed by six rounds with students from grades 3 to 10, aged 9 to 16.

Early game-play revealed a bias towards players who quickly accumulated points, while conversation cards, which could have helped balance the game, were largely unused. To address this, we introduced new ways to activate conversation cards, such as through water tanks and Panic tokens. We also increased the game's complexity by adding power-ups and debuffs to the hex chips, extending game-play beyond the initial 10–15 min. The original color coding in the hex chips (red for bad, green for good) was removed, as players quickly recognized the chips without seeing the activity itself, defeating the purpose of raising awareness. A guidelines chart listing both good and bad activities was introduced to offer quick reference during gameplay. We also increased and diversified the hex chip activities to ensure novelty and variation in every game round.

Feedback indicated that players enjoyed role-playing and reading conversation cards, as they featured idioms and phrases. However, we observed that players were disappointed when they encountered good activities, revealing an issue with the mental model formed. We asked the students questions before and after the play to assess the change in their awareness. We observed that many participants learned about new sustainability practices through the game while discussing various topics, such as using leaf plates, composting and minimizing consumption of non-biodegradable materials. Those who were familiar with these topics were explaining the reasons behind them to others. Players expressed intentions to implement this learning in their surroundings. One player proudly stated, "Humare ghar me ye follow karte hai" (We follow this in our household) regarding waste segregation. Another shared how they regularly donate old clothes and toys, further emphasizing the game's educational value. Parents reported that their children after going back home, talked about what they had learned in the game indicating the game's positive impact on information retention.

9   Conclusion and Future Work

To promote individual cleanliness and sustainability, we developed the board game 'Dhar-Pakad' for students aged 10 to 16. Evaluations show that the game effectively raises awareness, sparks discussions, and promotes decision-making on sustainable practices. In future work, we plan to expand evaluations to rural and underprivileged urban communities, translating the game into regional languages to assess its broader educational impact. We also aim to refine players' mental models around activity recognition and introduce multiple game levels based on their age.

Upcoming iterations will feature foldable maps with diverse settings-such as villages, cities, and schools-and incorporate additional administrative roles to deepen the educational experience. New mechanics will be introduced where early game decisions affect later outcomes, reinforcing the importance of long-term sustainable thinking. We also plan to conduct a long-term study to track retention and the implementation of good practices, with interviews from parents to evaluate the game's influence on children's behaviors.

References

1. United Nations, Department of Economic and Social Affairs, Sustainable Development: Ensure availability and sustainable management of water and sanitation for all. https://sdgs.un.org/goals/goal6. Accessed 04 Aug 2024
2. United Nations, Department of Economic and Social Affairs, Sustainable Development: Ensure sustainable consumption and production patterns. https://sdgs.un.org/goals/goal12. Accessed 04 Aug 2024
3. Swachh Bharat Mission Gramin Homepage. https://swachhbharatmission.ddws.gov.in. Accessed 04 Aug 2024
4. Rajsekhar, D., Manjula, R.: Swachh Bharat Mission: Awareness Strategies. Implementation and Issues, The Institute for Social and Economic Change (2023)
5. Pope, L.: Board Games as a Teaching Tool for Sustainability. Prescott College (2023)
6. DiPaolo, R., Pizziol, V.: Gamification and sustainable water use, the case of the BLUTUBE educational program. Simul. Gaming **55**(3), 391–417. https://doi.org/10.1177/10468781231181652
7. Lehtonen, T., et al.: On the role of gamification and localization in an open online learning environment. In: 15th Koli Calling Conference on Computing Education Research (2015)
8. NCERT Final syllabus on Health and Physical Education (Class I - X). https://ncert.nic.in/pdf/syllabus/. Accessed 04 Aug 2024
9. Karelia, G.: This Bengaluru start-up creates a game to make waste segregation fun. https://swachhindia.ndtv.com/bengaluru-start-creates-game-make-waste-segregation-fun-14062/. Accessed 04 Aug 2024
10. Realcast: Hide the Corpse. https://realcast.io/htc/. Accessed 04 Aug 2024
11. Amazon Prime Video, TVF(The Viral Fever): Panchayat. Season 2, Episode 3. https://www.primevideo.com/detail/Panchayat. Accessed 04 Aug 2024
12. ZA/UM: Disco Elysium, The Final Cut. https://discoelysium.com/. Accessed 04 Aug 2024

Branch Master: A Binary Search Tree Based Board Game

Vijayanand Banahatti$^{(\boxtimes)}$, Deekshaa Nim , Yash Karanjavkar ,
and Prasad Bokil

IDC School of Design, Indian Institute of Technology Bombay, 400076 Mumbai, India
{vijayanand.idc,deekshaanim,yash.karanjavkar,prasad.bokil}@iitb.ac.in

Abstract. Computational thinking helps to break down complex issues leading to solutions, learning this skill is essential to navigate in digital world. Learning through games is one strategy used in the past. This strategy is used in this board game (Branch Master) to explain binary search tree (BST) based searching and insertion operations. A strong connection between content and gameplay is created by employing an endogenous design based on BST operations to promote computational thinking in a social context. The game is built considering players know how to compare two numbers with minimalistic rules. The game has an inherent challenge due to conflict and competition which will make players engage throughout the game play.

Keywords: Computational Thinking · Binary Search Tree (BST) · Board Game

1 Introduction

As we embrace the digital age, developing computational thinking (CT) skills in everyone is essential and considered a crucial skill for the 21st century. It encompasses the ability to understand a problem and develop possible solutions that can be executed by either a human or a machine. Computer engineers do not just require CT, but everyone, and we should all learn to understand, and use this skill in our everyday lives [8]. National Education Policy (NEP) 2020 recommends that mathematics and computational thinking be given increased emphasis throughout the school years, starting with the foundational stage, through a variety of innovative methods, including the regular use of puzzles and games that make mathematical thinking more enjoyable and engaging [5]. Various learning strategies were used in the past to help students learn CT [4]. Game-based learning is one of the strategies used that has many characteristics of problem-solving, e.g., an unknown outcome, multiple paths to a goal, construction of a problem context, collaboration in the case of multiple players, and they add the elements of competition and chance [4]. We endorse game-based learning because games and game-based applications are becoming increasingly significant in cognitive training, learning, and educational interventions [6].

N. Rangaswamy et al. (Eds.): IndiaHCI 2024, CCIS 2338, pp. 63–72, 2025.
https://doi.org/10.1007/978-3-031-80832-6_5

Algorithms and data structures are fundamental subjects in computer science education. Students find these subjects challenging to comprehend and grasp digitally since they are typically taught through code writing, which not all students find enjoyable. The topic of the binary search tree (BST) was selected for game design, considering its importance in computer science education for efficient searching, insertion, and deletion operations.

2   Binary Search Tree Data Structure

A Binary Search Tree is a data structure used in computer science to organize and store data in a sorted manner. Each node in a Binary Search Tree has just two children: a left child and a right child, with the left child storing values less than the parent node and the right child carrying values larger than the parent node. This means that the left subtree of a node contains values that are smaller than the node's value, and the right subtree contains larger values. Due to this property, BSTs allow for efficient searching, insertion, and deletion by dividing the search space in half, making it an important data structure in computer science and many other fields. BST has the following rules.

- Each node has at most two child nodes representing two sub-trees.
- Every node's key is larger than all keys in its left sub-tree.
- Every node's key is smaller than all keys in its right sub-tree.
- There must be no duplicate key value of the nodes.

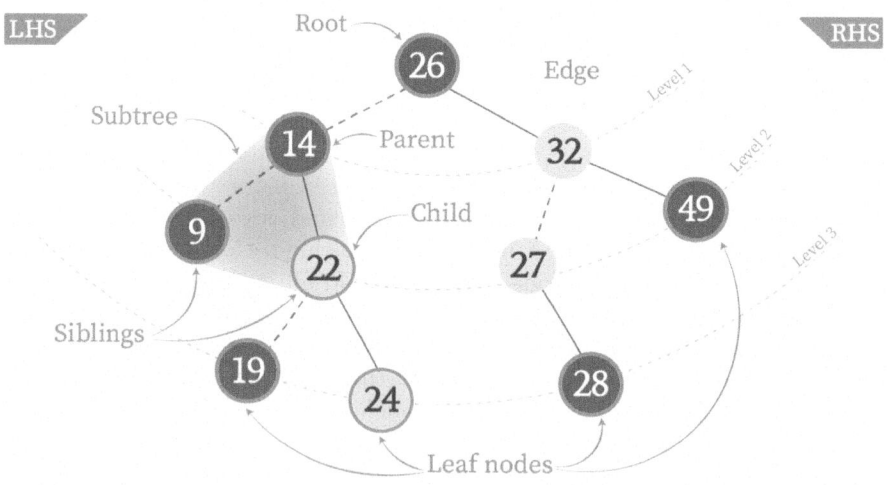

Fig. 1. BST node position explanation example

As shown in Fig. 1, BST has various terminology used to explain the nodes. Following list will explain these nodes in brief.

Root Node: This is the topmost node of the tree. A tree has exactly one root node. It serves as the starting point for many operations on the tree, such as traversals or searches.

Child Node: Nodes that connect to another node in a downward direction. For example, in a binary tree, a node can have at most two children (left and right child).

Leaf Node: Nodes that do not have any children.

Parent Node: For every node in the tree other than the root, one other node directly connects to it in an upward direction. This node is called its parent. Leaf nodes: The node which has a parent node but no children below it is called leaf node.

Level: is the number of parent nodes corresponding to a given node of the tree. It is the number of ancestors from that node until the root node. So, for the root node (topmost node), it's level is 0, since it has no parent node.

2.1   Search Operation Steps in BST

To search number "27" in Fig. 2 we start at the root note "26". We compare the value to be searched with the value of the root. If it's equal, we are done with the search. If it's smaller, we know that we need to go to the left subtree because in a binary search tree, all the elements in the left subtree are smaller, and all the elements in the right subtree are larger. In this example, "27" is larger than "26", so we go to the right side. In the next node, we have a value of "32", which is larger than "27", so we traverse to the left. We repeat this operation till no more traversal is possible, and if, at any iteration, the number (key) is found, then stop the search or else continue.

2.2   Insertion Operation Steps in BST

To insert number "23" in the existing BST as per Fig. 2 (b), we start at root node "26" and process the search operation as per Sect. 2.1 till we reach leaf node. In this case in Fig. 2 (b) leaf node is "24". Once leaf node is found, the new node is added as a child of the leaf node. As per Fig. 2 (b) new node "23" is added to the left of "existing leaf node "24" as its less than the value of parent node. Once the leaf node is reached, insert that particular value to its right or left based on the relation between value of the new node (to be inserted) and existing the leaf node's value.

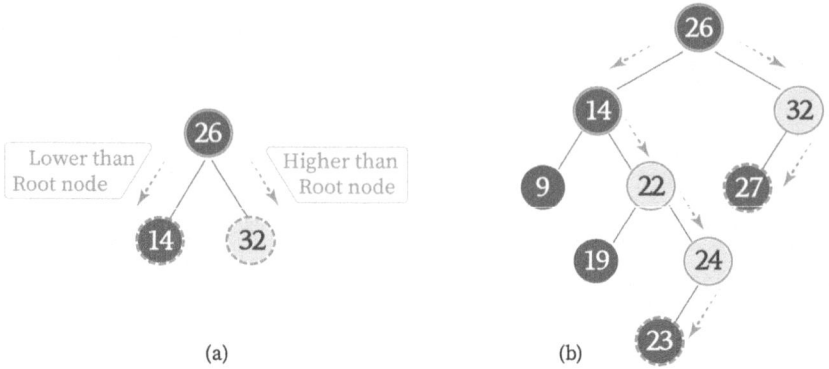

Fig. 2. Searching and Insertion operation in BST

3 Game Design

While planning BST based game, we wanted to have a tight coupling between content and gameplay. This sort of cohesion leads to games that are educational and enjoyable at the same time, making them effective. Such games are called endogenous wherein the game elements emerge from the content, create cohesion [1]. Board games are games with rules, a playing surface, and tokens enabling interaction between or among players as players look down at the surface and face each other [2]. As per Berland and Duncan playing board games in a social setting with friends engages players in computational thinking [3]. This motivated us to use an endogenous game design approach to create a board game to teach binary search tree operation such as searching and insertion.

3.1 Initial Game Design

As binary search tree is visualised as tree. So, we used the same tree concept to prepare our game board as shown in Fig. 3. We used white sheet as board where we can draw lines and circles using pencil/pen. For playing purpose we used coins made up of paper having number printed on them in the range of 1 to 51. We kept the coins in the closed opaque pouch and players take out one coin at a time from the pouch turn by turn and place it on the board by drawing line and circle on the paper as per the rule mentioned in Sect. 2.1 and 2.2. Please refer Fig. 3 used in one play session where we started with "26" number coin as root node. Once all the coins are placed on the sheet players can check the correctness of the placement of the coins as per the rule/algorithm mentioned in Sect. 2.1 and 2.2.

Advantages: The game played in cooperative mode and player learned together about the BST algorithm.

Limitations: The initial design of the game was to learn together and there was no winner getting elected at the end of the session. The game board was not fixed so players need to draw as game progress, and it was creating confusion with the clutter in the placement of lines and circles. We observed that there was no challenge and hence it was less engaging.

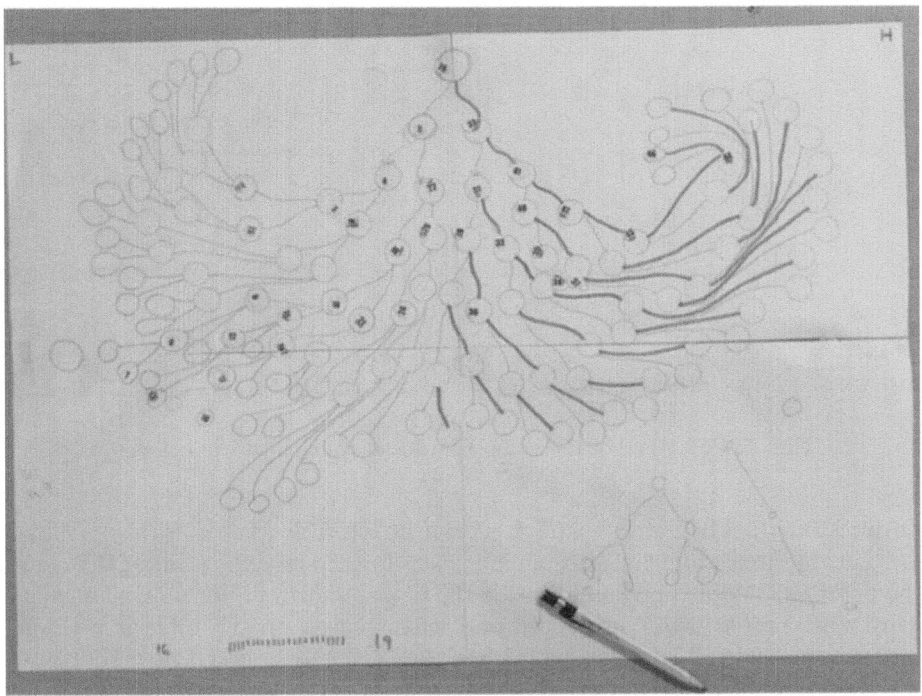

Fig. 3. Game prototype created for play session

3.2   Final Game Design

The game must be challenging to engage and immerse the players in the game play which was not the case with initial version of the game. The main functionality of the game is challenge. To introduce challenge, we decided to use competition and conflict mechanism in the final game design [7]. In the final design we decided to have a fixed game board to level 6. Also, the game board was created with all circles and lines present, so players can focus on game play and not drawing. Branch Master contains a game board, 51 tokens that have two colors on them, a pouch to keep coins, and 2-coin holders to temporarily hold the coins which play-ers draw from the pouch. The prototype of the game was shown in Fig. 4 and the Final design with all the components of the game are shown in Fig. 5 and Fig. 6 including the box and rule book.

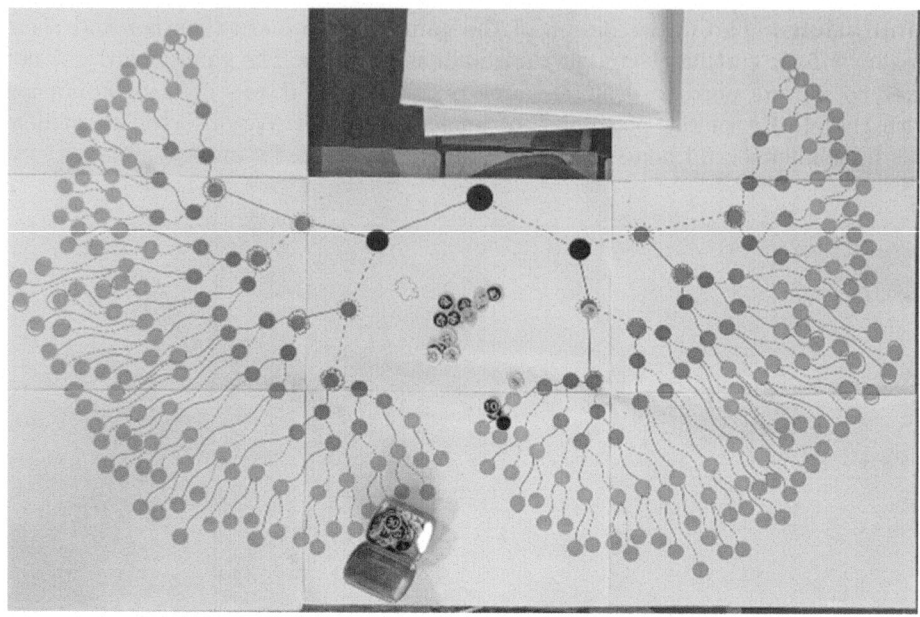

Fig. 4. Prototype of the game board and coins with two colors

Game Board: The game board as shown in Fig. 5 is created with predefined positions of circles and lines to make it easy for the payers to place the coins. The board is foldable and can fit inside the box as shown in Fig. 6 (a). The game board was created using sun board and when placed on the table it will look as shown in Fig. 5. The game board has SAFE ZONE marked near root node which is the area where players cannot replace other players coin.

Coins: coins were created using acrylic material with same number printed on either side with two different colors as shown in Fig. 5 and Fig. 6 (c).

Pouch: One non-transparent pouch to keep all the coins as shown in Fig. 6 (b) and (c).

Coin Holder: Having three slots to keep the coins which players draw from the pouch as shown in Fig. 6 (d).

4   Game Play

Before the game starts, each player picks one of the two colors: Orange or Green. It's important because it decides what color they want to use in the game. The objective is to place maximum coins having same color on the board at the end of the game play.

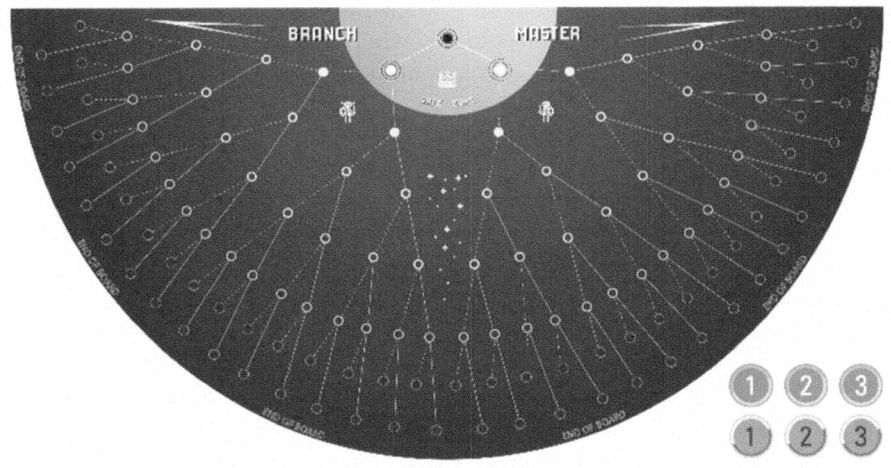

Fig. 5. Final Game board with 6 level and sample three coins

(a)   (b)   (c)   (d)

Fig. 6. Game box items. (a) Game box, (b) Coin pouch, (c) Coins, (d) Coin holder

Starting Position: To begin the game, put a coin with a number (like 26) in the middle on the game board. This coin is at the very start of our game journey, like the first step on a path.

Turn Order: First mover is decided using coin toss. The winner of this toss gets to start the game and pick coins from the pouch first.

Initially both players draw three coins blindly from the pouch to start the game. Players maintain a hand of three coins throughout the game using coin holder. After placing a coin on the board, they replenish their hand by drawing a coin from the pouch. Players can draw a coin, examine its number, and strategically place it on the board. Strategy revolves around analysing the initial coin number and evaluating opportunities for replacing opponents' coins at leaf nodes. The game concludes when all players have used up their draw coins and finalized their placements/replacements. The winner is determined by the player with the highest number of colour coins showing on the board at the end of the game. If there's a tie, the player who has more of their coins at the leaf nodes wins.

4.1 Coin Placement Rule

Players begin by comparing the current number drawn from the pool (coins inside pouch) with the topmost root node, then follow the branch to place it accurately on the node as per the steps described in Sect. 2.1. If a player's number exceeds the root node's coin number, they position a coin on the right side of the root node. Conversely, if a player's number is lower than the root node's coin number, they position a coin on the left side of the root node. Coins positioned in the safe zone (area marked with yellow color) are irreplaceable. For example, as shown in Fig. 7 (a), let's say player B with green color decides to place coin number "27" from his coin holder. Already coins 14, 32, 49 were placed on board so she has to place it on left side of parent coin "32" as shown in Fig. 7 (a). This rule helped to understand searching as per the algorithm described in Sect. 2.1. But to add competition and conflict as part of challenge we have decided to create replacement rule.

4.2 Coin Re-placement (Flipping) Rule

Players can replace/flip their opponent's coins to her selected color coin to maximize her winning possibility. This replacement can only happen at a leaf node. An opponent coin is replaceable if no other coin has been placed below it and during player's turn that player's coin has the possibility to be placed below the opponent's coin based on the placement rule (Refer Sect. 4.1). Example text to replace a coin, let's say players have kept following coins dawn from pouch in following order 14, 32, 49, 27 and now new coin "28" is drawn by player A, then he/she can flip "27" as per Fig. 7 (a) and place "28" on right of "27" as shown in Fig. 7 (b and c).

Players can flip opponents' coins to match their preferred color before placing them back on the board. Then the player can place the coin which they have drawn below that flipped coin based on the placement rule. This will bring the player towards the winning condition faster as they get two coins of their color in one turn. Coins must adhere to placement rules; reaching the end of a branch removes the coin. Players replenish coins from a pouch, ensuring they always have three coins in their hand. The game ends when all coins (including the ones in the players' hand) are placed. The player who has the highest number of coins having his/her selected color facing upwards on the board, wins the game. When the player reaches level 6 (end of the board) while placement of coin then players must keep that coin outside the board as it cannot be placed on the existing board.

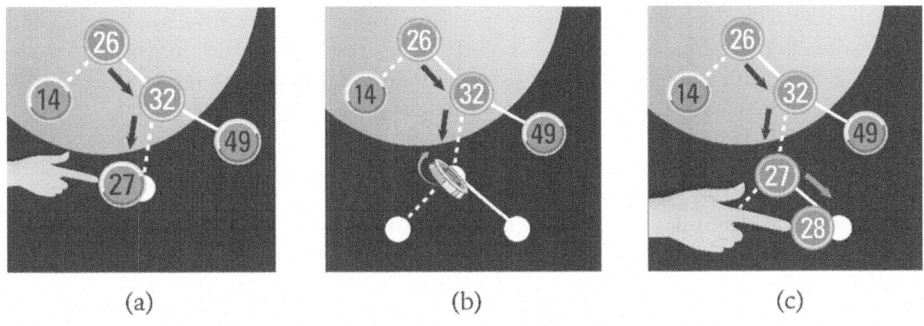

Fig. 7. Example of coin replacement

5   Conclusion

Branch master is an endogenous board game designed to help understand BST operation such as searching and inserting as part of computational thinking exercise. Fetching the coins from the pouch is based on chance, while making the right move to place/replace is strategic decision. The replacement (flipping) rule helps to add challenge as same number coin has 2 colors which give rise to conflict and competition. As the coins are fetched from the pouch turn-by-turn it will give rise to many possibilities arranging the coins on the board. Because of this, the game is unpredictable and new every time a player plays it, keeping players engaged in the game. One limitation of the current game play is the absence of deletion operation and will be considered in a later game version. Additionally, in future, play testing in schools needs to be conducted to find possible game enhancements and efficacy in teaching such concepts through board game.

Acknowledgments. We thank Nikhil Samant from CNC lab IDC, for his input and timely help in preparing the game coins. Our special thanks to Dr. Malay Dhamelia, Shruti Agarwal, and Madhuri Sasupilli for their feedback. We express our sincere gratitude to the IDC School of Design at IIT Bombay for lending us their facilities at game design studio and CNC lab.

References

1. Athavale, S., Dalvi, G.: Endogen: framework for designing endogenous educational games. In: Proceedings of DiGRA 2020 Conference: Play Everywhere. DiGRA, Tampere (2020)
2. Barbara, J.: Measuring user experience in multiplayer board games. Games Culture **12**(7–8), 623–649 (2017). https://doi.org/10.1177/1555412015593419
3. Berland, M., Duncan, S.: Computational thinking in the wild: uncovering complex collaborative thinking through gameplay. Educ. Technol. **56**(3), 29–35 (2016). http://www.jstor.org/stable/44430490

4. Hsu, T.C., Chang, S.C., Hung, Y.T.: How to learn and how to teach computational thinking: suggestions based on a review of the literature. Comput. Educ. **126**, 296–310 (2018). https://doi.org/10.1016/j.compedu.2018.07.004, https://www.sciencedirect.com/science/article/pii/S0360131518301799
5. Ministry of Human Resource Development, G.o.I.: National education policy 2020 (2020). https://www.education.gov.in/sites/upload_files/mhrd/files/NEP_Final_English_0.pdf. Accessed 14 Sept 2024
6. Prensky, M.: Digital Game-based Learning. McGraw-Hill (2001). https://books.google.co.in/books?id=kVG7AQAACAAJ
7. Sasupilli, M., Bokil, P.: Understanding the elements of challenge and skills in educational games. In: Vol. 16 No. 1 (2022): Proceedings of the 16th European Conference on Games Based Learnin. ACI, Lusófona University, Lisbon, Portuga (2022)
8. Wing, J.M.: Computational thinking. Commun. ACM **49**(3), 33–35 (2006). https://doi.org/10.1145/1118178.1118215

Right Turn: A Cybersecurity Serious Game with a Scenario-Based Assessment

Gokul Jayakrishnan$^{(\boxtimes)}$ (ID), Vijayanand Banahatti (ID), and Sachin Lodha (ID)

TCS Research, Tata Consultancy Services Ltd., Pune, India
{gokul.cj,vijayanand.banahatti,sachin.lodha}@tcs.com

Abstract. Security awareness programs and assessments often demonstrate high performance from the participants. Despite this, in real-life, security (cybersecurity) attacks often succeed because of some human error or poor judgment. We postulate that one reason for this difference is because the assessment methods grade the participants' awareness higher than it actually is. Unlike in question-based assessments, real life often presents scenarios involving several sub-decisions, each requiring careful attention. We attempted to assess the security awareness of enterprise employees by focusing on certain real-life scenarios and developed a security-oriented serious game called 'Right Turn'. The participants' game responses were assessed not just on a question-answer basis, but also on the overall correctness of the scenarios having multiple sub-decisions. Our exploratory study with 5,932 participants from an enterprise setting indicates that despite having good correctness in 'answering questions', the participants showed inferior performance in overall 'scenarios' within the game. In this paper, we provide a unique perspective on gauging the performance of security serious games.

Keywords: Serious Game · Scenario-based · Security awareness · Enterprise

1 Introduction

A vast majority of the awareness training focus does not go beyond an individual question-based approach. In real life, knowing the answer to a particular question or a situation might not be enough. There could be a chain of multiple situations constituting a scenario, and even a single incorrect decision in such a scenario could result in real life penalties. However, having proper awareness of a topic could lead to having better responses in real-life security scenarios and operating safely in cyber space [1]. Considering this, for a security scenario consisting of several decision-making steps, where 100% correctness is required, do users actually bother to respond correctly to all these decisions? This question motivated us to assess the security awareness of the employees of an IT consultancy organization. Our plan was in line with the requirements of the Corporate Security Office (CSO) of the organization under study, who had planned to gauge the security awareness of enterprise employees for formulating new training methods. Thus, we conducted an exploratory study using a purposeful game (serious game), 'Right Turn', to simulate six security scenarios (each containing several sub-decisions) and gauge the security awareness of employees in these scenarios.

N. Rangaswamy et al. (Eds.): IndiaHCI 2024, CCIS 2338, pp. 73–88, 2025.
https://doi.org/10.1007/978-3-031-80832-6_6

Any security-related mistake in real life would lead to a security incident, like a data breach. This is programmed into the game as well where 'water leakage' represents 'data leakage' or security incident.

Our research question (RQ) was: **Does correctness of answers to individual questions within an assessment guarantee the user's scenario-level security awareness?** Our study tries to measure this using correctness of a scenario as a whole, rather than just that of the individual questions that constitute the said scenario. Partial awareness of a security scenario could increase the chances of making mistakes to the constituting questions or situations. This RQ is relevant in the area of cybersecurity training and serious games since majority of them ask questions to the users and the correctness of their individual responses is often used to judge the effectiveness of the awareness method or training. Through our study, we report some insights on scenario-based assessment and also recommend an alternate way of gauging correctness in a security serious game, which could mimic real-life scenarios in context.

2 Related Work

The existing literature on user awareness games shows various methods where individuals are gauged and trained in cybersecurity concepts using games such as Anti-phishing Phil, Phishy, etc. [2–7]. They focus on how participants react to various situations and questions within the game, and appropriately equip them with the required knowledge. Sustaining the 'interest' of the learners is a key factor while learning cybersecurity concepts [8] and a 'serious fun' approach that combines real-world security implications within an appealing user interface (UI) is found to attract trainees' attention [8]. Purposeful games, often termed 'serious games', have played a big role in this as per several studies [2, 9–11]. 'Serious games' as defined by Zyda [12] are mental contests played with a computer and consist of specific rules. They use entertainment to further training, education, health, policies, and strategic objectives. They are games designed for a specific purpose, not just entertainment [13]. Studies with phishing awareness serious games, *PickMail* [14] and *What.Hack* [2] tested and trained users in how they identify several hints within emails to determine their legitimacy and differentiate them from phishing emails. The methodology used in these games is similar to identifying several situations (various elements such as sender's address, attachments, website links) within a scenario (the email).

There are a few gaps in the literature. For instance, these games do not show further analysis in how many users got the overall email scenarios correct (to 100%). Most of the serious games in security have these gaps. They gauge the user awareness in terms of answers to questions and certain scenarios, however, they do not measure how many scenarios (if it has scenarios) received perfect responses from the users, in other words, the 100% correctness for security scenarios. While this may sound farfetched, real life will require users to not make any mistake during a wide range of security scenarios. Doing so could increase the chances of a security incident or a cybersecurity attack. Thus, we focused on including the overall correctness for security scenarios while analyzing the participant data of our serious game.

3 Right Turn Game: Design and Development

The cognitive principle of learner motivation, as suggested by the Self Determination Theory (SDT) [15, 16], presents 'intrinsic motivation' that results from enjoyment of the game and 'extrinsic motivation' that results from external factors such as rewards and rules [17]. Our serious game was designed considering both these factors, with a familiar 'water-through-pipe' puzzle game mechanics [18–20] to provide intrinsic motivation and a sense of achievement, with the rewards (both in-game and external completion rewards) to promote external motivation. We chose a game over a nested questionnaire or other document-based methods due to its inherent ability to provide engagement and motivation [33]. The positive results from previous studies with serious games for cybersecurity education [2–7] also affected our decision. The game 'Right Turn' assessed users based on six security-related scenarios as shown in Table 1.

Table 1. Learning content focused within Right Turn.

Level	Scenario and Type (CS = Cybersecurity, GS = General Security)
1	Scanning an unknown QR code[a] that provides offers from a grocery store (CS)
2	Regarding the medium of sharing of confidential client documents within the organization (CS)
3	Security and privacy issues regarding unknown mobile applications (CS)
4	A situation involving a fire drill within the organization and the appropriate response needed (GS)
5	Regarding crisis management, business continuity plan (BCP) and managing work outages (GS)
6	Impact on work and possible unauthorized data leakage due to the device malfunction (GS)

[a]QR code or "Quick Response code" is a two-dimensional matrix code, with characteristics superior to a bar code [29, 30]. These codes have high data storage, and they enable fast scanning [31]. They are used to store website URLs, addresses, and other forms of data [32].

3.1 Learning Content

The scenarios focused on both cybersecurity and general security topics. Since this experiment was our initial exploratory study, we included a few security scenarios that the employees might encounter during work and a few that they might encounter both during and outside of work. These scenarios were finalized after careful consideration of certain security issues faced within the organization in the past and based on risk analysis done by the Corporate Security Group of the organization under study. Table 1 shows the scenarios used within the game. For example, in game level 1, 'QR Code' is focused, which in real life is a daily use case for enterprise employees as they perform transactions for purchases by scanning a QR code using their mobile applications. For each scenario, there are several situations that require decision-making (binary decisions like correct or incorrect). If all the individual decisions are correctly made, the game level will result in 'zero data leakage'.

3.2 Justification of "Water Leakage vs. Data Leakage" Analogy

We followed the 'water leakage' analogy for 'data leakage' because of their similar characteristics. In terms of water flow from source to destination, it is essential that every valve is properly turned to minimize leakage. Similarly, for data transfer from source to destination, all the controls like encryption, proper data classification etc. are essential to minimize unauthorized data disclosure and leakage. We compare the valves in pipes with the data controls. Comparing further, they may both start slow, but, due to gradual loss, can end up in causing considerable harm. Similar to how vulnerabilities in the pipe or valve can cause water leakage, security vulnerabilities (such as weak passwords or insecure networks) can cause data leakage. Both pipe system and data systems require constant vigilance, monitoring and maintenance. For data systems, the user also needs to be extremely cautious and vigilant about their actions. Immediate action is required to stop both water leakage and a potential data leakage scenario.

3.3 Game Overview

Figure 1 shows the game flow for Right Turn. The game has six levels as shown in Table 1. The game level begins when the user views the corresponding scenario description (as a pop-up message) and proceeds to click the "Play" button. The game level contains water tanks, pipes, and valves. To turn the valve, the player must hover over two arrows (containing response options to the security question), decide which one has the correct response, and then click on that arrow.

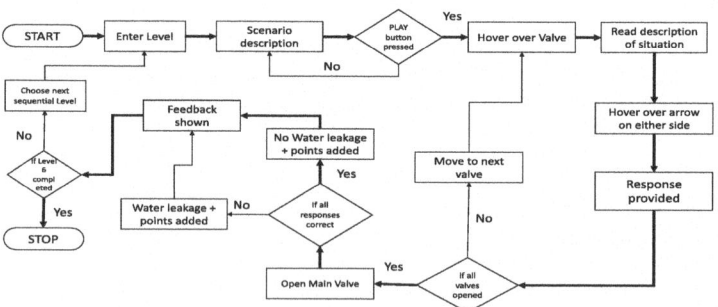

Fig. 1. The flow diagram for Right Turn game

3.4 Game Mechanics and Play

'Game Mechanics' can be simplified as the 'methods invoked by agents for interacting with the game world' [21, 22]. As per the Serious Game Design Assessment (SGDA) framework [21], game mechanics involves the goal of the game, reward system, obstacles/challenges, difficulty, and the win condition. As such, the goal in the game is to turn all valves in the scene so that the water flows from the source tank to the destination tank with no leakage (cf. Fig. 2.B).

Fig. 2. The Gameplay of Right Turn

To turn the valves in the correct direction, the player must carefully observe the security situation within the scenario (game level) and provide the correct decision using the left or right arrows (cf. Fig. 2.C and 2.D). The reward to the player is in the form of points, where 10 points get added for each correct response. If the player fails to provide the correct answer to the security scenario presented, the corresponding valve will turn in the wrong direction, resulting in water leakage (analogous to data leakage). For example, Fig. 2.A shows part of a scenario where the user receives an offer for scanning a particular code outside a grocery store. Now the four valves within the game level (cf. Fig. 2.B) denote four situations that are related to the scenario. The first valve poses the situation 'Validate the offer'. The two yellow arrows on both sides of the valve denote the proposed decision that could be taken by the customer of the grocery store (player). Figure 2.C shows the decision for the right arrow to 'Manually inspect the QR code' and Fig. 2.D shows the decision for the left arrow to 'Confirm with the shop manager' regarding the authenticity of the offer. Upon making the decision, the player can proceed to the next valve. Once all the valves are done, the player can turn the main valve (highlighted in red, cf. Fig. 2.B) after which, the water starts flowing from tank A to tank B (shown as an animation) and the game displays the correct responses for each situation as feedback to help the player reflect on their responses. The feedback for the situation is given in Fig. 2.E. If any response given by the player is incorrect, the corresponding valve will leak water (shown as water dripping animation), and water in tank B will be reduced (this reduction is calculated based on the percentage of incorrect answers). After this, the player proceeds to the next level where a different scenario and associated situations are shown. The game consists of six such scenarios as levels.

3.5 Design Process

We followed certain learning techniques such as 'cognitive feedback' and 'SGDA framework' to provide higher learnability:

Cognitive Feedback. (as emphasized by Ketamo and Kiili [34]): It is said to grab the player's attention and help them focus on the essential learning, thus helping in reflection, which is a learning science principle [23, 24]. Right Turn offers feedback at the end of each level for the player to identify their mistakes and reflect upon their decisions.

SGDA Framework. It suggests that the purposes of the game are well conveyed through the game design for greater player engagement [21]. Purpose, content, narrative, game mechanics, aesthetics, and framing are the six major components for assessing serious games as per the SGDA framework. While designing our serious game, we tried to match each of these components to the elements of the game to provide maximum engagement and learning.

Corporate Requirements. We had certain corporate requirements that influenced our design while creating the serious game such as: a) the ability to run on all browsers without installation of any special software or hardware, b) repurposable to adapt to various learning contexts, c) short duration (maximum of 10–15 min), and d) reduce cognitive overload on learners, so gameplay and controls must be kept very minimal without compromising learning and engagement. Our initial ideas included a platformer game [25], a 3D-interactive game, and a long-format role-playing game [26], but we finalized on the 2D, point-and-click game due to the corporate requirements.

3.6   Game Technology

The game was developed using the Unity Game Engine (Microsoft C# language, in Visual Studio Code). It was developed as a web-based game with WebGL build from Unity. The image assets and animations were made using Adobe Creative Cloud tools (Photoshop, Illustrator, and Animate). The game was deployed in the internal servers of the organization.

4   Study

4.1   Participants

The study participants consisted of employees of an Information Technology-related enterprise under study, who were informed through emails regarding the date of launch along with a trailer video of the serious game. Of the 5,932 participants who completed the game, 56.2% were males and 39.5% were females. 0.7% reported to be from the 'Others' category, and 3.6% did not respond to the question of 'gender' in their demographic survey. With regards to the educational background, 49.8% participants were from computer science or information technology (CS/IT) background and 41.2% were not, with 9% not responding to the question. The percentage of participants as per age-group is as follows: [20–29]: 59.4%, [31–40]: 30.7%, [41–50]: 6.1%, [Above 50]: 1.1%, with 2.7% of the participants overall providing no response.

The organization under study does not fall under the jurisdiction of an IRB, but we did abide by the privacy laws and did not collect any data on the participants. The game data was analyzed after assigning randomly generated 12-digit participant IDs to each participant, for anonymity. For research purposes, we requested the cumulative demographic data of participants. The same was informed to the participants before the start of the game. The participants could also opt out of providing responses to demographic questions by selecting 'I prefer not to answer this question'.

4.2 Reward Structure

The winners were rewarded daily for a period of 17 days from the date of initial launch of the game. 10 winners were selected daily (using a lucky draw) and were rewarded the organization's virtual currency (a coupon equivalent to $15) with which they could make purchases from online stores. There was also a 'bumper prize' for 10 participants (selected using a lucky draw from the list of all participants who completed) at the end of two weeks (a $45 coupon).

4.3 Procedure and Data Collection

The information about the game was sent as multiple notifications over email to the employees of the organization. The participants could voluntarily access the website link (within the organization's intranet) and enroll to play the game as per convenience. They could view the game on their web browsers, and play using keyboard or mouse. Prior to the game, the players were given a survey page to enter their demographic details (voluntary) to help with the data analysis. The other data collected includes the gameplay metrics such as the answers given by the participants for the various questions within the scenarios, and their game feedback survey responses (Likert scale).

5 Results

From our analysis of the participants' information collected, we measured the correctness percentage based on each game level. Since each scenario is represented as a game level, the terms 'scenarios' and 'levels' are used interchangeably in this section. Here, we report our initial analysis from the game data of 5,932 participants.

In the Right Turn game, all the levels except level 2 had four sub-decision points, and level 2 had three sub-decision points. Therefore, we calculated a 'normalized score' per level for comparison. Here, if a person gets all the three (or four) sub-decisions correct, then their scenario score would be '1'. This will be considered as an 'all correct' scenario, or a scenario with '100% correctness'. If they get one incorrect sub-decision in a scenario of three sub-decisions, their overall scenario score would be 0.66 and so on. If all the sub-decisions are incorrect, their scenario score would be '0'.

Using the above logic, we calculated the scenario-wise mean scores and also the percentage of participants who obtained '100% correctness' and 'zero percent correctness' per scenario (cf. Fig. 3.A). The mean scores per scenarios are shown as 0.57 (level 1), 0.69 (level 2) and so on. This is basically the mean of all questions per scenario, in other words, this is similar to the question-based assessment, where correctness of each question is identified and then averaged out for that level. Using this method, we found the overall mean score (for all the participants and all the scenarios) to be 0.65, or 65%

participants gave correct answer to the questions. Figure 3B shows the percentage of participants who correctly answered the individual sub-decisions (questions) per scenario, and it is generally found to be over 50%, with the highest being ~ 84% (in level 6). In terms of mean score per question, this comes to 0.65. We then measured the 'all correct' scenarios. Overall, out of the total 35,592 individual scenarios (six scenarios per participant, n = 5,932), a total of 10,270 scenarios scored 'all correct' (Fig. 3.A), coming to 28.9%, which is a tiny percentage. As per the Fig. 3.A, 13.45% participants made all correct sub-decisions for level 1, 32.99% for level 2 and so on. Comparing this with the percentage of participants who gave correct answers to individual questions (Fig. 3.B) shows that the former is very low.

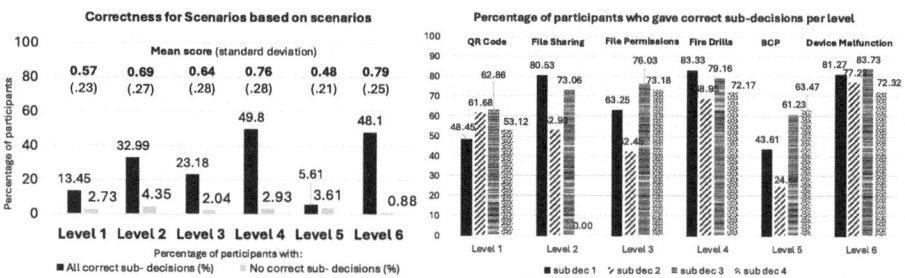

Fig. 3. A. Scenarios' correctness percentages, B. Correctness per individual sub-decisions

The details of scenarios and sub-decisions are provided in the Appendix. From Fig. 3.A we can also see that game levels 4 and 6 showed the highest percentage of 'all correct' sub-decisions. Game level 5 (BCP) showed the worst performance.

5.1 Demographics Analysis

Considering the overall mean correctness of scenarios among the genders, we found that females (M = 0.66, var = 0.07) show slightly higher mean over males (M = 0.65, var = 0.07). This was found to be statistically significant, despite having a small difference in the mean (Welch t-test, t(30,256) = −3.6, p < 0.01, here we considered overall scenarios for males (total N = 19,998) and females (total N = 14,052)). The effect size, Cohen's d = 0.03 here, meaning the gender difference in performance is minimal. Considering the percentage of participants who gave 'all correct' responses in all scenarios, females showed slightly higher percentage of 30.0% compared to males (28.4%). Similarly, considering the participants educational backgrounds, those with CS/IT background (M = 0.66, var = 0.07) performed slightly better than those with non-CS/IT background (M = 0.64, var = 0.07). We found a significant difference here, Welch t-test, t(31,192) = 6.0, p < 0.01, (a lower effect size, d = 0.06) when it comes to scenario-wise correctness. 30.4% of the CS/IT participants and 27.2% of the non-CS/IT category participants gave 'all correct' responses in all scenarios.

5.2 On Game Experience

The participants found the game to be engaging and educational, as seen from their game feedback responses. Many participants provided qualitative feedback such as 'classic design', 'nicely designed game', and 'very educational and in an interesting manner'. Some participants also agreed that gamified method of awareness is better than traditional methods. A Likert scale [27] game feedback response show that majority of the participants agree that the game is fun (M = 3.98, Var = .77), educational (M = 4.00, Var = .73) and is the preferred mode of cybersecurity assessment and awareness (M = 3.99, Var = .73) over other methods.

6 Discussion

The game results report that the at least 65% participants gave correct answers to the questions (sub-decisions), which can be considered as "question-wise responses" (cf. Fig. 3B). Considering all the scenarios, the percentage of 'all correct' scenarios is just 28.9%. The above findings show that there is a discrepancy when assessing the same intervention based on individual questions and individual scenarios. There could be chances that this behavior is reflected in real life as well. Awareness in an area of security should ensure that all the possible sources of insecure practices should be avoided. From Fig. 3. A, B, we answer our RQ that correct answers for questions alone within scenarios do not necessarily guarantee the complete awareness in that particular scenario, as 'all correct' scenarios are few. Our finding also augments the study [28], which states that a question-answer method alone cannot be used to judge the awareness of a cybersecurity topic. Based on our study, we suggest that the mode of assessment should also be upgraded. The assessment should prioritize scenario-wise understanding of the users. As per [28], we agree that security education must be targeted, actionable and provide feedback. We also found level 5 (BCP) to have the lowest performance, most likely because the majority of the users may not have encountered such a situation in real life and hence, they may require further training in that area. Our demographic analysis of participants' performance found slight differences among genders and educational background. We believe once we expand our study to a wider audience, these differences will become practically significant and would give insights on how to conduct demographics-targeted training.

6.1 Limitations and Future Work

In our enterprise-based exploratory study, we define scenario-wise correctness in terms of '100% correctness' of all the sub-decisions within that particular scenario. However, in certain security situations, this might not be needed. Further studies are required to formally define what constitutes a scenario in the context of security assessments and this could also change based on the demographics and skill level of the participants. We give a starting point to introduce the need for a scenario-based assessment, particularly in the domain of enterprise security awareness.

At present, our exploratory study does not include a control condition to compare the results with the game. We also do not have a knowledge retention test to see if the feedback provided during the game helped users understand the concepts. Moreover, we believe that more insights can be obtained with wider demographics. Regarding the game design, we believe the elements of pipe, valves, and the game environment could be updated in a future version of the game to provide a better aesthetics. The answer options contain two choices, which might give the users a fifty-fifty chance at getting the correct response. We will incorporate more multiple-choice questions in the next edition of the game to minimize the possibilities of a random bias. While we believe the participants were honest in their responses, we did not explicitly test if the reward system of the game has an impact on their performance. Further studies are required in this regard.

While we performed the initial analysis of the game-based data of the participants, we intend to analyze further on a deeper level. We plan on identifying the individual sub-decision-based performance of the participants and hope to find the reasons why certain sub-decisions performed poorly as compared to others. We plan to perform a comparative control condition where the game-based methodology will be compared with a nested questionnaire method. We also intend to create new security scenarios within the game. Our immediate step would be to conduct a delayed retention test, where we hope to gauge the understanding of the participants on the in-game security areas and to see the effects of the in-game feedback. Further plans include expanding the area of study to phishing, password security, and other areas of cybersecurity and privacy. Based on our exploratory study, we intend to update the training materials to focus more on security scenarios. Different kind of simulation-based tests will be incorporated as a part of employee awareness and their performance will be evaluated. While directly measuring user's online engagement is unethical, we will use these tests and certain simulations to gauge the participants' performance.

7 Conclusion

Our work in progress exploratory study with 'Right Turn' serious game focused on several security scenarios, each with multiple sub-decision-making steps, simulating real life scenarios. The study was targeted at an enterprise audience. We report that despite having a good performance in answering individual sub-decisions (or questions) within a scenario, the scenarios as a whole showed very poor performance. In other words, a small percentage of the participants got every sub-decision correct within all scenarios. This hints that most of the participants have a partial awareness of the respective security areas. Based on our study, we propose that the future security training and assessment methods focus on scenario-wise understanding of the users rather than question-answer-correctness approach because we believe that the former gives a better insight on how the user perceives the scenario (having multiple sub-decisions) in real life. This could augment a targeted training method. Our future work in this study includes performing further sub-decision-based analysis, a delayed retention test, a control condition, and expanding the study to a wider audience.

Appendix

The scenarios and the situations presented within each game level are given here. Some information (though fictional) has been redacted to protect the confidentiality of the organization under study. The six scenarios constitute the six levels in the game. When each level starts, the user will see the main scenario description as a pop-up message. After the user reads the scenario description and closes the pop up, the situations will be presented as valves. Upon mouse hover, the questions will appear on each valve that is found within the level, which the player will have to turn based on the answer. A screenshot of level 1 of the game is given below (Fig. 4):

Fig. 4. Screenshot of the game showing a sub-decision point. The option, as shown, pops up when the player hovers over right arrow for the third valve.

A.1 Scenario 1

"You are in a shop to purchase your monthly grocery. On the shop's outside wall, you see a poster with a QR code and text mentioning "Scan the QR code for 30% discount on all your purchases". The offer looks attractive to you. What will be the next steps you will follow?"

Situations within Scenario 1. (Displayed at each valve within the level)

1. Validate the offer
    Left Arrow: Confirm with shop manager
    Right Arrow: Manually inspect QR code
    Feedback: Checking with the shop manager before scanning the QR code will give extra assurance
2. Check for any known logo on the poster
    Left Arrow: A QR code with logo is authentic

Right Arrow: A logo is no guarantee that the QR is authentic

Feedback: A QR code, even with a logo, may not be authentic

3. Check pixel density of the QR Code

Left Arrow: Dense QR codes are authentic

Right Arrow: A dense QR does not guarantee authenticity

Feedback: Pixel density doesn't mean anything in a QR code

4. Auto redirection of URLs within QR codes

Left Arrow: Do not allow the scanner app to do auto redirection.

Right Arrow: Allow the scanner app to do auto redirection of URLs.

Feedback: The scanner application must not execute the QR code payload to avoid malicious execution

A.2 Scenario 2

"You are part of the team in the organization supporting a large deal for a US-based customer. Based on internal review, you did multiple last-minute changes in estimations, which has changed the overall cost for the program. You want to share the revised estimation sheet urgently with Jia, also part of bid team, working from customer location. Jia is more connected to customer emails than <organization's> emails. Detailed estimation sheet needs to be shared only to her, client partner and <redacted>, and not to the entire bidding team."

Situations within Scenario 2. (Displayed at each valve within the level)

1. How to send the file so that Jia does not miss it?

Left Arrow: Use WhatsApp, as Jia checks messages very often

Right Arrow: Use official email ID for business communication

Feedback: Sharing business information over social media is most vulnerable to information leakage

2. Which email ID to choose?

Left Arrow: Use customer email ID

Right Arrow: Use organization email ID

Feedback: Use organization's email ID for organization-related communication. You can drop a line to Jia on customer to check her organization's mails

3. How to restrict access to the file?

Left Arrow: Enable 'Do Not Forward' on the email

Right Arrow: Protect the file with <redacted>

Feedback: Do Not Forward' control permits recipients to download and share file. <redacted> can restrict access to certain users/period.

A.3 Scenario 3

"You received an invite to join one WhatsApp group from a known community group. After joining the new group, you get a Pulse measuring application .APK file which is a free mobile app for Android, and very efficient battery saver too."

Situations within Scenario 3. (Displayed at each valve within the level)

1. Configuring the App

    Left Arrow: Do not allow location and contact access

    Right Arrow: Allow location and contact access

    Feedback: For pulse measuring app, no contact or location information is required

2. Data storage

    Left Arrow: Allow the app to process the data locally

    Right Arrow: Allow the app to process the data on cloud

    Feedback: You have control over locally stored data

3. Permission to read SMS

    Left Arrow: Allow the app to read the messages

    Right Arrow: Do not allow the app to read the messages

    Feedback: For pulse measurement, SMS access is not required

4. Install.APK file

    Left Arrow: Install applications only through trusted app stores

    Right Arrow: Install.APK from the WhatsApp group chat

    Feedback: Known app store has control to detect fraudulent apps.

A.4 Scenario 4

"You are in a conference call with the customer on 5th floor of the <organization> office. This is a critical meeting with key stakeholders from customer side. At the same time, the admin officer of the building has made all necessary arrangements for the fire evacuation drill. Fire alarm starts followed by a PA announcement for associates informing them to evacuate the building since there is a fire. How will you respond?"

Situations within Scenario 4. (Displayed at each valve within the level)

1. Evaluate the situation

    Left Arrow: Ignore since it is just a drill

    Right Arrow: Decide to evacuate the building

    Feedback: By participating in drills, you are preparing to safeguard yourself in a real situation that may be life-threatening

2. When to evacuate?

    Left Arrow: Inform customer, disconnect the call and evacuate

    Right Arrow: Continue with call till Fire Marshal instructs you

    Feedback: Your safety is most important. Customers will appreciate you adhering to the norms.

3. How to evacuate quickly?

    Left Arrow: Take the nearest elevator

    Right Arrow: Use staircase

    Feedback: For your safety, you must use the staircase in case of a fire.

4. Upon exiting the building

    Left Arrow: Be at assembly point and wait for instructions

    Right Arrow: Find some place to continue customer call

    Feedback: Being not at assembly point, you may miss important instructions, which can be dangerous in case of real incident.

A.5 Scenario 5

"Team is providing production support services from <redacted> in <redacted>. Team has identified <redacted> office as an alternate site. It is 30 Kms away from <redacted>. There are stringent SLAs for incidents - Priority (P1) tickets to be resolved within <redacted>; P2 tickets in <redacted> and P3 tickets in <redacted>. Team has committed 25% of the services to be restored during any outage scenario. Team size is <redacted> and there are <redacted> seats reserved in the alternate site to handle any site outage scenario. Team conducts the site outage drills every quarter by visiting alternate site and tests network connectivity using their laptops."

Situations within Scenario 5 (Displayed at each valve within the level).

1. Managing SLAs (Service Level Agreements) in crisis
   Left Arrow: Possible with current set up
   Right Arrow: Not possible with current set up
   Feedback: Even if alternate site is in the same city, travel time to reach the alternate site to resume operations is not accounted
2. Effectiveness of drills
   Left Arrow: Not effective.
   Right Arrow: Effective since they are conducted quarterly
   Feedback: Drills tested only network connectivity. Performing actual work from alternate site will provide better assurance.
3. Assurance to handle agreed ticket volume during crisis
   Left Arrow: Plan is adequate
   Right Arrow: Plan is not adequate
   Feedback: Sufficient number of seats are planned at alternate site, in line with minimum business continuity objective of 25%
4. Way to meet stringent SLAs
   Left Arrow: Alternate site to be in the same campus to save travel time
   Right Arrow: Split support operations from 2 sites
   Feedback: Transfer of work to a team working from alternate site would be much quicker than moving people

A.6 Scenario 6

"You are working from a home on a critical project activity using <organization> provided laptop. Suddenly, your laptop stops functioning and you are unable to continue your work. How will you respond to the situation so that there is minimal or no impact on project deliverable?"

Situations within Scenario 6 (Displayed at each valve within the level).

1. Inform Manager
   Left Arrow: Call to seek further guidance
   Right Arrow: Send SMS to identify someone to take over
   Feedback: It is possible that SMS may not be read immediately. Calling the Manager can trigger immediate action.

2. Ensure work continues

    Left Arrow: Visit nearby Cyber-café to continue work

    Right Arrow: Transfer work to another associate

    Feedback: Working from a Cyber-café is not a secure option. Transferring work to another associate is a much better option.

3. Fix the issue with laptop

    Left Arrow: Fix the issue with self-help videos on YouTube

    Right Arrow: Seek help from <redacted> team

    Feedback: Fixing hardware issue yourself can void the warranty. Hence it is always advisable to seek help from <redacted> team.

4. Use an alternate device to get work done

    Left Arrow: Request IS team to provide an alternate asset

    Right Arrow: Complete work using personal laptop

    Feedback: personal device will not have required security controls. Using them for official purpose is also a security violation.

References

1. Amankwa, E.: Relevance of cybersecurity education at pedagogy levels in schools. J. Inf. Secur. **12**(4), 233–249 (2021)
2. Wen, Z.A., Lin, Z., Chen, R., Andersen, E.: What. hack: engaging anti-phishing training through a role-playing phishing simulation game. In: Proceedings of the 2019 CHI Conference on Human Factors in Computing Systems, pp. 1–12 (2019)
3. Sheng, S., et al.: Anti-phishing phil: the design and evaluation of a game that teaches people not to fall for phish. In: Proceedings of the 3rd Symposium on Usable Privacy and Security, pp. 88–99 (2007)
4. Gokul, C.J., Pandit, S., Vaddepalli, S., Tupsamudre, H., Banahatti, V., Lodha, S.: PHISHY-a serious game to train enterprise users on phishing awareness. In: Proceedings of the 2018 Annual Symposium on Computer-Human Interaction in Play Companion Extended Abstracts, pp. 169–181 (2018)
5. Jayakrishnan, G.C., Sirigireddy, G.R., Vaddepalli, S., Banahatti, V., Lodha, S.P., Pandit, S.S.: Passworld: a serious game to promote password awareness and diversity in an enterprise. In: 16th Symposium on Usable Privacy and Security (SOUPS), pp. 1–18 (2020)
6. Tupsamudre, H., et al.: GAP: a game for improving awareness about passwords. In: Göbel, S., et al. (eds.) JCSG 2018. LNCS, vol. 11243, pp. 66–78. Springer, Dordrecht (2018). https://doi.org/10.1007/978-3-030-02762-9_8
7. Hill Jr, W.A., Fanuel, M., Yuan, X., Zhang, J., Sajad, S.: A survey of serious games for cybersecurity education and training (2020)
8. Kam, H.J., Ormond, D.K., Menard, P., Crossler, R.E.: That's interesting: an examination of interest theory and self-determination in organisational cybersecurity training. Inf. Syst. J. **32**(4), 888–926 (2022)
9. Hart, S., Margheri, A., Paci, F., Sassone, V.: Riskio: a serious game for cyber security awareness and education. Comput. Secur. **95**, 101827 (2020)
10. Mittal, A., Gupta, M.P., Chaturvedi, M., Chansarkar, S.R., Gupta, S.: Cybersecurity Enhancement through Blockchain Training (CEBT)–a serious game approach. Int. J. Inf. Manag. Data Insights **1**(1), 100001 (2021)

11. Chettoor Jayakrishnan, G., Banahatti, V., Lodha, S.: GOVID: repurposing serious game for enterprise COVID-19 awareness. In: Proceedings of the 12th Indian Conference on Human-Computer Interaction, pp. 11–18 (2021)
12. Zyda, M.: From visual simulation to virtual reality to games. Computer **38**(9), 25–32 (2005)
13. Sawyer, B.: Serious Games: Improving Public Policy through Game-based Learning and Simulation. Foresight and Governance Project (2001)
14. Jayakrishnan, G., Banahatti, V., Lodha, S.: PickMail: a serious game for email Phishing Awareness training. In: Usable Security and Privacy (USEC) Symposium (2022)
15. Hart, S., Halak, B., Sassone, V.: MOTENS: a pedagogical design model for serious cyber games. arXiv preprint arXiv:2110.11765 (2021)
16. Deci, E.L., Ryan, R.M.: Self-determination theory: a macrotheory of human motivation, development, and health. Can. Psychol. **49**(3), 182 (2008)
17. Unkelos-Shpigel, N., Hadar, I.: Gamifying software development environments using cognitive principles. In: CAiSE Forum, pp. 9–16 (2015)
18. Plumber 3. Mobile Game. Appholdings. https://play.google.com/store/apps/details?id=com.Appholdings.Plumber3&hl=en_IN. Accessed 23 Sept 2024
19. Water Pipes. Mobile Game. Mobiloids. https://play.google.com/store/apps/details?id=com.mobiloids.waterpipespuzzle&hl=en_IN. Accessed 23 Sept 2024
20. Home Pipe. Water Puzzle. Mobile Game. Gameestudio. https://play.google.com/store/apps/details?id=com.gamee.homepiperescue&hl=en_IN. Accessed 23 Sept 2024
21. Mitgutsch, K., Alvarado, N.: Purposeful by design? A serious game design assessment framework. In: Proceedings of the International Conference on the Foundations of Digital Games, pp. 121–128 (2012)
22. Sicart, M.: Defining game mechanics. Game Stud. (8), 2 (2008). http://gamestudies.org/0802/articles/sicart. Accessed 23 Sept 2024
23. Donovan, Suzanne, M., Bransford, J.D., Pellegrino, J.W.: How People Learn: Bridging Research and Practice. National Academy Press, Washington, DC (1999)
24. Bellotti, F., et al.: Designing serious games for education: from pedagogical principles to game mechanisms. In: Proceedings of the 5th European Conference on Games Based Learning, pp. 26–34 (2011)
25. Bhosale, T., Kulkarni, S., Patankar, S.N.: 2d platformer game in unity engine. Int. Res. J. Eng. Technol. **5**(04), 3021–3024 (2018)
26. Ahmad, W.F.B.W., Shafie, A.B., Latif, M.H.A.B.A.: Role-playing game-based learning in mathematics. Electron. J. Math. Technol. **4**(2), 184–196 (2010)
27. Allen, I.E., Seaman, C.A.: Likert scales and data analyses. Qual. Prog. **40**(7), 64–65 (2007)
28. Bada, M., Sasse, A.M., Nurse, J.R.: Cyber security awareness campaigns: why do they fail to change behaviour? arXiv preprint arXiv:1901.02672 (2019)
29. Krombholz, K., Frühwirt, P., Kieseberg, P., Kapsalis, I., Huber, M., Weippl, E.: QR code security: a survey of attacks and challenges for usable security. In: Tryfonas, T., Askoxylakis, I. (eds.) HAS 2014. LNCS, vol. 8533, pp. 79–90. Springer, Cham (2014). https://doi.org/10.1007/978-3-319-07620-1_8
30. Soon, T.J.: QR code. Synth. J. **2008**, 59–78 (2008)
31. Tiwari, S.: An introduction to QR code technology. In: International Conference on Information Technology (ICIT), pp. 39–44. IEEE (2016)
32. Kieseberg, P., et al.: QR code security. In: Proceedings of the 8th International Conference on Advances in Mobile Computing and Multimedia, pp. 430–435 (2010)
33. Liu, Z.Y., Shaikh, Z.A., Gazizova, F.: Using the concept of game-based learning in education. Int. J. Emerg. Technol. Learn. **15**, 53 (2020)
34. Ketamo, H., Kiili, K.: Conceptual change takes time: game based learning cannot be only supplementary amusement. J. Educ. Multimedia Hypermedia **19**(4), 399–419 (2010)

Voice User Interface for Designing Inclusive Games for Children with Visual Impairment and Sighted Pupils

Monika$^{(\boxtimes)}$ ⓘ and Aakash Johry ⓘ

Department of Design, Indian Institute of Technology Delhi, New Delhi, India
monikasunariya1798@gmail.com

Abstract. Children with visual impairment (VI) face significant challenges in experiencing inclusive play due to limited accessibility to games. This study explores how Voice User Interfaces (VUIs), specifically Amazon's Alexa, can facilitate inclusive play experiences among visually impaired and sighted children. We conducted contextual inquiry studies and a series of co-design workshops with special educators and students with mixed visual abilities, identifying key challenges and deriving opportunities for game design on VUI. We shared a game prototype demonstrating a dynamic and inclusive play experience with a VUI in a low-resource environment. Through evaluation and testing, design insights and challenges are shared with the game development community, which will help them to develop accessible games relevant to Indian schools.

Keywords: Visually Impaired · Inclusive Play · Voice User Interface · Alexa

1 Introduction

Children with varying degrees of VIs face ongoing challenges in mainstream settings in participation, collaborative learning, and social engagement, to some extent because of the structure and design of assistive technologies [14]. One of the areas affected by this is the play experience. Interaction with peers is crucial for these children, not only for their development and enjoyment but also to exercise their right to participate in recreational, play, leisure, and sports activities which have historically been denied to those with sensory disabilities [3]. Earlier studies also mention the developmental delays children with visual impairment experience due to the lack of experiences with social/play and gross motor behaviors [22]. A large body of studies has been conducted on the use of play and games for learning for children with disabilities [5, 11, 12, 18, 21, 23] and visual impairment [13, 15, 19, 20] and on attempts to make new and existing digital games accessible, fun, and engaging for blind gamers using auditory and vibrotactile feedback [2, 8, 10, 13, 14, 16, 18, 24]. However, these studies are primarily focused on the developed regions: where largely people had access to technology, the internet, and accessibility tools, and at the same time focus largely on individual play. Accessible technologies and games often cater to specific user groups, such as those requiring

N. Rangaswamy et al. (Eds.): IndiaHCI 2024, CCIS 2338, pp. 89–98, 2025.
https://doi.org/10.1007/978-3-031-80832-6_7

accessibility support. This focus can hinder inclusion, as games designed for VI players may be overly simplified, resulting in a lack of engagement for sighted players [7]. There is a severe scarcity of research that examines the design and use of digital games for people with visual impairments in low-resource environments [9], which include both sighted and VI children.

For this study, we decided to explore the shared modality of audio along with scenarios where technologies like VUI can assist in designing inclusive play experiences among pupils with VI and their sighted peers. Specifically, we investigated how VUI devices like Amazon's Alexa can facilitate inclusive play in diverse group settings. We aim to understand the forms of support VUI devices can provide in these contexts. By co-designing VUIs for inclusive play experiences with a variety of stakeholders, including pupils with and without VIs and their educators, we seek to extend existing research in this area. This made our approach that doesn't prioritize the needs of one specific group. We did this by addressing the key research questions: 1) What are the current challenges to inclusive play experiences for visually impaired and sighted children? 2) How can VUI assist in an inclusive game experience?

We explored the potential of VUIs for inclusive play by discussing with experts and conducting contextual inquiries in a special school operated by the NGO Saksham to learn about challenges and barriers to inclusive play experiences. This special school offers tailored programs for different educational stages, including foundational learning, mainstream support, and higher secondary education. We engaged with special educators and two groups of students: one from mainstream schools and another that only had children with varied levels of VI. We then ran co-design workshops with these groups to learn about their challenges in inclusive play and understand their interaction with Alexa. From these activities, we derived a set of guidelines for the design of games, conducted an ideation session with a game designer and students to further develop the game concept, and prototyped and tested them with children with mixed visual abilities. This study contributes to 1) Identification of design space of how VUIs could be used to support inclusive play in low-resource environments. 2) A set of findings from the prototype testing provides a basis for designing play support for inclusive play through VUI.

2   State of the Art

Games for sighted players are typically visual, making them inaccessible for visually impaired players [25]. As a result, games that engage visually impaired and sighted children are rare as we lack options for play experiences in their shared modalities. This highlights the need to design opportunities that foster inclusive play between disabled and non-disabled players in heterogeneous settings in their shared modality like tactile interactions, auditory cues, and haptic feedback but at the same time are engaging. Voice-based interaction is primarily used in home environments to access online content, manage shopping, and control appliances. There is ongoing research on using voice-user interfaces for assistants with different personalities [25], helping the elderly with smart home assistance and error prevention [17], and for children in the educational context [15] to name some. Although VUIs offer a natural interaction method for individuals with VIs, their effectiveness for visually impaired and sighted students in inclusive play settings still needs to be explored.

Our initial research showed that young children with VI in the Indian context use technologies for independent functioning and educational contexts in mainstream settings. However, the use of technology for inclusive experiences is scarce, owing to socio-economic constraints [9]. Hence, the use of easily available technology for play experiences like VUI can significantly enhance access to inclusive play and shared engaging experiences.

3   Methodology

The initial study aimed to understand the currently available experiences, challenges, and barriers to inclusive play for visually impaired children by conducting contextual inquiry sessions and workshops with 2 groups of students 1) 7–12 years old and, 2) 12–16 years old, to understand their interactions with VUI. These sessions included focus group discussions and individual interviews, leading to the identification of several key issues including lack of resources, limited playtime, slow and non-dynamic play opportunities, and limited social interaction and mobility.

Following these initial observations, workshops were conducted to understand the functionality of Alexa and how children interacted with VUI and available games. In a series of workshops, children engaged with Alexa skills and VUI games, highlighting difficulties with language comprehension, the need for facilitator support, and the lack of prior concepts in play along with the challenges in the usability of Alexa. We also found these children never opportunity to explore the play space which is engaging, in groups, and allows gross motor behaviors.

A 120-min ideation workshop was conducted with 1 game designer with experience in designing for atypical children and other post-graduate students who had exposure to game design to conceptualize VUI game ideas. They formed four groups of three to brainstorm a wide array of concepts. These ideas were refined through bodystorming exercises to test feasibility and appeal. The focus was on developing audio-based interaction games to enhance sensory engagement and playability for young audiences. Concepts were then made and further iterated using all the learnings and observations. Initial testing was done on the Alexa stimulator post developing it on the Alexa Developer Console and then feedback from testing was incorporated into the gameplay mechanics (Fig. 1).

Fig. 1. Parts of the ideation workshop session: a) conceptualizing ideas, sharing and reflecting on inclusive games; b) body-storming game experiences.

4   Catch the Thief: Concept and Design

4.1   About the Game

"Catch the Thief" is a game meticulously designed to enhance interaction and gross motor behavior, for children of age 7–12. The game's structure and mechanics leverage a VUI facilitated by Alexa, providing an inclusive and engaging experience. The primary objective of "Catch the Thief" is for players to identify the "thief" among the group based on coded clues provided by Alexa. Players must use these clues to make an informed decision to attempt to catch the thief. Success in catching the thief earns points, promoting both cognitive and physical engagement.

4.2   Game Setup

For the formation, players stand in a circle, ensuring an arm's-length distance between each other and keeping their palms over the adjacent person's arms. Before starting the game, each player is instructed to remember the names of the individuals standing to their right and left, as this knowledge is crucial for decoding the clues. During the entire process, assistance was provided by the teacher who was involved in the supervision of the game.

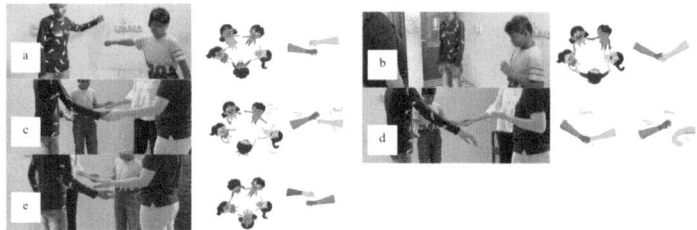

Fig. 2. Parts of the evaluation workshop session. Participants: a) stand at one arm's distance from each other; b) stand in circular formation; c) keep palms over the adjacent person's palm; d) react to clue and try to catch the adjacent person's palm; e) shuffle positions in further rounds

4.3   Game Mechanics

In the game, Alexa delivers clues in a coded format, specifying the name of the person adjacent to the thief and their precise location (left or right). Based on this information, players attempt to catch the thief by pointing towards the side where they believe the thief is located. Following each attempt, Alexa validates the attempt by querying its success. If the player correctly identifies the thief, they earn a point; if the attempt is unsuccessful, a point is deducted. Players who reach a predetermined point threshold may advance to higher difficulty levels or receive additional rewards, enhancing their engagement and motivation throughout the game.

4.4 Game Progression

The game introduces varying levels of difficulty to maintain engagement and challenge players' spatial reasoning skills. In the initial levels, the thief's position is restricted to the right of the chosen player. As players progress to advanced levels, the thief can be positioned on either side, increasing the complexity of the game. Additionally, to ensure fairness and further enhance the challenge, players shuffle their positions after every few rounds (refer the Fig. 2). This requires continuous adaptation and attention, promoting sustained cognitive and physical engagement throughout the gameplay.

5 Evaluation and Findings

An evaluation workshop was conducted to assess how the developed Alexa skill prototype supports inclusive play experiences. The skill was introduced to the participants across two different play contexts of 3 children with VI and their 2 sighted peers 1)with a facilitator, and 2) without a facilitator. The game, which lasted between 30–40 min, was facilitated by one TA for support and assistance. The play sessions were observed, and a short interview was conducted with the children and the teacher at the end of the session to gather their insights. Data was collected in the form of diary notes of the activity along with the videos during the testing. Observations were made around children's play behavior. At the same time, the game was evaluated against the usability heuristics for Speech-Based Smart Devices [7, 17].

5.1 Engagement with Alexa

On average, a typical session in one round of a game lasted for 15–20 min. The children were engaged with the application throughout the session and did not leave the session mid-way.

5.2 General + Conversation Style Observations

Agent Persona. It was observed during the initial round of play testing that there was no distinction between Alexa's generic persona and game facilitator persona. The use of language, sounds, and other stylistic elements gave Alexa a distinct agent persona just for the game, which the children found engaging. The variety of sound design (sound landscape, feedback tones) incorporated into the game was particularly enjoyed by the children.

System Status Clarity. Different tones were used for different actions and use cases in the game, providing clear game status information. This aided the children in understanding the stage and progress in the game. This included: round start music, waiting state music, and winning/losing music.

Multiple Responses or Non-response and Game Termination. Alexa effectively communicated situations where there were multiple responses, no responses, and when the game was about to switch off due to inactivity. This clarity prevented confusion and helped maintain engagement. But in certain cases, Alexa stopped without any question or prompt. This is illustrated as follows:

Alexa: Sorry, I didn't understand the response. Can you repeat?

(Wait)

Alexa: I didn't get you. We will stop the game if there is no response.

Action Confirmation. Before registering scores, Alexa confirmed game actions such as "catch" or "miss," ensuring that players were aware of the outcomes of their attempts. An interesting thing was that some children tried to change their responses for fun. This interaction is illustrated as follows:

Engaging Tone. One notable shortcoming in the initial rounds of texting was Alexa's default voice, which lacked the excitement and engagement needed for the game. The new recorded voice, incorporates Hindi and English phrases, emphasizing the excited and disappointed expression of the persona. This version was more engaging and aided comprehension. The conversational style of the newly recorded voice was similar to how their facilitators and teachers interacted with them, making it more relatable and easily understandable for the children.

Alexa: (Music) Was it a 'Catch' or a 'Miss'?

Participant: Miss.

Alexa: Oho(disappointed), no problem, try next time.

Alexa: (Music) Was it a 'Catch' or a 'Miss'?

Participant: Catch.

Alexa: WOHOO (excited), Good job (Excited)!! You have a point.

5.3   Guiding, Teaching, and Offering Help + Feedback and Prompts

Alexa's "Catch the Thief" game effectively guides users through each step, subtly cueing desired responses and preventing confusion. The game teaches users various commands organically, enhancing the experience with natural, conversational interactions. By using these strategies, the game ensures users remain engaged, informed, and supported throughout their play. An example of such interaction is illustrated as follows:

Alexa: It is time to shuffle. Shuffle your places.

Alexa: Are you ready for the new round or need more time?

Participant: More time.

Alexa: Okay, I will wait. Tell me whenever you are ready.

5.4   Errors

The game effectively uses concise prompts and intelligent input confirmation to keep interactions clear and engaging. However, the system is also challenged with handling low speech recognition confidence, leading to repeated re-prompts and frustration. Multimodal feedback may not be fully utilized, limiting the engagement of users who rely on visual or tactile cues. Also, since children act mischievously to deviate from the game flow, an error correction mechanism must be so that it can easily navigate mistaken conversations.

5.5 Speed of Speech

There were recurring challenges related to the speed of speech with Alexa's stimulator experience which then required some children to wait and hear the instructions and communications from Alexa for the next steps but they did enjoy the fast speed during the gameplay, which suggested the need of varying speaking rate in different contexts, and makes speech rate as one of the design element for Alexa as mentioned in some earlier studies [1, 6].

5.6 Engagement with Alexa

While children showed engagement across all play contexts in the "Catch the Thief" game, their experiences showed notable differences. With a facilitator present, children felt a sense of comfort, as the facilitator could offer personalized guidance based on their strengths and weaknesses. The feedback from Alexa and encouragement from the facilitator complemented each other well, leading to higher motivation and playfulness. However, this dynamic sometimes fostered a sense of adult authority, causing hesitation among children who waited for assistance, or approval before acting. Despite this, children relied on the facilitator to ensure fair play and trusted them to maintain the integrity of the game. In contrast, during unsupervised play conditions, children were able to complete the game independently, proceeding at their own pace. Playing independently with Alexa made children appear more competitive. They responded similarly to game prompts and engaged in chit-chat between turns, indicating comfort with the game environment. The absence of a facilitator allowed for more spontaneous and autonomous interactions, highlighting the children's ability to navigate the game confidently and competitively. This independent gameplay with Alexa demonstrated that children could effectively engage with the VUI, promoting a more self-directed play experience gradually.

5.7 Overall Feedback on the Application

In follow-up interviews, most children enthusiastically responded when asked if they enjoyed themselves, expressing joy in trying a new technology. They particularly appreciated the soundscape and Alexa's expression tones, as evident in their positive reactions during testing in the form of physical movements and body language. Except for one fully blind participant, others confidently engaged in the play from the beginning; he also developed confidence after a few rounds.

Facilitators acknowledged that the activities encompassed new elements and forms of play for these children and were designed in a way that encouraged physical movement and inclusivity. The application was found to be usable, and children were able to use it independently, apart from a few instances where they sought support. For example, some children found the audio instructions in the final game to be lacking clarity and being fast in speech delivery and had difficulty continuously counting the points gained. Overall, the application successfully promoted engagement and inclusivity, demonstrating its potential as a valuable tool for play.

6   Discussion and Way Forward

The "Catch the Thief" game demonstrates the potential of VUI technology to create engaging and inclusive play experiences for children with VIs beyond the existing home and educational setting and adds to the learnings of the digital play space in the low-resource landscape of India [9]. By leveraging VUI, the game offers a dynamic and interactive environment that allows children to participate on an equal footing with their sighted peers. This study builds on Metatla et al.'s research on designing VUI for educational experiences, expanding its application to fun and leisure activities. It underscores the capacity of VUI to facilitate mobility and provide accessible experiences that go beyond static interactions, thereby broadening the scope of VUI's applicability. The game's design fosters constant engagement and active participation, highlighting the possibility of giving autonomy to children participating in the game for the conversation with the voice assistant rather than to the agent as observed earlier in the study where it was mentioned to be one-sided [1]. This reflects the transformative potential of VUI in inclusive play and experiences.

The present study also had several limitations pertaining to a homogeneous sample size, confined to participants from a single organization. This lack of diversity may have biased the findings, not fully representing the wider population of children with VIs from different geographical and socio-economic backgrounds. The game faced several technical issues during the evaluation, such as abrupt stops due to inactivity, fast rate of speech, and unclear audio instructions. These interruptions affected the overall user experience and highlighted the need for further refinement. For the game experience, further refinement in giving more autonomy to the user in the play experience and reducing the current involvement of Alexa is needed for a more engaging inclusive experience.

The "Catch the Thief" game demonstrated significant potential in promoting engagement and inclusivity for children with VI. This study highlights the broader implications of VUI technology in creating independent, dynamic, interactive, and accessible play experiences. While further validation is necessary, the initial findings suggest that VUI applications can play a crucial role in enhancing the quality of life for children with VIs by providing opportunities for inclusive and interactive play.

Disclosure of Interests.   The authors have no competing interests to declare that are relevant to the content of this article.

References

1. Abdolrahmani, A., Kuber, R., Branham, S. M.: "Siri Talks at You": an empirical investigation of voice-activated personal assistant (VAPA) usage by individuals who are blind. In: Proceedings of the 20th International ACM SIGACCESS Conference on Computers and Accessibility, pp. 249–258. Association for Computing Machinery, New York, NY, United States (2018)
2. Archambault, D., Ossmann, R., Gaudy, T., Miesenberger, K.: Computer games and visually impaired people. Upgrade **8**(2), 43–53 (2007)
3. Barron, C., et al.: Barriers to Play and Recreation for Children and Young People with Disabilities. Exploring Environmental Factors. De Gruyter Open Poland, Warsaw, Poland (2017)
4. Carvalho, J., Guerreiro, T., Duarte, L., Carriço, L.: Audiobased puzzle gaming for blind people. In: Proceedings of the Mobile Accessibility Workshop at MobileHCI (MOBACC), San Francisco, USA (2012)
5. Charlton, B., Williams, R., McLaughlin, F.: Educational games: a technique to accelerate the acquisition of reading skills of children with learning disabilities. Int. J. Spec. Educ. **20**, 66–72 (2005)
6. Choi, D., Kwak, D., Cho, M., Lee, S.: "Nobody Speaks that Fast!" an empirical study of speech rate in conversational agents for people with vision impairments. In: Proceedings of the 2020 CHI Conference on Human Factors in Computing Systems (Honolulu, HI, USA,), pp. 1–13. Association for Computing Machinery, New York (2020)
7. Wei, Z., Landay, J.A.: Evaluating speech-based smart devices using new usability heuristics. IEEE Perv. Comput. **17**(2), 84–96 (2018)
8. Gutschmidt, R., Schiewe, M., Francis Zinke, F., Jürgensen, H.: Haptic emulation of games: haptic Sudoku for the blind. In: Proceedings of the 3rd International Conference on PErvasive Technologies Related to Assistive Environments, pp. 1–8. Association for Computing Machinery, New York (2010)
9. India, G., O, A., Diwakar, N., Jain, M., Vashistha, A., Swaminathan, M.: Teachers' perceptions around digital games for children in low-resource schools for the blind. In: Proceedings of the 2021 CHI Conference on Human Factors in Computing Systems, pp. 1–17. Association for Computing Machinery, New York (2021)
10. Kim, J., Ricaurte. J. TapBeats: accessible and mobile casual gaming. In: The Proceedings of the 13th International ACM SIGACCESS Conference on Computers and Accessibility (Dundee, Scotland, UK) (ASSETS 2011), pp. 285–286. Association for Computing Machinery, New York (2011)
11. Lin, C.-Y., et al.: Augmented reality in educational activities for children with disabilities. Displays **42**, 51–54 (2016). https://doi.org/10.1016/j.displa.2015.02.004
12. Markey, C., Power, D., Booker, G.: Using structured games to teach early fraction concepts to students who are deaf or hard of hearing. Am. Ann. Deaf **148**, 251–258 (2003)
13. Metatla, O., Bardot, S., Cullen, C., Serrano, M.: Robots for inclusive play: co-designing an educational game with visually impaired and sighted children. In: CHI 2020: CHI Conference on Human Factors in Computing Systems, Honolulu, USA (2020)
14. Metatla, O., Cullen, C.: Bursting the assistance bubble: designing inclusive technology with children with mixed visual abilities. In: The 2018 CHI Conference. Association for Computing Machinery, New York (2018)
15. Metatla, O., Oldfield, A., Ahmed, T., Vafeas, A., Miglani, S.: Voice user interfaces in schools: co-designing for inclusion with visually-impaired and sighted pupils. In: CHI 2019: Proceedings of the 2019 CHI Conference on Human Factors in Computing Systems, Association for Computing Machinery, pp. 1–15 (2019)

16. Miller, D., Parecki, A., Douglas, S.: Finger dance: a sound game for blind people. In: Proceedings of the 9th International ACM SIGACCESS Conference on Computers and Accessibility (Tempe, Arizona, USA) (Assets 2007), pp. 253–254. Association for Computing Machinery, New York (2007)
17. Pednekar, S., Dhirawani, P., Shah, R., Shekokar, N., Ghag, K.: Exploring voice user interfaces for seniors. In: 3rd International Conference on Intelligent Communication and Computational Techniques (ICCT), pp. 1–8. IEEE (2023)
18. Roth, P., Petrucci, L., Assimacopoulos, A., Pun, T.: From dots to shapes: an auditory haptic game platform for teaching geometry to blind pupils (2000)
19. Sánchez, J., Elías, M.: Science learning in blind children through audio-based games. In: Engineering the User Interface, pp. 1–16. Springer, London (2009)
20. Sánchez, J., Saenz, M., Garrido, J.: Usability of a multimodal video game to improve navigation skills for blind children. In: ACM Transactions on Accessible Computing (TACCESS), vol 3, no. 2, pp. 1–29. Association for Computing Machinery, New York (2010)
21. Saridaki, M., Gouscos, D., Meimaris, M.: Digital game-based learning for students with intellectual disability. In: Games-Based Learning Advancements for Multi-Sensory Human Computer Interfaces: Techniques and Effective Practices, pp. 304–325 (2009)
22. Schneekloth, L.H.: Play environments for visually impaired children. J. Vis. Impair. Blind. **83**(4), 196–20 (1989)
23. Simpson, E.: Video games as learning environments for students with learning disabilities. Children Youth Environ. **19**, 306–319 (2009)
24. Sjöström, C.: Using haptics in computer interfaces for blind people. In: CHI 2001 extended abstracts on Human Factors in Computing Systems, pp. 245–246. Association for Computing Machinery, New York (2001)
25. Smith, B.A., Nayar, S.K.: The RAD: making racing games equivalently accessible to people who are blind. In: Proceedings of the 2018 CHI Conference on Human Factors in Computing Systems, pp. 1–12. Association for Computing Machinery, New York (2018)
26. Tangmanee, K., Teeravarunyou, S., Buaban, N.: Voice User Interface (VUI): A Review of Present and Potential Voice Assistant (VA) applications (2020)

Gamifying Mental Well-Being Assessment: A New Approach for College-Going Students Using the 'Oxford Happiness Questionnaire'

Renuka Singh$^{(\boxtimes)}$ (iD), Harsh Mohan Shrivastava (iD), M. Krishnadas (iD), and Aakash Johry (iD)

Department of Design, Indian Institute of Technology Delhi, New Delhi 110016, India
renuka.singh.iitdelhi@gmail.com

Abstract. Mental well-being is a critical aspect of overall health, particularly for college-going students, who face increasing levels of stress, anxiety, and depression. The Oxford Happiness Questionnaire (OHQ) has been a standard tool to assess mental health in multiple contexts, including educational settings. However, the self-reported nature of the OHQ leads to challenges like lack of engagement and the occurrence of biases. Conversely, gamification is a concept that has proven to be effective in increasing engagement. Therefore, this study proposes a novel approach by incorporating gamification strategies with OHQ to enhance user engagement and assess the mental well-being of college-going students. A gamified application called "The Mirror" has been developed using a 'research-through-design' approach. The study utilized a mixed-method methodology to compare the traditional OHQ with the gamified application in terms of user engagement and experience. Results from a pilot study indicate that the gamified OHQ increased engagement and provided a more enjoyable and personalized assessment experience compared to the traditional format. The findings suggest that integrating gamification into the OHQ can improve its efficacy as a self-guided questionnaire, making it more effective in assessing mental well-being. Future research with larger sample sizes and real-world testing is recommended to further refine the gamified application and validate its effectiveness.

Keywords: Gamification · Oxford Happiness Questionnaire · Mental Well-being · Assessment · College-going Students

1 Introduction

Mental well-being has emerged as a pressing global concern, impacting people of all ages and diverse backgrounds [1]. While physical health has been traditionally the main focus of healthcare systems worldwide, the significance of mental well-being is now gaining the recognition it deserves on a global scale [2]. For college-going students, it is recognized as a critical aspect of their overall health and academic success [3]. With the rising cases of stress, anxiety and depression among this population, there is an urgent need for creating innovative tools which can effectively assess the mental well-being of the college-going students.

© The Author(s), under exclusive license to Springer Nature Switzerland AG 2025
N. Rangaswamy et al. (Eds.): IndiaHCI 2024, CCIS 2338, pp. 99–107, 2025.
https://doi.org/10.1007/978-3-031-80832-6_8

When researching on mental well-being, broaching topics like "depression" can evoke strong emotional reactions, potentially dissuading individuals from discussing their vulnerabilities and leading to the dissemination of inaccurate information [4]. In light of this, the Oxford Happiness Questionnaire (OHQ) has emerged as a valuable resource. It capitalizes on the universal value placed on "happiness" by individuals [5]. It is a well-defined resource comprising a questionnaire with a standardized six-point Likert scale for responses [6]. This scale encompasses a balanced mix of affirmative and negative elements, which can be seamlessly incorporated into broader assessments [6]. While the OHQ provides valuable insights into an individual's emotional state and overall life satisfaction, it does have certain limitations that should be taken into account while interpreting its findings. These limitations include (1) *Response format limitations:* a page with 29 questions, make it difficult for the participants to grasp the essence of each question [7], and (2) *Not engaging in nature*: paper-based format lacks user engagement compared to the web-based interactive formats among students [8]. These limitations should be addressed from a methodological perspective. This opens an opportunity to investigate *how to improve the engagement and efficacy of OHQ,* as this would help in assessing the mental well-being of a large number of the population. In this study, we chose to focus *only on enhancing the engagement aspect of OHQ,* which might also have a positive effect on its efficacy but that is beyond the scope of this paper.

In this paper, we experimented with a gamified version of OHQ as a *self-guided interactive prototype,* and studied its effect on the engagement of the users. Gamification has been used here in particular, because research has shown that it has the potential to increase a user's engagement [9]. It has a tendency to motivate users for active participation, maintain their interest throughout the assessment process, give users a sense of achievement after completion of each task, etc. [9]. This study presents the design of a gamified application that aims to leverage the power of visual-auditory narrative to enable users to identify their own thinking patterns and create a sense of cognitive awareness. In order to investigate this, the study tries to answer *how gamified application can enhance the engagement of the Oxford Happiness Questionnaire among the college-going students.*

2   Design Case - Using Gamification for Better Engagement

The design case described here is a gamified application called "The Mirror", as a part of a Research-through-Design (RtD) [10] study. It has been developed based on a hypothesis that *"gamified OHQ allows better engagement than the traditional OHQ".* The design of the gamified application was guided by a set of semi-structured interviews with six college-going students, conducted after they filled the paper version of traditional OHQ (The Oxford Happiness Questionnaire [6]). These interviews aimed to identify challenges in the traditional OHQ, which can be improved in the gamified version of it. Participants reported that the paper version felt too generic, making it monotonous, though questions were comfortable to answer without any hesitation. Some students found certain questions unclear and had trouble understanding what was being asked, making them lose interest mid-way. Many emphasized the importance of anonymity, saying that 'knowing their responses would be confidential' made them more willing to share their true thoughts and experiences.

Using the learnings from the interviews, *a gamified application has been developed named "The Mirror"* (see Fig. 1). In this application, gamification was implemented through the use of "narratives", as in research it had shown improvement in instructional outcomes when applied to instructional contexts [11]. Narratives also help in reading and remembering the content easily and more accurately than expository texts [11]. *The Mirror* uses a digital interface where the participant interacts with the narrator 'a mystical object- mirror'; which can also be seen as a metaphor to let people reflect about themselves. To deal with the monotony, audio/visual feedback format has been used, which also reduces the cognitive burden of the user [12]. To make questions clear to understand and more engaging, they were integrated into a narrative and divided into seven segments based on Freytag's narrative framework [13]: (1) Exposition, (2) Challenge, (3) Effort, (4) Crisis, (5) Solution, (6) Control, and (7) Triumph /Normalcy/Catastrophe. Freytag's narrative framework has been used here especially because it helps in enhancing the engagement, if used with visual communication [12]. It has been proven to be a powerful tool used in many fields like science communication, advertising, games, etc., which allows designers to communicate in a more compelling way, than presenting in a flat style [12].

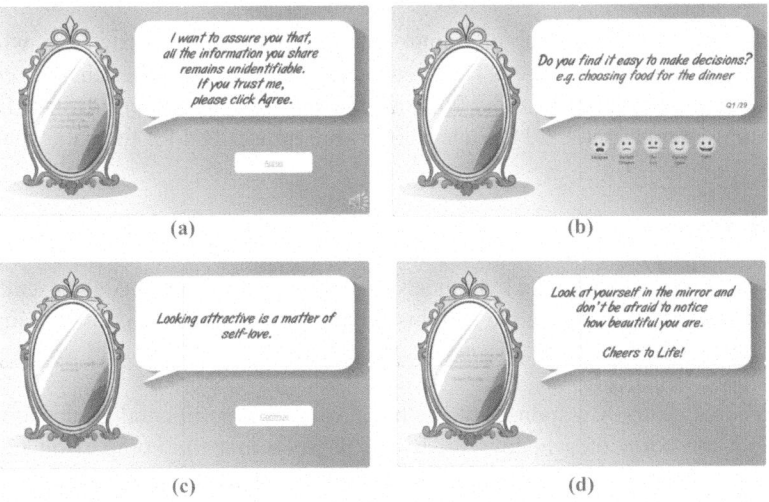

Fig. 1. Glimpse of the gamified application "The Mirror". (a) Protagonist introduction, (b) Question with example to assist in understanding the question, (c) Intervals in between questions after each segment, (d) Closing statement at the end of the questionnaire

In the application, the protagonist/narrator is a 'mirror' (see Fig. 1a) which guides the user through all segments, and also helps them with the supporting examples to understand the questions easily (see Fig. 1b). Five-scale emoji [14] has been used to collect the user-response (see Fig. 1b). After each section, motivational quotes are shown (see Fig. 1c) to create a supportive and encouraging atmosphere.

3   Methods

To check the hypothesis, we propose a mixed-methods methodological approach. In this paper, we report the learnings from a pilot study which included 6 participants who were students of IIT Delhi. These participants were selected using purposive sampling, ensuring diversity in gender (male = 3, female = 3), age (ranging from 18 to 30 years), and academic programs (undergraduate = 3, postgraduate = 3). Informed consent was obtained from all participants and ethical procedures were followed to ensure safety and privacy of participants. The study consisted of three sequential phases: experiment, survey and interview.

Experiment. In this introductory phase, participants were divided into two groups - a control group and an experimental group. The control group received *traditional OHQ*, while the experimental group received *gamified application "The Mirror"*. Basic instructions on how to fill out the questions were given initially, later, they were left alone to engage with either the traditional OHQ or the gamified application.

Survey. After completing the experimental phase, participants were given a feedback survey form (modified version of User Engagement Scale [15], see Annexure-I) to gauge user engagement in both mentioned experiments.

Interview Phase. A semi-structured interview was planned for participants who have completed the initial two phases. The feedback on their experience, challenges faced during the experiment, suggestions for potential improvements were recorded, which took about 5–10 min. Later, all the interviews were transcribed for thematic analysis.

4   Findings

The findings aimed to assess the hypothesis if gamified OHQ enhanced the user engagement. Additionally, the qualitative insights are presented leading to possible improvements in the gamified application to assess the mental well-being of college-going students, more effectively.

The feedback survey responses for both control and experimental groups are shown in Fig. 2 in the form of a histogram. It can be seen that the comparison reflects a higher rating for *gamified application,* in categories focusing on the positive side of user experience, like: 'the time I spent using Form/Application just slipped away', 'this Form/Application was attractive', 'this Form/Application was aesthetically appealing', 'this Form/Application appealed to my senses', 'using Form/Application was worthwhile', 'my experience was rewarding'. It also shows a slight decrease in the factors which indicate negative characteristics (highlighted by the dotted box in Fig. 2), and an equal level rating in the category 'I was absorbed and interested in this experience'. Through this, it can be seen that there are initial indications that show an increase in the engagement of *gamified application "The Mirror"* compared to the *traditional OHQ*. However, the results of the pilot study need to be extended by increasing the number of participants and testing in different educational contexts.

The study also collects in-depth qualitative data from the thematic analysis of 'semi-structured interview transcribed notes'. For both the traditional OHQ and the gamified

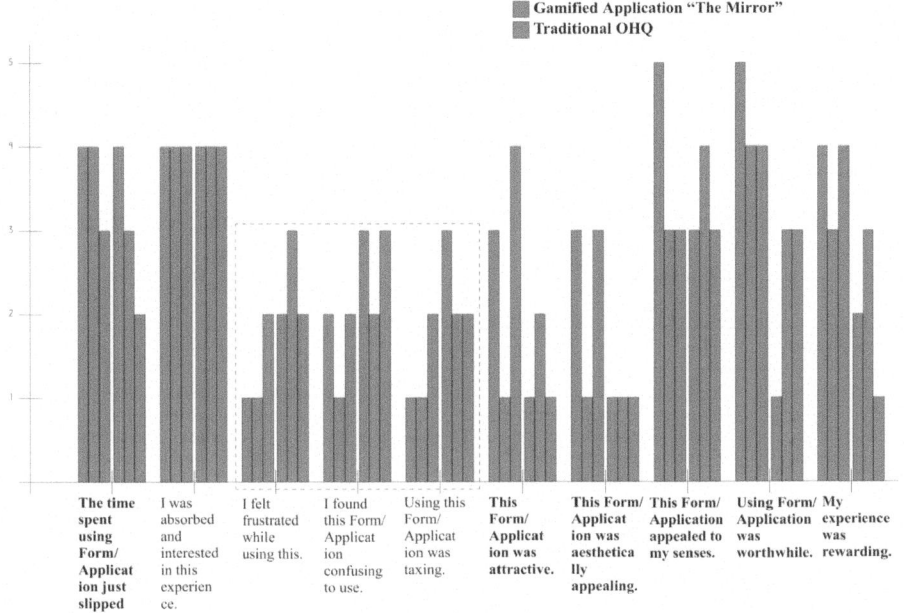

Fig. 2. Participant responses who were introduced to the gamified application (green) and traditional OHQ (red). (Color figure online)

application, notes were grouped using the themes and codes outlined below (Table 1), which are hypothesized to be important in the participant's interaction. Three broad themes relating to traditional OHQ emerged: (1) *Unveiling Delight through Curiosity:* Participants reported questionnaires were enjoyable and reflective, as it evoked pleasant memories, encouraged introspection, and revealed layers of insights that enriched their perspectives; (2) *Redefining Engagement in Sequential Tasks:* Participants pointed out that the structured and numbered format, though intended for organization, often felt monotonous, leading to disengagement and occasionally triggered negative memories; and (3) *Empowering Communication by Strategic Questioning and Gracefulness*: Participants emphasized on the need for a more refined and effective communication process, with suggestions for improved presentation and a call for more engaging approaches.

For gamified application "The Mirror", four broad themes emerged: (1) *Content is Supportive:* Participants valued the strategically placed in-between supportive texts for improving comprehension and engagement, and praised the use of emojis for their emotive power which made the interaction more engaging; (2) *Appraisal for Structure of Questions:* The structure of the questions was generally well-received with participants acknowledging its coherence and logical flow, they also pointed that intervals between questions act like commas or periods giving everyone a moment to think; (3) *Challenges with Visual Aspects and Information Delivery:* Participants highlighted several challenges like reduced interactivity and engagement with the main character "Mirror" due to integration of multiple communication modes, cognitive load due to rough transition between the use of text and audio, and confusion due to the questionnaire's overwhelming length; and (4) *Scope for Improvements:* Participants unanimously called for improved aesthetics, including mixed-gender voice-overs, vibrant visuals, and a proper closure to the questionnaire to ensure a cohesive narrative.

Table 1. Thematic findings for "Traditional OHQ" and "Gamified Application".

Traditional OHQ

S.No.	Themes	Codes
1	Unveiling Delight through Curiosity	- Down the memory lane - Happy moments remembered - Positive experiences - Interesting experiences - Happy moments from the past - Unbothered by questions - Interesting questionnaire - Motivating questions - Thought-provoking questions
2	Redefining Engagement in Sequential Tasks	- Structured and numbered questionnaire - Impact of structure and format - Monotonous format - Not really engaging - Non-engaging - Negativity and less enthusiasm - A subtle reminder of bad memories
3	Empowering Communication by Strategic Questioning and Gracefulness	- Incremental motivation for thoughtful responses is necessary - Random targeting of questions can be avoided - Can be improved with neutral questions - Presentation of questions can be enhanced - Introspection - Subjectivity in questions - Difficulty in immediate response - Challenges in questionnaire completion - Need for clarification in question interpretation - Questions not in the right direction - Presentation could have been better - Could have been more interesting

Gamified Application

S.No.	Themes	Codes
1	Content is supportive	- Helping text in between - Text helping and uplifting - Ease to understand - Smooth interactions - Positive engagement
2	Appraisal for Structure of Questions	- Intervals are perceived as levels of questions - Structure was ok - Intervention being retrospective
3	Challenges with Visual Aspects and Information Delivery	- Mirror image is less interactive - Unnoticed mirror - Length of questionnaire was not understandable - Length of questionnaire - Little hassle to navigate between audio and text - Too much text to read - Aesthetics was not impressive - Visual factors having a negative effect on answers of OHQ
4	Scope for Improvements	- Different examples based on different questions (suggestions) - Need for multiple audios for more inclusion - Need for a proper conclusion - Suggestion to put the text in the center with mirror in focus

These findings are indicative in nature, which needs to be validated by increasing the participants size in future. Despite that, the study illuminates the nuanced challenges that will help future designers to address and enhance the user experience in multimodal interaction scenarios, especially in case of gamified application for the assessment of mental well-being.

5 Discussion

The biases in traditional OHQ have been documented in this study as well, which has been reported in earlier literature [8]. The pilot study showed positive results indicating the potential of gamifying the OHQ and similar assessment tools. It is worth noting that these results are only indicative in nature and would need extensive testing to validate the findings further. Additionally, there is a need to also look at the effect of gamification on the efficacy of answering OHQ. Apart from the trends seen in the survey, a number of insights were revealed through qualitative analysis of the follow-up interviews. This included positive response for supportive content and improved overall structure, while identifying scope for further improvement in the use of multi-modal feedback. The participants also pointed out that the 29 questions in the questionnaire required a lot of individual focus, unlike the traditional OHQ, where participants could see all the questions at once and choose which ones to answer first. The examples with each question helped most of the participants in understanding the context, even though they recognized that the questions were still somewhat subjective. Participants appreciated the audio narration in the gamified application noting that it made the experience engaging and personalized, but they also recommended adding audio options with voices from different genders to make it more inclusive for everyone. Conversely, suggestions for the traditional OHQ concentrated on structural improvements.

The study had several limitations apart from the limited number of participants. The result might be influenced by the fact that the study took place in a controlled lab setting. It is important to note that participants were specifically invited for the study, which differs from the real-world use of the traditional OHQ where individuals respond independently in a genuinely self-reported manner. To truly understand how well the gamified application works in the assessment of mental well-being, it is important to compare it with the traditional method in real-world settings. Furthermore, the gamified OHQ includes features like 'motivational quotes' that could affect the user's happiness levels during the test. Future studies can look into the interactional effects of introduced parameters like digital medium, motivational quotes and gamification on engagement and effectiveness of such survey instruments. It would be interesting to also look into the psychological impact of the gamified interface of such surveys.

Thus, deferring these considerations to later studies empowers researchers to fine-tune the gamified application to better meet the needs of a diverse audience while maintaining its effectiveness.

6   Conclusion

In this paper, we presented a gamified application "The Mirror", an interactive OHQ to help in assessing the mental well-being of a larger number of college-going students. The study investigates the effect of gamification and whether this approach can improve the engagement of existing traditional paper-based OHQ. It has been found that the gamified application indicated a positive effect on enriching the engagement, elevating the user experience, solving the confusion related to the 29 questions by making them easy to understand and more personal to the users, as compared to the traditional OHQ. These findings suggest that combining the OHQ with gamification strategies can increase the efficacy of self-guided surveys, by incorporating strategies that contribute to greater engagement and reflective thinking on the questions.

Annexure. Link to access - https://drive.google.com/file/d/1LSIciRVnJPU3BqdYdSmnymS4Gj 0IoXNd/view?usp=sharing.

References

1. Pierce, M., et al.: Mental health before and during the COVID-19 pandemic: a longitudinal probability sample survey of the UK population. Lancet Psychiat. **7**, 883–892 (2020). https://doi.org/10.1016/S2215-0366(20)30308-4
2. World Health Organization: Integrating mental health into primary care: a global perspective. World Health Organization (2008)
3. Senger, K., Srivastava, P.: Mental depression emerging as an arduous challenge encountered by the students: a comprehensive review of literature. Math. Stat. Eng. Appl. **70**(2), 999–1009 (2021)
4. Small, M.L.: Someone to Talk to. Oxford University Press, Oxford (2017)
5. Barber, J.E.: An examination of happiness and its relationship to community college students' coping strategies and academic performance. Morgan State University (2010)
6. Hills, P., Argyle, M.: The Oxford Happiness Questionnaire: a compact scale for the measurement of psychological well-being. Personality Individ. Differ. **33**(7), 1073–1082 (2002). https://doi.org/10.1016/S0191-8869(01)00213-6
7. Medvedev, O.N., Siegert, R.J., Mohamed, A.D., Shepherd, D., Landhuis, E., Krägeloh, C.U.: The Oxford happiness questionnaire: transformation from an ordinal to an interval measure using Rasch analysis. J. Happiness Stud. **18**, 1425–1443 (2017)
8. Lalla, M., Ferrari, D.: Web-based versus paper-based data collection for the evaluation of teaching activity: empirical evidence from a case study. Assess. Eval. High. Educ. **36**(3), 347–365 (2011)
9. Liu, D., Santhanam, R., Webster, J.: Toward meaningful engagement. MIS Q. **41**(4), 1011–1034 (2017)
10. Stappers, P.J., Giaccardi, E.: Research through design. In: The Encyclopedia of Human-Computer Interaction, pp. 1–94. The Interaction Design Foundation (2017)
11. Armstrong, M.B., Landers, R.N.: An evaluation of gamified training: using narrative to improve reactions and learning. Simul. Gaming **48**(4), 513–538 (2017)
12. Yang, L., et al.: A design space for applying the Freytag's pyramid structure to data stories. IEEE Trans. Visual Comput. Graphics **28**(1), 922–932 (2021)

13. Freytag, G.: The Technique of the Drama, 1863. Johnston Reprints (1968)
14. Alismail, S., Zhang, H.: The use of emoji in electronic user experience questionnaire: an exploratory case study (2018)
15. O'Brien, H.L., Cairns, P., Hall, M.: A practical approach to measuring user engagement with the refined user engagement scale (UES) and new UES short form. Int. J. Hum Comput Stud. **112**, 28–39 (2018)

A Methodological Discourse
on Second-Order Nature in Board Games

Malay Dhamelia[✉] and Girish Dalvi

IDC School of Design, IIT Bombay Powai, Mumbai 400 076, India
{malay.dhamelia,girish.dalvi}@iitb.ac.in

Abstract. In this paper we deliberate on the second-order nature of experiences in games, and contemplate around the epistemological and methodological challenges it creates for design researchers. Role of design research in game studies is examined and re-examined, to arrive at the proposition that design research in games should study experiences in relation to the game rules. Overall, the paper aims to initiate and expand a discussion around the approaches and methods which can further the epistemological imagination and methodological wherewithal.

Keywords: Second-order Design Problem · Second-order Analysis Problem · Player Experiences · Empiricism · Proceduralism · Experience Sampling Method · Retrospective Protocol Analysis · Onto-epistemic discussion

1 Introduction

Player experiences in games are a second-order design problem [24]. Designers can not design the experiences *directly*, but only through the design of rules[1], can they gauge the generated experiences. The experiences are not created, but they *emerge* when players interact with the game systems. The second-order distance between the rules and the emergent experiences creates epistemological and ontological challenges for design researchers [17].

---

[1] **Game rules as game structure**. Viewing games as systems, game structure entails the logics, mathematical structures, and the formal structures like mechanics, goals, feedback loops, etc. From an experiential perspective, game structures provide the necessary verisimilitude for the players, in which they can voluntarily enter the game world. In the case of board games, the game rules create the game structures.

N. Rangaswamy et al. (Eds.): IndiaHCI 2024, CCIS 2338, pp. 108–119, 2025.
https://doi.org/10.1007/978-3-031-80832-6_9

Design researchers are tasked with understanding the relation between the rules and the emergent experiences[2] [7,19,26,28]. This task faces an epistemological challenge in two ways. First, the experiences cannot be captured in their true fidelity. They are either reduced to other measurable quantities, like psycho-physiological measurements or questionnaire based measurements. If attempted to qualitatively capture them, the method becomes susceptible to biases like recall bias, memory bias, and so forth. That is, a player when articulates about her experiences, she may articulate only the highs and lows of the experience, she might rationalise the experience, and so forth. Secondly, once the experiences are captured, in order to study them in relation to the game rules, the design researcher has to traverse towards the rules – that is what set of rules are creating these experiences? how are they creating and so forth.

Through this deliberation, in this short paper, we propose to initiate a discourse around methods which can possibly attempt to address this epistemological gap in studying experiences in relation to the game rules. It expands the nature of second-order design space by the means of two methods. The discussions that arrive at the choice of methods provide a glance into the second-order design nature of the experiences.

We believe that the value of the paper lies in initiating a discussion in studying player experiences from a design perspective. While the epistemological challenge has been articulated by Howell and Stevens, we further this direction by exploring two methods – Retrospective Protocol Analysis and Experience Sampling Methods.

2   Design Research and Experiences

Howell and Stevens propose [17], on the ideas of Stolterman [27], that design research should focus on *the ultimate particular means to the ultimate particular ends*. In the case of games in their second-orderness, the ultimate particular ends

---

[2] **Shifted positions for design research.** It was recommended that pertaining to games, design research should study the formal and structural elements [2], since a designer designs the formal and structural elements. This approach has resulted in notable works like Patterns in Game Design [5], Building Blocks of Tabletop Games [14], The 400 Project [1], and so forth. However, a more recent discussion by William and Alexander [28], positions design research differently. They argue that design research should focus on the creation of aesthetics and experiences in games. This position echoes several from the game design scholarship. Jrvinen poses to game design research – "How could one set combinations of such variables as 'design drivers' - i.e. conduct emotion-centred design that proceeds from psychological principles to design and implementation of game elements and their interaction?" [19] Similarly, Cowley also attempts to find relations between the rules and the emergent experiences [7].

are the emergent experiences. As for the ultimate particular means, in this paper we consider events as the ultimate particular[3], as suggested by [3,10,19].

Formally, rules are considered as the ultimate particular means, for it is through the game structure, designers design the experiences. However, this proceduralist view assumes that the experiences are solely embodied in the structure and that by studying the structures, one can understand the emergence of the experiences [26]. However, in the study of the formal and procedural structures, players are seldom considered.

Players are not distanced from their experiences, like designers are. For players, the ultimate particular means to fun might not be rules. It can be argued that they experience fun and other player experiences by the means of gameplay[4]. Since gameplay is a structure of interactions emerging from the rules and is also a property of analytical import for the player experiences, gameplay can be considered as a particular means, if not the ultimate particular means of player experiences.

We propose that gameplay has to be studied in order to understand the experiences in relation the game structure. The analysis is not formal, that is gameplay is not a structure which creates these experiences, rather, a structure which emerges when players interact with the rule system. A player's experiences lies in interacting with and creating those structures. Such experiences while playing a game, as Dhamelia and Dalvi, argue are inner, intrinsic, idiopathic, and pristine [12]. To understand these experiences, they have to be studied close to real-time and in the context which they emerged as suggested by [8,15].

Protocol Analysis is a process tracing method [20]. It helps researchers to understand the process of an individual in terms of the decisions, the conditions in which they decide, and so forth. Experience Sampling Method affords researchers to analyse the experiences in the context of their occurrence. It is often used to study inner and pristine daily experiences. We employ the two

---

[3] **Events, or Ludic Events**, are a new way of concpetualising gameplays. Gameplay is chunked in different paradigmas. Formally, gameplay is considered to be composed of game states. Turns and turn-orders are a paradigma of game structure, the design of game structure. Both these paradigmas suit well for the understanding the game structure, it is does not capture the player experiences. Hence, they cannot really be used for studying relations of players and game structures. Ludic events, attempts to capture the game states, in relation to the player's experience. These events are fluid when compared to their formal and structural counterparts - states and turns. They can occur anytime and multiple times.

[4] Gameplay is a thoroughly discussed and debated concept without a strong or an established consensus. In this paper, we adhere to the Guardiola's working definition of gameplay [16] – "The Gameplay consists of the actions performed by the player when involved in a challenge. It emerges from the emotionally-charged interaction between the player and the game components." It is the structure of player interaction with the game system and with the other players in the game. Thus, gameplay includes the possibilities, results, and the reasons for the players to interact within the game.

Fig. 1. The setup used for the study. Retrospective Protocol Analysis and Experience Sampling Method – both were employed using the same setup. The game of *Battleship* is set up on the table.

methods to understand and explore their strengths and weakness given our goal of understanding experiences in relation to the game structure.

These methods were employed with two participants of age 23 and 25 years, with whom the researcher played the game of *Battleship*. The study was set up as shown in Fig. 1.

3   Protocol Analysis

Protocol analysis is a valuable method for understanding decision-making processes in various fields, including education, sports, and behavioral sciences [15]. In design sciences, this method has been used to gain insights into how designers approach their tasks [4]. Typically, designers are given a design or redesign task and asked to verbalize their thought process using think-aloud protocols. Alternatively, conversation protocols can be used, or a retrospective account can be obtained after the completion of the task. Although think-aloud concurrent protocol analysis is commonly used for design research, it poses challenges when studying gameplay, as it can reveal player strategies. For example, to think-aloud in a game of *Chess*, would reveal a player's strategies and affect the gameplay. To address this, a retrospective protocol analysis approach has been adopted [20]. In retrospective protocol analysis, the experience is re-constructed by the participant by viewing some portions of the recorded tasks.

3.1 Exploration Using Retrospective Protocol Analysis

Retrospective protocol analysis requires high-fidelity data streams that participants revisit to reconstruct the experience in retrospect. For our study, we recorded video of the game boards and hand movements of both the participant and researcher, capturing crucial details to enhance the in-game experience recreation. These videos were then merged into a composite video of both gameplays. The researcher and participant watched this video together, pausing at fun events during playback.

During these pauses, the researcher and participant addressed three questions: (1) current emotions, (2) motivations for progressing in the gameplay, and (3) thoughts at that specific moment in the video. These questions aim to explore the cognitive and affective aspects of fun [12]. Adequate probing questions were used to gather information, followed by a discussion. Each segment, consisting of questions, responses, and discussions, contributes to the overall retrospective analysis. The entire gameplay account is documented using an audio recorder.

4 Experience Sampling Method

Experience Sampling is a method used to capture the subjective experiences of individuals in their natural environments [6, 8, 13]. It focuses on studying patterns of behaviour within a population of experiences. Researchers typically use a beeper or sound as a trigger to collect data, and participants respond to questions when triggered. The trigger intervals can be random for studying subjective experiences or fixed for studying daily life. Event-contingent sampling is used to study specific events. Experience Sampling is commonly used in psychology, clinical studies, and personality research, but is less commonly used in design. In game design research, it has been used to under-stand in-game experiences, particularly flow in video games [23]. However, it has not been employed to study gameplay design from the perspective of players as designers.

4.1 Exploration Through Experience Sampling Method

To employ the Experience Sampling Method (ESM), the same researcher as the one in RPA played Battleship with the participant for the study employing ESM. However, participant and the researcher both had sample collection sheets as shown in Fig. 2 (in the appendix). Of the three types of experience sampling methods, we employed event-contingent ESM. During the gameplay, the researcher or the participant can trigger the beeper and the sample is collected by filling the details. Hence the first item is who triggered the sample collection – the researcher or the participant. ESM is assessed to have the same source bias and a survey-like item is introduced to overcome that bias. Hence, the second item to be responded to in the sample is a 10 point Likert scale on how much fun they have while playing when sample collection was triggered. Participants respond to three questions constant throughout the experience of playing the game- (1) what are the players feeling at the moment?, (2) what is motivating them to take the gameplay forward? and (3) what are you thinking at the moment?

5   Discussion

When we place players in the formal systems, the gameplay becomes the process to craft the structures of interactions, and events become the building blocks of the gameplay. Events have information about the rule set, about the player, and her experience. Although RPA and ESM can functionally and methodically yield events; the type of data collected, aspects of the gameplay captured, and the nature of events generated by the two methods are different.

ESM is an idiographic method that captures a within-person pristine experience during an activity. It collects data in-context and close to real-time from the same subject. The experience is captured and elicited from the participant in the situation. Whereas RPA first captures the experience, then participants mentally recreate the experience and elicit the details of it. Such a difference in the time of eliciting response from the participant creates many nuances in the quality and nature of data collected.

5.1   Comparison of the Data from the Two Methods

In RPA, participants recreate the experience by watching the video playback of the game-play. This recreation is mostly in terms of decision making during the gameplay. For example, the RPA participant talks about successes, failures, and rationalisations of them during the gameplay. "Once my ships were hit, [I got] slightly worried but I moved past it because it was very early in the game." Here the RPA participant is worried about a minor setback in his game and he rationalises the loss as the game is just beginning. However, attribution of the loss is on the game state and not on the perceived feeling about the loss. If we compare similar rationalisation captured through ESM, the data captured is much more rich. Referring to Table 1, the opponent has had a small success in the initial part of the game, yet, the participant not only rationalises and attributes to the game state, but he attributes to what his presupposition is with respect to participant success. Here, the participant is attributed to randomness or luck. Attributing loss or win to randomness is a significant insight as we understand what the person is exactly feeling and thinking about the event. Such nuances are captured through ESM.

In addition, ESM not only captures the experience at the trigger, but it also captures the data for antecedent and precedent experiences in the same way as it captures the experience at the trigger. For example, in above Table 1, the participant is hopeful about his strategy. To analyse his game state, we refer to the video and the audio recording to arrive that he is hopeful because there are many working parts of his strategy. He is hopeful about the working parts of the strategy and desires "to test his strategy further" and at the same time, finds a new strategy in the process. Thus, ESM data not only captures the feeling associated with the in-game decision making, but it also provides time based context in form of antecedent and precedent experiences. This strength of ESM helps in reducing the interpretative gap while analysing data as well.

In addition, ESM also provides further details of in-game interactions. In our study with RPA, we did not find the experience data about the opponent. In board games, other players play a crucial role as they make or break your game. To study such in-game interactions, ESM captures data about the experience generated from the opponents. For example, in Table 2 the sample demonstrates players have more fun when the opponent's efforts are not favourable for his gameplay.

The difference in experience data collected by RPA and ESM can also be attributed to the triggers. In both – RPA and ESM studies, participant and the researcher had the autonomy to call out a trigger. Upon the trigger, participant and the researcher write the samples (in the case of ESM) and discuss the experience (in the case of RPA). However, participants exercised their autonomy to trigger a collection of an experience sample (in the case of ESM) or a segment (in the case of RPA) in vividly different ways.

5.2   Effect of Triggers

In RPA, the trigger is called upon by the significance of a decision that led to the end game state of the participant-win or lose. In RPA, since players already know the outcome, all the events are rationalised with respect to the outcome. Players are no longer situated in the experience, but are analysing their moves and learning how to improve the game. Moreover, failures are not captured in the RPA as the experience is rationalised, unless they are pivotal and very significant.

Whereas in ESM, the participant triggered an experience sample collection based on his in-situ, close to real-time experience. In other words, experience samples are collected while the player is situated in the gameplay. The current experience is not contingent on the out-come of the game, it is purely a within-person, inner experience as it has unfolded by the dynamics of the gameplay. And experience of small failures like setbacks, moving away from the goal, and so forth is also collected. For example, "I feel excited and intrigued why I am

Table 1. Comparing similar samples from ESM and RPA

ESM Samples	RPA Samples
Happy that he (opponent) is focusing on the wrong part of the ocean	realisation about wrong opponent moves, happy about wrong opponent moves
I have to find a ship	Action without a plan
The strategy to cluster in one quadrant works w/ new players. i am also leaving 2 parts of the ocean	Realisation about working parts of the strategy

Table 2. Comparing similar samples from ESM and RPA

ESM Samples	RPA Samples
Hopeful about my strategy. Opponent got one ship but I think it was lucky and random	Hopeful, rationalising opponent success to overcome a setback, attributing to randomness
To test my strategy further	testing the strategy further–the successful parts of the strategy
Found a new strategy and I think it works	Finding a new strategy–replacing not working parts of the strategy with working parts

getting misses", "A bit disappointed about my attack strategy. Diagonal is not working.". Here, not only failures are captured, but also in-situ thoughts about how to navigate the problem are articulated by participants. As opposed to RPA, where the segment "I should not have tried going to the top-left quadrant at this moment" was the only recorded failure from participants. According to him, this was the pivotal moment that changed the game. The nature and quality of the data collected by the two methods are different. Upon applying reflexive thematic analysis to both the data, events are generated. We coded the data inductively and descriptively to create events based on thematic analysis, the nature and type of events is also vividly different.

5.3   The Nature of the Two Methods

Fun can be considered as a broad game aesthetic [25]. Although it is considered as one of the fundamental driver to the games, it is often under-theorised [11,25]. While there are several reasons of under-theorisation – ranging from considering fun as a trivial and frivolous experience to shying away from fun because of its monolithic nature – the implications are far severe. Fun is often conflated with pristine and well-articulated experiences like flow, enjoyment, engagement, involvement, and so forth. Several works analyse the conceptual differences among different pleasures to identify differentiating factors of the experience of fun [11,22]. They argue that fun is a pristine, inner experience a player creates while playing games.

Inner experiences are characterized by "anything that is going on in awareness at the particular moment , whatever is 'before the footlights of consciousness' at that moment" [9,18]. As opposed to outer experiences which are more objective and measurable like perceptions (like time, visual, etc.) and sensations (like auditory, olfactory, visual, etc.). Fun is a first-hand experience that is difficult to understand to third person nomothetic methods.

Studying in-game, inner pristine experiences like fun is difficult in games because of several reasons. The experience created by the game is highly subjective to the player. Players are self-aware and in the moment. Such experiences are fleeting, but significant to game designers and researchers to understand the experience of playing a particular game. To study such experiences, the method applied has to do away with its instrumental nature. In such cases, the nature of methods cannot be mere means to collect data; rather, the method should be the experience itself.

Second problem is that of the researcher involvement. Nomothetic and instrumental natured methods suggest researcher as the observer and inquirer of the phenomenon under study. Fun, being a pristine, inner experience created by interactions of players with the ludic structure, researcher can no longer remain a passive observer or a third person inquirer of the experience. Researcher needs to be an active participant of the experience that is created by the players by interacting with rules [24]. Researcher as an active participant is a fairly common tradition in critical analytic traditions of game research.

Hurlburt and Akhter suggest to use idiographic methods to understand the experience of a single person [18]. Descriptive Experience Sampling (DES) method is one such method which is capable to understand the inner and outer experiences. This paper proposes the use of DES method to study the experience of fun in terms of ludological events. It employs researcher as an active participant of the experience and considers methods not as a means to understand the experience rather than a way to collect data.

6   Comparison of Logistics and Practical Aspects

Experience Sampling Method is an intrusive method. The gameplay is interrupted when players write samples. It can be argued that the gameplay is affected by the filling the sample. Apart from interrupting the gameplay experience, ESM also takes more time per participant as well. Participant of the ESM study has to play the game while writing the samples, and then discuss the samples with researcher. Whereas Retrospective Protocol Analysis is not only less intrusive, it takes less time as well. Participant of the RPA study plays the game and then explicates the experience by watching the video.

7   Conclusions

This paper aims to initiate a discussion around the epistemological challenges a design researcher experiences while being in a second-order design space. We explored two methods – Experience Sampling Method and Retrospective Protocol Analysis to further the role of design research in games. We build this work on the arguments of William and Alexander [28] and Howell and Stevens [17].

While we explore the two methods and the second-order design space, we do not claim effectiveness of one method over the other. Additionally, a known critique of idiographic methods is smaller sample size. Here, we wish to direct the reader's attention towards the goal of idiographic studies. Such studies consider their sample space as the number of experience samples collected, as opposed to nomothetic studies where a part of experience is collected over a large population.

Idiopathic studies are also not used to generalise a particular relation, but to describe and develop the relationships.

This work can be furthered in several ways. First, protocols can be developed around the methods. Second, a more systematic comparison can be useful for the domain. Thirdly, we discuss the methods that can be used to study experiences in relation to the game structure. Developing on this approach and the methods, in their variants, offshoots, and modifications, can create a repertoire of a methods like Games Research Methods [21].

A Appendix

See Fig. 3.

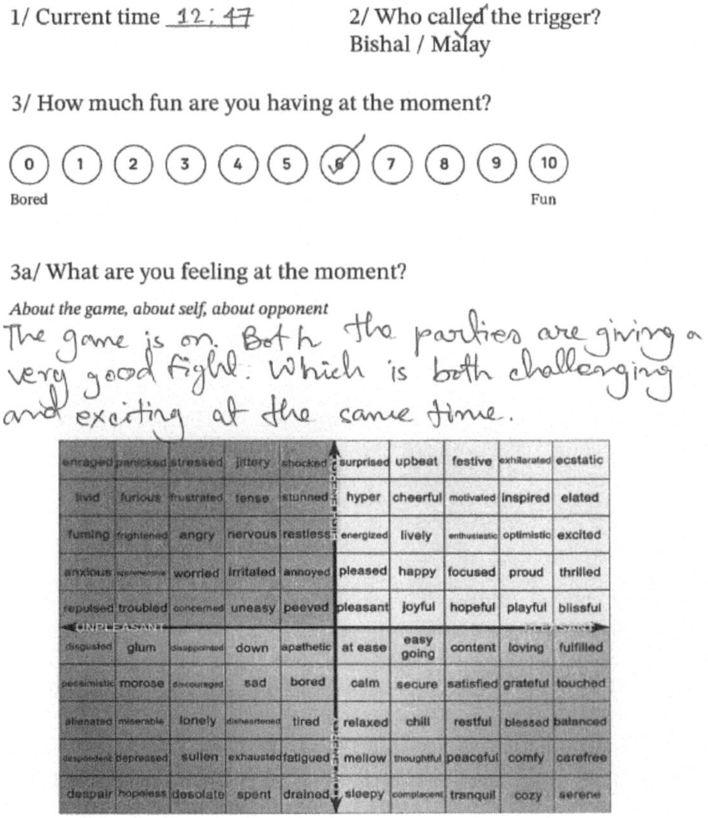

1/ Current time 12:47

2/ Who called the trigger?
Bishal / Malay

3/ How much fun are you having at the moment?

0 1 2 3 4 5 6 7 8 9 10
Bored — Fun

3a/ What are you feeling at the moment?

About the game, about self, about opponent

The game is on. Both the parties are giving a very good fight. Which is both challenging and exciting at the same time.

enraged	panicked	stressed	jittery	shocked	surprised	upbeat	festive	exhilarated	ecstatic
livid	furious	frustrated	tense	stunned	hyper	cheerful	motivated	inspired	elated
fuming	frightened	angry	nervous	restless	energized	lively	enthusiastic	optimistic	excited
anxious	apprehensive	worried	irritated	annoyed	pleased	happy	focused	proud	thrilled
repulsed	troubled	concerned	uneasy	peeved	pleasant	joyful	hopeful	playful	blissful
disgusted	glum	disappointed	down	apathetic	at ease	easy going	content	loving	fulfilled
pessimistic	morose	discouraged	sad	bored	calm	secure	satisfied	grateful	touched
alienated	miserable	lonely	disheartened	tired	relaxed	chill	restful	blessed	balanced
despondent	depressed	sullen	exhausted	fatigued	mellow	thoughtful	peaceful	comfy	carefree
despair	hopeless	desolate	spent	drained	sleepy	complacent	tranquil	cozy	serene

Fig. 2. Page 1 from a Sample Collection Form filled by the participant. Similar form is filled by the researcher.

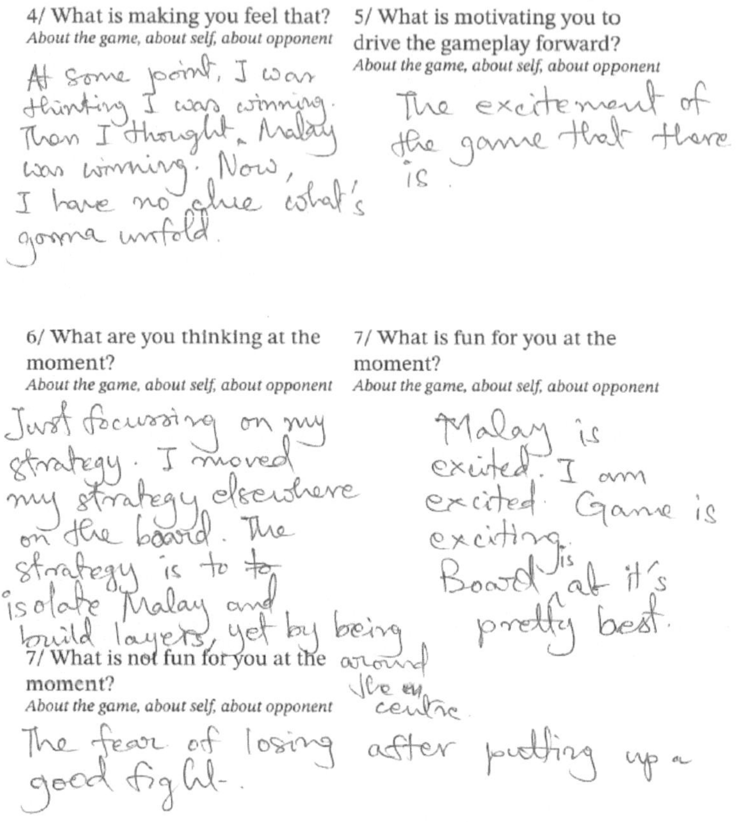

4/ What is making you feel that?
About the game, about self, about opponent

At some point, I was thinking I was winning. Then I thought, Malay was winning. Now, I have no clue what's gonna unfold.

5/ What is motivating you to drive the gameplay forward?
About the game, about self, about opponent

The excitement of the game that there is.

6/ What are you thinking at the moment?
About the game, about self, about opponent

Just focussing on my strategy. I moved my strategy elsewhere on the board. The strategy is to to isolate Malay and build layers, yet by being around the centre.

7/ What is fun for you at the moment?
About the game, about self, about opponent

Malay is excited. I am excited. Game is exciting. Board is at it's pretty best.

7/ What is not fun for you at the moment?
About the game, about self, about opponent

The fear of losing after putting up a good fight.

Fig. 3. Page 2 from a Sample Collection Form filled by the participant. Similar form is filled by the researcher.

References

1. The 400 Project. https://finitearts.com/Pages/400page.html
2. Aarseth, E.: Playing Research: Methodological approaches to game analysis. Artnodes **0**(7) (2007). https://doi.org/10.7238/a.v0i7.763
3. Anthropy, A., Clark, N.: A Game Design Vocabulary: Exploring the Foundational Principles behind Good Game Design. Pearson Education (2014)
4. Athavankar, U., Bokil, P., Guruprasad, K., Patsute, R., Yadav, S.: Reaching Out in the Mind's Space. In: Design Computing and Cognition '08 - Proceedings of the 3rd International Conference on Design Computing and Cognition, pp. 321–340 (2008). https://doi.org/10.1007/978-1-4020-8728-8_17
5. Bjork, S., Holopainen, J.: Patterns in Game Design. Charles River Media Game Development Series, Charles River Media, Hingham, Mass, 1st ed edn. (2005)
6. Conner, T.S., Tennen, H., Fleeson, W., Barrett, L.F.: Experience sampling methods: a modern idiographic approach to personality research. Soc. Pers. Psychol. Compass **3**(3), 292–313 (2009). https://doi.org/10.1111/j.1751-9004.2009.00170.x

7. Cowley, B., et al.: Experience assessment and design in the analysis of gameplay. Simul. Gaming **45**(1), 41–69 (2014). https://doi.org/10.1177/1046878113513936
8. Csikszentmihalyi, M.: Reflections on enjoyment. Perspect. Biol. Med. **28**(4), 489–497 (1985)
9. Csikszentmihalyi, M., Larson, R.: Validity and reliability of the experience-sampling method. In: Csikszentmihalyi, M. (ed.) Flow and the Foundations of Positive Psychology: The Collected Works of Mihaly Csikszentmihalyi, pp. 35–54. Springer, Dordrecht (2014). https://doi.org/10.1007/978-94-017-9088-8_3
10. Dhamelia, M., Dalvi, G.: Designing Fun Game Rules: A Formal Game Analysis Method. Digital Games Research Association, DiGRA 2022, 21 (2022)
11. Dhamelia, M., Dalvi, G.: Pleasures in games: conceptual analysis of fun and its constructs. In: Dhar, U., Dubey, J., Dumblekar, V., Meijer, S., Lukosch, H. (eds.) Gaming, Simulation and Innovations: Challenges and Opportunities. pp. 197–210. Lecture Notes in Computer Science, Springer International Publishing, Cham (2022). https://doi.org/10.1007/978-3-031-09959-5_17
12. Dhamelia, M., Dalvi, G.: Designerly ways of analysing gameplay and player experiences. In: Conference Proceedings of DiGRA 2023 Conference: Limits and Margins of Games Settings (2023)
13. Dimotakis, N., Ilies, R.: Experience-Sampling and Event-Sampling Research (2012)
14. Engelstein, G., Shalev, I.: Building Blocks of Tabletop Game Design: An Encyclopedia of Mechanisms. CRC Press, Boca Raton (2019)
15. Ericsson, K.A., Simon, H.A.: How to study thinking in everyday life: Contrasting think-aloud protocols with descriptions and explanations of thinking. Mind Cult. Act. **5**(3), 178–186 (1998). https://doi.org/10.1207/s15327884mca0503_3
16. Guardiola, E.: Gameplay definition: a game design perspective. Technical report (2019)
17. Howell, P., Stevens, B.: Epistemological Issues in Understanding Games Design, Play-Experience, and Reportage (2019)
18. Hurlburt, R.T., Akhter, S.A.: The descriptive experience sampling method. Phenomenol. Cogn. Sci. **5**(3–4), 271–301 (2006). https://doi.org/10.1007/s11097-006-9024-0
19. Järvinen, A.: Games without Frontiers: Theories and Methods for Game Studies and Design. Tampere University Press (2008)
20. Kuusela, H., Paul, P.: A comparison of concurrent and retrospective verbal protocol analysis. Am. J. Psychol. **113**(3), 387 (2000). https://doi.org/10.2307/1423365
21. Lankoski, P., Björk, S.: 3. Formal analysis of gameplay. Technical report (2015). https://doi.org/10.5555/2812774.2812779
22. Podilchak, W.: Distinctions of fun, enjoyment and leisure. Leis. Stud. **10**(2), 133–148 (1991). https://doi.org/10.1080/02614369100390131
23. Rowe, E., Shernoff, D.: The Finnish-US Network (FUN): studying flow in educational games & gamified learning environments. In: World Conference on Educational Multimedia, pp. 2502–2507. Association for the Advancement of Computing in Education (AACE) (2014)
24. Salen, K., Zimmerman, E.: Rules of Play: Game Design Fundamentals (2004)
25. Sharp, J., Thomas, D.L.D.: Fun, Taste & Games : An Aesthetics of the Idle, Unproductive, and Otherwise Playful (2019)
26. Sicart, M.: Against Procedurality. Game Stud. **11**(3) (2011)
27. Stolterman, E.: The nature of design practice and implications for interaction design research. Int. J. Des. **2**(1) (2008)
28. William, G., Alexander, M.: Towards Genre as a Game Design Research Approach (2017)

Student Research Consortium

Virtual and Human Influencers: Examining the Dimensions of Authenticity, Reliability, and Innovation in Consumer Perception

Rutu Patel[(⊠)]

International Fashion Academy Paris, Centre-Istanbul, Turkey
rutupatel1998@gmail.com

Abstract. This research explores the transformative role of virtual brand ambassadors in influencer marketing, driven by AI and CGI technologies. It investigates consumer perceptions of virtual influencers compared to human influencers, focusing on three major dimensions - authenticity, reliability, and innovation. Analyzing responses from an online survey and conducting an independent t-test methodology, the study examines the relative difference in influencing consumer perception and engagement with virtual and human influencers with reference to the key attributes. Through an in-depth literature review and empirical analysis, this paper contributes to understanding the evolving dynamics of virtual influencers in the digital marketing landscape.

Keywords: Virtual influencers · Human influencers · Consumer perceptions · Authenticity · Reliability · Innovation · AI

1 Introduction

Covid-19 pandemic has significantly altered our everyday lives as well as the marketing industry. The CMO Survey indicates that, in the aftermath of the pandemic, social media and influencer marketing will continue to expand for years to come [1]. The lockdowns and social distancing measures imposed during this period resulted in individuals spending increased amounts of time at home, leading to a substantial rise in social media usage. Due to the pandemic related regulations and restrictions, for example lockdown and social distancing, people have spent more time staying at home and using social media [2]. Social media became a critical plat form not only for entertainment but also for evaluating and purchasing products, underscoring its growing importance in post-pandemic marketing strategies Within this context, social media influencers have emerged as pivotal figures in marketing strategies, often perceived by consumers as more authentic and reliable than traditional celebrities. This perception has contributed to higher click-through rates (CTR) and conversion rates associated with brands endorsed by these influencers. This way of attracting customers is vital as, unlike traditional advertising [3], people trust an influencer in a way that is more like a friendship. Therefore, followers have a higher CTR and conversion [4].

N. Rangaswamy et al. (Eds.): IndiaHCI 2024, CCIS 2338, pp. 123–138, 2025.
https://doi.org/10.1007/978-3-031-80832-6_10

Despite the growth of these marketing strategies, COVID-19 related regulations and restrictions, for example social distancing, isolation and lockdown were obstacles to brands to produce marketing content. In the widespread of this situation, a virtual influencer received attention. Virtual influencers are computer-generated human beings or personas, often powered by artificial intelligence and CGI technology, who interact with audiences on social media platforms [5]. A virtual influencer is a digital avatar having human like appearance that interacts and communicates with consumers via digital media, and thus, it can be a great option for brands to endorse themselves to consumers via social media, regardless of pandemic situation. It is often designed as a high level of human likeliness in perspective of lifestyle, behavior and appearance but it is not a human [6]. A virtual influencer leverages an advantage for building an innovative brand image via social media in the minds of consumers [7].

According to market estimates, The Artificial Intelligence (AI) market industry is projected to grow from USD 128.1 billion in 2022 to USD 1,589.6 billion by 2030, exhibiting a compound annual growth rate (CAGR) of 37.0% during the forecast period of 2024–2032 [8]. Demand involving AI-forced answers that optimize advertising and marketing strategies, enhance client engagement and personalization, they are accountable for this growth. Previously exceptional for accuracy and efficiency, entrepreneurs can now also analyze considerable amounts of statistics, study client behavior, and customize campaigns via AI generation.

Though virtual influencers have certain advantages, there are several challenges to consider. Digital media experts pointed out the biggest potential challenge of virtual influencers is the lack of authenticity and reliability than human influencers [9]. Even though virtual influencers obtain high levels of human likeliness regarding its visual representation and storytelling of lifestyle, the VI fail to develop a sense of connection to human minds as they are AI generated personas. Thus, consumers may have second thoughts about the contents and brand endorsement by virtual influencers' nature [10]. But simultaneously, they are considered to me more innovative as they can implement the most distinctive ideas through 3-D modelling and CGI. Given these dynamics, a critical question arises: What factors distinguish virtual influencers from human influencers in the minds of consumers? Considering that authenticity, reliability, and innovation are essential elements of influencer marketing, it is crucial to explore how these factors influence consumer perceptions of virtual influencers compared to their human counterparts. To our knowledge, this area has not been extensively investigated. Therefore, this research seeks to enhance the understanding of consumer perceptions of virtual influencers, focusing on the dimensions of authenticity, reliability, and innovation relative to human influencers.

This paper consists of the following structure. First, the existing research related to the nature of influencer marketing and characteristics of virtual influencers are reviewed. After that, data gathering and analysis methods are described, and preliminary analysis results are discussed. Then, practical implication and limitation of the preliminary results is suggested.

2   Literature Review

2.1   Social Media Influencers as a Driving Force for Consumer Opinions

In the "People's Choice" Katz & Lazarsfeld developed the concept of the "Two-Step-Flow of Communication" previously, which is presented in detail in their work "Personal Influencer". According to this model, the dissemination of information via mass media takes place majorly in two steps. First step, opinion leaders receive the information from the mass media [11]. Second step, the received information as well as the personal interpretation and opinion of these opinion leaders is disseminated to the masses through various types of media. The principle of opinion leadership developed by Lazarsfeld & Katz can also be applied to influencer marketing on social media. Prominent influencers on social media can address many people due to their high reach and take on an important role in a networked and digitalized sphere. Accordingly, they can also influence consumers' opinions on brands and, for example, increase the brand visibility and awareness, intentions to buy products, provided the influencers are perceived as authentic, reliable, credible, competent and likeable by the recipients. In this context, influencer marketing represents the commercial use of the opinion leader concept by multiple brands [12]. Influencer marketing is a marketing strategy in which a firm selects and incentivizes social media influencers to engage their followers on social media in an attempt to leverage these influencers' innovation as well as reach to endorse the brands, with the ultimate goal of enhancing brand's visibility and performance.

The origins of virtual impact can be traced to the convergence of technology and creativity, as companies search for new ways to engage audiences in more crowded digital spaces One pioneering example is the "Lil Michela" (Figs. 1 and 2) virtual influencer by Los Angeles startup Brood. Introduced to the public via Instagram in 2016, Lil Michaela gained instant traction for her unique beauty and beautiful story, amassing a devoted following in the millions and currently has over 2.5 million followers on Instagram [13].

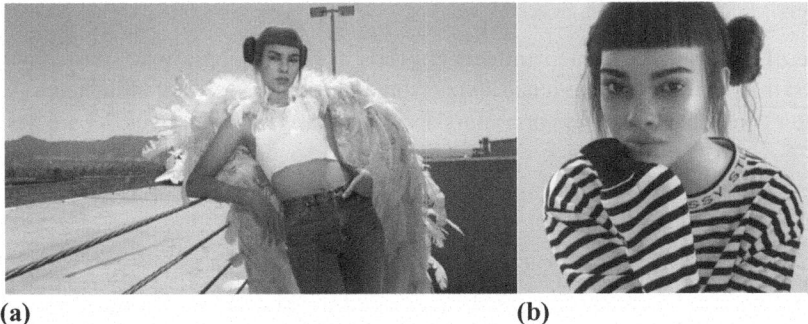

(a)   (b)

Fig. 1. (a and b) Image of "Lil Miquela," a virtual influencer created by the Los Angeles-based startup-Brud from her official social media account of "Lil Miquela"

2.2   Differentiation of Influencers – Human or Virtual Presence

In general, influencers refer to social media users with considerable numbers of followers who can potentially affect an individual's purchase intention. Fundamentally, these individuals are not built solely for marketing purposes, and they pursue a broader scope of outcomes, for example gaining the attention from audiences and creating customer engagement with their content [14]. Thus, they are distinguished from traditional celebrities in terms of their goal of using social media. They can be further classified depending on various factors.

Reachability. Within the social media influencer market one way of differentiating influencers is based on the size of their reach. Influencers are usually assigned to three different reach sizes: *Nano, Micro and Mega-influencers.* Nano-influencers are the category with the smallest reach of only a few hundred followers. In comparison to the other two categories, they often have a high level of personal identification and interaction with their follower count and therefore, a high level of credibility. Micro-influencers have a reach of a four- to five-figure range. This category of influencers is usually an expert in a niche or has a reliable connection with their followers. Consequently, they are of high interest for small or medium-sized brands as they have a high level of credibility. Mega-influencers have a follower range of several hundred thousand or even millions of people. They are more innovative and are the first choice for tier one brands, for example, big brands and luxury fashion houses, as they often help in increasing brand awareness and visibility. Thus, they reach a broad and diverse target group compared to the other two categories, however, they have a lower interaction rate and credibility due to their reach.

Category of Content and Niche. In addition to reachability, influencers can also be divided into different thematic categories they create content in, depending on which product category they promote intensively. For example, fashion and lifestyle influencers, beauty, and skincare influencers etc. Furthermore, there are numerous other typologies that could be considered, like, the communication behavior of influencers with their followers.

Nature of Existence. Human influencers (HI) are real people who exist physically based on their expertise, experience and personality. Whereas virtual influencers (VI) are computer generated characters or avatars designed to resemble humans. VI are designed by using AI and CGI technologies.

2.3   Virtual Influencers

Emphasizing that VI are autonomously controlled by AI and visually represented as an interactive, real-time rendered personas in a digital landscape [15]. From other authors, they are also explained as computer generated imagery (CGI)-influencers. The term computer generated imagery originates from the film industry and signifies 3D computer animations. Accordingly, a VI is not a real person like a SMI (Superhuman Machine Intelligence). A VI is an exclusive virtual entity that has been designed and created by AI agencies. For this, designers, social media managers and programmers work together and generate the VI attributes and character traits that resemble to a real person. VI contributions are controlled to varying degrees by algorithms. The VI background is entirely fictional and could be deliberately crafted to attend to a specific target group. Thus, VI can have multiple characters like a social activist. An example of this character profile is the VI @noonoouri which dedicated a whole Instagram Story Series to the Pride Month.

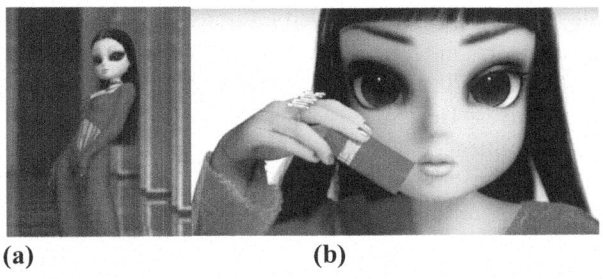

(a)   **(b)**

Fig. 2. (a) Image of Noonoouri for Versace, from official social media account of Noonoouri (b) Image of Noonoouri for Dior, from Luxury Daily

2D and 3D Virtual Influencers (VI). In the vast world inhabited by VI, we encounter two main categories: 2D and 3D models, each with its own unique and interesting aesthetic Animated characters and other 2D VI, available in color and graphics in two dimensions space. With stylized design, vibrant colors and exaggerated features, they captivate audiences with their quirky personas [16]. Previous study highlights how these avatars, with their quirky personalities and associated stories, resonate strongly with viewers who prefer engaging, visually appealing stories and video games.

In contrast, 3D VI are examples of technological marvels, created using advanced computer graphics (CGI) techniques to inhabit a life-like three-dimensional environment for these avatars, carefully crafted and refined in a simple and authentic way that blurs the lines a genuine digital illusion.

While 2D VI are more anime versions with quirky and loud looks, their 3D counterparts are comparatively more realistic and immersive. The industry experts have observed that both groups play an important and distinguishing role in reshaping the influencer marketing landscape, providing new avenues for brands to engage with consumers in the ongoing development of increasingly digital world [17].

Designing Character Profile of Virtual Influencers. Creating compelling narratives, profiles, and introductions offers powerful solutions to the authenticity dilemma surrounding true influencers. When complemented by rich background information, these digital personas add depth and richness, enabling viewers to explore their motivations, values and experiences and create deeper connections That part of the storytelling this not only increases the emotional resonance between true influencers and their audience but also creates a feeling of trust and authenticity. Furthermore, this methodology provides valuable insights into consumer preferences. By understanding the parts of the virtual influencer story that strongly speak to their audience, brands can gather valuable information about consumer interests, preferences, and values. This deeper understanding allows brands to tailor their messaging and what they present as best aligned with their target audience to be well rounded and maximize brand visibility.

Essentially, creating engaging background content for virtual influencers works as a multi-pronged approach. It strengthens the emotional connection between influencers and their audiences, provides valuable insights into consumer preferences, and increases brand visibility through messaging that aligns with audience interests and values.

Character Profile Mr. Ou. (Fig. 3), L'Oréal's First 2-D Virtual Brand Ambassador for Chinese Market. Mr. Ou (refer Fig. 3) is a 2-D anime character, who works in the Cosmetic and Beauty Industry. He is cautious about the environment and works on sustainability initiatives. He is a 24-year-old Chinese French entrepreneur. He is designed as a virtual influencer for Chinese market by the company L'Oréal for its endorsement. He will contribute to the social media content related to sustainability initiatives, eco-friendly ingredients and beauty trends.

Fig. 3. Image of L'Oréal's first 2-D virtual brand ambassador for Chinese market -Mr Ou., from The Business of Fashion

2.4   VI and its Correlation with Consumer Perception – A Comparative Study of VI and HI

Influencer marketing refers to a brand's activities leveraging social media resources to advance customer engagement and increase marketing performance through influencers on social media platforms like Instagram [18]. Covid-19 impacted consumers' social media marketing behavior, and now consumers are more likely to use social media platforms as a decision-making tool. Mason analyzed and found that consumers have a significant tendency of social media utilization behavior for identifying, comparing, evaluating, and purchasing products than before Covid-19 [2]. Over the past years, social media Influencers became a crucial element for social media marketing by brands [17]. Based on the social exchange theory, authenticity, homophily, and expertise (innovative content creation) of influencers have a positive impact on marketing outcomes such as loyalty to influencers, product attitude, authenticity and reliability and purchase intention. Lou & Yuan proposed an integrated model to explain the marketing effect of influencers via social media [19]. This model represents that innovative value of content results in trustworthiness, attractiveness, and similarity to followers have a positive impact on trust in branded posts which affects brand awareness and consumers' purchase intention as they find the products to be more authentic and reliable. Several literatures confirmed that authenticity and reliability are crucial elements of influencer marketing for achieving desirable marketing outcomes. Influencers' perceived authenticity and reliability is dependent on consumers' trust, because intuitively, if consumers feel an influencer is not real, they will not be able to draw a connection and will not be able to consider the influencer as an authentic source of trust. This could possibly a result of lack of emotions involved. At the same time, innovative content creation by influencers plays an important role in attracting new consumers and increasing reachability. The first factor that will attract consumers is the innovation and information in the content creation, later leading to the perceived credibility of the influencers (Table 1).

Table 1. Related work and previous findings on Virtual Influencer

Source	Theoretical Basis	Methodology	Main Findings	Major Factors Involved
Park et al. (2020), Journal of Marketing Research	Social Cognitive Theory, Self-Determination Theory	Survey, Interviews	Consumers perceive virtual influencers as authentic and relatable	Authenticity, Relatability, Visual Appeal
Smith et al. (2019), International Journal of Marketing	Social Identity Theory, Social Comparison Theory	Experiment, Content Analysis	Both human and virtual influencers are perceived with similar levels of trust and credibility	Trust, Credibility, Similarity with Audience
Lee et al. (2018), Journal of Consumer Psychology	Parasocial Interaction Theory, Social Influence Theory	Experiment, Observational Studies	Consumers show favorable attitudes towards virtual influencers and engage with their content more	Personality, Engagement, Content Quality
Johnson et al. (2017), Computers in Human Behavior	Uses and Gratifications Theory, Parasocial Interaction Theory	Survey, Content Analysis	Perception of authenticity was higher for human influencers while virtual influencers were seen as more engaging	Relatability, Authenticity, Engagement
Kim et al. (2020), Journal of Advertising Research	Elaboration Likelihood Model, Social Influence Theory	Survey, Experiment	Virtual influencers positively impact consumers' purchase decisions in the fashion industry	Credibility, Persuasiveness, Engagement

(continued)

Table 1. (*continued*)

Source	Theoretical Basis	Methodology	Main Findings	Major Factors Involved
Chen et al. (2019), International Journal of Advertising	Social Identity Theory, Source Credibility Theory	Survey, Focus Groups	Virtual influencers are perceived as credible and influential, leading to positive attitudes towards influencer marketing	Credibility, Influence, Brand Image
Wong et al. (2019), Journal of Business Research	Cognitive Dissonance Theory, Social Comparison Theory	Survey, Interviews	Gen Z consumers are influenced by virtual influencers but remain skeptical about their authenticity	Trust, Authenticity, Skepticism
Nguyen et al. (2018), Journal of Retailing and Consumer Services	Self-Determination Theory, Social Influence Theory	Survey, Content Analysis	Virtual influencers positively influence consumer attitudes and behavior in the retail sector	Trust, Engagement, Brand Loyalty

Particularly, identified the power of influencer marketing and its mechanism by comparing social media influencers and traditional celebrities such as movie celebrities. The authors also argued that consumers feel a stronger sense of connection to social media influencers than traditional celebrities, and the social presence mediates a relationship between influencer type and trustworthiness [16]. Through the research, authenticity and relatability are indicated as salient factors for social presence regarding to type of influencer. When people feel an influencer is real, they feel like the influencer is more feasible and attainable, and this perception leads to higher trustworthiness, brand awareness and purchasing decisions of consumers.

Additionally, virtual influencers can help to build innovative brand image, especially for young generations. With the use of AI and CGI, complicated and exaggerated concepts can be implemented resulting in a highly innovative brand endorsement. For example, a Korean public organization introduced a virtual influencer to appeal to the target market with an innovative and tech-sassy brand image. On 24th June 2022, the Korea Tourism Organization introduced "Yeo Lizzie' as the ambassador of Korea tourism via its social media channels for more innovation driven engagement with the audience. Yeo Lizzie is a 22-year-old virtual influencer. The organization has also previously appointed renowned celebrities like Son Heung-Min and EXO to its ambassadors. Nevertheless, the lack of authenticity and relatability is pointed out as its potential challenge. Although the key element of influencer marketing is authenticity of the influencers [16, 17, 19], consumers may perceive the virtual influencers as unrelatable and less authentic because they are not real humans. Arsenyan and Mirowsak investigated consumers' reaction toward virtual influencers on Instagram by drawing a comparison between three different types of Instagram influencers with respect to user engagement and reaction

[20]. They selected a 2D virtual influencer, a 3D virtual influencer, and a human influencer for their analysis. Among these three influencers, the users showed significant negative reactions toward the 3D influencer than the other two. Doubt of its nature and authenticity is the highest for 3D virtual influencers. Their work suggests that highly human-like virtual influencers are receiving high negative reviews for their nature, and this may cause uncanny valley phenomenon which affects triggers the negative reaction and doubt for the influencer's nature. This may harm the influencers' trustworthiness and decline brand loyalty and reduce reachability.

3 Background and Hypothesis Development

Based on the review of the existing literature and the underlying theories, it looks like there are multiple factors that affect virtual influencers on consumer perception in terms of authenticity, reliability, and innovation in comparison to human influencers. The content innovation of the influencers does help in greater customer engagement for the brands. The authenticity and reliability of the influencers further fuel this, impacting the purchase decision of customers. This paper results in drawing the focus on the factors that contribute to the significant opinion about authenticity, reliability, and innovation of virtual and human influencers. This forms the entire hypothesis of the study, which is being tested using a t-test through an online survey, as mentioned in the following methodology section. This led to the following hypotheses development:

3.1 Hypothesis

Null Hypothesis (H0). The use of virtual influencers does not significantly affect consumer perceptions of authenticity, reliability, and innovation compared to traditional human influencers.

Alternative Hypothesis (H1). The use of virtual influencers significantly influences consumer perceptions of authenticity, reliability, and innovation compared to traditional human influencers.

4 Methodology

The steps of the proposed methodology are as follows:

1. Online Survey
2. Paired t-test

4.1 Data Collection

The *online survey* was strategically distributed through purposive sampling to ensure a diverse representation across demographics, with a particular emphasis on individuals aged 18 to 35 years old to solicit unbiased opinions, especially from those actively engaged with influencer content. Out of the 180 respondents who participated, it was assumed that approximately 30 individuals, constituting approximately ±10% of the sample size, might have had little to no prior knowledge about virtual influencing. This exclusion allowed for a balanced representation of participants with varying levels of familiarity with the subject matter. Purposive sampling method was used to conduct a survey on design professionals, precisely fashion professionals and people who are engaged be influencer market. By employing a mix of Likert scale, matrix scale, and open-ended questions, the survey aimed to explore nuanced perspectives on authenticity, reliability, and innovation in influencer marketing. Following data collection, statistical analyses, including paired t-tests, were conducted to discern significant differences in consumer perceptions between virtual and human influencers. The methodology not only facilitated a deeper understanding of the factors responsible for consumer behavior but also provided valuable insights into the evolving landscape of influencer marketing. The segmentation of the questionnaire was made in a following way (Table 2):

Table 2. Segmentation of questionnaire

Segment	Description
Segment 1: Introduction	Introduction to the questionnaire and consent form
Segment 2: Demographic Information	Collecting demographic details of respondents
Segment 3: General Questions	Gathering general information about respondents' usage of social media and influencers
Segment 4: Hypothesis 1: Perception of Authenticity, Reliability, and Innovation (H1)	Assessing perceptions of authenticity, reliability, and innovation regarding virtual and human influencers
Segment 5: Hypothesis 2: Differential Influence (H2)	Evaluating if consumer perceptions of authenticity, reliability, and innovation are differentially influenced by virtual and human influencers
Segment 6: Conclusion	Concluding remarks and opportunity for additional comments

4.2 Data Analysis

Following data collection, statistical analyses, including paired t-tests, were conducted to discern significant differences in consumer perceptions between virtual and human influencers. The methodology not only facilitated a deeper understanding of the factors responsible for consumer behavior but also provided valuable insights into the evolving landscape of influencer marketing.

In our study involving 150 respondents, perceptions of authenticity regarding virtual influencers (VI) and human influencers (HI) were examined. Respondents attempted

Likert-scale questions in the survey to rate authenticity, reliability, and innovation for VIs and HIs. After collecting the data, we calculated mean and Standard Deviation (SD). Then we determined the mean differences (MD) of all the attributes by subtracting the mean ratings for HI from the mean ratings for VI. This revealed the direction and magnitude of the difference in perceptions.

Table 3. Data findings and calculation of authenticity, reliability and innovation

Attributes	Human Influencers	Virtual Influencers
Authenticity	Mean: 4.2	Mean: 3.4
	SD: 1.1	SD: 1.2
Reliability	Mean: 3.8	Mean: 3.3
	SD: 1.0	SD: 1.1
Innovation	Mean: 4.5	Mean: 3.5
	SD: 1.3	SD: 1.2

Paired t-Test for Authenticity. By using mean and standard deviation values from Table 3, we calculated the following values to conduct a paired t-test which is given by Eq. (1),

$$t = \frac{\bar{d}}{(SD/\sqrt{n})} \tag{1}$$

where,

t = t value

$\bar{d}$ = mean difference between virtual and human influencer ratings for each attribute which is given by Eq. (2)

SD = standard deviation of the differences

n = number of pairs (respondents)

Mean Difference

$$\bar{d} = VI_i - HI_i = 4.2 - 3.4 = 0.8 \tag{2}$$

Standard Deviation

The standard deviation of differences measures the variability in the paired observations (Table 3).

$$SD = \sqrt{\frac{SDVI2 + SDHI2}{2}} = \sqrt{\frac{(1.1 + 1.2)2}{2}} = \sqrt{1.325} \approx 1.15 \tag{3}$$

By using the values from Eq. (2) and Eq. (3) in Eq. (1) we get,

$$t = \frac{0.8}{\left(1.15/\sqrt{150}\right)} \approx 8.51$$

$$t_A \approx 8.51 \tag{4}$$

where $t_A = t$ value of Authenticity

Paired t-Test for Reliability. By using mean and standard deviation values from Table 3, we calculated the following values to conduct a paired t-test which is given by Eq. (1),

Mean Difference

$$\bar{d} = VI_i - HI_i = 3.8 - 3.3 = 0.5 \tag{5}$$

Standard Deviation
The standard deviation of differences measures the variability in the paired observations (Table 3).

$$SD = \sqrt{\frac{SDVI2 + SDHI2}{2}} = \sqrt{\frac{(1.0 + 1.1)2}{2}} = \sqrt{1.105} \approx 1.05 \tag{6}$$

By using the values from Eq. (5) and Eq. (6) in Eq. (1) we get,

$$t = \frac{0.5}{\left(1.05/\sqrt{150}\right)} \approx 5.81$$

$$t_R \approx 5.81 \tag{7}$$

where $t_R = t$ value of Reliability

Paired t-Test for Innovation. By using mean and standard deviation values from Table 3, we calculated the following values to conduct a paired t-test which is given by Eq. (1),

Mean Difference

$$\bar{d} = VI_i - HI_i = 4.5 - 3.5 = 1.0 \tag{8}$$

Standard Deviation
The standard deviation of differences measures the variability in the paired observations (Table 3).

$$SD = \sqrt{\frac{SDVI2 + SDHI2}{2}} = \sqrt{\frac{(1.3 + 1.2)2}{2}} = \sqrt{1.565} \approx 1.25 \tag{9}$$

By using the values from Eq. (8) and Eq. (9) in Eq. (1) we get,

$$t = \frac{0.5}{\left(1.05/\sqrt{150}\right)} \approx 5.81$$

$$t_I \approx 5.81 \tag{10}$$

where t_I = t value of Innovation

5 Results and Discussions

Attribute	Mean Difference $(\bar{d})$	Standard Deviation (SD)	t-value	Critical t-value (two-tailed) t_f, $D_F = 149$, $^-\alpha = 0.05$)	Result
Authenticity	0.8	1.15	4.4	8.51	Reject H_0
Reliability	0.5	1.05	4.5	5.81	Reject H_0
Innovation	1.0	1.25	4.6	9.80	Reject H_0

Here,
D_F = Degrees of Freedom
$D_F = n - 1 = 150 - 1 = 14$
α = Significance Level
The significance level for the test is 0.05. Since it is a two-tailed test, this α is split into two tails (0.025 in each tail).
Using a standard t distribution table, the critical value of D_F and $\frac{\alpha}{2} = 0.025$ (for a two-tailed test) is approximately,

$$t_{critical} = \pm 1.976$$

Critical t value ($t_{critical}$) exceeded the critical t-value of ±1.976, for all the three attributes – authenticity, reliability and innovation leading to the rejection of the null hypothesis (H_O) in each case. This indicates a significant difference in perceptions of authenticity, reliability, and innovation between virtual influencers and human influencers.

6 Conclusion

In this research, the aim was to compare consumer perceptions of human influencers (HIs) and virtual influencers (VIs) across three critical attributes: authenticity, reliability, and innovation within the fashion industry. Through a comprehensive analysis in volving paired t-tests, we found significant differences in how consumers perceive HIs and VIs. The results indicate that VIs are perceived as more innovative com-pared to HIs, which aligns with the growing trend of digital and AI advancements and the novelty associated with virtual personas. On the other hand, HIs are perceived as more authentic and reliable, highlighting the importance of human emotions and real-life experiences in influencer marketing. The findings provided valuable insights for marketers and brands looking to leverage influencer marketing strategies. Understanding the impact of these attributes on consumer perceptions can help in effectively targeting and engaging with different consumer segments. While VIs may attract audiences with their technological approach, HIs continue to align strongly with consumers who value authenticity and reliability as a strong customer engagement for a brand. Overall, the study underlines the evolving dimensions of the influencer marketing landscape and emphasizes the need for a balanced approach that considers the strengths of both human and virtual influencers. Overall, the study underlines the evolving dimensions of the influencer marketing landscape and emphasizes the need for a balanced approach that considers the strengths of both human and virtual influencers.

7 Discussion

This study reveals significant differences in how consumers perceive human influencers (HIs) and virtual influencers (VIs) across the attributes of authenticity, reliability, and innovation. VIs are perceived as more innovative, reflecting their appeal as personas with cutting-edge technology and digital creativity. Their ability to deliver visually compelling content and unique brand identities positions them as trendsetters in the influencer space. However, this innovation has some limitations. VIs are seen as less authentic and reliable compared to HIs, who continue to engage & resonate more deeply with consumers due to their real-life experiences and emotional relatability. The trust and credibility that HIs stimulate through genuine engagement remain vital in building long-term relationships with consumers. These findings suggest that while VIs offer creative opportunities for brands, HIs are imperative for developing trust and authenticity. Brands should consider leveraging & capitalizing the unique strengths of both influencer types to create balanced and effective marketing strategies.

8 Future Research

One potential area of research could be the long-term impact of influencer types on brand loyalty and consumer trust. Additionally, future studies could delve deep into the effectiveness of hybrid models that combine both human and virtual influencers in marketing campaigns. Studying factors that affect shaping consumer perceptions of His and VIs like cultural differences could also provide deeper insights, as cultural factors often play a significant role in social media consumption and technology adoption. Lastly, as technological advancement in virtual influencing continues to evolve, examining the ethical implications and consumer acceptance of highly sophisticated virtual personas will be crucial for the sustainable growth of influencer marketing in the future.

References

1. The CMO Survey. September 2022. (n.d.). https://cmosurvey.org/results/september-2022/

2. Mason, A.N., Narcum, J., Mason, K.: Social media marketing gains importance after Covid-19. Cogent Bus. Manag. **8**(1) (2021). https://doi.org/10.1080/23311975.2020.1870797
3. Khamis, S., Ang, L., Welling, R.: Self-branding, 'Micro-celebrity' and the rise of social media influencers. Celeb. Stud. **8**(2), 191–208 (2017). https://doi.org/10.1080/19392397.2016.1218292
4. Hajli, M.N.: A study of the impact of social media on consumers. Int. J. Market Res. **56**(3), 387–404 (2014). https://www.researchgate.net/publication/261098834_A_study_of_the_impact_of_social_media_on_consumers
5. Jin, S.V., Phua, J.: Following celebrities' tweets about brands: the impact of twitter-based electronic word-of-mouth on consumers' source credibility perception, buying intention, and social identification with celebrities. J. Advert. **47**(4), 436–449 (2018)
6. Wibawa, R.C., et al.: Virtual influencers: is the persona trustworthy? J. Manajemen Informatika (JAMIKA) **12**(1), 51–62 (2022). https://www.researchgate.net/publication/359814023_Virtual_Influencers_Is_The_Persona_Trustworthy
7. Kim, H., Park, M.: Virtual influencers' attractiveness effect on purchase intention: a moderated mediation model of the Product–Endorser fit with the brand. Comput. Human Behav. **143**, 107703 (2023). https://www.sciencedirect.com/science/article/abs/pii/S0747563223000547
8. Market Research Future: Artificial Intelligence (AI) Market Research Report - Forecast to 2032 (2022). https://www.marketresearchfuture.com/reports/artificial-intelligence-market-1139
9. Moustakas, E., Lamba, N., Mahmoud, D., Ranganathan, C.: Blurring lines between fiction and reality: perspectives of experts on marketing effectiveness of virtual influencers. In: 2020 International Conference on Cyber Security and Protection of Digital Services (Cyber Security) (2020). https://ieeexplore.ieee.org/document/9138861/
10. Belanche, D., Casaló, L.V., Flavián, M.: Human versus virtual influences, a comparative study. J. Bus. Res. **173**, 114493 (2024). https://www.sciencedirect.com/science/article/pii/S014829632300085 24Katz/Lazarsfeld (1955): Personal Influence. https://www.researchgate.net/publication/328078453_KatzLazarsfeld_1955_Personal_Influence
11. Katz, E., Lazarsfeld, P.F.: Personal Influence (1955). https://www.researchgate.net/publication/328078453_KatzLazarsfeld_1955_Personal_Influence
12. Leung, F.F., Gu, F.F., Li, Y., Zhang, J.Z., Palmatier, R.W.: Influencer marketing effectiveness. J. Mark. **86**(6), 93–115 (2022)
13. Drenten, J.: Celebrity 2.0: Lil Miquela and the rise of a virtual star system (2020). https://www.researchgate.net/publication/344791173_Celebrity_20_Lil_Miquela_and_the_rise_of_a_virtual_star_system
14. Brown, D., Hayes, N.: Influencer Marketing: Who Really Influences Your Customers? Elsevier/Butterworth-Heinemann (2008)
15. Sands, S., Campbell, C.L., Plangger, K., Ferraro, C.: Unreal influence: leveraging AI in influencer marketing. Eur. J. Market. **56**(6) (2022). https://kclpure.kcl.ac.uk/portal/files/167172729/Sands_et_al_2022_Unreal_influencer_EJM_Author_Accepted_Version.pdf
16. Jin, S.V., Muqaddam, A., Ryu, E.: Instafamous and social media influencer marketing. Mark. Intell. Plan. **37**(5), 567–579 (2019). https://doi.org/10.1108/MIP-09-2018-0375
17. Kim, D.Y., Kim, H.Y.: Trust me, trust me not: a nuanced view of influencer marketing on social media. J. Bus. Res. **134**, 223–232 (2021). https://doi.org/10.1016/j.jbusres.2021.05.024
18. Li, F., Larimo, J., Leonidou, L.C.: Social media marketing strategy: definition, conceptualization, taxonomy, validation, and future agenda. J. Acad. Mark. Sci. **49**(1), 51–70 (2021). https://doi.org/10.1007/s11747-020-00733-3
19. Lou, C., Yuan, S.: Influencer marketing: how message value and credibility affect consumer trust of branded content on social media. J. Interact. Advert. **19**(1), 58–73 (2019). https://doi.org/10.1080/15252019.2018.1533501

20. Arsenyan, J., Mirowska, A.: Almost human? A comparative case study on the social media presence of virtual influencers. Int. J. Hum. Comput. Stud. **155**, 102694 (2021). https://doi.org/10.1016/j.ijhcs.2021.102694

Chordex: A Wearable Chorded Keyboard for Malayalam

N. S. Abhiram$^{(\boxtimes)}$ (iD)

IDC School of Design, IIT Bombay, Mumbai 400076, India
abhiramns06@gmail.com

Abstract. Can a chorded keyboard improve text entry speed for Indian languages? This paper documents a wearable chorded keyboard for the Malayalam language and the longitudinal study conducted to evaluate the performance of the keyboard. We evaluated text entry speed among 18 users across 10 sessions. Our results indicate that participants were able to significantly improve their text entry speeds over time, demonstrating the potential of chorded keyboards for efficient text input in complex scripts. To the best of our knowledge, ours is the first study that evaluates a chorded keyboard for an Indian language.

Keywords: Text entry · Chorded keyboard · Malayalam · Indian languages · User testing

1 Introduction

Text input for Indian languages has been a challenging task due to the complexity of characters in many Indian scripts, often requiring multiple keystrokes to input a single glyph. For instance, the Hindi word स्त्री(= woman) may seem like a single glyph but comprises three consonants (स, त्, and र) and a vowel modifier (◌ी) that can collectively necessitate six keystrokes on most desktop keyboards [1]. Previous research has explored various innovative text input methods to address this challenge. *Swarachakra*, a soft keyboard designed for Indian languages, achieved a text entry speed of over 40 characters per minute (CPM) after 20 sessions in a study [1].

The Dravidian language Malayalam, primarily spoken in Kerala, a southern state in India, is renowned for its complex script. With over 56 basic letters and numerous ligatures, the script poses significant challenges for efficient text input. Traditional keyboards, which rely on a one-to-one mapping of keys to characters, are often inadequate for such a rich character set, leading to slower typing speeds and higher error rates.

Chorded keyboards have a wide range of potential applications in the Indian language context. In educational settings, they could enable faster learning of typing skills for Indian scripts, particularly for beginners [15]. Chorded keyboards are also well-suited for accessibility [8], as they allow one-handed operation, making them valuable for users with physical disabilities or when one hand is occupied. Additionally, these keyboards have applications in stenography and real-time transcription, as their ability to input characters with a single chord can significantly improve efficiency in fast-paced environments like court reporting [15].

While chorded keyboards have shown promise in enabling faster text entry through shorthand typing, their potential for Indian languages remains largely unexplored. The motivation behind this study is to investigate whether a wearable chorded keyboard designed specifically for the Malayalam language can enhance text entry speed compared to traditional input methods.

Furthermore, chorded keyboards can support multilingual typing by allowing seamless switching between different Indian scripts. This feature is particularly valuable in professional settings where multilingual communication is necessary. From an ergonomic perspective, chorded keyboards can reduce strain and fatigue, making them more suitable for long-term use compared to traditional keyboards.

Finally, in the realm of wearable technology, chorded keyboards can be integrated into devices like smartwatches, providing a practical solution for typing in regional languages. Their minimalistic design can also make them useful in assistive technologies for visually impaired users, offering tactile feedback for more intuitive text entry.

In this study, we present ChorDex, a wearable chorded keyboard designed for faster text input in Indian languages, with a focus on Malayalam. ChorDex leverages the dexterity of human hands to facilitate efficient typing using minimal finger movement, making it well-suited for compact, wearable technology. Our primary aim is to evaluate the performance of ChorDex in enabling users to type Malayalam, a complex script, more efficiently compared to traditional input methods.

The research questions addressed in this study are:

1. Can a wearable chorded keyboard improve text entry speed for the Malayalam language?
2. How quickly can users adapt to a wearable chorded keyboard for Malayalam text input?

2   Related Work

Previous research in text entry methods for Indian languages has primarily focused on virtual keyboards for touchscreens. Studies like Bhikne et al. [1] have explored the use of speech recognition to augment text entry speeds for Hindi, finding significant improvements over keyboard-only input. Additionally, the work by Joshi et al. [4] on Text Entry in Indian Languages on Mobile highlighted the limitations of traditional text entry methods and the potential for novel input strategies.

Text input methods for Indian languages face challenges due to the large number of characters and ligatures involved. Sowmya V.B [10] conducted a comprehensive study on input methods for Telugu, offering insights into various layouts and input method editors (IMEs). The study underscores the limitations of existing input methods for Indian scripts and presents the need for optimized layouts to improve typing efficiency. [9] describes the design and evaluation of the keyboard *Keylekh* for text entry in Indic scripts. Similarly, Malsattar et al. [11] conducted a usability study comparing *Swarachakra* with the traditional InScript layout, finding that *Swarachakra's* logical grouping of characters allows for faster adaptation and improved typing speed.

Chorded keyboards, such as the Twiddler and the Stenotype, have been studied for their potential to enhance text entry efficiency through chording (pressing multiple keys simultaneously). Lyons et al. [5] demonstrated the effectiveness of the Twiddler for one-handed text input, reporting significant improvements in typing speed after repeated practice. Their study revealed an average speed of 26.2 words per minute (WPM) after 400 min of practice, with some users reaching up to 67 WPM.

Additionally, research conducted by Jussi Tarvainen [6] on the GKOS chorded keyboard showed a remarkable improvement in typing speed among novice users, with participants achieving a 277% increase in typing speed after an eight-day learning phase. These findings highlight the promise of chorded keyboards for mobile devices and compact spaces where traditional QWERTY keyboards may be less practical.

Other input methods, like speech-to-text, predictive text input, and handwriting recognition, have also been explored for Malayalam. Speech-to-text systems, while promising, often faces difficulty due to the diverse accents and dialects of Malayalam speakers [12]. Predictive text input can reduce typing effort but may not be suitable for all contexts, especially where precise word choice is critical. Handwriting recognition offers a natural input method but requires sophisticated algorithms to handle the complex ligatures and variations in handwriting styles [13, 14]. Compared to these methods, chorded keyboards offer a balanced approach, combining the efficiency of key-based input with the compactness and ergonomic benefits of chording.

3   A Brief Background of Malayalam Language

Malayalam is recognized as one of India's 22 scheduled languages, predominantly spoken by the Malayali people in Kerala and in the union territories of Lakshadweep and Puducherry (Mahé district).

The State Institute of Languages in Thiruvananthapuram has conducted extensive research to identify the essential character components required for encoding Malayalam text [2]. The Style Book (Malayalam Achatiyum Ezhuthum), published by the State Institute of Languages [2], details the findings derived from a series of investigations. The Committee has approved the foundational Malayalam character set outlined in the Style Book (See Fig. 1).

Swarachakra is a soft keyboard designed for Indian languages, including Malayalam. It utilizes a circular layout to facilitate text entry through a combination of taps and gestures. While *Swarachakra* has shown promising results, it is limited to touch-based input on digital devices.

The need to explore alternative input methods, such as a wearable chorded keyboard, arises from the potential for increased typing speed and the ability to input text in various contexts, beyond just digital devices.

3.1 Malayalam Character Set

Vowels (13)

അ	ആ	ഇ	ഈ	ഉ	ഊ	ഋ
എ	ഏ	ഐ	ഒ	ഓ	ഔ	

Consonants (36)

ക	ഖ	ഗ	ഘ	ങ
ച	ഛ	ജ	ഝ	ഞ
ട	ഠ	ഡ	ഢ	ണ
ത	ഥ	ദ	ധ	ന
പ	ഫ	ബ	ഭ	മ
യ	ര	ല	വ	
ശ	ഷ	സ	ഹ	
ള	ഴ	റ		

Anuswaram, Visargam, Chandrakkala (3)

ം	ഃ	്

chillu (5)

ൻ	ൽ	ർ	ൾ	ൺ

consonant signs (4)

്യ	്ര		്വ

vowel signs (12)

ാ	ി	ീ	ു	ൂ	ൃ
െ	േ	ൈ	ൊ	ോ	ൗ

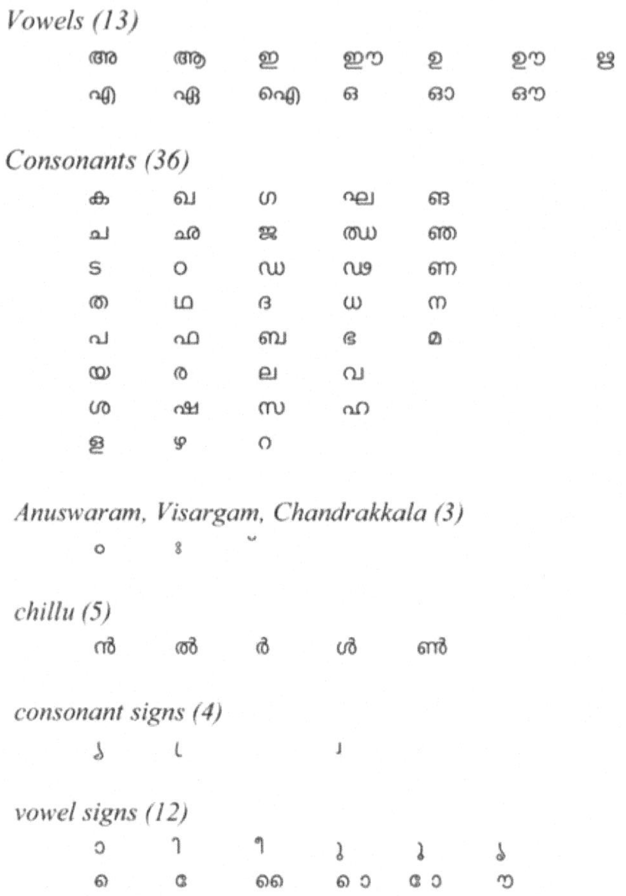

Fig. 1. Malayalam character set

4 Prototype Design

The prototype of the wearable chorded keyboard built by the author comprises ten joysticks, with two four-way joysticks allocated for the thumbs and the remaining eight accommodating two-way inputs for the fingers (see Fig. 2). The main body, created via 3D printing, features adjustable straps facilitating secure attachment to the user's hand, ensuring optimal comfort and stability during operation. The microcontroller employed in the prototype is the ESP32, chosen for its versatility and compatibility with the design requirements.

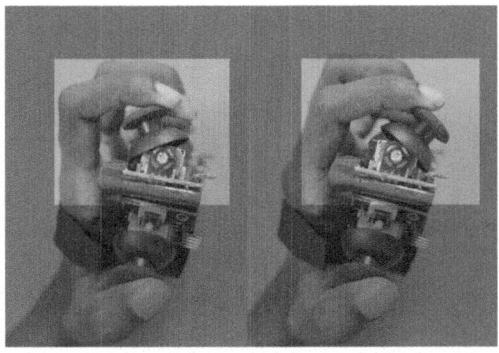

Fig. 2. Mechanism of the joystick keys and hand position.

Technical specifications of the prototype as shown in Fig. 3 include:

- Microcontroller: ESP32, chosen for its wireless capabilities and processing power.
- Keys: Five strategically placed keys that can be pressed in combinations to produce over 100 characters.
- Housing: A lightweight, ergonomic design that can be worn on the hand.

Fig. 3. Major components of the prototype. Joystick module and ESP32 microcontroller.

4.1 Design Iterations

The final design of the keyboard was developed through an iterative process, focusing on ergonomics, using mock-up models made from clay and other materials (see Fig. 4). Although the prototype used in the study featured straps to secure it to the user's hands (see Fig. 5), later design iterations were refined to naturally fit the hands without the need for straps.

The wearable chorded keyboard, named ChorDex, was developed to address the complexities of text input in Indian languages, particularly Malayalam. The name ChorDex reflects its focus on chording input and the dexterity required for efficient typing. Through careful ergonomic design and a refined key mapping system, ChorDex offers users an intuitive and efficient tool for faster text input.

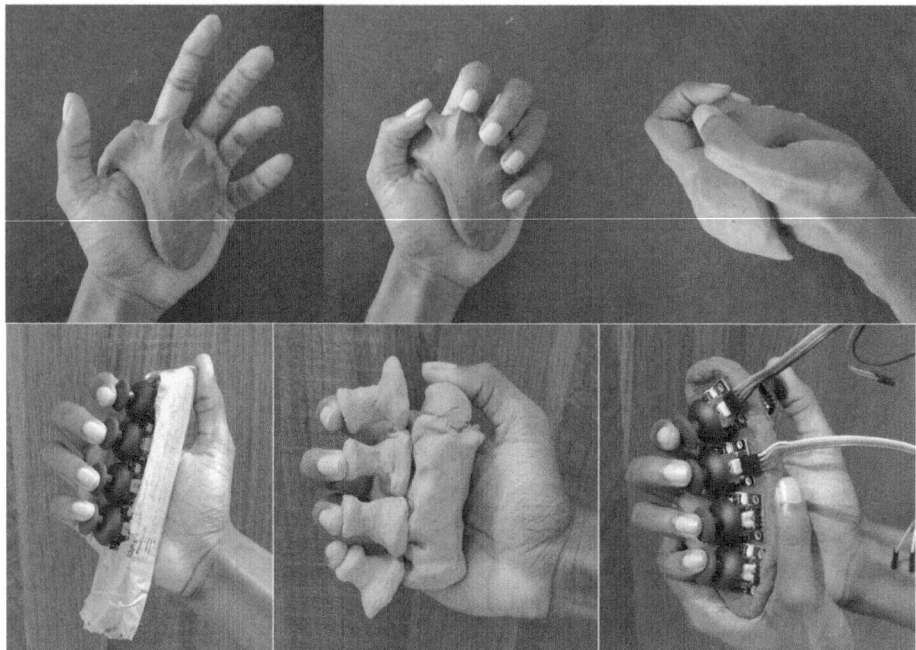

Fig. 4. Mockups that lead to the final design

Fig. 5. Final prototype of the wearable keyboard ChorDex used for the study

4.2 Mapping

The layout and mapping of the letters on the chorded keyboard are meticulously designed based on the frequency of usage of Malayalam characters and the ease of combinations [3]. Frequently used characters are assigned to more accessible combinations, aiming to facilitate faster and more efficient text input while minimizing the learning curve for users.

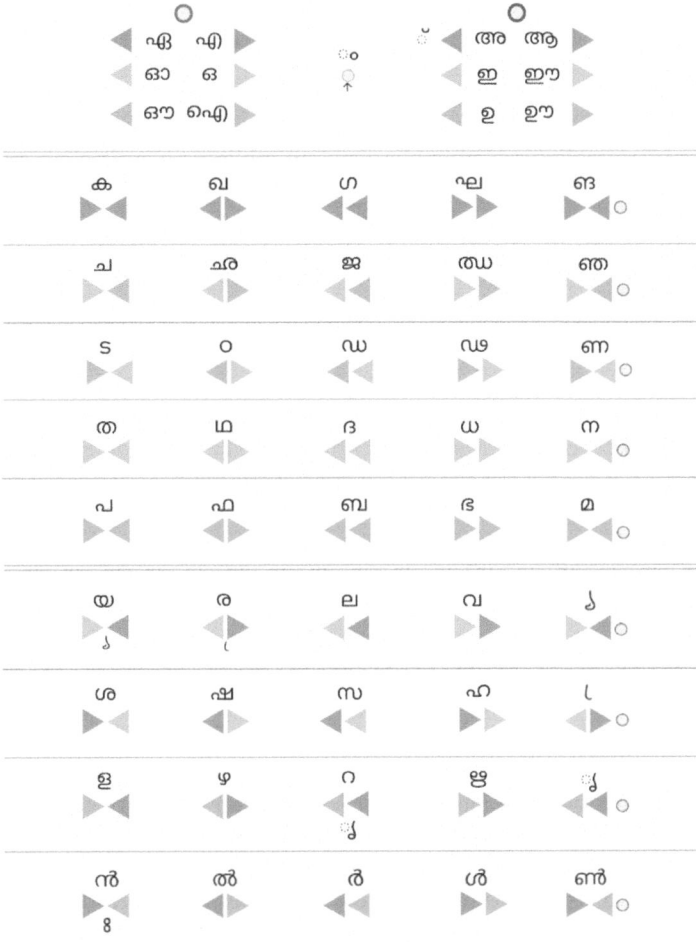

Fig. 6. Final Layout for the Malayalam chorded keyboard

The icon direction indicates the movement required for each key. Keys are color-coded as follows: orange for index fingers, yellow for middle fingers, and green for ring fingers. When a combination involves two keys, the icon on the left side represents keys pressed with the left hand, and the icon on the right side represents keys pressed with the right hand, assuming the hands are held facing each other. The circular icon denotes the use of thumb keys. For example, to type the letter " ക," press both index fingers inward. If you press a thumb key along with the index fingers, you will type the letter " ങ." (see Fig. 6).

The placement of keys in the keyboard is primarily based on the frequency of character usage in Malayalam. Frequently used characters are assigned to easily accessible positions, leveraging the stronger fingers for more common letters. For instance, the "ka" series is grouped together on the same fingers, and all vowels are controlled using a single finger for better memorability and ease of use (as illustrated in Fig. 6). This design reduces cognitive load and ensures that users can quickly adapt to the layout while improving typing speed.

Additionally, the mapping of characters was designed to consider learnability and accessibility. The ergonomic positioning helps in minimizing movement fatigue, particularly for longer typing sessions, which is crucial for sustained use in educational or professional environments.

5 Methodology

5.1 Participants

This section outlines the experimental design used to evaluate the effectiveness of the wearable chorded keyboard for Malayalam text input. The study followed a longitudinal design to assess user adaptation and performance over time.

The participants were recruited using community sampling. A total of 25 participants were initially recruited, of which 18 participants (11 males and 7 females, aged 20–25 years) successfully completed the study. The participants were native Malayalam speakers with no prior experience using chorded keyboards. No remuneration was provided to participants, and the experiment adhered to ethical guidelines by ensuring voluntary participation and informed consent.

5.2 Experimental Design

Each participant underwent an introductory session prior to the first session where participants practiced basic chording combinations. They were asked to type out each letter at least once and then their name or preferred words to familiarize themselves with the chorded keyboard. This was followed by the main transcription task, which involved typing a set of predefined Malayalam phrases. These phrases were selected to cover a range of linguistic structures, including common words, complex ligatures, and less frequent characters. This approach ensured a comprehensive evaluation of the keyboard's performance across different aspects of the Malayalam script. The sessions concluded with a short debrief where participants provided qualitative feedback on their experience.

The main longitudinal usability test consisted of 10 sessions, each requiring the participant to type out 9 phrases (#1–3- easy level phrases, #4–6 medium, #7–9 hard). of varying difficulty as given below.

1. 1. എവിടുന്ന് വരുന്നു
      (Evidunnu Varunnu)
2. 2. അവ☐ ചുറ്റും നൊ·ാക്കി
      (Avan Chuttum nokki)
3. 3. എനിക്ക് മനസ്സിലായില്ല
      (Enikku manassilayilla)
4. 4. കാണം വിറ്റും ഓണം ഉണ്ണണം
      (Kaanam vittum onam unnanam)

5. 5. അമ്മേ വകൈീട്ട് ചായക്കെന്താ
   (Ammee vaikeettu chayakkentha)

6. 6. കൊ·ാന്നാ□ പാപം തിന്നാ□ തീരും
   (Konnal paapam thinnal theerum)

7. 7. ഇതുപൊ·ാലൊ·ാരണ്ണം   കയറുപൊ·ാട്ടിച്ച്   കാട്ടീ   കറേി
   (Ithupolorennam kayarupottich kaattee keri)

8. 8. കട്ടവനെ കണ്ടില്ലെങ്കി□ കിട്ടിയവനെ പിടിക്കുക
   (Kattavane kandillenkil kittiyavane pidikkuka)

9. 9. ഇരുട്ട് വ്യാാപകമായി പ്രത്യക്ഷപ്പെട്ടിരിക്കുന്നു
   (Iruttu vyapakamaayi prathyakshappettirikkunnu)

For the first 4 sessions, participants had the option to keep the letter mapping with them during the test, while from the 5th session onwards, they continued without the aid of the mapping.

For the main typing tasks, 9 predefined Malayalam phrases of varying difficulty (easy, medium, and hard) were used in each session. Following a similar approach to Dalvi et al. [16] as a part of their protocol to evaluate virtual Indian language keyboards. These phrases were carefully selected to cover a wide range of linguistic structures, including common words, complex ligatures, and less frequently used characters. The selection process considered the frequency of use and linguistic complexity of the phrases. Additionally, the phrases were classified into three categories based on a difficulty index (DI), which accounted for factors such as typing difficulty, phrase length, and memorability. The DI score ranged from 3 to 9, with phrases classified as easy (DI = 3), moderate (DI = 4–5), and hard (DI = 6–9). These phrases were compiled from various sources, including Malayalam proverbs and dialogues from popular Malayalam movies.

The experimental environment was carefully controlled to minimize external distractions and ensure consistency across sessions. Participants were seated in a quiet room with consistent lighting and temperature conditions. They were provided with noise-cancelling headphones to eliminate auditory distractions. The experimental software was configured to provide visual feedback on typing performance without being intrusive, helping participants maintain focus on the task.

5.3 Measures

The primary measure was the text entry speed, calculated as the number of characters per minute (CPM). In addition, qualitative observations were made through direct observation of the participants' performance and follow-up interviews conducted after each session. Key performance indicators, such as error rates (measured by backspace usage) and time taken per session, were also documented.

6 Results

6.1 Text Entry Speed

Figure 7 shows the average CPM for the wearable chorded keyboard across 10 sessions, along with the 95% confidence interval. As participants became familiar with the keyboard layout, their text entry speed increased consistently. The average CPM for all participants after the 10th session was 85 CPM, a significant improvement from the first session. While a saturation point was not reached within the 10 sessions, the upward trend in CPM indicates that participants were continuing to improve their typing speed.

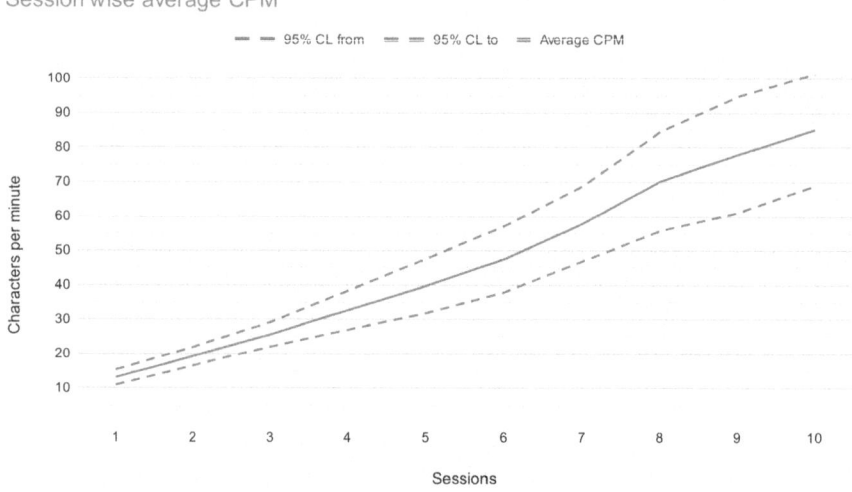

Fig. 7. Average CPM (Characters Per Minute) and 95% confidence intervals.

In comparison to other Indian language text input systems, such as the *Swarachakra* keyboard for Marathi, the wearable chorded keyboard for Malayalam demonstrated a considerable advantage in terms of typing speed. For example, in the longitudinal study of *Swarachakra*, the average CPM after 10 and 20 sessions was 35 CPM and 45 CPM, respectively [1]. By contrast, the final CPM in our study was much higher (see Fig. 7), emphasizing the potential of chorded keyboards to enhance text entry efficiency for Indian scripts.

6.2 Accuracy and Error Rates

In addition to CPM, error rates were analyzed based on the number of backspaces used during each session. The results show that the average backspace count across all sessions was 54, with a steady decrease as participants became more familiar with the keyboard. This reduction in backspace usage suggests that participants were making fewer typing errors as they progressed through the sessions. Figure 8 illustrates the decline in backspace counts over time, reinforcing the participants' growing accuracy in typing.

6.3 External Factors

Qualitative feedback from participants provided further insights into their experiences with the wearable chorded keyboard. Many participants expressed initial difficulty with

Session wise average backspace count

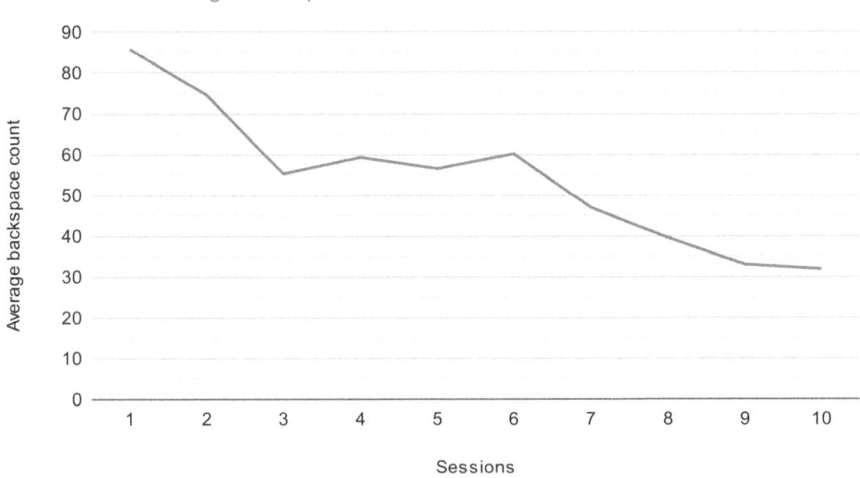

Fig. 8. Average number of backspaces counts in each session.

memorizing the character combinations but reported significant improvement by the 4th or 5th session. By this point, most users were able to type without relying on visual mapping, indicating that the learning curve for the keyboard was shorter than expected.

While 25 users participated in the study, 18 users completed the experiment strictly adhering to the protocol. Some users had difficulty with the size of the keyboard not fitting their hands properly. The experiment involved 1–2 h of typing time for each user. Total average time taken by all the users in each session is given in Fig. 9.

Additional observations revealed that participants with smaller hands experienced some discomfort when using the device, particularly when navigating certain key combinations involving the ring finger and little finger. This issue was noted as a potential area for future improvement, particularly in terms of adjusting the size of the device for better ergonomics.

7   Discussion

The results of this longitudinal study provide empirical evidence that a wearable chorded keyboard can significantly improve text entry speed for the Malayalam language. The observed increase in CPM over the course of the study suggests that users can adapt to the chorded keyboard with continued practice.

Compared to traditional keyboards, such as the QWERTY layout or virtual keyboards like *Swarachakra*, the wearable chorded keyboard demonstrated a significant advantage in terms of typing speed. As previously noted, the final CPM achieved by participants in this study (85 CPM) far surpassed the results from similar longitudinal studies on Indian language keyboards like *Swarachakra*, where CPM values were much lower

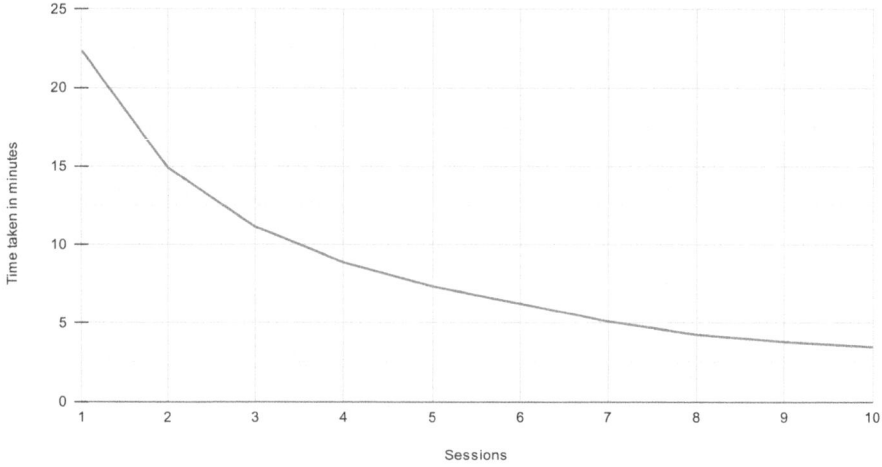

Fig. 9. Average time taken in each session in minutes

after comparable training sessions. This result highlights the efficiency of chorded input methods in contexts requiring fast and accurate typing of complex scripts. The wearable chorded keyboard offers the advantage of enabling text input in a wide range of contexts, beyond just digital devices. Additionally, the ergonomic design and wearable nature of the prototype allow for more natural and comfortable typing, potentially leading to higher typing speeds in the long run.

One of the notable qualitative findings from this study was the impact of hand size on typing performance. Participants with smaller hands faced difficulties when performing complex key combinations, especially when the ring or little finger was involved. This issue likely stemmed from the lack of adjustability in the keyboard's size, which affected comfort and ease of movement. Future iterations of the device should focus on improving the ergonomic design to accommodate users with varying hand sizes. Addressing this limitation would likely result in further improvements in typing speed and accuracy, particularly for users who found certain key combinations challenging.

The study found that participants were able to type without relying on the visual mapping from the 5th session onwards, indicating that the learning curve for the wearable chorded keyboard is relatively short. This is especially encouraging, considering the complexity of the Malayalam script. Previous studies on text entry systems, such as those by Tarvainen and Lyons et al. [6, 7] also observed significant improvements in typing speed after sustained practice. However, the progress shown in this study suggests that chorded keyboards can facilitate faster learning and higher proficiency than traditional text entry methods.

The success of this study has broader implications for the field of human-computer interaction and the design of input methods for complex scripts. The demonstrated adaptability and efficiency of the wearable chorded keyboard suggest that similar approaches could be explored for other Indian languages with rich character sets, such as Tamil, Telugu, and Kannada. Additionally, the portable, ergonomic design of the wearable keyboard makes it well-suited for use in mobile and wearable computing environments, where traditional keyboards are often impractical.

However, it is important to note that this study was limited to a participant group of young adults aged 20–25. A more diverse participant group, including users from different age ranges and typing proficiencies, could provide a more comprehensive understanding of the keyboard's usability across demographics. Future studies should also investigate the long-term usability of this keyboard in real-world applications.

7.1 Contributions

The primary contributions of this paper include the development and evaluation of a wearable chorded keyboard specifically tailored for the Malayalam script. By conducting a comprehensive empirical study with 18 participants, we have demonstrated significant improvements in text entry speed and accuracy, highlighting the potential of this innovative input method. Additionally, our study provides valuable insights into the user experience and learning curve associated with chorded keyboards, suggesting their applicability in various contexts where traditional input methods are inadequate. Furthermore, our findings contribute to the broader field of human-computer interaction by presenting a viable solution for efficient text entry in complex scripts, which can be extended to other Indian languages with similar character sets.

7.2 Future Avenues

Future work may focus on several key areas to further improve the wearable chorded keyboard. One direction involves refining the key mapping algorithm to optimize character combinations for speed and accuracy. Another area of interest is the integration of haptic feedback, which could provide users with tactile confirmation of key presses and further reduce error rates. Additionally, longitudinal studies with larger and more diverse participant groups need to be conducted to validate the findings and explore the long-term usability of the keyboard. Research may also investigate the potential of adaptive learning algorithms to personalize the key mappings based on individual user preferences and typing patterns.

While this study focused primarily on text entry speed, future research could explore other factors that may influence the overall typing experience, such as cognitive load, fatigue, and user satisfaction. Additionally, comparative studies with traditional input methods could provide further insights into the relative advantages and limitations of the wearable chorded keyboard.

Moreover, the application of this wearable chorded keyboard could be extended to other Indian languages, enabling a more inclusive and efficient text input experience across various linguistic communities. The influence of user demographics and training methods on typing speed could also be explored in further studies.

8 Conclusion

This study demonstrates the potential of a wearable chorded keyboard to improve text entry efficiency for the Malayalam language, which poses significant challenges due to its complex script. Through a longitudinal study involving 18 participants, we found that users were able to significantly improve their typing speed and accuracy over time. By the 10th session, participants achieved an average of 85 CPM, a noteworthy improvement compared to traditional or soft keyboards for Indian languages.

The ergonomic design of the wearable chorded keyboard played a key role in reducing strain during prolonged use, making it a viable option for both educational and professional environments. However, issues related to hand size, particularly for participants with smaller hands, indicate the need for future design iterations to accommodate a broader range of users. Addressing this limitation could further enhance the usability of the device and lead to even greater improvements in typing speed and comfort.ZIn conclusion, ChorDex offers a novel and effective approach to enhancing text input efficiency for the Malayalam language. By addressing the specific needs of complex script input, this study paves the way for innovative solutions that can significantly improve digital engagement and productivity in native languages. The broader implications of this research contribute to the field of human-computer interaction, highlighting the potential for such innovative input methods to be adopted widely across different linguistic contexts, ultimately fostering greater inclusivity and accessibility in digital communication.

Acknowledgments. I would like to express my sincere gratitude to Prof. Anirudha Joshi, IDC IIT Bombay, for his invaluable guidance and unwavering support throughout this project. His insights and encouragement were crucial in shaping this work.

References

1. Bhikne, B., Joshi, A., Joshi, M., Ahire, S., Maravi, N.: How much faster can you type by speaking in Hindi? Comparing keyboard-only and keyboard + speech text entry. In: IndiaHCI '18: Proceedings of the 9th Indian Conference on Human-Computer Interaction, pp. 20–28 (2018). https://doi.org/10.1145/3297121.3297123
2. Malayalam keyboard layout and character encoding Report of the Committee. Microsoft Word - Malayalam standardization report-final.doc (keralabhashainstitute.org) (2001). https://www.keralabhashainstitute.org/sites/default/files/inline-files/malayalam%20standardization%20report_2.pdf
3. Prema, S., Manu, J.: Frequency count of Malayalam characters and letters. Department of Linguistic University of Kerala. https://www.academia.edu/36857783/Frequency_Count_of_Malayalam_Characters_and_Letters
4. Joshi, A., Ghosh, S.: Text entry in Indian languages on mobile: user perspectives. In: IndiaHCI'14 Proceedings of the India HCI Conference, New Delhi, India. ACM Digital Library (2014). https://doi.org/10.1145/2676702.2676710
5. Lyons, K., Plaisted, D., Starner, T.: Expert chording text entry on the twiddler one-handed keyboard. In: CHI '04 Proceedings of the SIGCHI Conference on Human Factors in Computing Systems (2004). https://ieeexplore.ieee.org/document/1364695

6. Tarvainen, J.: Beginner performance with the GKOS chorded keyboard. Master's thesis, University of Tampere) (2010). https://trepo.tuni.fi/bitstream/handle/10024/81829/gradu04481.pdf?sequence=1
7. Lyons, K., Plaisted, D., Starner, T.: Twiddler typing: one-handed chording text entry for mobile phones. In: Proceedings of CHI. ACM Press (2004). https://doi.org/10.1145/985692.985777
8. Weller, J.I.: Dynamic one hand chord keyboard. Department of Informatics and Media, Uppsala University (2021). https://uu.diva-portal.org/smash/get/diva2:1598956/FULLTEXT01.pdf
9. Joshi, A., Ganu, A., Chand, A., Parmar, V., Mathur, G.: Keylekh: a keyboard for text entry in indic scripts. In: CHI '04: Proceedings of the SIGCHI Conference on Human Factors in Computing Systems, Vienna, Austria (2004). https://doi.org/10.1145/985921.985950
10. Sowmya, V.B.: Text input methods for Indian languages. Master's Thesis, International Institute of Information Technology, Hyderabad (2008). https://researchweb.iiit.ac.in/~sowmya_vb/msthesis.pdf
11. Malsattar, N., Emmadi, N., Joshi, M.: Testing the efficacy of an indic script virtual keyboard: swarachakra. In: IHCI '14: Proceedings of the India HCI Conference, New Delhi, India. ACM Digital Library (2014). https://doi.org/10.1145/2676702.2677203
12. Kavya, M.: Linguistic challenges in Malayalam speech recognition: Analysis and solutions. Ph. D. Thesis, APJ Abdul Kalam Technological University, Thiruvananthapuram (2023). https://kavyamanohar.com/documents/Kavya-phd-2023.pdf
13. Pius, N.K., Johny, A.: Malayalam handwritten character recognition system using convolutional neural network. Int. J. Appl. Eng. Res. **15**(9), 918–920 (2020). https://www.ripublication.com/ijaer20/ijaerv15n9_05.pdf
14. Alex, M., Das, S.: An approach towards Malayalam handwriting recognition using dissimilar classifiers. Procedia Technol. **25**, 224–231 (2016). https://core.ac.uk/download/pdf/82467761.pdf
15. Tabe, H.T., Materechera, E.K.: Academic writing technique: the influence of stenography on students' academic performance in higher education. Cogent Educ. **11**(1) (2024). https://doi.org/10.1080/2331186x.2024.2306883
16. Dalvi, G., et al.: A protocol to evaluate virtual keyboards for Indian languages. In: Proceedings of the 7th Indian Conference on Human-Computer Interaction (IndiaHCI '15). Association for Computing Machinery, New York, NY, USA, pp. 27–38 (2015). https://doi.org/10.1145/2835966.2835970

The Role of Social Media in Fostering Social Movements: Assessing User Experience (UX) Elements for Effective Mobilization in Bangladeshi Digital Activism

Md. Arif Billah[1]([✉]) and Rifat Rahman[2]

[1] Jatiya Kabi Kazi Nazrul Islam University, Mymensingh 2224, Bangladesh
`arif_20122410@jkkniu.edu.bd`
[2] Bangladesh University of Engineering and Technology, Dhaka, Bangladesh

Abstract. In today's era of contemporary activism, social media (SM) platforms are becoming an essential medium for fostering social movements and activism, especially in growing regions like Bangladesh, where digital connectivity is rapidly expanding. This study explores the intricate relationship between various user experience (UX) elements, including hashtags, banners, information cards, reels, videos, captions, and live streams, and their efficacy in driving social change through digital activist campaigns on social media in Bangladesh. By leveraging both online and offline surveys, this research employs a quantitative approach to examine the behavior of regular social media users in Bangladesh. Key findings from this study suggest that strategically designed visual UX elements, such as videos or reels and social media banners, significantly influence the efficacy of activist campaigns on social media, demonstrating their ability to stimulate social change. Efficient user experience (UX) can help accomplish social change goals by enhancing user engagement and disseminating information. This study offers valuable insights for UX practitioners in Bangladesh who wish to utilize social media as an opportunity to facilitate constructive social change.

Keywords: User experience · Social media · Digital activism · Social change · Bangladesh

1 Introduction

In both developed and developing countries, access to technology has significant advantages in areas such as education, health, information accessibility, and economic growth. This has led experts to consider it a fundamental 'human right'. During this period of technological progress, social movements are undergoing a transformation, shifting from conventional street protests to embracing the dynamic realm of online social media (SM) platforms. Numerous studies from both advanced and emerging nations demonstrate that individuals who participate in civic and political activities, such as engaging in protest behavior, are regular users of various SM platforms (Bekkers et al., 2011; Earl & Kimport, 2011; Pearce & Kendzior, 2012; Valenzuela et al., 2012; Seongyi & Woo-Young,

© The Author(s), under exclusive license to Springer Nature Switzerland AG 2025
N. Rangaswamy et al. (Eds.): IndiaHCI 2024, CCIS 2338, pp. 154–171, 2025.
https://doi.org/10.1007/978-3-031-80832-6_12

2011). Within the past 15 years, critics, the media, western governments, and the tech industry have portrayed Facebook and other SM platforms as a means of promoting democratic change in dictatorial nations during times of political turmoil. In fact, the Arab Spring events catapulted SM into the forefront of global attention as a possible instrument to foster democratization (Wells & Deejay, 2021). There are numerous of positive and negative aspects to this technology-driven transformation in social movements. The positive aspect is in the ability to promptly and effortlessly bring attention to any societal abnormality on social media, mobilizing popular sentiment against it and compelling policymakers to take substantial measures to eradicate it. But a significant danger is that ongoing or emerging confrontations could escalate on the internet as a result of false information or hate speech, which is further magnified by algorithms that promote negativity, and ultimately spill over into the real world. But whether it describes people's favorable, negative, or any other perspectives, the user experience (UX) elements found on SM platforms, such as hashtags, banners, info cards, reels, videos, captions, and live streams, play a crucial role in shaping these movements.

Bangladesh, a rapidly developing nation in Southeast Asia, is currently experiencing a substantial digital revolution. SM platforms, which include Facebook, Twitter, Instagram, etc., play a crucial role in facilitating enhanced communication in Bangladesh as an essential requirement for digitization. These platforms are essential for individuals to effortlessly obtain up-to-date information and convenient access to a vast online repository of knowledge. In January 2024, Bangladesh had 52.90 million active SM users, and the total number of SM users had grown by 9.7 million individuals, or a 22.3 percent increase, from early 2023 to the beginning of 2024 (Kemp, 2024). As a result of this rapid adoption, SM apps have significantly influenced the personal, social, and national aspects of life in Bangladesh.

Online activists utilize diverse UX components to engage with one another and disseminate their movement across different social media platforms, which later turned into a massive street protest. These UX elements serve as manifestations of their emotions and articulate their sentiments and viewpoints regarding a particular phenomenon. Through the process of sharing, posting, reacting, and engaging with these UX elements, each movement gradually grows in size, progressing from a small to a large scale. This study aims to explore the role of several SM platforms in promoting activism for social transformation in Bangladesh by investigating how various UX elements on these platforms contribute to this process. A quantitative approach was employed in this study by administering a survey through Google Form to an estimated sample of 216 individuals residing in both urban and rural regions of Bangladesh. We selected UX elements based on similar components found on Bangladesh's most frequently used SM platforms. To ensure an effective analysis, we performed descriptive and inferential analyses on the data using a Friedman test. The results essentially suggest that the adoption patterns of SM show a noticeable difference between users in urban and rural areas. Additionally, individuals of all ages and backgrounds have a strong preference for visual material, especially movies and reels, to stimulate engagement.

1.1 Objectives of the Study

• To evaluate the common UX elements used by Bangladeshi online activists.

- To pinpoint the key UX element that holds the most potential to influence any movements in Bangladesh.
- To investigate the perceived effectiveness of UX elements in promoting activism in Bangladesh.

1.2   Contribution of the Study

- This research focuses specifically on the UX elements that improve user involvement in mobilization efforts. It also adds to the current understanding of how UX design and digital activism overlap with one another.
- It offers specific insights that might guide the development and execution of more efficient digital activist campaigns adapted to the socio-cultural and technological context of Bangladesh.
- This study also highlights the significance of UX in attaining social change goals. It bridges the gap between interaction design and social effect, emphasizing the potential of well-crafted digital experiences to generate significant societal results.

1.3   Common UX Elements Used in Various SM Platforms in Bangladesh

According to Kemp (2023), The top four SM sites in Bangladesh in terms of traffic are Facebook, YouTube, Instagram, and LinkedIn. At the start of 2023, Meta's advertising resources revealed that there were 43.25 million Facebook profiles in Bangladesh. However, as of early 2023, there were 34.40 million YouTube users in Bangladesh, according to improvements to Google's advertising tools. In a surprising turn of events, LinkedIn's planning tools revealed that their potential ad reach in Bangladesh climbed by 1.3 million (+28.3 percent) from 2022 to 2023, while Instagram's potential ad reach in Bangladesh stayed the same during the same time period. Common interaction elements observed on these SM platforms include hashtags, social media banners, information cards, videos and reels, real-time live streaming, and captions.

Hashtags: A hashtag is generated by placing a hash symbol (#) before a word or keyword phrase. Social media posts employ it to aid those with similar interests in locating them via keyword or particular hashtag searches. It serves to attract attention to SM posts and stimulate engagement (O'Brien, 2023).

Social Media Banners: A social media banner is a visual element that draws attention to specific acts or information. It has the potential to influence user behavior and increase engagement. Digital advertising primarily uses SM banners. According to Hayes (2022), digital banner advertising is defined as the use of a rectangular graphic display that spans across the top, bottom, or sides of a website or SM platform.

Information Cards: It is also a precisely designed visual element that includes essential information excerpts or interactive components, such as surveys or concise pieces of information. Information cards provide succinct and easily understandable information that can enhance decision-making and content engagement.

Videos and Reels: Video has completely transformed the field of multimedia, fundamentally altering the manner in which we consume and engage with information.

Streaming video on social media sites is readily available to smartphone users, enhancing the consumption of knowledge by making it more dynamic and interesting, hence boosting the user experience (Swiderska, 2024). Reels are short vertical videos, ranging from 15 to 90 s in length, that users can produce, edit, and share on their SM profiles. Reels, in contrast to SM stories (typically seen on Facebook and Instagram), offer the advantage of remaining visible for 24 h and facilitating easy saving or sharing. Instagram introduced reels on August 5th, 2020, with a duration of 15 s, to compete with the video craze on TikTok.

Live Streams: Live streams are a type of video streaming that occurs in real time, allowing interaction between the broadcaster and the viewers on SM sites. It facilitates real-time, interactive experiences that encourage active participation and the development of emotional connections within the community.

Captions: Captions are used on SM platforms to provide contextual information, explanations, or commentary for visual media such as photographs and videos. It improves comprehension and availability of visual content, allowing for conversation and participation.

2 Literature Review

A multitude of research, both domestic and foreign, have been carried out aimed at investigating the correlation between social media (SM) and social movements. According to Encyclopedia Britannica (2024), SM refers to the online platforms, including social networking and microblogging websites, that enable users to engage in mass communication by sharing various forms of content, such as information, ideas, personal messages, images, and videos. And social movement indicates to a loosely structured yet persistent effort to promote or hinder a change in the structure or values of society (Smelser et al., 2024). The majority of research undertaken on the above issues indicates that current improvements in internet technologies, as well as the presence of SM platforms like Facebook, Twitter, YouTube, etc., have empowered millions of people to effectively mobilize and utilize information. As a result, we refer to gatherings of a large number of individuals with the goal of instigating or opposing societal transformations as 'digital activism'.

The contribution of SM platforms in effectively organizing social or political movements has garnered significant attention in academic research. According to Hwang & Kim (2015), social networks enable the efficient and extensive dissemination of information, allowing like-minded individuals to leverage and maximize their collective influence. Social networks are widely regarded as a highly successful means of not only spreading information, but also engaging new volunteers in social causes (González-Bailón et al., 2011). Thus, they are considered one of the primary venues for engaging in activism today. Marandici (2022) asserted that, Twitter and other SM platforms enable the process of thoughtful discussion, the preservation of historical events, and the widespread sharing of information during protests. These platforms connect users from many countries and assist in the coordination of protests that take place offline. Also, in accordance with Castillo-Esparcia et al., (2023), social media has significantly impacted political activity globally by providing a platform for citizens to voice their thoughts, participate in grassroots collective action, and collaborate with other activists. In several instances that have been observed all around the world, social media has been recognized to play a significant role in the mobilization of movements. For instance, the Arab Spring relied on social media for mobilization, communication, and coordination. It also diffused revolutionary ideas inside and outside the affected countries. Social media also strengthened Arab nations' shared identity, which helped revolutionary ideas proliferate (Tudoroiu, 2014). In another study, Khamis & Vaughn (2012) emphasize the importance of Facebook in spreading information and organizing people during the Tahrir Square protests in Egypt. Additionally, they also highlight the significance of Facebook pages and groups as "safe spaces" for protesters to gather, serving as a unique platform for unrestricted expression of ideas unlike any other (p. 157). Moreover, several studies have shown that the Black Lives Matter (BLM) movement has proven the efficacy of SM platforms, Twitter in particular, in rallying support from all over the world and coordinating protests (Ince et al., 2017; Carney, 2016; Wilkins et al., 2019).

It is evident that Bangladesh is an ideal instance of a recently digitalized country where SM platforms have greatly contributed to numerous social and political movements. Dhaka University (DU) students, Bangladesh's oldest and largest institution, blocked critical capital areas in April 2018 to demand quota reform. The cops severely assaulted and injured protesting students. This news spread across social media, such as Facebook pages, groups, and accounts where DU students provided live updates every few minutes. Protesters and activists used SM before they turned to traditional media. Facebook and other SM news feeds sparked this movement (Khan, 2018). The utilization of SM as a catalyst for social or political transformation is a relatively recent phenomenon in Bangladesh. Few studies has been looked at on this topic, with notable examples including the Shahbagh movement, which called for the prosecution of war criminals (Sinha, 2013; Zamir, 2014; Zaman, 2018; Roy, 2018), the student movement advocating for safer roads (S. Rahman, 2018), and the #MeToo movement (Hassan et al., 2019).

In July 2024, after an order by the High Court of Bangladesh, declaring the scrapping of the quota system illegal, students from DU again started protesting against government job quota system. Once again, the police and government troops launched an assault on the general students and began firing arbitrarily. The students used Facebook's 'group formation' feature on SM to garner significant public support for quota reform, and they began disseminating various photos and videos that exposed the brutality of the government troops. As a result, this movement rapidly spread over the entire country. Simultaneously, footage containing several inflammatory comments from prominent government officials and ministries, including the Prime Minister of Bangladesh, rapidly circulated on SM platforms. The campaign quickly intensified, and within a month of the student quota reform movement, it evolved into a single demand for the government's step down. This demand garnered support from individuals across every class and profession. At last, as a result of severe demonstrations, Sheikh Hasina, the Prime Minister of Bangladesh, resigned on August 5, 2024, concluding her 15-year tenure (bdnews24.com, 2024; Amnesty International, 2024).

Numerous studies have also explored the use and significance of specific UX components in bolstering social or political movements via SM platforms. As described by Yang (2016), a notable advancement in digital activism in recent times is the emergence of 'hashtag activism'. Hashtag activism occurs when individuals generate a substantial volume of postings on social networks using a shared word or phrase, accompanied by a hashtag that serves as a call to action for social or political causes. The integration of the interconnected influence of hashtags and the communal act of storytelling has the potential to transform the online sharing of personal experiences into a force that amplifies the impact of a collective movement (Clark, 2016). Another study conducted in Malaysia reveals that various elements of SM platforms, particularly Instagram, have varying effects on user engagement. Videos had the most significant influence on user engagement, followed by images with people and images without people. Moreover, users generally respond favorably to informational textual content (W. N. A. Rahman et al., 2022). Furthermore, it implies that social media influencers have a significant impact on both consumption-based (e.g., viewing) and creation-based (e.g., content creation) engagement.

Although the crucial role of SM platforms in promoting digital activism has been studied, there is a lack of study on the specific UX elements on social media that have the greatest impact on mobilization efforts. Besides, the study in question is more limited in a developing nation like Bangladesh, where the widespread use of diverse social media platforms like Facebook, Instagram, and Twitter has a profound impact on society and is influencing societal norms and behaviors in a new manner (Ahmed, 2024). To have a comprehensive understanding of modern activism, it is crucial to recognize the fundamental user experience (UX) components and how they are employed on various social media platforms to mobilize social movements, organize demonstrations, and coordinate protests. This study aims to explore this phenomenon in the context of Bangladesh, focusing on a lack of research highlighted in the current literature.

3   Materials and Methods

The study utilized a quantitative methodology. To ensure a representative and thorough knowledge of how UX elements promote digital activism in Bangladesh, we used a stratified random sampling strategy. The target population consisted of Bangladeshi SM users who were engaged in or aware of digital activism. Demographic factors such as age, gender, geographic area, and occupation determined the stratification to accurately represent the diverse population of SM users. A final sample size of 216 participants, estimated using G*Power, is considered sufficient to guarantee a satisfactory level of statistical power for the inferential analysis. G*Power is an independent power analysis software designed for various statistical tests frequently employed in the fields of social, behavioral, and biomedical sciences (Faul et al., 2009). This chosen sample size enhances the capacity to apply the findings to a larger population.

We collected the data for this study directly from primary sources using a cross-sectional survey, utilizing both a virtual instrument (a Google Form) and an offline instrument (an in-person survey questionnaire). The study was conducted in multiple areas of the Mymensingh district, covering Bhaluka Upazila, Trishal Upazila, and Mymensingh

Sadar Upazila. The survey questionnaire consisted of a total of 22 questions, which were divided into four groups. The initial part of the survey obtained demographic information, while the latter two sections obtained data on SM usage, engagement in activism, rating, and period of interaction with UX elements, depending on their effectiveness in encouraging activism. Finally, we also assessed the perceived effectiveness of UX elements. As this study is based on a quantitative technique, it facilitates the organized arrangement of acquired data and the successful completion of coding activities.

After the data collection process, the self-reported data was checked by social media researchers to reduce bias in the data. We followed the adjudication procedure to ensure high accuracy and reliability in the collected data. We also examined the responses manually to remove error-prone responses, such as choosing a fixed response for all questions. For data analysis, we used both descriptive and inferential methodologies, performed statistical analysis on the organized data, and presented the findings in the report using the software programs 'MS Excel' and 'SPSS'. Anyway, the study was scientifically focused on the moral and ethical principles of social obligation (Žukauskas et al., 2018). Considering the complex nature of the research process, we conducted this study in accordance with research ethics. We maintained strict confidentiality, ensured a harmonious environment during interviews, encouraged voluntary participation in the survey, and respected the respondents' privacy (Yip et al., 2016).

4   Findings of the Study

Using cross-sectional study data, this section thoroughly investigates the behavior of regular social media users in Bangladesh. It specifically focuses on how the UX components of SM platforms affect individuals' participation in various movements. This study primarily displays and analyses the data using a univariate approach. The presentation utilized both bar charts and column charts to depict the essential information. The presentation primarily used percentage analysis and frequency distribution to present the data.

4.1   Demographic Variance in SM Use and Activism Engagement

Demographic data is considered essential in any research endeavor because it provides valuable insights into the overall status and conditions of the people in question. However, the subsequent part comprises demographic data pertaining to the respondents' gender, age, and geographical location.

216 individuals' demographic data is presented in Table 1, which is divided equally by gender (50% male, 50% female), age, and location. Each age group (18–25, 26–35, 36–45, and 46 +) accounts for 25% of the sample. The geographic distribution is balanced, with 50% in cities and 50% in rural or isolated locations. This uniformly distributed sample enables thorough and impartial scrutiny across various demographic dimensions.

Table 2 provides an extensive analysis of the utilization of several social media platforms in Bangladesh, divided by gender. With 100% and 81.9% of the participants engaged, Facebook and YouTube are the dominant platforms in the market. Instagram

Table 1. Demographic information

Variables		Frequency	Percentage (%)
Gender	Male	108	50
	Female	108	50
Age Range	18–25	54	25
	26–35	54	25
	36–45	54	25
	46 year or older	54	25
Geographic Location	Urban or City Area	108	50
	Rural or Remote Area	108	50

[**Source:** Online & Field Survey in Bhaluka Upazila, Trishal Upazila, and Mymensingh Sadar Upazila, Mymensingh; February-April, 2024]

Table 2. Gender and Most Used Social Media Platforms

	Facebook	Twitter	Instagram	YouTube	TikTok	LinkedIn	Snapchat	Total
Male	108	4	43	89	39	14	1	108
Female	108	4	44	88	42	11	2	108
Total	216	8	87	177	81	25	3	216
Percentage	100%	3.7%	40.3%	81.9%	37.5%	11.6%	1.4%	100%

and TikTok exhibit significant usage, with 40.3% and 37.5% of users, respectively. Conversely, only a small portion of users utilize Twitter and LinkedIn (3.7% and 11.6%, respectively), while Snapchat trails behind at 1.4%. This distribution highlights the prominence of visual and video content platforms in social media consumption patterns across genders.

Table 3. Gender and Types of Activism Participation

	Human Rights	Environmental Protection	Gender Equality	Women Safety	Social Justice	Political Campaigns	Total
Male	95	44	38	34	86	46	108
Female	96	40	36	33	87	42	108
Total	191	84	74	67	173	88	216
Percentage	88.4%	38.9%	34.3%	31%	80%	40.7%	100%

Table 3 delineates the level of involvement in different types of activism according to gender. Human rights and social justice are the primary focus of activism, with 88.4%

and 80% of individuals involved in these areas, respectively. Political campaigns and environmental conservation generate significant interest, with participation percentages of 40.7% and 38.9%, respectively. However, advocacy pertaining to gender equality (34.3%) and women's safety (31%) garners comparatively less participation.

Table 4. Age Range and Most Used Social Media Platforms

	Facebook	Twitter	Instagram	YouTube	TikTok	LinkedIn	Snapchat
18–25	54	7	29	39	12	22	3
Percentage	25%	87.5%	33.3%	22%	14.8%	88%	100%
26–35	54	1	17	30	9	3	0
Percentage	25%	12.5%	19.5%	16.9%	11.1%	12%	0%
36–45	54	0	13	54	31	0	0
Percentage	25%	0%	14.9%	30.5%	38.3%	0%	0%
46 and older	54	0	28	54	29	0	0
Percentage	25%	0%	32.2%	30.5%	35.8%	0%	0%

According to Table 4, Facebook has a global appeal, as 25% of all age groups use it. Among younger demographics, Twitter has the highest usage rate (87.5%), whereas usage among elderly demographics is quite low. Instagram engagement levels fluctuate, reaching a peak of 33.3% among users aged 18–25. Users' engagement on YouTube rises with age, reaching 30.5% in the oldest age categories. TikTok is most popular among younger users, with 38.3% of its users falling within the 36–45 age bracket. The majority of people who use LinkedIn are in the 18–25 age range (88%), whereas the youngest demographic utilizes Snapchat completely. Using this distribution, we can see that different age groups have different social media involvement patterns, as well as varying tastes and preferred platforms.

Table 5 reveals that human rights and social justice are continuously significant issues, with nearly equal engagement of roughly 25% across all age groups for human rights and participation varying from 24.3% to 26% for social justice. Among those aged 36–45, the level of engagement in environmental preservation reaches its maximum point at 27.4%. In contrast, the involvement in political campaigns is relatively stable, with the highest participation rate of 26.1% seen among individuals aged 18–25 and 26–35. However, there is a consistent level of gender equality and women's safety throughout all age groups, with minor differences.

Adoption of various social media platforms in both urban and rural areas is shown in the Table 6. Half of urban participants use Facebook, and 96% use LinkedIn, indicating their broad popularity in metropolitan regions. Adoption on Instagram follows at 77%, while TikTok and YouTube have significant but relatively smaller user bases at 33.3 and 55.4%, respectively. The urban areas have the highest percentage of Snapchat users, at 100%. Facebook is also at 50% in rural regions, while YouTube is at 44.6%, reflecting the predilection for video material among rural residents. With 66.7% of users, TikTok

Table 5. Age and Types of Activism Participation

	Human Rights	Environmental Protection	Gender Equality	Women Safety	Social Justice	Political Campaigns
18–25	48	20	18	17	45	23
Percentage	25.1%	23.8%	24.3%	25.4%	26%	26.1%
26–35	48	21	18	16	43	23
Percentage	25.1%	25%	24.3%	23.9%	24.9%	26.1%
36–45	48	23	19	17	42	20
Percentage	25.1%	27.4%	54.7%	25.4%	24.3%	22.7%
46 and older	47	20	19	17	43	22
Percentage	24.6%	23.8%	25.7%	25.4%	24.9%	25%

Table 6. Geographic location and Most Used Social Media Platforms

	Facebook	Twitter	Instagram	YouTube	TikTok	LinkedIn	Snapchat	Total
Urban	108	8	67	98	27	24	3	108
Percentage	50%	100%	77%	55.4%	33.3%	96%	100%	
Rural	108	0	20	79	54	1	0	108
Percentage	50%	0%	23%	44.6%	66.7%	4%	0%	

shows a higher preference for short-form video content, making it the most popular platform in rural areas. Instagram and LinkedIn have far lower adoption rates in rural locations compared to urban ones, while Snapchat and Twitter have almost no adoption at all.

Table 7. Geographic location and Types of Activism Participation

	Human Rights	Environmental Protection	Gender Equality	Women Safety	Social Justice	Political Campaigns	Total
Urban	108	54	43	43	98	47	108
Percentage	56.5%	64.3%	58.1%	64.2%	56.6%	53.4%	
Rural	83	30	31	24	75	41	108
Percentage	43.5%	35.7%	41.9%	35.8%	43.4%	46.6%	

Table 7 illustrates a useful comparison of activism engagement in rural and urban areas. In most types of activism, people in urban areas are more involved; for example, 56.5% of urbanites are activists for human rights, and 64.3% are activists for environmental conservation. On the flip side, engagement is high in rural regions, especially when it comes to political campaigns (46.6% of the population). However, there is a low and consistent dedication to the causes of gender equality and women's safety in both urban and rural areas.

Table 8. Average time spend on SM platforms based on Age Range

	2 h	3 h	4 h	5 h	Over 5 h
18–25	4	2	4	16	28
Percentage	13.8%	7.4%	8.5%	26.7%	52.8%
26–35	5	0	13	16	19
Percentage	20.7%	0%	27.7%	26.7%	35.8%
36–45	11	8	14	15	5
Percentage	37.9%	29.6%	29.8%	25%	11.3%
46 and older	8	17	16	13	0
Percentage	27.6%	63%	34%	21.7%	0%

Table 8 illustrates that over half (52.8%) of 18- to 25-year-olds spend over 5 h on social media every day, decreasing with age. The 26–35 age group also shows substantial engagement, with 35.8% spending over 5 h. 37.9% of 36–45-year-olds spend 2 h and 29.8% spend 4 h, a more even distribution. For those 46 and older, 63% spend 3 h on social media, which decreases as time goes on.

Finally, a descriptive analysis reveals the frequency at which a sample of 216 respondents engage with activism-related information on social media. According to the statistics, respondents tend to actively engage with content connected to activism. On a scale where 1 represents rare or no involvement, 2 indicates occasional engagement, and 3 signifies frequent engagement, the average score was 2.27. This indicates that, on average, respondents tend to sporadically interact with activism-related information on social media. The standard deviation of 0.779 shows a considerable amount of variability around the mean. Overall, these findings demonstrate a significant degree of interest in and involvement in activism on social media platforms.

4.2   The Efficiency and Regularity of UX Elements

Figure 1 displays the efficacy ratings of several SM elements used by regular Bangladeshi SM users, which indicate the level of user involvement. The categories of 'videos or reels' and 'social media banners' are particularly notable, with 50% and 60% of respondents evaluating them as highly effective or effective, respectively, showing their significant impact. On the other hand, respondents varied in their scores for 'caption rating' and 'live stream rating', with a significant number finding them neutral or ineffective. Specifically, 78% of respondents rated captions as neutral or ineffective, while 59% expressed a similar sentiment towards live streaming. 'hashtags' and 'information cards' demonstrate modest success, with 42% and 40% of respondents, respectively, rating them as effective.

Fig. 1. Comparison of user ratings about the efficacy of several SM interaction elements.

This analysis highlights the ever-changing nature of the interaction landscape, where visual content surpasses text-based solutions in terms of perceived impact.

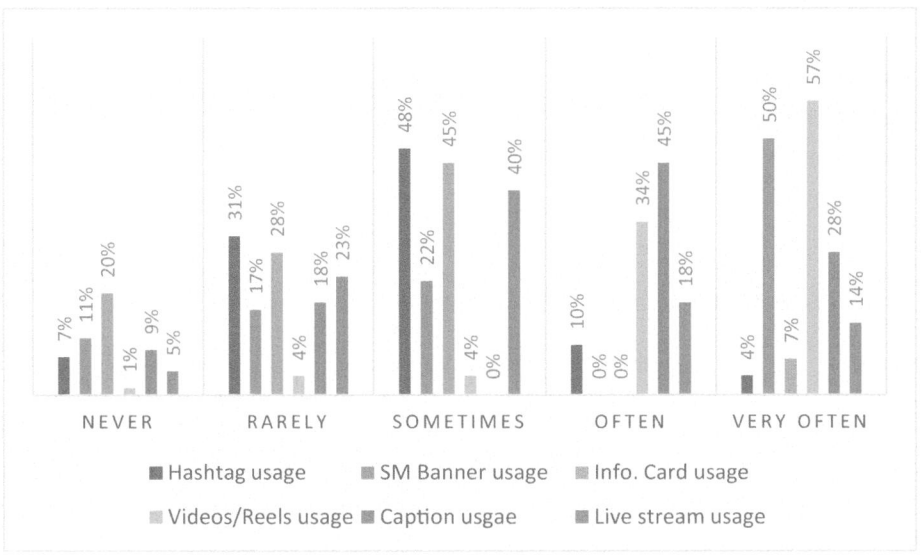

Fig. 2. Frequency of use for various SM elements.

As shown in Fig. 2, videos or reels are the most commonly used element—91% of users use them often or very often. Additionally, 50% of users frequently use social media banners. Hashtags and information cards, on the other hand, exhibit more irregular use; a noteworthy 28% and 31%, respectively, rarely ever use these tools. While live streams exhibit a balanced distribution of use, with no dominant frequency but a tendency toward occasional use, it is noteworthy that 45% often and 28% very often use captions.

Furthermore, we have performed an inferential study, specifically using the Friedman Test, to explore the disparities in user assessments regarding the perceived efficacy of different user experience (UX) elements on social media platforms. The Friedman test serves as a non-parametric substitute for the one-way ANOVA with repeated measures. It is employed to assess disparities across groups when the measured dependent variable is in ordinal form.

Hypotheses for the Friedman Test

- **Null Hypothesis, H_0:** There is no statistically significant difference in the median ratings of the UX components on SM sites.
- **Alternative Hypothesis, H_a:** At least one pair of UX components has different median ratings.

Table 9. Friedman's Two-Way Analysis of Variance by Ranks

UX Element	Mean Rank
Hashtag Rating	3.35
SM Banner Rating	3.95
Info. Card Rating	3.44
Videos/Reels Rating	4.85
Caption Rating	2.41
Live Stream Rating	3.00

Table 10. Friedman's Two-Way Analysis of Variance by Ranks Summary

Total N	Test Statistic	Degree of Freedom	Asymptotic Sig.
216	261.743	5	1.66×10^{-54}

According to the data from Tables 9 and 10, significant differences among the UX elements were found ($\chi2$ (5) = 261.743, p < .001). Descriptive statistics reveal varying mean ratings across the components: Videos and reels had the highest mean rank (4.85), while caption ratings had the lowest mean rank (2.41), indicating a less favorable rating compared to other components. SM Banner Rating (mean rank = 3.95) and Live Stream Rating (mean rank = 3.00) also showed notable differences in ratings. This suggests that users perceive videos and reels more positively than captions, as well as providing strong evidence to reject the null hypothesis in favor of the alternative, indicating a statistically significant disparity in the median ratings of the UX components on SM sites.

When examining the level of agreement about the impact of UX aspects on the effectiveness of activism efforts, we found a significant majority. Specifically, 52% of participants expressed either agreement or strong agreement, indicating a prevailing positive sentiment towards these features. Only a small portion of the participants (16%) stated neutrality, and dissent was infrequent (2%), with no participants vehemently disagreeing. In addition, 82% of users expressed that activist content on social media motivated them to engage in action, while 18% stated a lack of such an incentive.

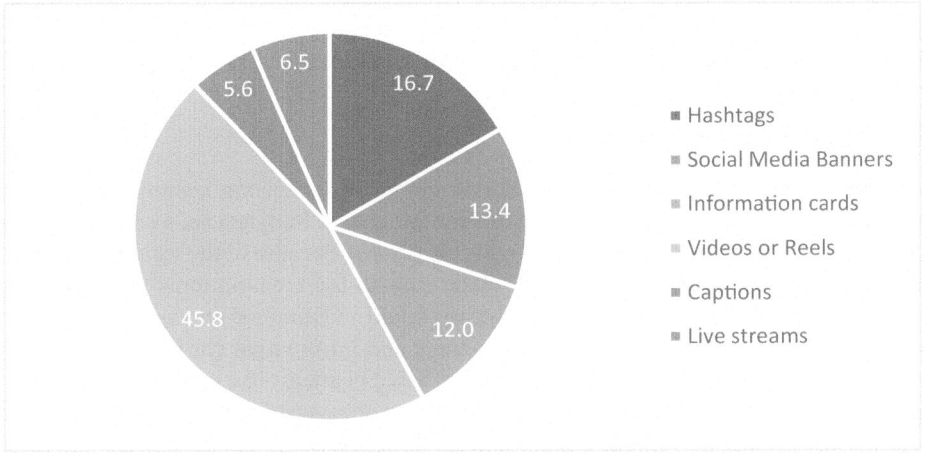

Fig. 3. User preferences for various UX elements on SM.

Finally, Fig. 3 displays a pie chart illustrating user preferences for six UX elements on social media. The figure clearly shows that videos or reels are the most preferred element, accounting for almost half of the total preference share (45.8%). Hashtags account for 16.7% of the significant components, followed by social media banners at 13.4% and information cards at 12.0%. Captions and live broadcasts lag behind, accounting for 5.6% and 6.5%, respectively. These findings highlight once again the varied yet imbalanced nature of user engagement across different UX elements. Videos or reels are clearly the leading factor in driving user interaction and fostering social or political initiatives in Bangladesh.

5   Discussion of the Study

This study serves as an initial phase in quantifying the capacity of various user experience elements on social media platforms to participate in social movements in Bangladesh. The SM tools were initially launched to facilitate communication and played a crucial role in cultivating personal connections and encouraging social engagement. However, the results of this study provide a thorough understanding of how user experience elements on social media platforms influence user engagement and activism among regular social media users in Bangladesh. The SM adoption patterns demonstrate a clear distinction between urban and rural users, with platforms such as LinkedIn and Snapchat being more widespread in urban areas while TikTok prevails in rural settings. It also elucidates that activism, particularly in human rights and social justice, remains actively involved across different demographic groups, with varying levels of involvement in political campaigns and environmental protection. The influence of visual information, namely videos and reels, on captivating users and promoting activity is clearly apparent, with a significant preference observed across all demographic groups. In contrast, textual components like captions and live streaming have a diminished effect, highlighting a transition towards more dynamic and visually-oriented modes of communication. These findings underscore the importance of interactive and visual content in social media strategies that promote activism, emphasizing the necessity for platform-specific approaches to maximize user engagement and impact in diverse demographic contexts.

5.1 Design Implications

The analysis's findings highlight a number of significant design implications for improving UX components on social media platforms targeted at Bangladeshi users. Platforms should give features such as videos and reels top priority because of the significant desire for visual material. They should also include easy-to-use creation tools and a smooth integration into the user feed. Additionally, we should add minimal, engaging, and easily understandable designs to social media banners and information cards to ensure their impactful usage. Different live-streams or text-based elements like captions work better in different situations. Making these parts easier to access, more interesting, and more relevant to the situation might make them more appealing to users, possibly through AI-driven personalization and content adaptation. Given the urban-rural divide in platform adoption, we advise a distinct strategy: urban-centric characteristics could leverage sophisticated features like LinkedIn integration and Snapchat-like ephemeral content, while rural users could benefit from easily accessible, minimal tools that facilitate short-form video content like TikTok. Besides, though focused on Bangladeshi users, the findings from this study can be broadly applied to other developing nations with similar socio-cultural and infrastructural challenges. Prioritizing visual content like videos and reels is crucial, as it appeals to users with varying levels of digital literacy. According to Opp (2023), Lower technology adoption in LDCs (Least Developed Countries) is a result of insufficient levels of digital skills and competences. A poor adoption and usage of digital technology is a result of students in some LDC nations having a higher than average self-assessment of their digital literacy. The Internet is used for commercial purposes by 7% of Africans on average, with a range of 1% in Rwanda to 20% in Senegal. In LDCs, less than 10% of the population purchases online. So, simplified content creation tools can empower users in these areas, where many are new to social media platforms.

5.2 Limitations

However, this study has some limitations. Despite conducting the selection process with great attention to detail, the results from individual regions may not accurately represent the overall perception of social media in Bangladesh. Expanding the sample size to include diverse regions of Bangladesh can enhance the likelihood of extrapolating these findings. Furthermore, there are numerous other models for technology acceptance. For instance, (Venkatesh & Davis, 1996) developed the UTAUT model, which includes more components, providing a more comprehensive explanation of this occurrence.

However, surprisingly Twitter usage in Bangladesh was found to be lower compared to other social media platforms. Several recent studies, including Park (2013), Gleason (2013), and Park & Kaye (2017), have demonstrated that Twitter is the predominant SM channel utilized for protests. In agreement with the recommendations of Akter & Islam (2019), it is essential for future research to prioritize studying the differences in social media usage for protests between rural and urban areas in Bangladesh and beyond. Additionally, it is crucial to continue evaluating the Technology Acceptance Model (TAM).

Another issue arises while dealing with misinformation, disinformation, and polarization in social media data. As we investigate users' perceptions towards different UX elements for fostering social movements on social media, dealing with misinformation and polarization is out of the domain for our study. We will explore this issue in the future. Again, our study only examines the quantitative findings, and qualitative analysis will be performed in future studies.

6 Conclusion

In essence, this study emphasizes the crucial role of UX elements in enhancing the effectiveness of social media-based activist campaigns in Bangladesh, a region now experiencing substantial digital growth. It enriches the academic discourse by improving our understanding of how UX elements affect digital activism and emphasizing the significance of culturally appropriate designs tailored to Bangladesh's socio-cultural dynamics. To better understand the efficacy of digital activism, future research must analyze the long-term effects of UX components and their interactions with other contextual factors. This study not only strengthens the theoretical foundation of UX in social movements but also provides practical knowledge for enhancing the design and execution of successful digital campaigns in developing areas.

References

Ahmed, I.: Social media usage in Bangladesh. Bangladesh's digital footprint in the age of social media saturation. The Daily Star (2024). https://www.thedailystar.net/opinion/views/news/bangladeshs-digital-footprint-the-age-social-media-saturation-3585071

Akter, S., Islam, M.: Perceived value of social media in students' participation in social movement: a developing country perspective. Digit. Libr. Perspect. **35**(3/4), 244–258 (2019). https://doi.org/10.1108/DLP-06-2019-0023

Amnesty International. https://www.amnesty.org/en/latest/news/2024/07/what-is-happening-at-the-quota-reform-protests-in-bangladesh/. Accessed 06 Aug 2024

bdnews24.com. https://bdnews24.com/sport/de9c98bcffad. Accessed 06 Aug 2024

Bekkers, V., Beunders, H., Edwards, A., Moody, R.: New media, micromobilization, and political agenda setting: crossover effects in political mobilization and media usage. Inf. Soc. **27**(4), 209–219 (2011). https://doi.org/10.1080/01972243.2011.583812

Britannica: The editors of encyclopaedia. "social media". Encyclopedia Britannica (2024). https://www.britannica.com/topic/social-media. Accessed 08 Jun 2024

Carney, N.: All lives matter, but so does race: black lives matter and the evolving role of social media. Humanit. Soc. **40**(2), 180–199 (2016). https://doi.org/10.1177/0160597616643868

Castillo-Esparcia, A., Caro-Castaño, L., Almansa-Martínez, A.: Evolution of digital activism on social media: opportunities and challenges. Profesional de La Información **32**(3), 3 (2023). https://doi.org/10.3145/epi.2023.may.03

Clark, R.: "Hope in a hashtag": the discursive activism of #WhyIStayed. Fem. Media Stud. **16**(5), 788–804 (2016). https://doi.org/10.1080/14680777.2016.1138235

Earl, J., Kimport, K.: Digital Enabled Social Change: Activism in the Internet Age. Contemporary Sociology-a Journal of Reviews—CONTEMP SOCIOL vol. 41 (2011). https://doi.org/10.7551/mitpress/9780262015103.001.0001

Faul, F., Erdfelder, E., Buchner, A., Lang, A.-G.: Statistical power analyses using G*Power 3.1: tests for correlation and regression analyses. Behav. Res. Methods, **41**(4), 1149–1160 (2009). https://doi.org/10.3758/BRM.41.4.1149

Gleason, B.: #Occupy wall street: exploring informal learning about a social movement on twitter. Am. Behav. Sci. **57**(7), 966–982 (2013). https://doi.org/10.1177/0002764213479372

González-Bailón, S., Borge-Holthoefer, J., Rivero, A., Moreno, Y.: The dynamics of protest recruitment through an online network. Sci. Rep. **1**(1), 197 (2011). https://doi.org/10.1038/srep00197

Hassan, N., Mandal, M.K., Bhuiyan, M., Moitra, A., Ahmed, S.I.: Nonparticipation of Bangladeshi women in #MeToo movement. In: Proceedings of the Tenth International Conference on Information and Communication Technologies and Development, pp. 1–5 (2019).https://doi.org/10.1145/3287098.3287125

Hayes, A.: What is banner advertising? Definition and how it works. Investopedia (2022). https://www.investopedia.com/terms/b/banneradvertising.asp

Hwang, H., Kim, K.-O.: Social media as a tool for social movements: the effect of social media use and social capital on intention to participate in social movements. Int. J. Consum. Stud. **39**(5), 478–488 (2015). https://doi.org/10.1111/ijcs.12221

Ince, J., Rojas, F., Davis, C.A.: The social media response to black lives matter: how twitter users interact with black lives matter through hashtag use. Ethn. Racial Stud. **40**(11), 1814–1830 (2017). https://doi.org/10.1080/01419870.2017.1334931

Kemp, S.: Digital 2023: Bangladesh. DataReportal – Global Digital Insights (2023). https://datareportal.com/reports/digital-2023-bangladesh

Kemp, S.: Digital 2024: Bangladesh. DataReportal – Global Digital Insights (2024). https://datareportal.com/reports/digital-2024-bangladesh

Khamis, S., Vaughn, K.: We are all khaled said: the potentials and limitations of cyberactivism in triggering public mobilization and promoting political change. J. Arab Muslim Media Res. **4**, 145–163 (2012). https://doi.org/10.1386/jammr.4.2-3.145_1

Khan, M.: How the quota reform movement was shaped by social media. The Daily Star (2018). https://www.thedailystar.net/star-weekend/opinion/how-the-quota-reform-movement-was-shaped-social-media-1568212

Marandici, I.: Collective action, memories of 1989, and social media: novel insights from Moldova's twitter revolution. Communis. Post-Commun. **56**(1), 82–104 (2022). https://doi.org/10.1525/cpcs.2022.1716515

O'Brien, C.: How to use hashtags effectively on social media. Digital Marketing Institute (2023). https://digitalmarketinginstitute.com/blog/how-to-use-hashtags-in-social-media

Opp, R.: Committing to bridging the digital divide in least developed countries. UNDP (2023). https://www.undp.org/blog/committing-bridging-digital-divide-least-developed-countries

Park, C.S.: Does Twitter motivate involvement in politics? Tweeting, opinion leadership, and political engagement. Comput. Hum. Behav. **29**(4), 1641–1648 (2013). https://doi.org/10.1016/j.chb.2013.01.044

Park, C.S., Kaye, B.K.: The tweet goes on: interconnection of Twitter opinion leadership, network size, and civic engagement. Comput. Hum. Behav. **69**, 174–180 (2017). https://doi.org/10.1016/j.chb.2016.12.021

Pearce, K.E., Kendzior, S.: Networked authoritarianism and social media in Azerbaijan. J. Commun. **62**(2), 283–298 (2012). https://doi.org/10.1111/j.1460-2466.2012.01633.x

Rahman, S.: How social media breeds social movements. The Daily Star (2018). https://www.thedailystar.net/news/opinion/perspective/how-social-media-breeds-social-movements-1618270

Rahman, W.N.A., Mutum, D.S., Ghazali, E.M.: Consumer engagement with visual content on Instagram: impact of different features of posts by prominent brands (2022). https://services.igi-global.com/resolvedoi/resolve.aspx?doi=10.4018/ijesma.295960, https://www.igi-global.com/article/consumer-engagement-visual-content-instagram/295960

Roy, A.D.: Shahbag stolen? third force dynamics and electoral politics in Bangladesh. South Asia Res. **38**(3_suppl), 1S-24S (2018). https://doi.org/10.1177/0262728018791698

Seongyi, Y., Woo-Young, C.: Political participation of teenagers in the information era. Soc. Sci. Comput. Rev. **29**(2), 242–249 (2011). https://doi.org/10.1177/0894439310363255

Sinha, A.: Millions of people on the streets of Bangladesh #Shahbag movement. Youth Ki Awaaz (2013). https://www.youthkiawaaz.com/2013/03/millions-of-people-on-the-streets-of-bangladesh-shahbag-movement/

Smelser, N.J., Turner, R.H., Killian, L.M.: Social movement. Encyclopedia Britannica (2024). https://www.britannica.com/topic/social-movement

Swiderska, O.: Video in multimedia—Best practices. Publuu (2024). https://publuu.com/knowledge-base/video-in-multimedia/

Tudoroiu, T.: Social media and revolutionary waves: the case of the arab spring. New Polit. Sci. (2024). https://www.tandfonline.com/doi/abs/10.1080/07393148.2014.913841

Valenzuela, S., Arriagada, A., Scherman, A.: The social media basis of youth protest behavior: the case of Chile. J. Commun. **62**(2), 299–314 (2012). https://doi.org/10.1111/j.1460-2466.2012.01635.x

Venkatesh, V., Davis, F.D.: A model of the antecedents of perceived ease of use: development and test. Decis. Sci. **27**(3), 451–481 (1996). https://doi.org/10.1111/j.1540-5915.1996.tb00860.x

Wells, T., Deejay, A.: How activists are using Facebook in Myanmar for democratic ends, but Facebook itself also facilitated hate speech. Melbourne Asia Review, Edition 7, 2021 (2021). https://doi.org/10.37839/MAR2652-550X7.1

Wilkins, D.J., Livingstone, A.G., Levine, M.: Whose tweets? The rhetorical functions of social media use in developing the black lives matter movement. Br. J. Soc. Psychol. **58**(4), 786–805 (2019). https://doi.org/10.1111/bjso.12318

Yang, G.: Narrative agency in hashtag activism: the case of #BlackLivesMatter, commentary. Media Commun. (2016). https://doi.org/10.17645/mac.v4i4.692

Yip, C., Han, N.-L.R., Sng, B.L.: Legal and ethical issues in research. Indian J. Anaesth. **60**(9), 684 (2016). https://doi.org/10.4103/0019-5049.190627

Zaman, F.: Agencies of social movements: experiences of Bangladesh's shahbag movement and hefazat-e-Islam. J. Asian Afr. Stud. **53**(3), 339–349 (2018). https://doi.org/10.1177/0021909616666870

Zamir, M.H.: Diffusion of protest information in twitter during shahbag movement of bangladesh. Proc. Am. Soc. Inf. Sci. Technol. **51**(1), 1–4 (2014)

Žukauskas, P., Vveinhardt, J., Andriukaitienė, R., Žukauskas, P., Vveinhardt, J., Andriukaitienė, R.: Research ethics. In: Management Culture and Corporate Social Responsibility. IntechOpen (2018). https://doi.org/10.5772/intechopen.70629

Key Dimensions for Human-Robot Interaction in XR for Rescue Robots

V. S. Rajashekhar$^{(\boxtimes)}$ ⓘ

Department of Design, Indian Institute of Technology, Kanpur, Uttar Pradesh, India
raja23@iitk.ac.in

Abstract. The post-earthquake search operation requires faster response by the rescue team since several lives need to be saved quickly. Designing the Human-Robot Interaction (HRI) for Extended Reality (XR) requires knowledge of virtual and remote environments. While interacting with the virtual and remote environments, the user's perspective needs to be addressed based on the scenario. This work focuses on selecting the six key dimensions for XR-based remote HRI. Then, we arrive at the conditions in the local environment and map the key dimensions for each of them. This will help the rescue team face post-earthquake search operations with the available XR technologies.

Keywords: Human Robot Interaction · Extended Reality · Rigid bodied robots · Soft robots

1 Introduction

1.1 Human-Robot Interaction

The Human-Robot Interaction (HRI) for rescue robots is essential since they must encounter unpredictable and harsh conditions that require humans to act. A review on the advances and challenges in HRI has been presented in the works of *Obaigbena et al.* [25] in the year 2024. A review of the status and challenges of HRI prior to 2016 can be referred to in the works of *Sheridan et al.* [1]. It reports that the rapid evolution of robots and computers requires continuous research and up-gradation in HRI. Also, an HRI survey before 2008 can be referred to in the works of *Goodrich et al.* [3]. In the works of *Murphy et al.* [2], the field studies with fire rescue teams in Tampa, Florida, and the World Trade Center were done, where the response provided insights about the challenges faced in HRI, such as operator errors and the need for improved interfaces. In the works of [4], the HRI research done before the year 2004 is presented. The work discusses the need for physical interaction in achieving coordination, particularly by citing examples like the *MS DanceR*, a dance partner robot designed for ballroom dancing. It also emphasizes the need for robots to interpret human intentions and background information to improve their collaborative nature. Before this, in 1992, a book on HRI was published [8], which deals with the importance of human factors in

N. Rangaswamy et al. (Eds.): IndiaHCI 2024, CCIS 2338, pp. 172–186, 2025.
https://doi.org/10.1007/978-3-031-80832-6_13

robotics, including safety and usability. It also discusses various programming modes designed for different user expertise levels. Prior to this, there were a few works on HRI in the 1980s which can be referred to in the following articles [5–7].

1.2 Natural Disasters where HRI in Extended Reality is Needed

This work focuses on building HRI design in extended reality (XR) for post-disaster rescue robots. There are several natural disasters that can be categorized as geophysical, hydrological, meteorological, climatological, biological, and extraterrestrial [9]. The disaster focused on in this work is an earthquake, which is a geophysical disaster. More specifically, this work deals with the post-earthquake search operations. It is to be noted from the works of *Tadokoro et al.* [10] that a number of survivors were rescued even five days after the Hanshin-Awaji earthquake. The authors of the paper believe that robots can aid in search operations. It can travel through the debris and search for survivors, which is difficult for humans to perform. When robots are being used, an effective HRI is required, which is planned using XR in this work.

1.3 Robots in Search and Rescue Operations

The robots used in search and rescue (SAR) operations are briefly explained in the works of *Chitikena et al.* [11]. Unmanned aerial vehicles can give a bird's-eye view of the environment and create a map of the region. The rescue team can transport relief materials using unmanned surface vehicles over the water bodies. The unmanned guided vehicles are used to explore the damaged buildings and search for survivors. The unmanned amphibious vehicles can be used for missions involving land and water bodies. The robots were used in the past to explore several collapsed buildings due to earthquakes and other reasons. The HRI for robot-assisted SAR operations post the unfortunate World Trade Center attack in the year 2001 has been reported in the works of *Casper et al.* [12]. It highlights the importance of logistics, user experience, and cognitive fatigue in rescue operations. The work also describes the importance of perceptual user interfaces by utilizing visual and audio channels effectively. Then, in the works of *Nagatani et al.* [13], the robots used in the nuclear accident at the Fukushima Daiichi nuclear power plants after the earthquake in March 2011 have been reported. The tracked mobile robots named *Quince* were used since they had multi-terrain climbing capability. In Italy, in August 2016, after the earthquake, semi-humanoids mounted on wheeled robots were used for search operations inside damaged buildings [14]. In 2017, after the earthquake in Mexico, the rescue team used snake robots to search for survivors inside the debris [15]. The camera was fitted to the head of the robotic snake and the live feed was given to the screen at the operator end. Since sunshine was falling on the screen, an artificial shadow had to be created to view the live feed on the screen. Multi-modal interaction with the robot can overcome this kind of situation. Therefore, we perform planning for the HRI design using XR for rescue robots in this work.

1.4 Role of Extended Reality in Enhancing Human-Robot Interaction

The use of extended reality (XR) for applications such as robotics and entertainment has recently increased. A systematic literature review of the field (XR) applied to digital twins and robotics has been presented in the works of *Feddoul et al.* [16]. The taxonomy for virtual, augmented, and mixed reality has been done and reported in the works of *Walker et al.* [17]. The human-in-loop approach for XR-enhanced human-robot collaboration has been presented in the works of *Karpichev et al.* [18]. The mobile robots can be tele-operated using the XR technology as shown in the works of *Batistute et al.* [19]. In works of *Wang et al.* [20], the systematic review of the XR-based HRI, have been presented.

1.5 Gaps in the Literature

Although there are works that present the robots being used in the search and rescue operations, the usage of XR as a medium for tele-operation and virtual control is yet to be implemented. There are various factors that are involved in the process of using XR for rescue robots. The role played by them during the time of crisis and their selection at critical times is crucial. Also the merits and demerits of using soft and rigid bodied robots during the search operation needs to be understood. In this work, the key dimensions for the proposed method is discussed in detail. The main contribution of this paper is the Sankey diagram (Fig. 3) which aids the search team to decide on the XR implementation process post the earthquake. The key dimensions of the XR-based remote HRI have been presented in this work, and a Sankey diagram has been drawn considering the search operations during the post-earthquake conditions.

1.6 Structure of the Paper

The rest of the paper is organized as follows. Section 2 discusses the problems the robots face during the search operations. Section 3 describes the robots considered for the search operations. The selection of key dimensions for XR-based remote HRI is explained in Sect. 4. The mapping of key dimensions as a Sankey diagram is presented in Sect. 5. Finally, the discussion is done in Sect. 6, and the concluding remarks are presented in Sect. 7.

2 Problems Faced During Search Operations in the Past

The search and rescue team face several problems due to the uncertainties in the terrain created by the debris after the earthquake. A few of them are discussed here, which would be helpful while mapping the key dimensions in Sect. 4.

2.1 Nature and Size of the Robot

In the works of *Tadokoro et al.* [10], it is mentioned that compressed crushes (debris) are of size 0–30 cm. Then, the sparse crushes are of size 30–100 cm, and damaged structures are of size above it. A combination of this crush is found when a building collapses. In recent years, the approximate appearance of a building after it collapses can be predicted. A real and simulated image of a building after collapse can be seen in the works of *Grunwald et al.* [21]. It is not possible for a single robot to pass through all types of debris voids since their performance will be affected. A smaller robot (fits inside a volume of $30\,\mathrm{cm}^3$) would move slower and cover a lesser distance, but on the other hand, a bigger robot (fits inside a volume of $100\,\mathrm{cm}^3$) would not be able to enter and explore smaller voids. In the unfortunate World Trade Center building collapse after the attack, three kinds of robots were used for search operations [12] to overcome this situation. They are micro-robots (*MicroTracs and MicroVGTV*), mini robots (*Foster-Miller Solem*), and man-portable robots (*Foster-Miller Talon, Inuktun Pipe Crawler, Inuktun Mini-Disruptor, iRobot ATRV, and SPAWAR Urbot*). In the search operation post the Italy earthquake [14], semi-humanoid mounted on a four-wheeled mobile robot with a size of *$134\,cm \times 80.8\,cm \times 103.7\,cm$* was used since it had to enter into the partially damaged house and the void was huge enough to accommodate the robot. In the post-Mexico earthquake search operation, a sleek snake robot, as shown in the article by *Whitman et al.* [15] was used for the search operation. This had the ability to enter the voids and produce a video feed to the operator. Thus, the nature and size of the robot play an important role since the situation is highly uncertain. Also, using multiple robots of different sizes and capabilities will aid in a better search operation.

2.2 Connectivity with the Robot

In the search operations, the communication of the robot with the operators is very important. If it is partially lost or completely lost, then there is no use for the robot, even if it functions effectively. The wired communication is better when reliability and stability are important during communication. The wireless communication provides greater flexibility and mobility, which enable operators to control robots from a distance without being tethered. During the urban SAR response at the World Trade Center [12], both wired and wireless communication methods were utilized for operating the robots. This was because, during the deployment of the *Solem* robot, there were multiple instances of communication loss, which lasted for significant periods. In the Fukushima Daiichi nuclear power plant incident [13] interestingly, the highly radioactive environment of the reactor building led to the usage of a combination of wired and wireless communication between the robots and the operator. During the search operations after the Italy earthquake, the robot was controlled wirelessly inside the house that was damaged. It can be referred to in the works of *Negrello et al.* [14]. On the other hand, during the post-Mexico earthquake search operation, the snake robot that was used had a wired communication. It can be referred to in the works of

Whitman et al. [15]. Thus, based on the situation and condition, the robot was established to perform the search activity using wired or wireless connectivity.

2.3   Interaction with the Robot

The human-robot interaction during the World Trade Center (as presented in the works of [12]) response involved a combination of control interfaces (joystick and buttons), video feedback (screen), and audio communication (two-way audio system). The robots used in the Fukushima Daiichi nuclear power plant incident [13] had visual feedback during teleoperation. In the post-Italy earthquake search operation (as presented in [14]), the teleoperator wore an Oculus Rift headset, which provided visual feedback from the ZED camera of the robot. The system computed the orientation of the head of the teleoperator using an inertial sensor, while the wrist pose and hand closure level were sent to the control module. This information was sent to the control inputs for the joints in the robot, which enables the operator to manipulate the upper body of the robot effectively. The snake robot that was teleoperated during the Mexico (as presented in [15]) earthquake used two joysticks and twelve buttons for input and a display screen as an output device. It can be observed that in different situations, different modes of interaction were used to communicate the intent with the robot. Thus, it can be concluded that different robots need different methods of interaction and development times. Hence, HRI can be designed in XR for these robots to save the development cost involved.

3   Robots Used for the Study

Several robots were developed for search operations after disasters. From the materials standpoint, they can be classified as rigid-bodied and soft-bodied robots. In the works of [23], a method for simulating rigid and soft-bodied robots is presented. For initial testing purposes, we develop a rigid-bodied and soft-bodied snake robot. It can be seen in Fig. 1.

3.1   Rigid Bodied Robots

These are robots that are made of rigid bodies or linkages. This field is mature and well-established in both modeling and experimental analysis. It was used in the search operation during the disasters as mentioned in [12–15]. This robot can survive harsh and unstable environments that occur in post-disaster situations. They have more precise control over their movements, which is required to traverse narrow gaps. The payload capacity of these robots is also high; hence, more equipment, such as sensors, can be attached to them. They can apply force that helps move significantly heavy debris when encountered in the path. These robots are durable and can withstand wear and tear. The speed of these robots is fast, which aids in faster search operations. The robots used in [12,13] had tracks that helped traverse high obstacles.

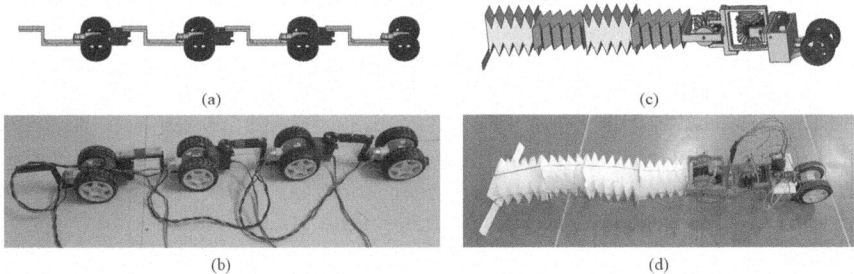

Fig. 1. The two robots to be used in the study. The rigid-bodied snake robot (a) CAD model (b) The physical prototype. The soft-bodied snake robot (c) CAD model (d) The physical prototype

On the other hand, these robots have certain limitations. They have limited flexibility, meaning there are limited degrees of freedom. This severe drawback makes the robot unsuitable for functioning in unknown complex terrains. The weight of these robots is high and hence can not be used for search operations in some instances [12]. The power consumption of these robots is high, which makes them survive for a limited duration. They either need to be recharged, or the batteries need to be replaced. They also have the possibility of being stuck in debris in specific scenarios. When they interact with survivors, they may harm them due to their rigid nature. Also, since disasters happen rarely, these robots must be maintained, which is costly. Therefore, these conditions must be considered before a rigid robot can be selected for post-earthquake search operations.

In this work, we use a rigid-bodied snake robot, which is shown in Fig. 1 (a,b) for motion in flat surfaces (planar snake robot) and crossing trenches. This robot can be used to search and inspect partially collapsed buildings. We chose the snake robot for our study because it has a distributed load (minimal ground pressure), is sleek, negotiates sharp turns, and can perform tasks without disturbing the debris. It can function even if one of the actuators fails to actuate. Although this version could be better, the future version can climb stairs, pipes, and slopes on the path.

3.2   Soft Bodied Robots

The works of [22] describe a small-scale soft robot capable of walking, crawling, and jumping. When mounted with sensors, lots of this size can be used to explore small voids. However, the field is yet to develop for them to be used in such scenarios. The soft robots can adapt to tight spaces due to their soft nature. They are less prone to damage by collision or impacts by small debris. They are ideal for delicate tasks, making them gently handle fragile objects. Also, it does not cause harm to survivors when it interacts with them. Then, it can traverse uneven surfaces with ease. Integrating sensors with the robot is easily possible due to its soft and flexible nature. The cost of manufacturing these robots is lower, and they can be easily manufactured. The collaboration of the robot with rigid and other soft robots is possible.

On the other hand, this robot can carry a limited payload, which is a considerable drawback. It also lacks strength, which is crucial for lifting heavy payloads. Due to its soft nature, it is prone to wear and tear. The precise control and manipulation of soft robots are more challenging than rigid robots. Some soft robots operate on pneumatics or hydraulics, which makes the setup huge. These robots are slow and can not be used for rapid search operations. The exposure to extreme temperatures, chemicals, and harsh environments damages the soft robot. The use of soft material makes maintenance and repair work more challenging than that of rigid robot counterparts.

In this work, we use a soft snake-like robot, presented in Fig. 1 (c,d). The functioning of the robot is presented in [26], where it can be used as a soft manipulator and soft snake robot. The rescuer can use the manipulator (with the camera as an end effector)rescuer to insert inside the debris to find survivors and bigger voids. If bigger voids are found, then the snake robot form of the robot will be sent inside for the search operation. Thus, this robot serves a dual purpose for the rescue team.

4   Key Dimensions for XR-Based Remote HRI

It is essential to select the key dimensions required for XR-based remote HRI to make the interaction possible. This is done based on the work in [20]. The position of the user, virtual environment, and the remote environment are shown in Fig. 2. The XR technologies are present in the enhancement location and interact using several modes of data representation. The XR devices are operated using interaction modalities. The user views the virtual environment using the XR devices. The way how the user sees the virtual world is known as the user perspective. The robots are present in remote locations and perform the tasks that the user instruct to do. We can now see each key dimension and its types.

4.1   XR Technologies

The usage of virtual reality (VR), augmented reality (AR) and mixed reality (MR) for disaster management are presented in [24]. VR technology provides users with a three-dimensional, graphical environment by enabling interaction through headsets and motion controllers. The AR is a technology that overlays digital information in the real world in real time. It also uses headsets to project the information. The MR is a technology that combines real and virtual worlds, allowing physical and digital objects to exist in the same place and interact in real time with a fixed frame of reference. Cave automatic virtual environment is a technology with an enclosure with display devices, and the environment is projected on it. The user views inside the cave as if it were a reality. Mobile AR

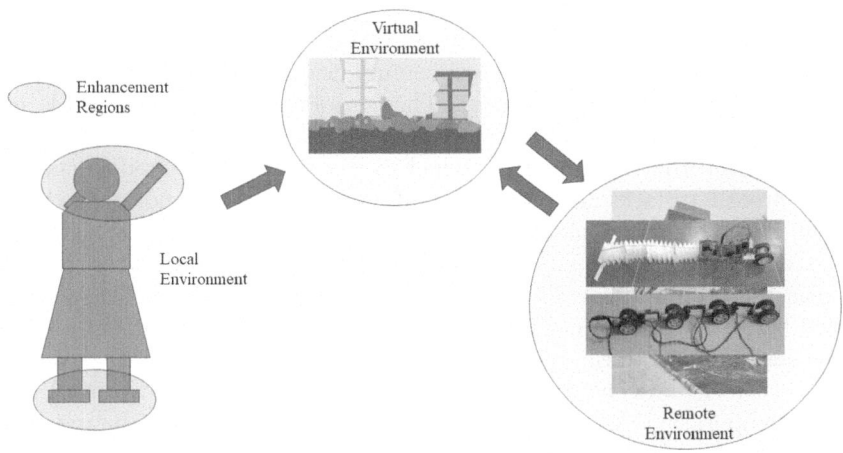

Fig. 2. The user is in the local environment with the XR technologies. They interact with the virtual environment and, in turn, with the remote environment

is a technology where a phone is used as a display screen to project augmented objects over the physical world captured by the camera. The XR is an umbrella term that covers VR, AR, MR, Cave, and mobile AR and uses multi-modal interaction with the environment. These technologies can be used to understand damaged buildings better during post-earthquake search operations.

4.2   Interaction Modalities

The environments viewed using the XR technologies must be interacted with for better decision-making. There are several input devices, and they are listed in [20]. The hand-held controllers are commonly used to interact with the VR devices. Then, using gestures from human fingers is identified when interacting with the XR devices. The hand-held joystick can be used to operate the movement of the robot. The haptic devices get force feedback from the given virtual environment. The motion capture system is used to interact with the whole human body. 2D screens such as mobile devices, tablets, and projector screens display the virtual world. The gloves fitted with sensors can interact with the virtual world. The movement of the head of the human can be used to interact with the virtual world by looking at different perspectives. The eye trackers are used to track the eyes and can be used as an input interface. Due to situational impairments that might arise in the physical environment (disaster area), the XR technology must be able to operate using an alternate interaction modality along with what it is designed to work with.

4.3   Virtual Interface

Several virtual interfaces are mentioned in [20]. A digital twin is a common virtual interface. Here, there is real-time communication between the remote robot, the virtual robot, and the operator. The sensors play an essential role in this type of interface. The user gets real-time feedback from the robot and operates the virtual robot accordingly, which is parallelly transferred to the remote robot. Direct interfaces are used where 3D reconstruction is not needed and are cost-effective. The combination of a digital twin and a 3D reconstruction interface is done in a remote environment so that the user can better understand the disaster environment. Similarly, the direct and 3D reconstruction interface is used better to understand the natural environment in the virtual world. The 3D reconstruction interface is done to overlay the virtual world on the physical world. A virtual control room can also be created using the control buttons and other operating devices. This would save the cost of constructing multiple prototypes before building the final model. The context-aware AR interface conveys information or step-by-step instructions to users as they wear the device and look at the physical world. Thus, this kind of virtual interface can be used during the post-earthquake search operations to understand the situation and perform the search operation.

4.4   User's Perspective

After establishing the virtual interface, the remote condition from the user perspective needs to be studied [20]. The decoupling with the robot is a perspective where the user moves the input device in the hand, which in turn moves the robot in the real world. The vision is attached to the robot from the perspective of being coupled with the robot. The user sees the objects seen by the robot in real time. From a dynamic perspective, different users view the virtual world differently. The bird-eye view shows the aerial view of the location in the real world. Thus, these perspectives are essential from the rescuer's standpoint since each gives different views of information about the same location in the disaster region.

4.5   Robots and Task Classification

The robots used for the search operation and their tasks are explained. Using robots for search operations can make the process faster [11].

Robot Used for Search Operation. About seven robots are listed in [20] on a generic basis. Of these, four can be used for the search operations. The mobile ground robots can search for survivors inside the collapsed buildings. A robotic arm attached to it can also be used for the same purpose as in [14]. The double-arm robots can be used along with mobile robots. Aerial vehicles such as drones can be used to get a bird-eye view of the environment. Thus, these four types of robots can be effectively combined with the search operation after the disaster.

Task Classification for the Robots. Several tasks must be done for an effective search operation. The navigation must be planned so the robots can plan how to traverse the environment. Scanning the environment is necessary for identifying voids in the damaged buildings and possible survivors trapped inside collapsed buildings. The search task is done using several search algorithms in the literature. The grabbing, picking, and placing of small debris or objects in the path is very important for the robot to pass through the environment. Thus, these four tasks are helpful for the robots that are involved in the rescue operations.

4.6   Enhancement Locations and Types

The enhancement locations and their types help the rescuer to interact with the virtual world. The enhancement locations refer to the local space where the control and perception of the robot happen. The enhancement types refer to the mode of communication with the rescuer.

Enhancement Locations: The enhancement location provides and exchanges information about the virtual and real environment to the rescuer. The virtual object is given as a feed to the user for better visualization of the environment. The real robot is operated under user supervision using the input modalities. The user has a view of the real environment. The user communicates with another user for better operation through dynamic perception. While using digital twins, virtual robots are projected to the user. The virtual environment is projected to the user for a better understanding of the condition of the damaged site. Thus, users use these enhancement locations to learn about the environment.

Enhancement Types: The primary purpose of the enhancement type is to communicate the intent to the rescuer. It can be a voice, where the user's speech can be processed and sent as a signal to the robot. A video feed can also be used and process computer vision algorithms. The robot can display text to the user as an output medium. The user can use a ray-emitting device to mark the boundaries for the robot to move. In the virtual world, objects can be highlighted for better understanding. The field of haptics can be used for input and output feedback from and to the robot. The real objects can be enhanced and represented graphically in the virtual world. Instead of showing a human and considering privacy issues, the avatar can communicate with human like images. There can be 3D objects that can be used as input devices for the robot. Thus, a feasible enhancement type can be chosen based on the situation where the robot is used and where the rescuer is present.

5   Mapping the Key Dimensions

The key dimensions for the XR-based remote HRI were chosen and discussed in Sect. 4. In this section, we present a Sankey diagram that represents the flow

of information from one stage to another. It is shown in Fig. 3. The blue blocks
show the elements of XR technologies. The red and the yellow blocks show the
elements of interaction modalities and robot types, respectively. The magenta
blocks show the elements of task classification for the robots. The orange and
green blocks show the elements of the user perspective and virtual interface.
The violet and black blocks show the elements of the enhancement locations
and types.

Among the XR technologies, except mobile AR, the rest of the technologies have better interfacing with the interaction modalities. Mobile robots and
mobile robots with robotic arms have a better interface with most of the interaction modalities when compared to double-armed robots and drones. Navigation,
environmental scanning, and searching are possible using all four robots considered for the rescue operations. All the robots except the mobile robot do the
grabbing, picking, and placing. The four user perspective elements are utilized
in all the tasks performed by the robot. All the virtual interface elements except
the context-aware AR can be interfaced with the user perspective. These virtual
interface elements are connected to the enhancement locations and their types,
as shown in Fig. 3. This is the relationship between the key elements related to
XR-based remote HRI.

Thus, by using this Sankey diagram, one can make decisions before the rescue
operations. At times of situational impairments, one can cut down the elements
in the Sankey diagram. A flow diagram can be created with the rest of the
available elements. It can consider the rescuer's experience and the available
resources in hand. The Sankey diagram drawn here was done by writing a Python
program. It can also be modified if a new interaction modality or a new type of
robot is introduced.

6   Discussion

The selection of key dimensions for HRI in XR for rescue robots has been done
in this work. This is done based on the parameters in the works of *Wang et al.*
[20]. The mapping of the key dimensions, which was done in Sect. 5, has to be
made after the following assumptions: The robot's size and nature (rigid or soft)
and connectivity with the robot. These parameters are not directly a part of
XR technology and are not included in the Sankey diagram. The snake robots
presented in Sect. 3 will be a part of the search operation.

If a trapped survivor needs to be shown to the rescuer, the following path can
be chosen. It is shown in Fig. 4. Since the physical condition of the survivor is not
known, the image captured by the camera can be converted to an avatar. This can
be transferred to the virtual environment. Then, a direct and 3D reconstruction
of the avatar and the environment can be done. The view can be coupled with
the mobile robot that performs the search. A joystick can control the robot in
the virtual world using a virtual reality head-mounted display. Thus, the key
dimensions from the Sankey diagram were selected for the XR-based remote
HRI.

Fig. 3. Sankey diagram: The visualization of the flow of relationship between key dimensions for the XR-based remote HRI (Color figure online)

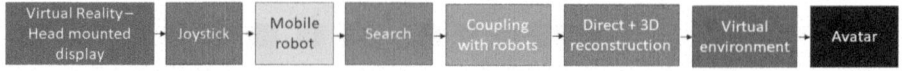

Fig. 4. An example where the avatar is viewed using the virtual reality head-mounted display

6.1   Applications and Advantages

The use of HRI design for XR in the virtual world has the advantage of simulating different types of buildings with various debris properties. It can also be used to train rescuers, which does not require the physical setup. Since the virtual environment is used, many types of robots can be simulated. By doing so, the cost of developing robots will be reduced drastically. Using artificial intelligence (AI), the size of the voids in the debris can be determined, and the best robot to traverse through can be determined. The AI can also be used to find parameters and factors that identify the optimal set of sensors in the scene. Also, many people can view the scene from different viewpoints, which is known as a dynamic perspective. The search team can send the robotic hardware to the site. They can operate the robot from a remote location, which means that their physical presence is not required in the site.

7   Conclusion

This work presents a Sankey diagram representing the relationship between the key dimensions of XR-based remote HRI. The problems faced during the search operations were discussed. Two snake robots were presented and planned to be used for the search operations. The six key dimensions for XR-based remote HRI were presented in detail. The mapping of these dimensions was done and represented using the Sankey diagram. This was followed by discussing an example. Thus, this work presented a method to map the dimensions for XR-based remote HRI, mainly focusing on post-earthquake search operations.

References

1. Sheridan, T.B.: Human-robot interaction: status and challenges. Hum. Factors **58**(4), 525–532 (2016)
2. Murphy, R.R.: Human-robot interaction in rescue robotics. IEEE Trans. Syst. Man Cybern. Part C Appl. Rev. **34**(2), 138–153 (2004)
3. Goodrich, M.A., Schultz, A.C.: Human-robot interaction: a survey. Found. Trends Human-Comput. Interact. **1**(3), 203–275 (2008)
4. Kosuge, K., Hirata, Y.: Human-robot interaction. In: 2004 IEEE International Conference on Robotics and Biomimetics, pp. 8–11. IEEE, Shenyang, China (2004)
5. Ghosh, B.K., Helander, M.G.: A systems approach to task allocation of human-robot interaction in manufacturing. J. Manuf. Syst. **5**(1), 41–49 (1986)

6. Kazerooni, H.: Stability and performance of human-robot interaction. In: Proceedings of IEEE International Conference on Systems, Man and Cybernetics, pp. 494–497. IEEE, Cambridge, MA, USA (1989)
7. Harless, M., Donath, M.: Intelligent safety system for unstructured human/robot interaction. In: Robotics Int of SME, pp. 19–9 (1985)
8. Rahimi, M., Karwowski, W. (eds.): Human-Robot Interaction. Taylor and Francis Inc, London (1992)
9. Chaudhary, M.T., Piracha, A.: Natural disasters-origins, impacts, management. Encyclopedia **1**(4), 1101–1131 (2021)
10. Tadokoro, S. (ed.): Rescue robotics: DDT project on robots and systems for urban search and rescue. Springer (2009)
11. Chitikena, H., Sanfilippo, F., Ma, S.: Robotics in search and rescue (SAR) operations: An ethical and design perspective framework for response phase. Appl. Sci. **13**(3), 1800 (2023)
12. Casper, J., Murphy, R.R.: Human-robot interactions during the robot-assisted urban search and rescue response at the world trade center. IEEE Trans. Syst. Man Cybern. B Cybern. **33**(3), 367–385 (2003)
13. Nagatani, K., et al.: Emergency response to the nuclear accident at the Fukushima Daiichi Nuclear Power Plants using mobile rescue robots. J. Field Robotics **30**(1), 44–63 (2013)
14. Negrello, F., et al.: Humanoids at work: the walk-man robot in a post-earthquake scenario. IEEE Robot. Autom. Mag. **25**(3), 8–22 (2018)
15. Whitman, J., Zevallos, N., Travers, M., Choset, H.: Snake robot urban search after the 2017 Mexico City earthquake. In: 2018 IEEE International Symposium on Safety. Security, and Rescue Robotics (SSRR), pp. 1–6. IEEE, Philadelphia, PA, USA (2018)
16. Feddoul, Y., Ragot, N., Duval, F., Havard, V., Baudry, D., Assila, A.: Exploring human-machine collaboration in industry: a systematic literature review of digital twin and robotics interfaced with extended reality technologies. Int. J. Adv. Manufact. Technol. **129**(5), 1917–1932 (2023)
17. Walker, M., Phung, T., Chakraborti, T., Williams, T., Szafir, D.: Virtual, augmented, and mixed reality for human-robot interaction: a survey and virtual design element taxonomy. ACM Transact. Human-Robot Interact. **12**(4), 1–39 (2023)
18. Karpichev, Y., Charter, T., Najjaran, H.: Extended Reality for Enhanced Human-Robot Collaboration: A Human-in-the-Loop Approach. arXiv preprint arXiv:2403.14597 (2024)
19. Batistute, A., Santos, E., Takieddine, K., Lazari, P.M., Da Rocha, L.G., Vivaldini, K.C.T.: Extended reality for teleoperated mobile robots. In: 2021 Latin American Robotics Symposium (LARS), 2021 Brazilian Symposium on Robotics (SBR), and 2021 Workshop on Robotics in Education (WRE), pp. 19–24. IEEE, Natal, Brazil (2021)
20. Wang, X., Shen, L., Lee, L.: A Systematic Review of XR-based Remote Human-Robot Interaction Systems. arXiv preprint arXiv:2403.11384 (2024)
21. Grunwald, C., et al.: Reliability of collapse simulation: comparing finite and applied element method at different levels. Eng. Struct. **176**, 265–278 (2018)
22. Hu, W., Lum, G.Z., Mastrangeli, M., Sitti, M.: Small-scale soft-bodied robot with multimodal locomotion. Nature **554**(7690), 81–85 (2018)
23. Kriegman, S., Cappelle, C., Corucci, F., Bernatskiy, A., Cheney, N., Bongard, J.C.: Simulating the evolution of soft and rigid-body robots. In: Proceedings of the Genetic and Evolutionary Computation Conference Companion, pp. 1117-1120. ACM, Berlin, Germany (2017)

24. Khanal, S., Medasetti, U.S., Mashal, M., Savage, B., Khadka, R.: Virtual and augmented reality in the disaster management technology: a literature review of the past 11 years. Front. Virtual Reality **3**, 843195 (2022)
25. Obaigbena, A., Lottu, O.A., Ugwuanyi, E.D., Jacks, B.S., Sodiya, E.O., Darao-jimba, O.D.: AI and human-robot interaction: a review of recent advances and challenges. GSC Adv. Res. Rev. **18**(2), 321–330 (2024)
26. Rajashekhar, V.S., Rajesh, A., Athaaillah, M.I.A., Prabhakar, G.: Serpentine Synergy: Design and Fabrication of a Dual Soft Continuum Manipulator and Soft Snake Robot. arXiv preprint arXiv:2407.04802 (2024)

User Experience for Inclusion: Analysis of WCAG 2.2 in Pharmacy App for Visually Impaired Group

Shibanee Mishra🆔 and Shanu Sharma(✉)

School of Planning and Architecture, Bhopal, India
shanusharma@spabhopal.ac.in

Abstract. The boom in the Indian e-commerce market has changed how people typically shop since the COVID-19 pandemic. Ensuring accessibility is a must for e-commerce platforms to create inclusive experiences and equitable access to digital spaces. However, many companies overlook a portion of their customer base, namely the visually impaired. A significant number of web platforms in India lack alternative text for non-text content (e.g., images, audio, and video), keyboard accessibility, and screen reader compatibility which affects the smooth navigation of various e-commerce platforms. The WCAG 2.2 (Web Content Accessibility Guidelines) has a set of guidelines and success criteria to ensure that websites and digital content are accessible and usable. However, it needs more emphasis on improving the overall experience for visually impaired users who rely on screen readers to shop for products and services on e-commerce platforms. Based on a comprehensive literature review, user studies, and UX audits, we identify specific shortcomings in the guidelines and how AI can be incorporated further into e-commerce systems to enhance accessibility. Our findings suggest a more holistic approach to accessibility that includes user testing, real-world user scenarios, and integration of emerging technologies like AI, including chatbots and image identification.

Keywords: WCAG · E-commerce UX · Pharmacy App · Accessibility · Visual Impairment · Accessibility framework · Inclusive experience

1 Introduction

Online shopping has changed how we purchase products and services by offering a wide selection at our fingertips, making it simple and accessible. While this innovation has made access to goods and services more convenient than ever before, people with visual impairments do not experience the same ease. Studies have found that nearly 94% of e-commerce websites are inaccessible, including those of major brands such as Nike, Lowes, H&M, etc. [12]. Imagine the frustration of placing online medication orders, only to find that the website is not readily accessible! That is the reality for 35 million Indians (2.55% of the population) who are visually impaired, with 0.24 million being children and 4.95 million (0.36% of the total population) classified as blind [1]. These statistics highlight that accessibility to e-commerce platforms is essential to meet the diverse needs of this substantial segment of the population.

Nevertheless, many online retailers overlook the needs of this significant demographic, resulting in websites riddled with accessibility issues. In 2022, around 4,500 ADA-related lawsuits were filed [2].

The Web Content Accessibility Guidelines 2.2 WCAG 2.2 covers a broad range of recommendations for making web content more accessible. Following these guidelines makes applications more perceivable, operable, understandable, and robust than for individuals with visual impairments [10].

This paper aims not only to address these accessibility issues of a pharmacy ordering application (here, we took the case of the TATA 1 mg app) but also to enhance its user experience. The study began by analyzing the process of placing medicine orders through the application. Some identified drawbacks include missing text labels for voice search, which often forced users to rely on manual typing, a lack of guidance for using the camera to take pictures of prescriptions, and long wait times to speak with pharmacists.

Consequently, additional features were suggested to maximize these tasks, such as:

- Integrating 'Seeing AI' (an app that uses the mobile camera to identify people and objects, audibly describing them for people with visual impairment) allows users to independently take pictures of prescriptions and upload them in the pharmacy ordering app.
- Using a barcode scanner feature (from the Seeing AI app) to scan and automatically input names of medicines' names for direct search.
- Combining chatbots and screen readers like Talkback to assist with entering data such as symptoms or scheduling doctor's appointments, thus reducing the wait time for customer support.

2   Review of Literature

In 'E-Commerce Website for the Visually Impaired' (Anagha S. Kulkarni, 2023), it is proposed to make all user inputs voice-based to save visually impaired users from the discomfort of keyboard typing. This solution aims to enhance the accessibility of e-commerce websites by enabling voice interaction as the primary mode of input.

The paper 'Visually Impaired Friendly E-commerce Website' (Mallika Chand, 2019) emphasizes the importance of providing methods by which visually impaired individuals can navigate e-commerce websites and make purchases independently. This study utilized speech recognition technology, achieving an accuracy rate of 70%.

According to 'A Survey Based on an E-Commerce Website for Visually Impaired People' (Sarbanshu Sanyal, 2022), a variety of machine learning techniques were applied to facilitate the use of voice commands and simple hovering over the computer screen by visually impaired consumers throughout the entire e-commerce process, from registration to payment.

'E-commerce Usability Guidelines for Visually Impaired Users' (Elisa Prati, 2021) provides structured guidelines to improve the usability of e-commerce for visually impaired users, thus offering a more customized shopping experience.

Amazon, the e-commerce giant, has integrated several accessibility features into its devices and digital platforms. These include a Voice Search feature, allowing users to search for products using the app's microphone icon, text size adjustment for users of screen magnifiers, compatibility with screen readers like VoiceOver on iOS and TalkBack on Android, and features like one-click ordering and Alexa voice commands that further enhance the shopping experience for visually impaired users by streamlining tasks such as adding items to the cart and tracking orders [7].

With Simple 1-Tap Checkout on Myntra, visually impaired users can complete their purchases more quickly by reducing their cognitive load during the checkout process. This feature eliminated the need to scroll through multiple form fields or navigate interactive buttons, minimizing time-consuming screen reader interactions [8].

While this paper focuses on designing applications for users with visual impairments, it primarily emphasizes enhancing the user experience, differentiating it from other studies. It also addresses the limitations of WCAG 2.2 guidelines, proposing the integration of AI technologies like Seeing AI for image recognition and barcode scanning, alongside chatbots and screen readers, to simplify the process of ordering medicine. In addition, the paper emphasizes the importance of incorporating different tones (e.g., sympathetic, informative, friendly) in screen reader voices—an aspect that is not extensively covered in WCAG 2.2, but which could be addressed in future revisions.

3   Methods of Data Collection

3.1   Secondary Research

To begin, we conducted secondary research on how visually impaired people navigate e-commerce platforms, the challenges they encounter, and whether these platforms have evolved to meet their specific needs. We further deepened our understanding by attending the Axe-con 2024 on digital accessibility, where we participated in a session led by Collin Wong, a blind-by-birth accessibility consultant at Gotomedia. His insightful perspectives on why digital accessibility is often failing and his emphasis on the need to integrate accessibility at every stage of development provided us with a new direction for our research. Although we identified potential focus areas during this phase, we needed to gather more primary research before finalizing any conclusions. Given the limitations of our secondary research, we started approaching blind schools, and NGOs in Bangalore, India, to conduct one-on-one interview sessions for an in-depth study.

3.2   Primary Research

We employed a mixed methodology encompassing both qualitative and quantitative approaches along with a UX audit and usability testing to gain a comprehensive understanding of the gaps and potential solutions.

For quantitative research, a survey was circulated among 124 participants in the age group of 18–55 years of age living in Tier 1 cities in India with a range of vision abilities, from visually impaired to normal vision. For the visually impaired participants, the survey was circulated with the help of a visually impaired teacher from Sri Rakum School for the Blind, Bengaluru, who was part of a self-help group for the sighted underprivileged. They were mostly local people speaking Kannada and were also comfortable with English. For people with normal vision, we circulated it among our colleagues and acquaintances in Bangalore, Mumbai, and Delhi to get a wider perspective. The survey focused on specific, measurable questions, such as the comfort level in using pharmacy-ordering apps, the participants' most preferred pharmacy app, etc.

Qualitative research was conducted through contextual inquiry and focus group discussions to explore users' lived experiences, uncovering their struggles, frustrations, and emotional responses to e-commerce platforms. The qualitative study included 27 participants from Sri Rakum School for the Blind, Bengaluru (Fig. 1).

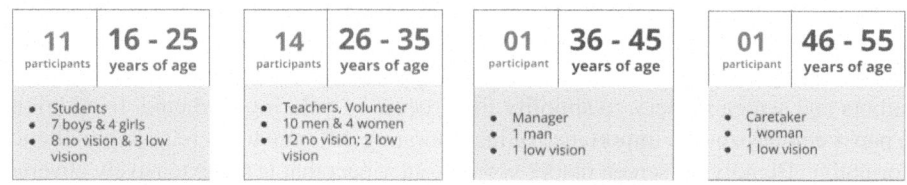

Fig. 1. Demographics showing the age and vision level of participants from Sri Rakum School for the Blind, Bengaluru.

Common questions asked during both the qualitative and quantitative research phases included:

1. Name, Age, Occupation, Family members
2. How do you typically purchase medicines: online, in-store, or with assistance?
3. How do you navigate and use mobile applications as a visually impaired user?
4. Have you ever used e-commerce applications for shopping? If yes, can you share your experience?
5. Which e-commerce application do you use most frequently?
6. What challenges do you encounter while using mobile apps, particularly for online shopping, due to your visual impairment?
7. What specific features or improvements would enhance your experience and make your shopping more accessible and user-friendly?
8. Have you ever purchased medicines online? If not, how do you usually buy medicines? Do you need to require assistance?

Usability testing was conducted using the Android Accessibility Scanner application, which adheres to WCAG 2.2 guidelines. This test identified approximately 30% of accessibility issues, with common problems including empty text labels, improperly sized touch targets, and insufficient contrast between foreground and background colors (Fig. 2).

A detailed UX audit was performed to evaluate the overall user experience beyond just usability heuristics. This involved step-by-step navigation done using a screen reader to place an order on the TATA 1mg app, providing a holistic view of the challenges faced by visually impaired users when shopping online.

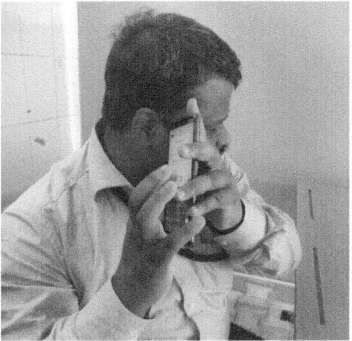

Fig. 2. Focused group discussions with faculty members with visual impairments from Sri Rakum School for the Blind, Bengaluru (left). A teacher demonstrated how he used Talkback to navigate through applications (right).

4   Research Synthesis

Key findings from quantitative research: Most participants with vision impairments reported needing assistance when purchasing medicines online, which is why they rarely opt for online shopping independently. In contrast, most people with normal vision frequently used TATA 1 mg as their preferred medicine-buying app, with many purchasing medicines more than 10 times a year. These users found the app very accessible and easy to navigate. However, individuals with vision impairments needed more confidence in navigating the app.

Key problems mentioned by the participants (qualitative research): Most participants expressed a preference for traditional shopping over online shopping due to their need for assistance when shopping online. Despite this, there was a clear interest in overcoming these challenges and adopting online shopping, particularly for purchasing medicines. Among the available apps, TATA 1mg emerged as the top choice for many participants. The Care Plan (a membership subscription) was beneficial, as it facilitated medicines reordering and provided excellent customer support via call. However, accessibility issues within the app remained a significant barrier, leading to continued dependence on customer support, friends, or relatives when making purchases.

Figure 3 highlights the major sentiments observed during the interviews involved in the qualitative research. These sentiments were recorded and transcribed to reflect participants' beliefs and attitudes, contributing to the research objective. The data was coded into two categories: semantic, which focused on explicit, straightforward interpretations of the data, and latent codes, which addressed implicit or unlying meanings.

Fig. 3. Majorly observed sentiments towards online shopping by the participants involved in qualitative research (contextual inquiry).

Participant Statement	Semantic Codes	Latent Codes
I have learnt various assistive technologies to operate these smartphones	Use of assistive technology	Willingness to learn
I am using Talkback and google Assistant to send messages and online browsing of products	Specific assistive technology usage (TalkBack & Google Assistant)	Preference for familiar tools
We have never used online shopping	No prior online shopping experience	Fear of the unknown
We need assistance while online shopping	Difficulty with online shopping independently	Need for accessibility features
Recently, Talkback is not supporting Facebook, so we have stopped using such apps	Specific accessibility issue with app	Frustration with lack of universal compatibility
We don't have knowledge regarding what type of/ color dress will look	Lack of confidence in selecting products online	Need for product recommendations or visualization tools
For medicines, someone mostly gets it from nearby pharmacy for me. If the meds are not available at the moment I have to wait for the supply.	Reliance on traditional methods for most purchases	Limited access to online options
We are unsure what will look good on us.	Lack of confidence in selecting products online	Need for personalized shopping experiences
Wo dukaan wale bhaiya bata dete he me isme achha lagunga.. to online shopping kyun karun? (Shopkeeper tells me what looks good, why should I shop online?)	Reliance on physical store assistance	Preference for in-person interaction and personalized service
One perk of online shopping is discounts and branded clothes. That's why I love shopping from there, but I need assistance.	Motivated by discounts and brands	Need for accessibility features despite benefits
Concentrating on accessibility is going to improve the lives of all! Not just specially abled people.	Positive attitude towards accessibility	Understanding of the broader impact of accessibility

Fig. 4. Organizing the sentiments from contextual inquiry and focus group discussions to semantic and latent codes.

Figure 4 shows a brief categorization of responses to codes. After organizing the responses from the qualitative research and aligning them with the affinity mapping, several common themes emerged. These themes provided a deeper understanding of participants' experiences and highlighted significant insights within the data.

The five main themes identified from the thematic mapping were:

1. Accessibility and Technology
2. Barriers to Online Shopping
3. Alternative Shopping Strategies
4. Motivations and Preferences
5. Overall Impact

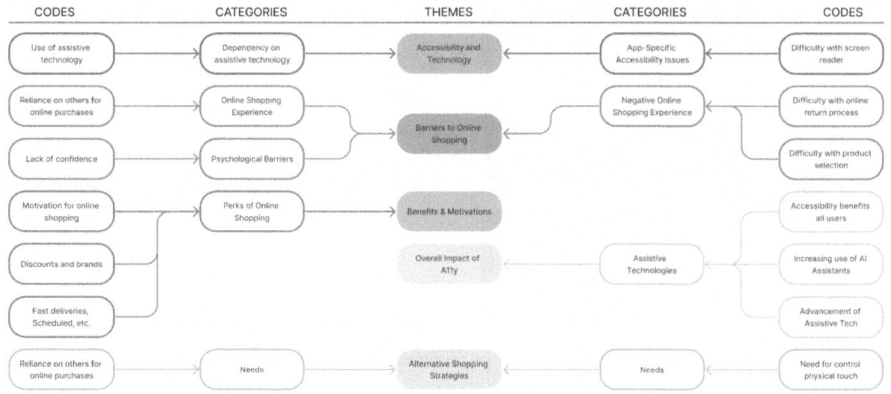

Fig. 5. Chart showing thematic mapping derived from the responses from the qualitative research.

Figure 5 illustrates how the problems identified by participants during the qualitative research resulted in the formation of a pattern (or themes). This thematic mapping was instrumental in focusing on each theme individually, enabling a more structured approach to addressing the challenges visually impaired users face in online shopping.

5   Findings of Usability Testing

Finding from automated Usability Testing of the TATA 1MG app:
    Some of the results that show its failure were as follows:

1. Figure 6 shows the Home page of the TATA 1mg application focusing on its accessibility issues and WCAG 2.2 compliance.
2. Figure 7 emphasizes the Search page of the TATA 1mg application showing missing text labels of the voice typing, and low contrast ratios of text labels.

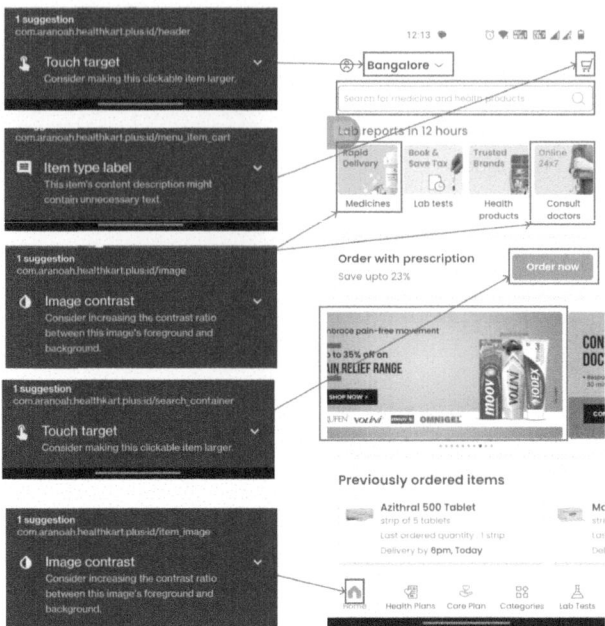

Fig. 6. The TATA 1mg application's Home page shows accessibility issues and WCAG compliance. This test was done on 15 April 2024.

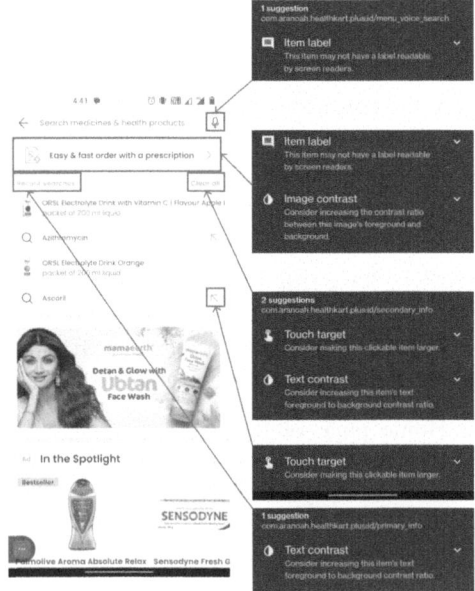

Fig. 7. The search page of the TATA 1mg application shows missing text labels of the voice typing, and low contrast ratios of text labels, thus, failing WCAG guidelines. This test was conducted on 15 April 2024.

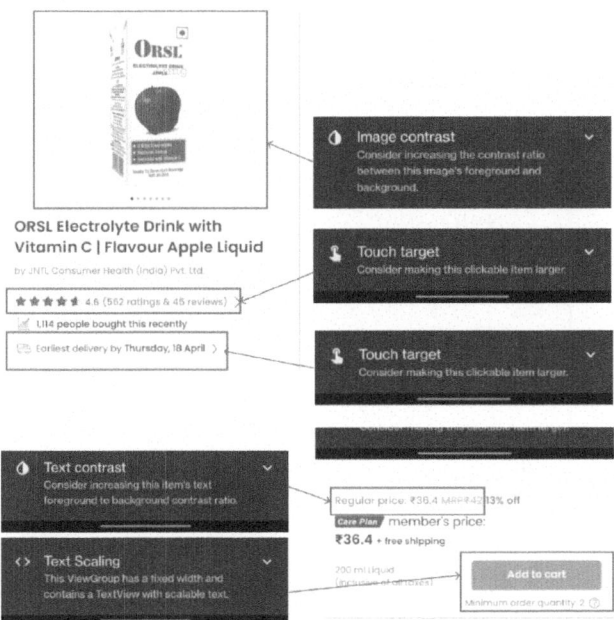

Fig. 8. The product description page of the TATA 1mg application shows low text and image contrast, missing text labels, smaller touch targets, and an inadequate touch target for the 'add to cart' button, failing WCAG guidelines. This test was conducted on April 15, 2024.

3. Figure 8 talks about the Product description page of the TATA 1mg application showing a lack of image contrast and missing text labels, smaller touch targets, low text contrast, and touch target of the 'add to cart' button.
4. Figure 9 talks regarding the previously ordered items page of the TATA 1mg application that has low text contrast ratios, a smaller touch target, and a need for text scaling of CTA buttons like to add to cart, and adding items buttons.

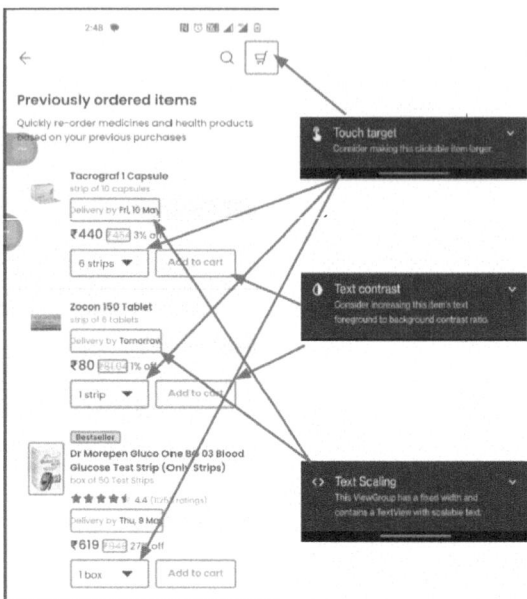

Fig. 9. The previously ordered items page of the TATA 1mg application shows low text contrast ratios, smaller touch targets, and a need for text scaling of CTA buttons like "Add to Cart" and "Add Items." This test was conducted on 15 April 2024.

Finding from manual Usability Testing of the TATA 1MG app:
Some of the results of the UX audit were as follows:

1. Figure 10 focuses on the Home page of the TATA 1mg application, highlighting the difficulties faced while navigating through the screen.
2. Figure 11 shows the lack of alternate text labels for the medicine image on the Product Description page (PDP) of the TATA 1mg application.
3. Figure 12 discusses the Product Description page (PDP) of the TATA 1mg application, showing how users were unable to skip some information, leading to cognitive overload and a drop in conversion rates.
4. Figure 13 shows the process of adding products to the cart in the TATA 1mg application, which lacks a visual hierarchy. This issue prevents users from skipping texts, leading to cognitive overload.

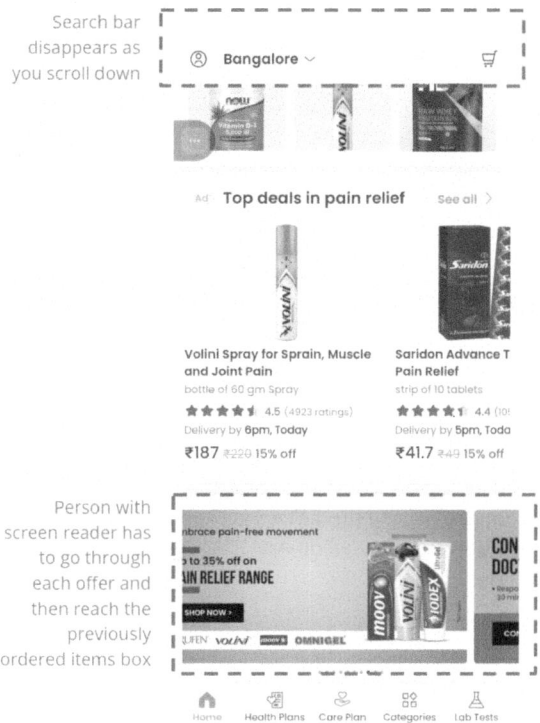

Fig. 10. The home page of the TATA 1mg application shows navigation difficulties. This test was conducted on April 21, 2024.

This integrated approach not only addressed immediate usability concerns but also contributed to the strategic development of user-centered designs that meet both functional and emotional user needs, ultimately leading to more intuitive, effective, and satisfying user interactions with digital platforms.

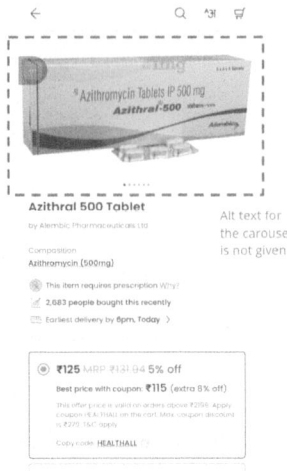

Fig. 11. The product description page of the TATA 1mg application lacks alternate text labels for the medicine image. This test was conducted on April 21, 2024.

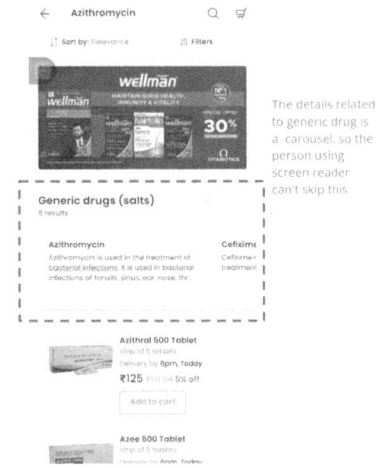

Fig. 12. The product description page of the TATA 1mg application shows how the user is unable to skip some information which leads to cognitive overload and a drop in conversion rates. This test was done on 21 April, 2024

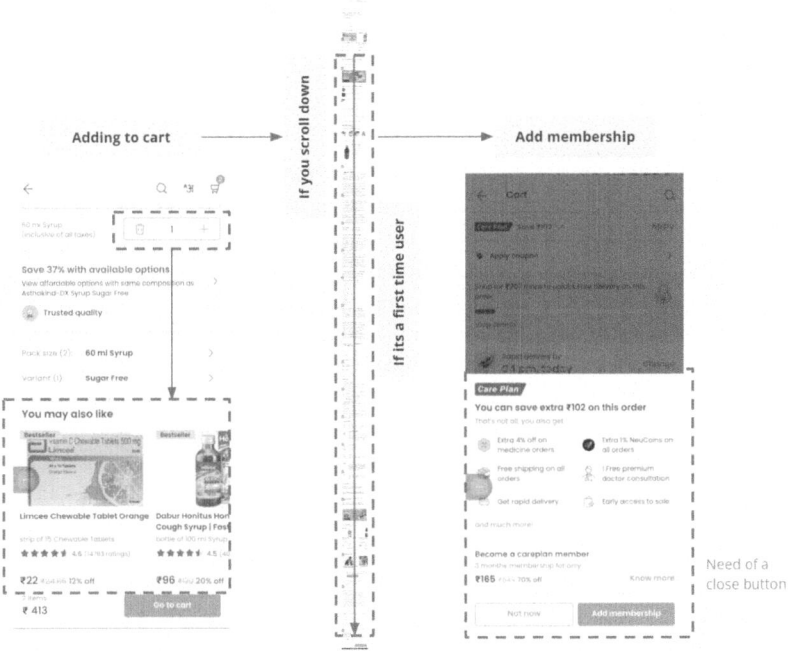

Fig. 13. The process of adding products to the cart in the TATA 1mg application shows a lack of visual hierarchy. This test was conducted on April 21, 2024.

6 Discussions

The TATA 1mg app is specially designed to assist Visually impaired users in navigating e-commerce applications with ease. With advancements in AI, integrating more advanced AI chatbots, error-free image recognition, and other emerging technologies can further enhance the app's usability, providing better navigation and a more seamless experience for the users. For example, to ease the process of searching for a medicine's name, a barcode scanner feature is proposed that would help the user scan the barcode present on the medicine strip. The barcode is a tactile one attached to the medicine strip or bottle. To scan it, the user can feel it, point the mobile camera at it, and choose the barcode scanner feature. With the help of Seeing AI, the scanner scans the barcode and inputs the medicine name in the search bar. Also, taking a picture of the prescription using the Seeing AI camera, which assists the user in framing the image with the help of image recognition, would make uploading the prescription easier for the user. Looking ahead, major e-commerce companies such as Nike, Lowes, and H&M could adopt similar technologies to improve the accessibility of their digital platforms, which would not only increase usability for visually impaired users but also expand their global customer base.

This study also highlights the need for designers worldwide to focus not only on visual aesthetics but also on the functionality of the products they are designing. By prioritizing both, they may contribute to a more inclusive world, assuring that digital places are accessible to everyone, regardless of their ability.

7 Conclusion

The contributions of this paper were threefold; (1) Findings from two evaluations, including an online survey of 124 respondents from Tier 1 cities across India and contextual interviews and focus group discussions with 27 visually impaired individuals from Bangalore, aged 18 - 55 years. (2) The exploration of AI technologies, such as chatbots, and image recognition tools (e.g., the Seeing AI app), which could streamline the data entry process for tasks like doctor consultation and medicine searches, simplifying user interactions and enhancing accessibility, and (3) the proposal to add emotional nuance to the tone of the screen readers, such as Talkback, to improve the overall user experience. For example, in the case of a medicine ordering application, the tone of the screen reader could convey empathy, making the user feel more human-like.

As WCAG 2.2 guidelines focus on the four principles of accessibility— Perceivable, Operable, Understandable, and Robust [11]— this paper suggests an expansion of these guidelines to include customizable screen reader tones for specific applications. As visually impaired individuals often rely on screen readers to access information, working on just the interface part is not enough, focus on sound design is a must. Hence, these enhancements could further improve the user experience for visually impaired individuals by making their interactions with e-commerce platforms feel more personal and less automated.

8 Expected Outcome

The outcome of this paper is a comprehensive analysis of the 'TATA 1mg app' designed specifically for people with visual impairments, ensuring not only accessibility but also customization based on their unique needs. The app aims to empower users by enabling them to purchase medicines from the brands they want, schedule doctor appointments, and book tests independently, with their device, thus boosting their confidence. Features such as ease of accessing coupons and discounts instead of going through multiple screens, further enhance the user experience by reducing cognitive load and making the online shopping process for medicines more streamlined and hassle-free.

Additionally, this app has the potential to benefit the elderly population who may have lost their vision due to conditions like glaucoma or diabetic retinopathy. Providing greater accessibility, it can also support TATA 1mg in expanding its market reach, contributing to revenue growth as more users, including those with visual impairments and elderly individuals, can use the app seamlessly.

Acknowledgments. Thank you to all volunteers, students, teachers, and colleagues who contributed to this paper. This work was part of our Master's final year thesis dissertation, supported by the School of Planning and Architecture, Bhopal. We would also like to thank our project guide, Dr. Shanu Sharma, and the faculty members of our respected institution, Aman R Xaxa, Dr. Monikuntala Das, and Dr. Sukanta Majumdar.

References

1. Sharma, M., Khanna, R., Singh, M.P.: Current estimates of the economic burden of visual impairment in India. Indian J. Ophthalmol. **70**(6), 1199–1206 (2022). https://doi.org/10.1097/IOP.0000000000002000
2. UsableNet: Decoding digital accessibility lawsuits in 2023: key trends & strategic insights. UsableNet Blog (2023). https://blog.usablenet.com/decoding-digital-accessibility-lawsuits-in-2023-key-trends-strategic-insights. Accessed 13 Sep 2024
3. Kulkarni, A.S., Bhandari, M.S.: E-commerce website for visually impaired. Int. J. Research Appl. Sci. Eng. Technol. **10**(7), 1200–1210 (2022). https://www.ijraset.com/research-paper/e-commerce-website-for-visually-impaired
4. Sharma, A., Singh, R.: Improving web accessibility for visually impaired users. In: 2020 IEEE Conference on Software Engineering, pp. 1–5. IEEE, New York (2020). https://ieeexplore.ieee.org/document/9114617
5. UsableNet: Accessibility features of Amazon in their e-commerce platform and digital devices. UsableNet Blog (2022). https://www.accessibility.com/blog/accessibility-features-of-amazon-in-their-e-commerce-platform-and-digital-devices. Accessed 13 Sep 2024
6. W3C: WCAG 2.1 implementation report. https://www.w3.org/WAI/WCAG21/implementation-report/implementation?implementation_id=146. Accessed 13 Sep 2024
7. Accessibility.com: Accessibility features of amazon in their e-commerce platform and digital devices. https://www.accessibility.com/blog/accessibility-features-of-amazon-in-their-e-commerce-platform-and-digital-devices. Accessed 13 Sep 2024
8. Myntra: Myntra for ultimate festive fashion convenience. Myntra Blog (2022). https://blog.myntra.com/myntra-for-ultimate-festive-fashion-convenience. Accessed 13 Sep 2024
9. McMillan, R., Xiao, X.: The economic cost of digital accessibility lawsuits. Soc. Sci. Res. Netw. (2020). https://doi.org/10.2139/ssrn.3621166
10. Lee, H., Park, S.: Improving web accessibility for the visually impaired through AI. In: Kang, D. (ed.) HCI International 2021, LNCS, vol. 12712, pp. 246–257. Springer, Cham (2021). https://doi.org/10.1007/978-3-030-78092-0_18
11. W3C: Web content accessibility guidelines (WCAG) 2.2. https://www.w3.org/TR/WCAG22/. Accessed 13 Sep 2024
12. Baymard Institute: Accessibility benchmark for e-commerce websites. https://baymard.com/blog/accessibility-benchmark-launch. Accessed 13 Sep 2024

Enhancing Dining Experiences with Augmented Reality and Olfactory Technology

Aarav Balachandran, Kritika Gupta, and Prajna Vohra[✉]

Indraprastha Institute of Information Technology (IIIT), Delhi, India
prajna21345@iiitd.ac.in

Abstract. This study aims to explore the integration of Augmented Reality (AR) and olfactory technology to enhance dining experience in restaurants. We present ARoma, an 'AR Olfactory Menu Application" for Indian cuisine which provides users with 3D visualisation of dishes, detailed ingredient and nutritional information, and historical context, as well as an olfaction device to deliver the aroma of the dishes. Our research compares the traditional menu experience with AR menus and ARoma, aiming to understand how these technologies affect customers' perceptions of food quality, dining enjoyment, and immersion. Our user study involved a sample size of 30 participants, divided into two groups. Group A compared traditional menu experiences with AR menus, while Group B experienced traditional menus followed by ARoma. Using this control group study and mixed-method approach, including quantitative surveys and qualitative interviews, we found that AR menus and olfactory elements significantly enhance the dining experience by providing detailed and engaging information. Our findings suggest that AR and olfactory technology can significantly improve customer satisfaction and engagement in the food industry.

Keywords: Augmented Reality · Olfaction · AR-Menu · Dining Experience · Olfactory devices · Scent Dispersion

1 Introduction

1.1 Augmented Reality in the Food Industry

Augmented Reality (AR) revolutionizes how we interact with the world around us, seamlessly integrating digital elements into our physical environment. It enhances our perception and interaction with reality by overlaying computer-generated content onto real-world objects [11]. In technical terms, AR is defined as a real-time view of the physical world environment that has been enhanced by adding virtually generated information. By superimposing virtual objects upon the real world in real-time, AR improves the user's perception of the real world [13]. AR technology has applications across various industries, transforming how

N. Rangaswamy et al. (Eds.): IndiaHCI 2024, CCIS 2338, pp. 202–225, 2025.
https://doi.org/10.1007/978-3-031-80832-6_15

businesses operate and interact with customers. In the food industry context, AR holds a strong potential by creating digital menus that allow customers to visualize dishes in 3D before ordering, receive detailed ingredient information, and enjoy interactive, immersive dining experiences that combine the physical and digital worlds [3,26].

Traditional menus often fall short of conveying the essence of dishes, relying on limited textual descriptions or static images. This can lead to misunderstandings and unmet expectations among customers. Customers may struggle to visualize the actual portion size of a dish, which can result in either over-ordering or under-ordering. Static images might fail to effectively communicate the texture, colour and presentation of a dish. Moreover, essential details about the dishes' ingredients, potential allergens and nutritional information are often missed out in restaurant menus due to their limited scope [15,19,33] for providing detailed and extensive information.

AR-based food menus offer a transformative approach to tackle these shortcomings of traditional menus. Marker-based AR, or recognition-based AR, functions by identifying distinct patterns or user-defined images to trigger augmentation. These markers, whether on paper or physical artifacts, are swiftly recognized and analyzed by cameras [38]. By utilizing marker-based menus, users can unlock interactive, three-dimensional representations of menu items simply by scanning them with their smartphones. This offers customers with an immersive dining experience with realistic and informative depictions of dishes, including details like ingredients, nutritional content, and even pricing [4]. With the help of realistic 3D visualisations, customers can correctly judge the portion size of the dishes as well as get accurate information about their presentations. Extra information regarding the dishes ingredients and nutritional values can also be more easily incorporated in an AR based smartphone application with the help of buttons and drop-downs. AR menus also transcend language barriers, as food items are visually represented as 3D models, making them universally understandable. This not only aids in decision-making but also fosters trust and loyalty among customers.

1.2   Olfactory Approach as an Extension to AR

Conventional AR systems tend to work on only two significant senses: visual and auditory. Today, AR is not only limited to visual and auditory stimuli but can also be extended to different senses by incorporating haptic and olfactory elements. Multi-sensory media, unlike traditional AR systems, focuses on providing fully immersive interactions with the user, thus improving user experience [32].

While numerous applications and devices have been developed for these senses, there remains a significant gap in AR applications targeting the olfactory and gustatory senses, largely due to the inherent complexities involved [14]. Olfaction holds a unique power to evoke emotions and memories, enriching immersive environments [5,22,24]. Combining AR with olfaction can create genuinely immersive dining experiences where users visualise and smell virtual representations of dishes. This integration of sensory stimuli elevates dining to a multi-sensory journey, enhancing enjoyment and engagement [24]. Despite its importance, most existing AR systems in the food industry focus solely on visual and auditory elements, neglecting the powerful impact of smell on the dining experience. This oversight represents a significant gap in both the market and academic research.

1.3 Introducing ARoma: An AR Olfactory Menu Application

Previous research has shown that AR menus can improve customer satisfaction by offering interactive 3D visualizations of food items. Early AR efforts included translating menus and displaying 3D food models with limitations such as language constraints and limited dish representation [7,36]. Subsequent developments incorporated QR codes and unique markers to enhance interactivity and provide detailed information about dishes, including ingredients and nutritional data [4,29]. However, these systems have often focused on general applications rather than specific cuisines. Despite advancements, there remains a notable gap in AR applications for complex cuisines like Indian food. Additionally, while olfactory integration in AR is emerging, its application in dining experiences is still limited [6,12]. This study aims to fill this gap by introducing ARoma, an innovative Augmented Reality Olfaction Menu Application designed specifically for Indian cuisine, that not only provides users with 3D visualizations of dishes but also incorporates an olfactory device to deliver the aroma of the dishes. By combining visual, informational, and olfactory elements, ARoma seeks to create a more immersive and multi-sensory dining experience. ARoma aims to enhance the dining experience by providing 3D visualizations of dishes along with detailed ingredient and nutritional information. This information is crucial for individuals with dietary restrictions, including those with specific religious dietary beliefs, especially in a diverse country like India. Additionally, the application includes the historical background of each dish, making the dining experience not only more immersive but also educational and culturally enriching. This feature is particularly beneficial for tourists, offering them a deeper understanding and appreciation of Indian culinary traditions. To further augment the immersive experience, we have developed and integrated an olfactory device with ARoma. This device allows users to experience the aromas of the dishes, adding a powerful sensory dimension to the dining experience. By combining visual, informational, and olfactory elements, ARoma aims to create a holistic and engaging dining experience for restaurant customers.

The goal of this project is to leverage AR and olfactory technology to contribute to social good, particularly in the context of Human Computer Interaction (HCI). By making dining experiences more informative, and enjoyable, we hope to increase immersiveness, enhance cultural appreciation, and improve overall customer satisfaction in the food industry. The research questions that we aim to address through our study are as follows:

RQ1- How does the AR experience provided by ARoma affect customers' perceptions of food quality and dining enjoyment compared to traditional menus?

RQ2- How does the multi-sensory experience, including both AR and olfactory technology provided by ARoma, affect customers' perceptions of food quality and dining enjoyment compared to traditional menus?

By addressing these research questions, we aim to provide insights into the effectiveness of ARoma in creating a more immersive and satisfying dining experience for customers. Our study will explore the potential of AR and olfactory technology to transform traditional dining. Ultimately, we hope that our findings will contribute to the broader field of HCI by demonstrating how multi-sensory technologies can be used to improve user experiences and promote social good in diverse cultural contexts.

2   Related Work

2.1   AR Menu

AR technology has emerged as a promising solution as it combines the real-world environment with computer-generated content, offering an interactive and immersive experience for diners by enhancing the dining experience. Early applications of AR in restaurant settings focused primarily on menu translation and basic 3D visualization [36]. For instance, a study had a mobile application that could translate Chinese menus into English and display 3D models of food items. While innovative, this approach was limited to a single language and could only render a few 3D models simultaneously [7]. As the technology evolved, researchers began exploring more comprehensive restaurant AR applications. In parallel developments, a digital food menu application using AR technology used unique stickers bearing the restaurant's name and logo as image targets to trigger the display of 3D food models [29]. This allowed for efficient recognition and tracking of restaurant-specific markers. They also proposed a system with features like real-time tagging, an interactive menu, and a food identifier. Their application allowed users to view 3D models of dishes by scanning a restaurant logo or marker, providing additional information such as prices, ingredients, ratings, and recipe videos. However, this system was still confined to a single restaurant's menu items. More recently, another research study developed an AR-based android application that uses QR codes as markers to display 3D food models from restaurant menus [4]. This offers greater flexibility in terms of the number of dishes that can be augmented, as QR codes can store more data than traditional fiducial markers [38]. Their system allows customers to visualize dishes in 3D along with price, ingredient, nutritional, and calorie information. The authors conducted a user experience evaluation, which showed positive results for criteria such as attractiveness, efficiency, and interactivity. A research study examined the potential of AR-integrated menus to create healthier dining experiences. Their research highlighted the growing concern for healthy eating habits among consumers, both at home and when dining out. They proposed that AR technology could be used to provide detailed nutritional information and health-related data directly on the menu, helping diners make more informed

choices [9,10]. This approach not only caters to the increasing health consciousness of consumers but also positions restaurants to play a role in addressing
public health concerns such as obesity and diabetes.

2.2   Integration of AR with Emerging Technologies

The integration of AR with other technologies has opened up new possibilities
for enhancing the dining experience. For instance, a study developed "Menu
Guide," an AR smartphone application that combines optical character recognition (OCR), sentiment analysis, and AR technology [30]. Their system scans
traditional paper menus using OCR, performs sentiment analysis on customer
reviews, and then projects ratings for each dish using AR. This innovative approach not only enhances the customer experience by providing instant feedback
on menu items but also offers valuable insights to restaurateurs about their most
popular and least preferred dishes. As these technologies continue to evolve,
there is a growing need to understand user acceptance and adoption. Based on
this, a study applied the Unified Theory of Acceptance and Use of Technology
(UTAUT) model to evaluate user acceptance of AR menu systems [10]. Their
findings indicated that Performance Expectancy was the strongest determinant
of user acceptance, suggesting that the perceived usefulness of AR menus in
enhancing the dining experience is crucial for their widespread adoption. While
AR menu systems have been developed for various cuisines and dining experiences, there is a notable lack of focus on Indian cuisine. This gap is significant given the complexity and diversity of Indian food. AR menus designed for
Indian restaurants could offer unique benefits, such as ingredient breakdowns
and region-specific information [18,25]. This will allow diners to interact with
each component and learn about its origin and flavour profile. This could help
demystify the vast array of Indian dishes for unfamiliar diners, showcasing the
intricate blends, cooking methods, and regional variations that make Indian cuisine rich and diverse.

2.3   User Experience of AR Applications

User experience (UX) in AR applications plays a pivotal role in shaping how
users interact with and adopt these systems across various domains. As AR
technology has progressed, the emphasis has shifted from the novelty of virtual
overlays to how effectively and intuitively users can engage with these digital
elements in real-world contexts [8,28]. However, no such studies specifically evaluated the user experiences of AR menus. On the other hand early AR systems,
such as mobile apps designed for gaming, often faced limitations in usability
and scalability, impacting the overall user experience [20]. The evolution of AR
has brought with it new challenges and opportunities in UX design. Research
by another study emphasized that while mobile AR applications introduced an
exciting way to engage with contextual data, their user experience evaluations
revealed significant hurdles in terms of physical ergonomics, UI consistency, and

user control. Users often found early AR applications captivating but cumbersome, with the novelty wearing off quickly when interaction proved inefficient or unintuitive [17]. Another key element in evaluating AR UX is the standardization of AR interfaces and interactions to ensure consistency and reliability across platforms. A study emphasized the need for AR standardization from a UX perspective, focusing on crucial factors like ergonomics, usability, immersion, and safety [31]. Their proposed Ux4AR framework aims to provide a roadmap for evaluating user experience in AR systems by assessing input modalities (visual, auditory, tactile, and kinesthetic) and output elements (visual and haptic feedback). This framework highlights how key UX factors such as input accuracy, ease of use, and visual consistency are integral to ensuring users can interact effectively with AR applications across diverse scenarios. More recently, studies have demonstrated the growing sophistication of AR experiences by comparing the UX of AR applications to conventional digital interfaces. Their research showed that AR can deliver enhanced engagement, particularly in areas like stimulation and novelty, which are key drivers for user satisfaction [35]. In their experiment involving the IKEA Place AR app, users reported higher levels of enjoyment and a deeper connection to the task, compared to traditional web interfaces. This highlights how AR can transform routine tasks into more immersive and engaging experiences, provided the system is easy to use and responsive. Another important aspect of UX in AR is the need for seamless interaction between digital and physical environments. It was also found that despite the advantages of AR in creating stimulating experiences, challenges remain in making the user interface both intuitive and powerful enough to handle complex interactions [35]. Ensuring that users can easily control the digital elements without experiencing frustration is essential for the widespread adoption of AR applications. In contrast to these evaluations, we try to conduct detailed qualitative interviews to evaluate the user experience.

2.4 Combining AR and Olfactory Devices

The integration of olfactory systems in HCI has seen significant advancements, with various innovative approaches aimed at enhancing user experiences through the incorporation of smell. Our research builds upon these by combining AR and olfaction within the context of restaurant menus. While previous systems have focused on general olfactory interactions, wearable technologies, or isolated scent delivery mechanisms [5,6,12,21,27,37,40], our study specifically targets the dining experience in restaurants. We aim to develop an AR olfactory menu application, ARoma, that integrates visual AR elements with advanced olfactory technology to create a comprehensive and immersive dining experience. This combines visual, informational, and olfactory elements to enhance customer engagement and satisfaction in restaurant settings. Unlike systems primarily focusing on scent diffusion or wearable technology, ARoma will leverage AR to provide a visual context for the olfactory experience. Furthermore, while generalized applications offer broad control over scent emission, our research narrows the focus to the specific needs and opportunities within the dining sector. By synthesizing the lessons learned from these diverse olfactory systems and applying them to the unique challenges of restaurant menus, we aim to create a novel, multi-sensory experience that enhances the dining process [16]. This integration of AR and olfaction in a practical, real-world context represents a significant step forward in applying olfactory HCI systems. A similar approach was employed in a study incorporating an advanced olfactory display system to enhance the sensory experience [23]. This system utilizes techniques to deliver precise and controlled scent emissions. The core of the olfactory display is based on a capillary arrangement and drive circuit, this allows for the controlled release of aromas corresponding to selected menu items. This system employs a heat-based approach for scent dispersion, chosen for its simplicity and cost-effectiveness. Temperature-controlled phase transitions in polymers regulate the release of essential oils and other aromatic compounds. The olfactory display is designed to be compact and easily integrated into the dining table setup, with wireless Bluetooth connectivity allowing seamless communication with the Virtual Food Menu (VFM) application [23]. This sophisticated olfactory system enables the creation of controlled bursts of scents with varying intensities, providing users with a nuanced and immersive aromatic experience that complements the visual AR elements of the virtual menu.

3   Design Process

The design process for ARoma involved several steps. Initially, we designed a mobile based AR menu application incorporating integral design features such as 3D visualizations and information overlays. This was followed by the creation of the prototype of an olfactory device allowing customers to experience the aromas of the AR menu dishes. Finally, to integrate the olfactory device with the AR menu, we switched from the mobile application to a kiosk-style setup for ARoma.

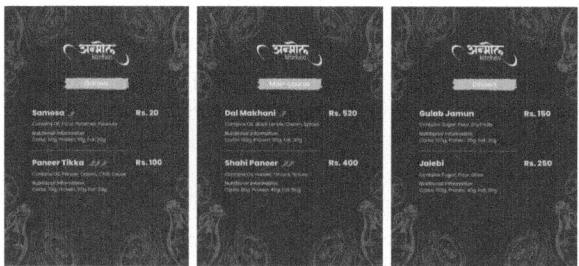

Fig. 1. Traditional Restaurant menu

3.1   AR Menu Application

The AR menu application was designed to offer users an engaging and informative restaurant dining experience to customers. The menu leverages AR to present users with interactive 3D visualizations of various food items in the menu, along with displaying detailed information about the ingredients and nutritional value of each dish. The application also delves into the cultural history behind it. This immersive approach aims to enhance customer engagement and facilitate informed decision-making. Our prototype for the AR menu consisted of three dishes of Indian cuisine namely Samosa, Dal Makhni and Gulab Jamun (refer Fig. 2).

Design Features: The key design features of the interactive AR menu application include the 3-dimensional representation of food items and the digital informative overlays highlighting ingredients, nutritional information and cultural significance of the dishes. It also focuses on the emotional and sensory aspects of dining, aiming to evoke a sense of excitement and anticipation through the immersive AR interface.

The 3D assets for the food items were sourced from Sketchfab [34]. These 3D assets were superimposed on the respective dish menu cards, with each menu card displaying the corresponding dish in the AR menu (refer Fig. 3). By utilizing these assets, we could accurately represent a diverse variety of dishes in our AR menu prototype. This aspect of virtual plating adds a new dimension to the dining experience, enabling users to engage with the menu more tangibly and interactively. The 3D representations of the dishes provide customers with accurate information about the size, colour, texture and presentation of the actual dishes. Moreover, the 3D assets in the AR menu were designed to rotate, allowing users to view the dish from all angles and see it in its entirety. This immersive feature helps customers make more informed decisions and feel a deeper connection to the cuisine.

Fig. 2. Menu cards which act as AR markers

It can be challenging to include extensive textual information in traditional printed menus (refer to Fig. 1) without leading to a cluttered and visually overwhelming user experience. There is less scope for including text-heavy information such as cultural significance of a dish in printed menus. In contrast, including interactive and informative digital overlays within the AR menu prototype overcomes these limitations. The application displays these overlays using different buttons. The AR interface displays the name of the food item along with its price. The overlays offer insights into the ingredients, nutritional value, and cultural value of the food dish. They further enhance the user experience by allowing information to be easily accessible, interactive, and visually engaging, in contrast to traditional menus. For instance, the use of buttons ensures a clean and organized display of information, reducing cognitive load compared to text-heavy paper menus. Our AR menu prototype prominently displays a label indicating whether each dish is vegetarian or non-vegetarian. A spice level indicator is also included to consider individuals with different levels of spice tolerance (ref Fig. 4).

Including the list of ingredients in the dishes on the menu was crucial for several reasons. Providing detailed information about the ingredients ensures that users can make informed choices about ordering food items that align with their dietary needs and preferences. This feature also acknowledges and respects religious nutritional restrictions, ensuring that users with specific religious beliefs can navigate the menu in adherence to their religious dietary practices. Additionally, this is particularly helpful for those who have allergies to specific food items or ingredients, as they can conveniently identify and avoid potential allergens. While the AR menu serves the functional purpose of highlighting various allergens, it also contributes to a sense of safety and assurance for users, which is an emotional aspect often overlooked in traditional dining experiences. The immediate visual display of this information through AR enhances user trust and confidence in their food choices, bridging a crucial gap between data and experience.

The dish's nutritional value includes calories, carbohydrates, fat, and protein. Providing this information empowers users to make healthier choices and promotes transparency and accountability, ensuring that users know the nutritional content of their chosen dishes. When users are made fully aware of what they are consuming, it enhances their dining experience by reducing uncertainty and fostering confidence in their eating choices. AR's capability to visually present nutritional data, such as trans fats or fiber content, provides an enhanced user experience that goes beyond static descriptions, making it easier for users to comprehend and act upon the information. This feature supports health-conscious decision-making in an engaging and interactive format, unlike traditional menus, which can be overwhelming with textual data.

The AR menu also displays the cultural importance of the food items. Exploring the historical background of menu items adds depth and context to the dining experience. It allows users to appreciate different dishes' cultural significance and heritage. This enhances the dining experience by fostering a deeper connection to the cuisine and its origins. This section talks explicitly about the dish's origin, as many dishes have deep-rooted ties to specific regions, each with its culinary traditions and flavours. By highlighting the regional significance of menu items, users gain insights into the diverse culinary landscape.

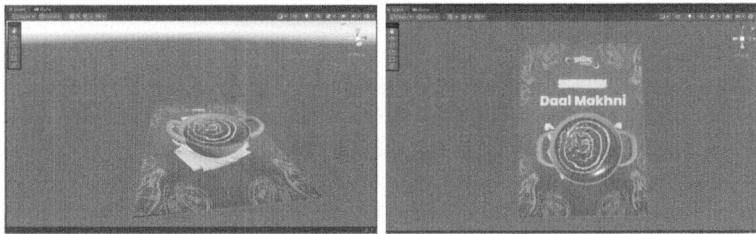

Fig. 3. 3D visualisation of Dal Makhni in ARoma

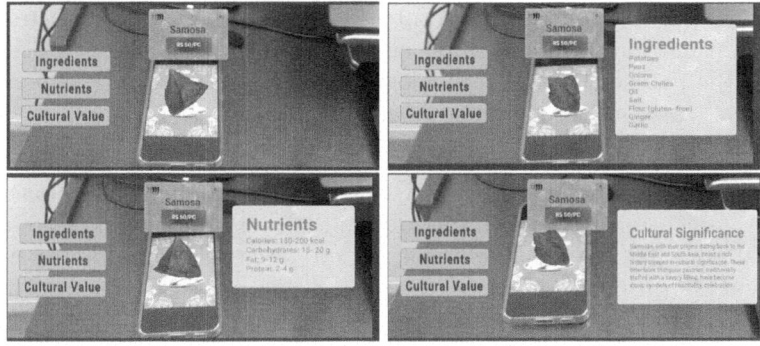

Fig. 4. Samosa in ARoma with buttons for ingredients, nutrients and cultural value

Mobile Application (Prototype 1): The initial prototype of the AR menu was developed as a mobile application, aiming to provide a personal and portable dining enhancement tool. The mobile app enabled users to interact with 3D models of food items and access detailed information overlays through their smartphones. The user interface featured intuitive buttons for revealing dish names, prices, ingredients, nutritional values, and cultural backgrounds. This initial prototype focused on creating an engaging and informative dining experience by allowing users to visualize and learn about their food choices directly from their mobile devices, promoting informed decision-making and enhancing overall satisfaction. Additionally, the mobile application was designed to evoke positive emotional responses through its interactive elements, offering a sense of novelty and discovery as users explored the various AR features.

Kiosk Application (Prototype 2): After the mobile application's initial testing phase, we identified the potential to further enhance the dining experience by integrating an olfaction device, which was not feasible with the mobile application due to technical and logistical constraints. To achieve this, we transitioned to developing a kiosk-like application. This stationary setup allowed us to integrate the olfaction device with the AR menu, enabling users to experience the aroma of the dishes along with the visual and informational AR features.

The kiosk application retained all the interactive features of the mobile prototype, with additional sensory engagement through the olfaction device. This setup provided a more immersive and holistic dining experience, where users could see, learn about, and even experience the aroma of the dishes before ordering. The larger interface of the kiosk also allowed for a more detailed and user-friendly interaction, catering to a broader audience in a restaurant setting. An important use case for this kiosk setup could be its deployment in restaurants as a fun and engaging element for customers. Such a setup not only enhances the dining experience but also serves as a unique attraction, drawing in customers interested in a novel way to explore the menu. Such a setup can distinguish restaurants from their competitors, potentially increasing customer satisfaction.

By iterating from a mobile application to a kiosk application, we aimed to maximize the potential of AR technology in enhancing the dining experience to increase user satisfaction and engagement.

Technical Implementation. The AR menu application was developed using the Unity game engine [39], with the Vuforia SDK [2] enabling marker-based AR functionality of ARoma. For the mobile prototype, users could interact with 3D models and information overlays on their smartphones, designed using Figma [1]. In transitioning to the kiosk version, we integrated additional hardware, such as a screen display and an olfaction device, to enhance sensory engagement. This required synchronizing visual and olfactory outputs to maintain an intuitive interface while expanding the immersive dining experience.

3.2   Olfaction Device

The prototype of the olfaction device was devised to bring the idea to life using a plastic container, cardboard, a motor, Arduino, and scents from various food items. The process involved enclosing a sample of the scent-spreading substance within a partitioned container with an open front and a perforated back (refer Fig. 5). This feature is activated based on the dish chosen by the user and released the corresponding scents to provide a multi-sensory dining experience. The idea stemmed from the understanding that food selection is not solely based on visual appeal, but also other sensory stimuli, significantly the aroma of the food item. [24]. The scent disposal mechanism in the prototype operates by having different sections for each dish's scent. We carefully selected fragrances that represent the Indian experience in some way. Each fragrance was meant to transport users to culturally significant moments. The scents are created using spices, essential

Fig. 5. A prototype of the olfaction device with ingredients of dishes for the scents. The lid has a servo motor attached for its rotation which is controlled using an Arduino.

oils, or ingredients that have distinctive smells specific to the dishes. Once the user views a dish on the AR menu, it triggers the Arduino to rotate the lid of the cylindrical olfaction device, positioning the corresponding section with the dish's scent in the open area. This allows users to experience the aroma of the dish.

4   Methodology

To investigate the impact of ARoma on customers perceptions of food quality and dining enjoyment, we designed a controlled experiment involving two groups of participants (refer Fig. 6). The study aimed to compare traditional menus, AR menus, and ARoma (AR menus with olfactory integration).

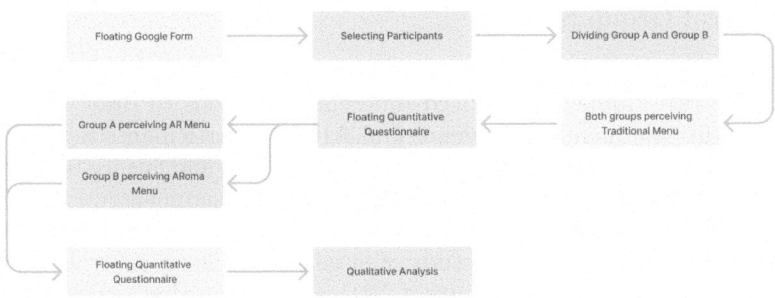

Fig. 6. Flow Diagram of the User Study

4.1   Participants

We floated a Google form across various social media platforms and community groups to recruit participants for our control group study. The form collected basic demographic information and asked if the individual would like to participate in the study. Individuals who volunteered by submitting the form were contacted and invited to participate. A total of 30 participants were recruited for the study out of which 17 were female and 13 were male. The participants were randomly divided into two groups of 15 each, ensuring that both groups had a diverse representation of participants in terms of age and gender. The demographic information can be found in Table 1. All participants had prior experience dining in restaurants but had varied familiarity with AR technology. Given the exploratory nature of our study and the aim to gather preliminary insights, this pilot study was designed with a relatively small sample size of 30 participants to test the feasibility and initial impact of ARoma. The small sample size, while limiting generalizability, was appropriate for this phase and provides a foundation for larger-scale studies to validate and expand upon these findings.

Table 1. Demographic Information of Study Participants

Group	Female	Male	Average Age
Total Participants	17	13	28.8
Group A	9	6	29.66666667
Group B	8	7	27.93333333

4.2   Control Group Study

The study was conducted in a controlled environment simulating a restaurant setting. The two groups experienced different conditions to draw comparisons between traditional menus, AR menus and ARoma. Participants were randomly assigned to one of two groups to mitigate selection bias and ensure balanced representation of demographic variables. The random assignment was carried out using a computerized randomization procedure to maintain fairness and control over group characteristics. The study was conducted in a controlled environment designed to simulate a restaurant setting, ensuring that external variables did not influence participants' experiences. The same quantitative questionnaire was used for both the groups to maintain consistency in how the participants experiences were measured.

Group A: Participants in Group A were first presented with the traditional menu consisting of Indian cuisine dishes. They were given sufficient time to review the menu and make their perceptions based on the textual descriptions and static images provided. Once they completed this task, participants were asked to fill out the quantitative questionnaire (refer Table 2) assessing their experiences with the traditional menu. Next, the participants were introduced to the AR menu mobile application. They were guided on how to use the AR application to view the 3D representations of the dishes and explore the additional information about each dish (ref Fig. 7). After reviewing the AR menu, participants were asked to fill out the same quantitative questionnaire regarding their experiences with the AR menu. Finally, we evaluated the user experience through detailed qualitative interviews to gather in-depth feedback and insights into their experiences with both menu types.

Group B: Participants in Group B followed a similar procedure with the addition of olfactory enhancement in ARoma. Initially, they were presented with the traditional menu and given time to review and evaluate it. They filled out the quantitative questionnaire assessing their experiences with the traditional menu once they were done. Next, participants were introduced to the ARoma setup. They were instructed on using ARoma to visualize the dishes in 3D, access detailed information, and experience the olfactory device that emitted the corresponding scents of the dishes. After interacting with ARoma, participants were asked to fill out the same quantitative questionnaire about their experiences ARoma. Finally, we captured the user experiences of the users through qualitative interviews were conducted to delve deeper into their experiences and gather detailed feedback on the impact of the multi-sensory experience.

Fig. 7. AR Menu user study with a participant

5   Results

5.1   Quantitative Results

The quantitative analysis of the study was done using a Likert scale based questionnaire (refer Table 2). To analyze the quantitative data collected from the

Table 2. Quantitative Interview Questions and Rating Scale

S.No	Interview Questions	Scale (1 to 10)
1	How would you rate the visual appeal of the menu?	1 (Very Poor) to 10 (Excellent)
2	How easy was it to understand the dish descriptions on the menu?	1 (Very Difficult) to 10 (Very Easy)
3	How satisfied are you with the amount of information provided about the dishes (ingredients, nutritional content etc.) on the menu?	1 (Very Unsatisfied) to 10 (Very Satisfied)
4	How well do you think the menu conveys the portion size of the dishes?	1 (Very Poorly) to 10 (Very Well)
5	How well does the menu convey to you the texture, colour and presentation of the dishes?	1 (Very Poorly) to 10 (Very Well)
6	How would you rate your overall dining enjoyment, immersivity, and engagement with the menu?	1(Very Poor) to 10 (Very enjoyable, immersive and engaging)

Likert scale-based questionnaires, statistics were calculated, including mean and standard deviation for each menu type (traditional, AR, ARoma). To assess the significance of the differences in participants' perceptions between the different menu types, a paired sample t-test was conducted. This test was used to compare the scores from the traditional menu with those from the AR menu in Group A and with ARoma in Group B (refer to Tables 3 and 4). This method was chosen because the same participants rated both menu types within each group, making it necessary to use a paired sample t-Test. The paired sample t-Test allowed us to evaluate whether the differences in mean scores between the traditional menu and the AR/ARoma menus were statistically significant. The average scores shown for each participant represent the average scores for the six Likert based questions asked to the participants. The quantitative analysis reveals a significant difference in the participants' perceptions and satisfaction between traditional menus, AR menus and ARoma.

In Group A, where participants were exposed to both traditional and AR menus, the average score for the traditional menu was 5.72, while the AR menu received a significantly higher average score of 8.2 (refer Table 3). This indicates a notable improvement in the overall dining experience when using AR, and had a p value of 9.27×10^{-11}. This extremely low p-value indicates a highly significant difference, suggesting that the AR menu greatly enhanced participants' dining experience compared to the traditional menu. Similarly, in Group B, which compared traditional menus with ARoma, the traditional menu received an average score of 5.82, whereas ARoma achieved an even higher average score of 8.97 (refer Table 4). Group B indicated a p value of 7.48×10^{-11}, which also reflects a significant improvement in the overall dining experience when olfactory stimuli were added to the AR menu. These results suggest that the AR and ARoma menus significantly enhance participants' perceptions of food quality, ease of under-standing dish descriptions, satisfaction with the information provided, and the overall dining experience, including visual appeal, engagement, and immersivity.

To determine if there was a significant difference between the experiences of participants in Group A (AR menu) and Group B (ARoma menu), a t-test was conducted. This method was chosen as it does not assume equal variances between the two groups, making it more appropriate for our data, where vari-ances might differ due to the different sensory experiences offered by AR and ARoma. The comparison between Group A's AR menu scores and Group B's ARoma scores resulted in a p-value of 4.50×10^{-5}, indicating a statistically sig-nificant difference between the two groups. This suggests that adding olfactory stimuli in the ARoma menu further enhanced participants' perceptions and sat-isfaction compared to the AR menu alone. A summary of the p-values from the statistical tests conducted can be found in Table 5.

Table 3. Average Quantitative Scores out of 10 and Standard Deviations for Group A (Traditional Menu vs. AR Menu)

Participant No.	Traditional Menu (Avg. Score)	AR Menu (Avg. Score)
1	5.67	9.17
2	5.67	7.33
3	5.83	8.50
4	6.00	8.83
5	6.67	8.17
6	5.33	8.17
7	5.50	8.17
8	6.00	8.17
9	5.33	8.00
10	5.33	8.33
11	6.00	8.00
12	5.83	7.67
13	6.17	8.33
14	5.50	8.50
15	5.00	7.67
Mean Score	5.72	8.20
Standard Deviation (SD)	0.42	0.46

5.2 Qualitative Results

The participants were interviewed after experiencing both the traditional menu and the AR menu (Group A), or the traditional menu and ARoma (Group

Table 4. Average Quantitative Scores out of 10 and Standard Deviations for Group B (Traditional Menu vs. ARoma)

Participant No.	Traditional Menu (Avg. Score)	ARoma (Avg. Score)
16	5.83	9.50
17	6.33	8.17
18	5.00	9.00
19	5.83	9.17
20	5.50	8.33
21	6.33	8.83
22	6.00	9.67
23	6.00	8.67
24	5.00	9.17
25	5.67	9.17
26	5.83	8.83
27	6.83	8.67
28	5.33	8.83
29	6.00	9.50
30	5.83	9.17
Mean	5.82	8.98
Standard Deviation (SD)	0.49	0.42

Table 5. Summary of p-values from Statistical Tests

Comparison	Statistical Test	p-value
Group A: Traditional Menu vs. AR Menu	Paired Sample t-Test	9.27×10^{-11}
Group B: Traditional Menu vs. ARoma	Paired Sample t-Test	7.48×10^{-11}
Group A: AR Menu vs. Group B: ARoma	t-Test	4.50×10^{-5}

B). The interviews were recorded and transcribed for a detailed content analysis. The interview transcripts were coded to identify recurring themes related to immersivity, engagement, decision-making, and the role of olfaction. The themes identified were Visual Appeal and Engagement, Information Richness, Immersivity, Role of Olfaction and Overall Enjoyment and Satisfaction.

Visual Appeal and Engagement: Participant 1 from Group A noted, "The traditional menu was just text and a few pictures. It wasn't very engaging. I couldn't really imagine what the dish would look like or how much food there would be." In contrast, Participant 2, also from Group A, remarked, "The AR menu was amazing! The 3D images made the dishes look so real. I spent more time looking at the menu because it was so interactive." This sentiment was echoed by Participant 16 from Group B, who stated, "The addition of smell made it even more engaging. It was like I could almost taste the food just by smelling it."

Information Richness: Participants frequently mentioned the limited information available in traditional menus. Participant 4 from Group A said, "The traditional menu didn't give much information about the dish's ingredients. I didn't learn anything about the history or cultural significance of the dishes." However, Participant 5, who used the AR menu, commented, "The AR menu provided so much more information, like the ingredients and nutritional facts. I loved learning about the history of the dishes. It made the dining experience richer." Similarly, Participant 18 from Group B, who used ARoma, noted, "With ARoma, I got all the details plus the smell. It was a complete sensory experience."

Immersivity: Participant 7 from Group A described the traditional menu as "just functional. It didn't add to the dining experience." They further mentioned, "It was just reading and choosing. Nothing immersive about it." Conversely, Participant 8 from Group A stated, "The AR menu made me feel more connected to the food. Seeing the dishes in 3D was like a preview of the meal." This was further enhanced in Group B, as Participant 20 highlighted, "ARoma was something else. The smells combined with the visuals made it feel like the dish was right in front of me, even before I ordered it."

Multi-sensory Experience: Participant 10 from Group A noted, "The AR menu was great for visualizing the food, but I think adding smell would take it to the next level." This addition was particularly appreciated by Group B participants. Participant 22 remarked, "The olfactory element was incredible. It triggered memories and made me more excited about the food." Participant 25 added, "The smell made it feel so real. It wasn't just about seeing the food; it was about experiencing it even before it arrived."

Overall Satisfaction: Participant 13 from Group A summed up their experience by saying, "The AR menu definitely made the dining experience better. I felt more informed and engaged." Group B participants expressed even higher satisfaction. Participant 28 commented, "ARoma was a game-changer. The combination of visuals and smells made dining so much more enjoyable. It was immersive and informative, and I felt more connected to the dishes."

The qualitative analysis indicates that both AR and ARoma significantly enhance the dining experience by providing more detailed information, increasing engagement, and creating a more immersive and multi-sensory environment. The olfactory element in ARoma, in particular, played a significant role in enhancing the overall immersivity and enjoyment of the dining experience.

6   Discussion and Future Work

6.1   Interpreting the Impact of AR Menu on Customer Perceptions

Our first research question (RQ1) aimed to understand how the experience provided by our AR menu affects customers' perceptions of food quality and dining enjoyment compared to traditional menus. The quantitative results clearly demonstrate a significant preference for AR menus over traditional ones, with Group A participants rating AR menus considerably higher (8.2) than traditional menus (5.72).

This substantial difference in ratings aligns with previous studies that show AR menus enhance engagement, information richness, and decision-making processes compared to traditional menus [4,7,29]. AR menu's ability to present dishes in a more vivid and interactive manner appears to create a more compelling and enjoyable menu-browsing experience. These results are consistent with findings from earlier AR applications in restaurant settings, which also noted that AR technology improves customer interaction with menu content and provides a more immersive experience [36]. For instance, applications that use AR to display 3D models and detailed nutritional information have been reported to increase customer satisfaction and support healthier dining choices [9,10]. The qualitative data further illuminates why AR menus were preferred. Participants consistently reported that our AR menus provided a more comprehensive understanding of dishes, their ingredients, and nutrients, allowing them to make more informed decisions. Moreover, including cultural context and historical significance of dishes added depth to the dining experience, connecting customers to the culinary heritage behind each meal. This enriched information not only educated diners but also enhanced their appreciation for the food's cultural roots. The increased information availability, encompassing nutritional facts and cultural narratives, seems to boost confidence in food choices and create a more meaningful dining context, potentially leading to higher satisfaction with the overall dining experience.

6.2   Evaluating the Multi-sensory Experience of ARoma

Our second research question (RQ2) explored how the multi-sensory experience provided by ARoma affects customers' perceptions compared to traditional menus. Adding olfactory stimuli to the AR experience further amplified the positive effects observed with visual AR alone, as evidenced by the even higher ratings for ARoma (8.97) compared to traditional menus (5.82) in Group B.

This significant improvement highlights the synergistic effect of combining visual and olfactory stimuli, creating a more immersive and realistic representation of dishes. This finding is in line with research that combines AR with other emerging technologies, such as olfactory displays, to enhance user experience by engaging multiple senses [5,6,21,23,27]. The multi-sensory preview provided by ARoma seems to create a more immersive and realistic representation of dishes, potentially leading to heightened expectations and enjoyment of the actual meal.

The qualitative data reveals that the olfactory component adds depth to the dining experience by engaging emotions and memories. This emotional engagement appears to create a more profound connection to the food, potentially influencing not just immediate perceptions but also long-term memories of the dining experience. Furthermore, the increased excitement reported by participants using ARoma indicates that the multi-sensory preview builds anticipation for the meal. These results are consistent with other studies that emphasize the potential of olfactory integration to create immersive and memorable experiences in HCI systems [12, 16, 37, 40]. The inclusion of scent appears to not only improve immediate perceptions but may also positively impact long-term memories of the dining experience.

While it is true that information such as portion sizes and textual information like cultural backgrounds and nutritional information can be presented through traditional printed menus, the addition of AR in this study provided an immersive and interactive dimension that text alone cannot achieve. For example, participants could visually gauge portion sizes through 3D representations and experience the cultural essence of dishes not only through text but also through sensory engagement, which added depth to their understanding and appreciation. Additionally, the AR interface allows for a cleaner and more organized user experience compared to printed menus. Information can be layered and accessed through intuitive buttons, enabling users to explore details such as ingredients, cultural backgrounds, or dish preparation methods without cluttering the main menu display.

Moreover, our study sought to address the gap in existing research on olfactory systems by focusing on the dining experience in restaurants. While the previous systems explored in our literature review concentrate on general olfactory interactions, wearable technologies, or isolated scent delivery mechanisms [5, 6, 12, 21, 27, 37, 40], our study aimed to integrate these in an AR based menu specifically tailored for restaurants. The results of our study confirm that such a system - ARoma - significantly enhances the dining experience by providing a more immersive, engaging, and informative interaction with the menu.

6.3   Practical Implications

The implications of AR and olfactory technologies extend beyond enhancing customer engagement. They also have practical benefits for the restaurant industry. AR menus can provide valuable information, such as nutritional content, allergen information, and ingredient breakdowns without overwhelming the user with textual data, and directly at the point of decision, promoting healthier eating habits [9, 10]. Furthermore, by creating interactive and culturally enriched dining experiences, these technologies can cater to the growing consumer demand for more personalized and informative dining options.

ARoma, in particular, has the potential to revolutionize how diners perceive and select their meals, making it a valuable tool for restaurants aiming to differentiate themselves in a competitive market. This aligns with industry trends that favor technological innovation to enhance customer satisfaction and loyalty.

6.4   Future Implications

Moving forward, our development will focus primarily on refining the olfactory delivery mechanisms of ARoma. We plan to expand the application's content to include a broader spectrum of cuisines and dietary preferences, making ARoma more inclusive and adaptable to diverse user needs. This approach aims to address the gap in AR menu research for diverse food cultures, such as Indian cuisine, which remains under-explored in AR applications [18, 25]. Another potential enhancement involves adapting the prototype to a more sophisticated scent dispersal system. This would be possible by exploring specific diffusion techniques to release and absorb the smell. This would help in reducing the amount of smell that is released [40]. Additionally, integrating an ultrasonic sensor to detect user presence would activate the device, ensuring the scent reaches the user precisely when needed. This setup would allow for controlled and efficient scent dispersal, providing a more immersive and engaging dining experience.

Moreover, our current study does not fully capture the depth of qualitative insights regarding user experiences. To address this gap, we plan to conduct an in-depth focus group study to gain a more comprehensive understanding of user preferences and interactions. This approach will help us refine the design and functionality of ARoma to better meet diverse and evolving user expectations.

7   Conclusion

The clear preference for AR menus and ARoma over traditional menus observed in this study has significant implications for the restaurant industry and dining experiences. These technologies have the potential to enhance customer engagement, improve decision-making, and create more memorable dining experiences. By providing rich visual and olfactory information, ARoma could lead to increased customer satisfaction and potentially influence dining habits and culinary appreciation on a broader scale. Its ability to integrate cultural, nutritional, and olfactory information represents a novel step forward in restaurant technology, promoting inclusivity and health consciousness. As these technologies continue to develop, they may reshape the landscape of the restaurant industry and our relationship with culinary experiences.

References

1. Figma (2024). https://www.figma.com. Accessed 20 July 2024
2. Home - engine developer portal. https://developer.vuforia.com/. Accessed 20 July 2024
3. Ahn, S., Santosa, S., Parent, M., Wigdor, D., Grossman, T., Giordano, M.: Stickypie: A gaze-based, scale-invariant marking menu optimized for ar/vr. In: Proceedings of the 2021 CHI Conference on Human Factors in Computing Systems, pp. 1–16 (2021)

4. Amin, S.N., Shivakumara, P., Jun, T.X., Chong, K.Y., Zan, D.L.L., Rahavendra, R.: An augmented reality-based approach for designing interactive food menu of restaurant using android. In: Artificial Intelligence and Applications, vol. 1, pp. 26–34 (2023)
5. Amores, J., Maes, P.: Essence: Olfactory interfaces for unconscious influence of mood and cognitive performance. In: Proceedings of the 2017 CHI Conference on Human Factors in Computing Systems, pp. 28–34 (2017)
6. Amores Fernandez, J.: Olfactory interfaces: toward implicit human-computer interaction across the consciousness continuum. Ph.D. thesis, Massachusetts Institute of Technology (2020)
7. Arioputra, D., Lin, C.H.: Mobile augmented reality as a chinese menu translator. In: 2015 IEEE International Conference on Consumer Electronics-Taiwan, pp. 7–8. IEEE (2015)
8. Balani, M.S., Tümler, J.: Usability and user experience of interactions on vr-pc, hololens 2, vr cardboard and ar smartphone in a biomedical application. In: Chen, J.Y.C., Fragomeni, G. (eds.) Virtual, Augmented and Mixed Reality: 13th International Conference, VAMR 2021, Held as Part of the 23rd HCI International Conference, HCII 2021, Virtual Event, July 24–29, 2021, Proceedings, pp. 275–287. Springer International Publishing, Cham (2021). https://doi.org/10.1007/978-3-030-77599-5_20
9. Balasubramanian, K., Konar, R.: Moving forward with augmented reality menu: changes in food consumption behaviour patterns (2022)
10. Balasubramanian, K., Kunasekaran, P., Konar, R., Sakkthivel, A.M.: Integration of augmented reality (AR) and virtual reality (VRd) as marketing communications channels in the hospitality and tourism service sector. In: Adeola, O., E. Hinson, R., Sakkthivel, A.M. (eds.) Marketing Communications and Brand Development in Emerging Markets Volume II: Insights for a Changing World, pp. 55–79. Springer International Publishing, Cham (2022). https://doi.org/10.1007/978-3-030-95581-6_3
11. Batat, W.: How augmented reality (ar) is transforming the restaurant sector: Investigating the impact of 'le petit chef" on customers' dining experiences. Technol. Forecast. Soc. Chang. **172**, 121013 (2021)
12. Brooks, J., Lopes, P.: Smell & paste: Low-fidelity prototyping for olfactory experiences. In: Proceedings of the 2023 CHI Conference on Human Factors in Computing Systems, pp. 1–16 (2023)
13. Carmigniani, J., Furht, B., Anisetti, M., Ceravolo, P., Damiani, E., Ivkovic, M.: Augmented reality technologies, systems and applications. Multimedia Tools Appl. **51**, 341–377 (2011)
14. Erkoyuncu, J., Khan, S.: Olfactory-based augmented reality support for industrial maintenance. IEEE Access **8**, 30306–30321 (2020)
15. Filimonau, V., Krivcova, M.: Restaurant menu design and more responsible consumer food choice: An exploratory study of managerial perceptions. J. Clean. Prod. **143**, 516–527 (2017)
16. Fiore, A.M., Yah, X., Yoh, E.: Effects of a product display and environmental fragrancing on approach responses and pleasurable experiences. Psychol. Market. **17**(1), 27–54 (2000)
17. Irshad, S., Rambli, D.R.A.: User experience evaluation of mobile ar services. In: Proceedings of the 12th International Conference on Advances in Mobile Computing and Multimedia, pp. 119–126 (2014)
18. Jain, A., Bagler, G.: Culinary evolution models for Indian cuisines. Phys. A **503**, 170–176 (2018)

19. Kuo, F.F., Li, C.T., Shan, M.K., Lee, S.Y.: Intelligent menu planning: Recommending set of recipes by ingredients. In: Proceedings of the ACM Multimedia 2012 Workshop on Multimedia for Cooking and Eating Activities, pp. 1–6 (2012)
20. Lacoche, J., Villain, E., Foulonneau, A.: Evaluating usability and user experience of ar applications in vr simulation. Front. Virt. Real. **3**, 881318 (2022)
21. Lei, Y., Lu, Q., Xu, Y.: O&o: A diy toolkit for designing and rapid prototyping olfactory interfaces. In: Proceedings of the 2022 CHI Conference on Human Factors in Computing Systems, pp. 1–21 (2022)
22. Maggioni, E., Cobden, R., Dmitrenko, D., Hornbk, K., Obrist, M.: Smell space: mapping out the olfactory design space for novel interactions. ACM Transact. Comput.-Human Interact. (TOCHI) **27**(5), 1–26 (2020)
23. Magrey, B.S., Chauhan, A., Ramneet: Enhancing dining experiences: Virtual food menu with aroma dispenser integration. In: 2023 Global Conference on Information Technologies and Communications (GCITC), pp. 1–5 (2023). https://doi.org/10.1109/GCITC60406.2023.10426287
24. Miotto, L.: Using scents to connect to intangible heritage: engaging the visitor olfactory dimension: three museum exhibition case studies. In: 2016 22nd International Conference on Virtual System & Multimedia (VSMM), pp. 1–5. IEEE (2016)
25. Nanjangud, A., Reddy, M.: The test of taste': New media and the 'progressive Indian foodscape. J. Creative Commun. **15**(2), 177–193 (2020)
26. Nazmi, N.A.M., Rizhan, W., Rahim, N.: Developing and evaluating ar for food ordering system based on technological acceptance evaluation approach: a case study of restaurant's menu item selection. Int. J. Eng. Trends Technol. **70**(5), 1–8 (2022)
27. Niedenthal, S., Fredborg, W., Lundén, P., Ehrndal, M., Olofsson, J.K.: A graspable olfactory display for virtual reality. Int. J. Hum Comput Stud. **169**, 102928 (2023)
28. Olsson, T., Lagerstam, E., Kärkkäinen, T., Väänänen-Vainio-Mattila, K.: Expected user experience of mobile augmented reality services: a user study in the context of shopping centres. Pers. Ubiquit. Comput. **17**, 287–304 (2013)
29. Rane, P., Usmani, A.: Digital food menu application for restaurants based on augmented reality. Int. Res. J. Eng. Technol. **8**(3), 2651–2654 (2021)
30. Reddy, A.D., Nath, A.K., Aditya, T., Kumar, A., Sebastian, A.: Menu guide: An ar application for smartphones. Int. Res. J. Comput. Sci. (IRJCS) **6**(06) (2019)
31. Ritsos, P.D., Ritsos, D.P., Gougoulis, A.S.: Standards for augmented reality: a user experience perspective. In: International AR Standards Meeting, pp. 1–9 (2011)
32. Rodrigues, J.M., Ramos, C.M., Pereira, J.A., Sardo, J.D., Cardoso, P.J.: Mobile five senses augmented reality system: technology acceptance study. IEEE access **7**, 163022–163033 (2019)
33. Rule, A.F.: Food labeling; nutrition labeling of standard menu items in restaurants and similar retail food establishments (2014)
34. Sketchfab: Sketchfab (2023). https://sketchfab.com/. Accessed 20 July 2024
35. Stumpp, S., Knopf, T., Michelis, D.: User experience design with augmented reality (ar). In: Proceedings of the ECIE 2019 14th European Conference on Innovation and Entrepreneurship, pp. 1032–1040 (2019)
36. TEJ, M.B., Bellam, K.: Augmented reality restaurant menu. Int. J. Comput. Sci. Eng. Inform. Technol. Res. **12**(1), 29–40 (2022)
37. Tomasi, D.: Olfactory virtual reality (ovr) for wellbeing and reduction of stress, anxiety and pain (2021)

38. Uma, R., Sirisha, U., Varshaa, V.: Marker based augmented reality food menu. In: 2022 1st International Conference on Computational Science and Technology (ICCST), pp. 967–971. IEEE (2022)
39. Unity Technologies: Unity (2023). https://www.unity.com Accessed 20 July 2024
40. Wang, Y., Cui, Z., Gong, H., Chen, T.: Olfackit: A toolkit for integrating atomization-based olfactory interfaces into daily scenarios. Int. J. Human–Comput. Interact., pp. 1–20 (2023)

Exploration of Gesture-Based Text Input System for Indic Languages

Amrita Das[✉][iD]

National Institute of Design, Gandhinagar, India
amritadas1302@gmail.com

Abstract. Many innovative text input methods exist but are scarce in Indian languages. In this paper, we aim to explore a novel text input method for the Malayalam language. This method is gesture-based, where specific hand movements using the natural demarcations of the hand are mapped to particular characters, which enables typing. This is implemented using an image processing program to track key points on our hands, which allows us to distinguish between different gestures accurately. We conducted a study to identify which gestures provide higher accuracy, and least confusion. Using the results, we mapped the gestures to Malayalam and conducted an empirical longitudinal study, which analyzed the speed and accuracy of this prototype. This method yielded a 40+ CPM, which is comparable to similar text input studies in other languages. This technology can be further developed to assist users in various ways, such as providing a communication guide or aiding in daily activities.

Keywords: Indic Text Input · Computer Vision · Longitudinal Study

1 Introduction

Designers have grappled with the challenge of creating an effective text input system for Indic scripts since the advent of typewriters, continuing into the current era of computers and mobile devices.

Here, we aim to investigate an alternative text input method that goes beyond the conventional keyboard. In the initial phase of our research, we examined a set of 16 potential gestures to determine their suitability for our proposed input method. Utilizing a confusion matrix, we assessed the accuracy of each gesture, allowing us to identify those that met our criteria for acceptability. Following this selection process, we mapped the identified gestures to the corresponding characters in the Malayalam script. To evaluate the efficacy of this text input system, we conducted an empirical longitudinal study, measuring its performance over time. Notably, our system achieved a characters per minute (CPM) rate of 40+, which is comparable to similar text input studies conducted in other languages. However, we acknowledge that we currently lack sufficient data for direct comparisons with studies specifically focused on Malayalam. Thus, through this paper, we make the following contributions-

N. Rangaswamy et al. (Eds.): IndiaHCI 2024, CCIS 2338, pp. 226–243, 2025.
https://doi.org/10.1007/978-3-031-80832-6_16

- We present a confusion matrix that reveals the accuracy of various hand gestures for text input.
- We develop a system that effectively maps Malayalam characters to corresponding hand gestures.
- We evaluate the system's performance, achieving a character per minute (CPM) rate of 40+, comparable to similar studies in other languages.

2   Related Work

Text input is an extensive field of study in HCI. With the advent of mobile phones, there was a shift in research to virtual screens in the early 1990s. Early work involved the use of styluses. For example, Zhai et al. [14] proposed a method for touchscreen-based speed writing where users could learn shorthand gestures for words. With the advent of smartphones and virtual reality headsets, text input studies moved to these devices. Vertanen et al. [12] proposed a sentence-based text entry approach achieving a 41 CPM on a smartwatch-sized keyboard 40 mm wide for novice users.

In recent years, gesture-based text input systems have gained traction as innovative alternatives to traditional typing methods. One prominent example is iHand [4], which utilizes a hand gesture recognition algorithm to enable text input through simple gestures captured by a wearable device's RGB camera. Another approach involves the development of virtual keyboards and mice that operate based on hand movements, allowing users to perform actions like selecting characters and executing commands through gestures [11]. Additionally, systems like Tilt-based Gesture Keyboards facilitate single-handed text entry by detecting tilt movements, enhancing usability on larger devices [13]. Text input in the Virtual Reality(VR) world [3,9] is usually done with VR headsets and hand-held controllers.

While much research has been done in English text input studies, a lot still needs to be done in text input in Indian languages. Keyboard layouts for Indian languages began with the evolution of typewriters. The Inscript layout was the first specifically designed for Indian language computing, modeled after typewriter designs, and optimized for two-handed typing. The phonetic nature of Inscript allows a person who knows how to type in one Indian script to type in any other Indian script, making it easy to learn [1].

Another notable keyboard is Keylekh [6], which offers a unique structure for data input in Indic scripts, diverging from standard keyboard layouts. While Inscript can be challenging for first-time users, Keylekh's non-QWERTY design presents its difficulties.

As virtual keyboards became more prevalent, the Swarachakra keyboard [7], designed for typing in various Indic scripts, has gained popularity due to its usability for touch-screen devices. Other notable soft keyboards for Indian languages include the Unified Virtual Keyboard developed by C-DAC for the

Android platform, supporting multiple Indian languages, and the Indic Phonetic Keyboards introduced by Microsoft in Windows, allowing users to type in ten Indian languages using phonetic transliteration.

However, the current methods for text input in Indian languages still have limitations. The Inscript layout, while phonetic, can be difficult for first-time users, while Keylekh's non-QWERTY design may not be intuitive for those accustomed to standard keyboard layouts. The need for innovative text input methods in Indian languages arises from these limitations, as well as the growing demand for efficient and user-friendly typing solutions that can cater to a diverse user base and encourage greater participation in digital spaces.

Although these innovative methods are being developed, it is particularly difficult to create a Malayalam keyboard due to several reasons. The complex script of Malayalam, which includes numerous conjunct characters, poses significant challenges for keyboard design. These limitations underscore the need for alternative innovative text input systems for Malayalam that can provide a more efficient and user-friendly typing experience.

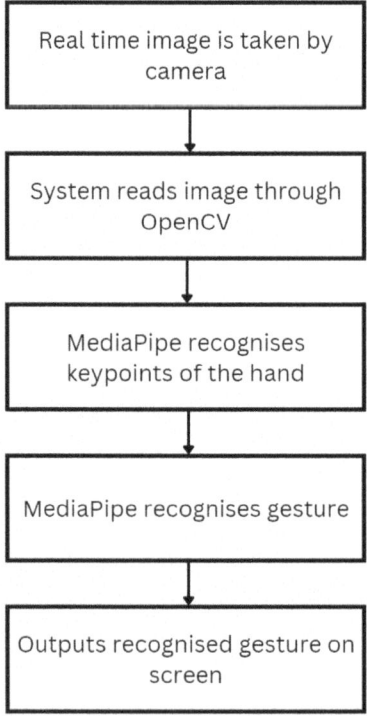

Fig. 1. System Flowchart

3 Proposed Model

This section presents the proposed model and the basic workflow of the system.

3.1 Flowchart

The workflow begins with the user making a hand gesture in front of a camera (a laptop webcam or an external camera). The camera captures the movements in real-time, and the images are processed using OpenCV, a computer vision library (Fig. 1). OpenCV provides advanced image processing techniques such as background subtraction, skin color detection, and contour analysis. These methods help accurately locate and track the hand in video frames, which is essential for recognizing gestures effectively in real time. Following this, MediaPipe is employed to recognize key points of the user's hand. Mediapipe Hands is a pre-trained machine learning library used to infer 21 3D landmarks of the hand from a single frame (Fig. 2). The library's robustness against occlusions and varying hand orientations enhances the accuracy of gesture recognition, even in challenging scenarios [15]. Each recognized point is then mapped to a predefined set of gestures that have been previously established within the system. Finally, the system outputs the recognized characters onto the screen, allowing the user to see the results of their gestures in real-time.

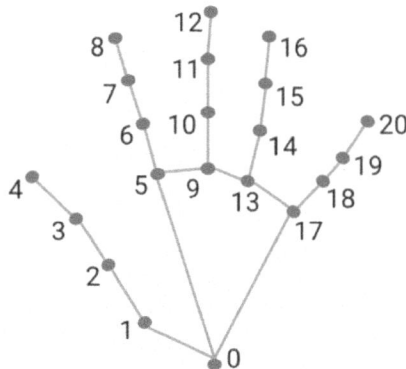

Fig. 2. 21 Key Points predefined in MediaPipe

3.2 Definition of Gestures

The following actions are proposed-

1. **Single Tap-** this is the simplest action that involves using the thumb to gently tap on one demarcation on a finger in the open palm of a hand. This action is proven to have the highest accuracy.

2. **Long Press**- the long press is the action where a tap is prolonged for longer than 1 s. This time interval can be changed, depending on what is convenient. The long press action works well for a few data points and can be used to accommodate more characters if necessary.
3. **Nail Tap**- for the nail tap, the user must use their thumb to tap the nail of their fingers in such a way that the folded finger is bent sufficiently.
4. **Closed Fist/Shift**- to accommodate more characters, one hand could be folded into a fist while the other is used to make the gestures alternatively.

To determine the optimal key points for mapping to Malayalam, we conducted a study and created a confusion matrix to evaluate the accuracy of gesture detection, allowing us to select the most accurate gestures.

4 Study 1 - Understanding Which Gestures are Better Identified

In this section, we conduct experimental testing in a real environment and assess the performance of our proposed system in terms of recognition, accuracy, and learnability. At this stage, we focus on recognizing the key points with higher accuracy and low error, so that we can use this system as a text input method for Malayalam later.

4.1 Users and Study Context

We recruited 20 participants (10 female, 10 male) aged 18 to 25 from the local university community. All participants were right-handed and had normal or corrected-to-normal vision. None reported any physical limitations that would affect their ability to perform hand gestures. Participants provided written informed consent and received a small monetary compensation for their time. In this study, we maintained consistent lighting conditions using overhead LED lights set to a cool color temperature (5000 K) to minimize glare on the screen. The camera used was a smartphone camera mounted on a phone stand positioned above the table, facing downwards (Fig. 3) to effectively capture the participants' hand movements while they interacted with the interface. Each participant was seated in a standard ergonomic chair, positioned 60 cm from the screen, with both hands placed flat on the table's surface. This setup ensured optimal visibility of the participants' hand movements and interactions, creating a controlled environment conducive to accurate data collection. Each participant was seated at a table facing a monitor displaying the gesture recognition system. The experimenter first explained the purpose of the study and demonstrated the 16 target gestures (see Fig. 4). Participants were then asked to place their open palms flat on the table, directly below the camera. Participants completed 16 trials, each consisting of performing a specific gesture with their hand against one of four colored backgrounds (red, green, black, and white). Left and right hands were consecutively used for each change of background. The order of gestures and background colors was randomized for each participant. As depicted

Table 1. Confusion Matrix Table

Actual \ Predicted	01	02	03	04	05	06	07	08	09	10	11	12	13	14	15	16
01	82	18	0	0	0	0	0	0	0	0	0	0	0	0	0	0
02	0	97	03	0	0	0	0	0	0	0	0	0	0	0	0	0
03	0	13	83	0	0	0	2	0	2	0	0	0	0	0	0	0
04	0	0	03	88	7	2	0	0	0	0	0	0	0	0	0	0
05	0	0	02	2	78	15	0	2	0	0	0	0	0	0	0	0
06	0	0	03	0	5	90	0	0	2	0	0	0	0	0	0	0
07	0	0	0	0	0	3	85	2	6	0	0	2	0	0	2	0
08	0	0	0	0	0	3	8	72	2	0	2	3	0	0	0	0
09	0	0	0	0	0	0	0	2	96	0	2	3	0	0	0	0
10	0	0	0	0	0	0	2	2	3	86	3	3	0	0	0	0
11	0	2	0	0	0	0	0	0	12	3	68	15	0	0	0	0
12	0	0	0	0	0	0	0	0	1	0	3	87	0	0	0	0
13	5	0	3	0	0	0	0	0	0	0	0	0	92	0	0	0
14	0	0	2	15	0	0	0	0	0	0	0	0	2	81	0	0
15	0	0	0	0	0	0	3	0	0	0	0	0	0	0	97	0
16	0	0	0	0	0	0	0	0	3	2	0	0	0	0	0	95

in Fig. 4, the 16 key points selected for this study were 01, 02, 03, 04, 05, 06, 07, 08, 09, 10, 11, 12 and the nail points 13, 14, 15, and 16. After each gesture, participants returned their hands to the resting position on the table. The experimenter verbally prompted participants to perform the next gesture in the sequence. The entire session lasted approximately 30 min per participant.

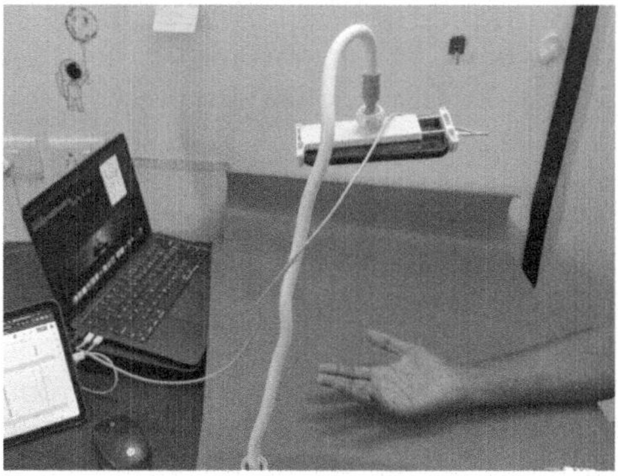

Fig. 3. Testing Setup

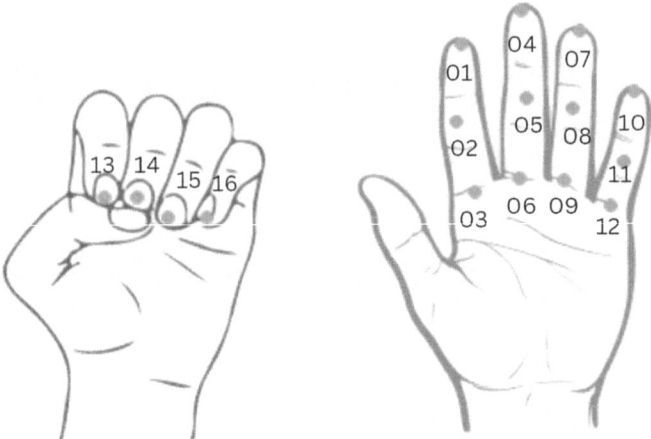

Fig. 4. Key points numbered

4.2   Confusion Matrix

In the context of our study on gesture recognition, the confusion matrix serves as a crucial tool for determining the most accurate gestures performed by participants. The diagonal elements of the matrix represent the instances where the predicted gestures match the actual gestures, indicating correct classifications. By analyzing these values, we can identify which gestures were recognized accurately and which ones were frequently misclassified.

4.3   Observations

- From Table 1, it was observed that gestures 02, 09, 13, 15 and 16 have the highest accuracy of >90%. These points are present either on the tip of the finger or the lowest point.
- Gestures 05, 08, and 11 have the lowest accuracy of <80%. These key points are in the middle of the middle, ring, and little finger respectively. This could be caused by inefficient depth perception due to the overlapping of the fingers.
- It was observed that there was no significant difference in the key point prediction due to the change in the background color. Mediapipe requires sufficient color contrast between the skin and the background [10], and in all 4 cases(white, black, green, and red), the contrast was sufficient.
- Some confusion was observed amongst users in the duration of the long press gesture, with users holding the gesture for longer than 1 s, which led to inaccurate predictions. Due to this observation, we decided to discard the long press action.

Using these observations, we selected the gestures with the highest accuracy and discarded those with low accuracy. From Table 2, the gestures highlighted in

Table 2. Gesture Accuracy Percentages

Accuracy Percentage

02	97
15	97
09	96
16	95
13	92
06	90
04	88
12	87
10	86
07	85
03	83
01	82
14	81
05	78
08	72
11	68

blue are those with higher accuracy and they are used for further developments in this study. The remaining gestures highlighted in grey are discarded. The discarded key points lie in the middle of the middle, ring, and little finger. The varying performance of certain gestures compared to others may be attributed to technical challenges or human error. Currently, the underlying causes of these differences remain unclear. However, future studies may provide insights into why some gestures demonstrate superior performance over others.

5 Further Developments

5.1 Key Mapping and Naming

Figure 5 gives us the references for naming each hand gesture. The Naming is given as follows:

- A three-letter name would be used to represent each single tap. The first letter would indicate which hand should be used to press the key (L for left, R for right), while the second letter designates the specific finger to use (Index, Middle, Ring, or Pinky).
- For a closed-fist(shifted) tap, the second letter would be capitalized, while for a regular tap, it remains in lowercase. The third letter indicates the finger position (1, 2, 3, or 4).
- For example, 'Lm3' represents a regular tap on the 3rd point of the middle finger in the left hand. Similarly, 'RR1' denotes a shifted tap on the 1st point of the Ring finger in the right hand.

– By counting these keys, we can determine that each hand will have a total of 16 keys, including both shifted and unshifted, resulting in a combined total of 64 keys.
– Figure 5 shows us a detailed view of Key mapping and the naming convention.

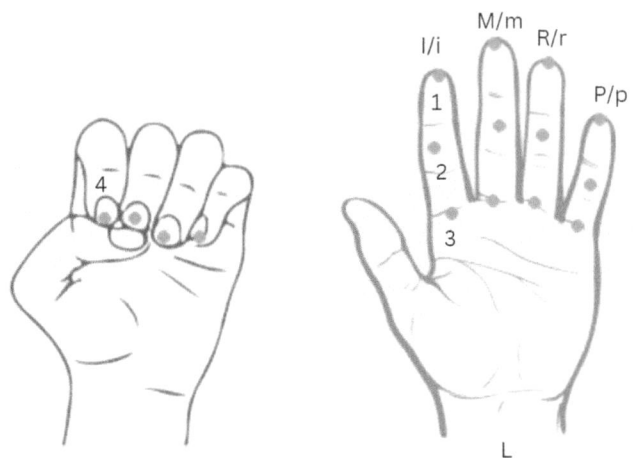

Fig. 5. Naming Reference for the Left hand

Following this notation, we take a look at the Malayalam script before mapping the characters onto the key points.

Malayalam Script. To develop a keyboard layout and character-encoding scheme for Malayalam, the initial phase involves establishing a clear definition of the character set. The Malayalam character set consists of 13 vowels and 36 consonants. Vowels are classified into short vowels and long vowels. Chillu characters are a set of 5 letters that represent a consonant without the inherent 'a' vowel. They are used for certain native Malayalam words. Alpaprana and Mahaprana are terms used to classify Malayalam consonants based on their aspiration: Alpaprana consonants are unaspirated (e.g. ka, cha, ta, tha, pa), and Mahaprana consonants are aspirated (e.g. kha, chha, ta, thha, ffa).

In this mapping,

– The first two fingers of the left hand (index, middle) are dedicated to vowels, with 'a' starting at the lower key point of the index finger and long vowels mapped as shifted taps on the same key point ('aa' in this case).
– Consonants begin with 'ka' on the lowest point of the left-hand ring finger, with the Mahaprana consonant 'kha' also mapped on the same key point, using a shifted press. The next two consonants, 'ga' and 'gha', are mapped

Table 3. Malayalam vowels mapping

Table 4. Malayalam consonants mapping

Li1	Lr1
LI1	LR1
Li2	Lr3
LI2	LR3
Li3	Lp1
LI3	LP1
Lm1	Lp3
LM1	LP3
Lm3	Rp1
LM3	RP1

to the top key point of the ring finger. This pattern is repeated for each set of consonants.

– Consonants from 'sa' to 'rra' are arranged as shifted taps on the key points on the nails.

Tables 3 and 4 show examples of this mapping of vowels and consonants onto the key points using the naming convention given in Fig. 6., respectively.

Figure 6 depicts the key mapping in detail. The middle key points of the middle, ring, and little finger have been removed based on the results from Table 2.

6 Theoretical Evaluation

To calculate the theoretical typing speed for the keyboard, KLM model [8]was used.

6.1 GOMS-Model (KLM)

Assumption. The user will type the given phrase using the provided keyboard setup, checking each character on the screen and reviewing the feedback at each step.

Challenge. Some operator time had to be calculated, the estimated time cannot be taken.

Operator time to be calculated included keystroke, shifted keystroke and long press. The operator time for the mental operator is taken as the estimated time i.e., use 1.2 s.

Operator Sequence. The calculation is done by making the user type only letters in fixed random order 10 times and calculate the time taken for typing it the 11th time.

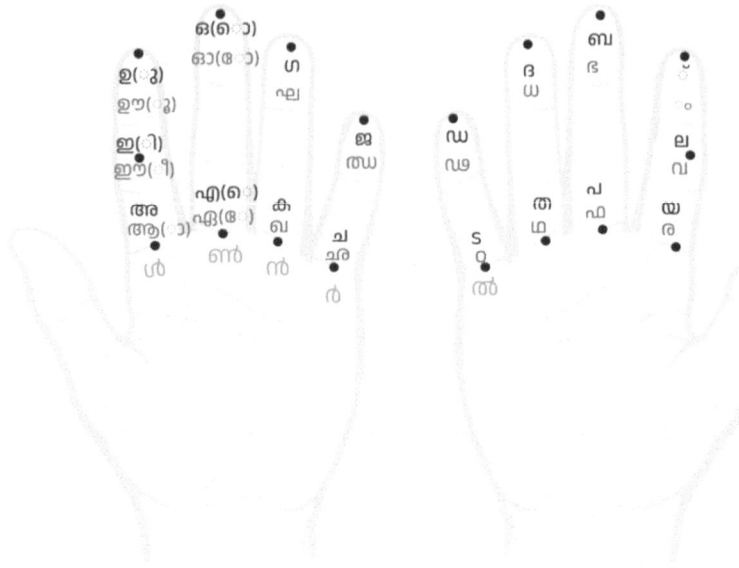

Fig. 6. Key Mapping

- Initiate entry (M)
- Move hands to typing pose (H)
- Type [Example Phrase](9K)

The above phrase also includes normal keystroke (K); Shifted keystroke (S) (Additional cognitive or physical time gap for shifted characters); Long-press (L); Mental perception looking at the layout and character (M).

Phrase Selection. To make the calculation easier we selected a particular phrase for calculating time which has no long-pressed keys.

Calculation. The calculation is done by making the user type only letters in fixed random order 10 times and calculate the time taken for typing it the 11th time.

K - order [Example Phrase]
time = 12.09 s, keystroke = 22, average = .54 s
S - order [Example Phrase]
time = 24.67 s, keystroke = 26, average = .948 s
For typing the phrase "Example Phrase" (when double consonants and vowel signs are taken as one character for mental operators) Time taken (mental operator) = m + 7k + k + 5k + s + k + 8k + k + 6k + 14 m
= 29k + s + 15 m = 29 x .54 + .94 + 15 × 1.2 = 34.60 s
Note: - The method used to calculate the time of key press and shifted key press are arbitrary and thus cannot be verified experimentally.

7   Study 2 Empirical Evaluation

We assess the learnability of the system alongside the associated gestures, while also calculating the accuracy, error rate, and text input speed.

7.1   User Selection Criteria

Native Malayalam speakers who could read and write fluently in Malayalam were chosen. Participants from the ages of 18 to 27 years old were chosen who were easily adapted to technology and had faster learnability. Importantly, none of the participants had participated in the previous study. 6 users- 3 male and 3 female were chosen based on ease of recruitment to facilitate the study's logistics.

7.2   Protocol

For the study, 150 unique Malayalam phrases following a similar approach to Dalvi et al. [5] were identified. This phrase set also included Malayalam proverbs and conversation from Malayalam movies. The proposed phrase set was further evaluated and analyzed by Malayalam linguistic specialists.

Objective. The goal of the accelerated empirical study was to calculate the learnability of first-time users, calculate the typing speed, and estimate the occurrence of errors.

The protocol involved several steps, including training, self-exploratory sessions, and 10 longitudinal usability test sessions, followed by two open-loop usability tests. The evaluation process for each user typically lasted between two to three weeks. The tests were conducted on an Apple laptop, which ran the prototype. It was connected to a phone whose camera served as the hand-tracking device and was secured in place on top of the laptop using a phone holder, with the camera facing downwards (as shown in Fig. 7). To aid in the evaluation process, we used a tool that allows for customized phrase sets for each user and provides metrics such as error rate and typing speed created by Manjiri Joshi. For the Interface, an illustrated image of the key mapping is displayed on the left side while the right side displays a text box and the phrase the user should type.

The selection for usability testing was limited to six users because of various factors such as the availability of users who were willing to participate in the testing daily and the limitations of the testing setup, which could only accommodate a certain number of people per day. The first session involved providing users with training on how to use the prototype to type a phrase using gestures. Users were taught about the functioning of the prototype, as well as how to perform each gesture effectively to achieve optimal results.

During this training, a moderator guided the user through a set of 10 predefined words in a specific order (training words). The moderator demonstrated each word and then asked the user to type it. If the user was unable to type the word correctly, the moderator would repeat the demonstration or instructions as needed. Once the user could type all 10 words, they were deemed to be "trained" on the keyboard. After the training, the users explored the keyboard for 5 min by themselves. At this time, the user could type whatever they like. If necessary, the moderator may suggest the user type their name, their friends or siblings' names, etc.

Fig. 7. Testing Setup

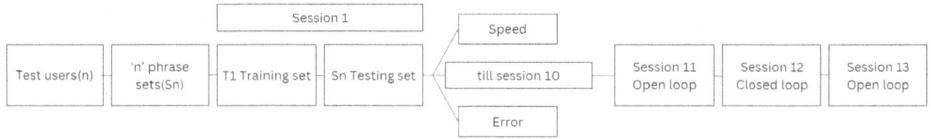

Fig. 8. Evaluation Protocol

The Longitudinal Usability Test (LTU) [2] commenced on the same day as the training session and required participants to type ten phrases consecutively during each session. The time taken to complete each phrase was recorded to calculate typing speed in characters per minute (CPM). Each phrase could only be attempted once, and participants did not receive immediate feedback regarding their speed or time after each phrase. Instead, the cumulative time for all phrases was presented to the user upon the completion of the usability test.

During the LTU, the moderator refrained from providing any assistance; however, a self-exploration session was offered either before or following the LTU to help users acclimate to the new keyboard. Given that the keyboard was a novel product, this preliminary session alleviated potential confusion.

Following the initial LTU session, participants were required to complete an additional ten sessions, one per day. After each session, a qualitative assessment was conducted to identify any challenges or issues encountered by the user during the LTU. This feedback was crucial for evaluating the effectiveness of the prototype for each user. To ensure consistency in testing, there needed to be no gaps exceeding one day between sessions, even in cases where a user was unavailable on specific days.

Upon completion of the first ten sessions (Fig. 8), the eleventh session was conducted as an open-loop study, during which participants were not provided with transcribed feedback. The twelfth session was a closed-loop usability test, and the thirteenth and final session was again an open-loop usability test. The open-loop study was designed to ascertain the maximum achievable typing speed with the prototype, free from any constraints imposed by the system.

8 Result

8.1 Typing Speed

Figure 9 shows the session-wise average typing speed in characters per minute (CPM) for the keyboard. We clearly observe that during LTU sessions 1–10, the speeds of users improve rapidly. In session 11, there is an exponential increase in speed. The mean speed in peak LTU session 11 seems to be justified by the open-loop study conducted particularly in this session. The CPM range of each user varied from 10 to 40 in each session, with accidental key presses being one of the factors accountable for this variation. At session 11, the CPM was reported to be nearly 50, at 49.95. This result provided insights into the speed of learnability while adapting to a new text input method. The speed of typing each phrase was higher in the open loop session due to a lack of feedback. In session 13, which would be an open-loop study, these differences are expected to be resolved, and narrower variations could be observed, although the study is yet to be conducted.

8.2 Error

Calculating the uncorrected error rate created another set of problems. As the users were learning the tool, they immediately learned the phrase characters and the characters' location in the hand. The error percentage noticeably decreased in subsequent sessions (Fig. 10), but the errors in the initial sessions were primarily a result of unintentional keystrokes. As demonstrated here, users can reduce the likelihood of such errors through repeated practice. However, the calculated errors cannot be used to determine the accuracy of the keyboard in general, but rather only for this specific prototype. The values indicate a significant reduction in error percentage, but it should be noted that the limitations of the prototype largely contribute to the errors. Nevertheless, the prototype's learnability has helped to improve its accuracy.

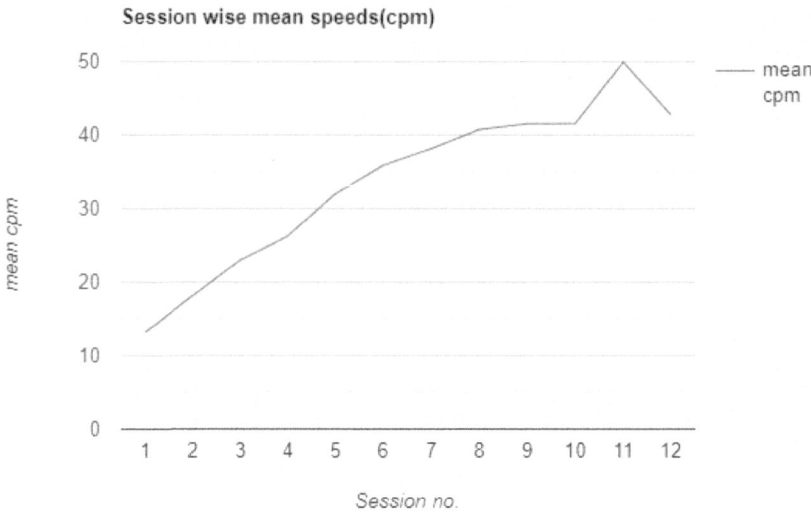

Fig. 9. Session Wise Mean Speeds

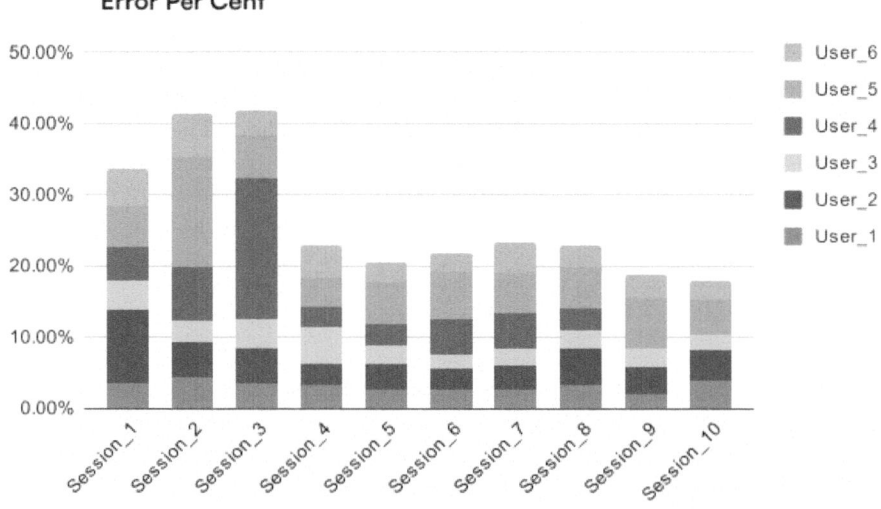

Fig. 10. Error Percent graph

8.3   Qualitative Observations

After extensive practice with the prototype, it was discovered that the effectiveness of its operation greatly depended on the user's hands. Specifically, the position of key points tracked in the hands varied due to differences in factors such as length and movement. While users adapted to this variability, reachability was another critical issue that had to be considered. For example, a user may not be able to reach the lowest point of their little finger, resulting in low accuracy and typing speed. At first, users experienced hand fatigue, but this problem disappeared in the later stages of testing. To address this, the setup was adjusted to ensure maximum comfort, with the user's chair raised and the laptop lowered so that their hands rested on the table at a comfortable height in line with the camera. Unfortunately, accidental taps were a significant drawback of the prototype, with users inadvertently triggering key presses by resting their hands on the table. This resulted in typos and the need for additional backspacing, negatively impacting the typing experience.

9   Conclusion

The preliminary investigation indicates that the proposed design possesses the potential to become a fully functional text input method. However, the medium through which the device operates needs to be further examined to create a more convenient hardware-free device for users.

The idea presents ample opportunities for future studies and research to enhance the layout design and delve deeper into micro-interactions for typing. For instance, during an early stage of research, sliding was found to be a promising interaction, but further research was hampered by prototype limitations. Additionally, more sophisticated programs can be developed to improve hand identification and key point tracking accuracy.

Furthermore, the existing prototype can be adapted for other Indic languages by deciding the layout based on frequency-based character mapping. This concept may also be applied in the field of augmented and virtual reality to develop a typing experience using a wristband. By utilizing an IR camera sensor to detect fingers, visually impaired individuals can identify their finger points and use them to input data into a virtual keyboard. The layout of the keyboard would need to be memorized by the user to identify the letters, but once memorized, typing would become as natural as for a sighted person. The technology can be further developed to assist users in various ways, such as providing a communication guide or aiding in daily activities. With continued research and development, this innovative technology has the potential to significantly enhance the quality of life for people with disabilities.

In conclusion, the proposed design demonstrates promising results as a fully functional text input method. However, further research is necessary to optimize the hardware-free device and enhance the overall user experience. The concept presents exciting opportunities for future studies, particularly in the areas of layout design, micro-interactions, and hand identification accuracy. Additionally, the adaptability of the prototype to other Indic languages and its potential applications in augmented and virtual reality highlight its versatility and impact. With ongoing research and development, this innovative technology can revolutionize the way individuals, especially those with disabilities, interact with digital interfaces and improve their overall quality of life.

Acknowldegement. I would like to express my sincere gratitude to Rohith T for his invaluable contributions to this project, which spanned from the initial development phase to the evaluation stage. His involvement was integral throughout the entire course of the work. I would also like to acknowledge Mohammed Anas, who has contributed immensely on the development of the prototype. I take this opportunity to express my profound gratitude and deep regards to my guide, Prof. Anirudha Joshi for their exemplary guidance, monitoring, and constant encouragement throughout the course of this project. I also take this opportunity to express my thankfulness towards Manjiri Joshi for their valuable guidance, particularly in the development of the evaluation system. I would like to thank all the users who have dedicated their valuable time to conducting the usability tests.

References

1. Report of the committee for standardization of keyboard layout for Indian script-based computers (1984)
2. Bharath, P.A., Jadhav, C., Ahire, S., Joshi, M., Ahirwar, R., Joshi, A.: Performance of accessible gesture-based Indic keyboard. In: Human-Computer Interaction-INTERACT 2017: 16th IFIP TC 13 International Conference, Mumbai, India, 25–29 September 2017, Proceedings, Part I, pp. 205–220. Springer (2017)
3. Boletsis, C., Kongsvik, S.: Controller-based text-input techniques for virtual reality: an empirical comparison (2019)
4. Chu, Q., Chen, C.P., Hu, H., Wu, X., Han, B.: iHand: hand recognition-based text input method for wearable devices. Computers **13**(3), 80 (2024)
5. Dalvi, G., et al.: A protocol to evaluate virtual keyboards for Indian languages. In: Proceedings of the 7th Indian Conference on Human-Computer Interaction, pp. 27–38 (2015)
6. Joshi, A., Ganu, A., Chand, A., Parmar, V., Mathur, G.: Keylekh: a keyboard for text entry in Indic scripts. In: CHI 2004 Extended Abstracts on Human Factors in Computing Systems, pp. 928–942 (2004)
7. Joshi, M., Joshi, A.N., Emmadi, N., Malsattar, N.: Swarachakra keyboard for Indic scripts (tutorial). In: Proceedings of the 1st International Conference on Mobile Software Engineering and Systems, pp. 5–6 (2014)
8. Kieras, D., et al.: Using the keystroke-level model to estimate execution times. University of Michigan, 555 (2001)
9. Nguyen, A., Bittman, S., Zank, M.: Text input methods in virtual reality using radial layouts. In: Proceedings of the 26th ACM Symposium on Virtual Reality Software and Technology, pp. 1–3 (2020)
10. Sánchez-Brizuela, G., Cisnal, A., de la Fuente-López, E., Fraile, J.-C., Pérez-Turiel, J.: Lightweight real-time hand segmentation leveraging mediapipe landmark detection. Virtual Reality **27**(4), 3125–3132 (2023)

11. Sandhya, B.R., Amrutha, C., Ashika, S.: Gesture recognition based virtual mouse and keyboard. In: International Conference on Advances in Communication Technology and Computer Engineering, pp. 25–36. Springer (2023)
12. Vertanen, K., Memmi, H., Emge, J., Reyal, S., Kristensson, P.O.: VelociTap: investigating fast mobile text entry using sentence-based decoding of touchscreen keyboard input. In: Proceedings of the 33rd Annual ACM Conference on Human Factors in Computing Systems, pp. 659–668 (2015)
13. Yeo, H.-S., Phang, X.-S., Castellucci, S.J., Kristensson, O., Quigley, A.: Investigating tilt-based gesture keyboard entry for single-handed text entry on large devices. In: Proceedings of the 2017 CHI Conference on Human Factors in Computing Systems, pp. 4194–4202 (2017)
14. Zhai, S., Kristensson, P.-O.: Shorthand writing on stylus keyboard. In: Proceedings of the SIGCHI Conference on Human Factors in Computing Systems, pp. 97–104 (2003)
15. Zhang, F., et al.: MediaPipe hands: On-device real-time hand tracking. arXiv preprint arXiv:2006.10214 (2020)

Integration of Social Design with ICT to Promote Sustainability

Anubha Sharma[1]([✉]), Divy Sharma[1], Vikshita Jain[1], Aastha[1],
Kanan Agarwal[1], Kinshuk Agarwal[2], and Anisha Absolom[3]

[1] Ajay Kumar Garg Engineering College, Ghaziabad, Uttar Pradesh, India
anubhaa.sharma27@gmail.com
[2] Indian Institute of Foreign Trade, Kakinada , India
[3] Indian Institute of Technology Hyderabad, Sangareddy, Telangana, India
https://www.akgec.ac.in/

Abstract. This study will explore and combine information Communication Technology (ICT) with Social Design principles. The aim is to promote sustainable use of water through AquaAlert, a smart water management system. AquaAlert caters to monitoring real-time water usage, detecting water leakage, and providing actionable insights to users to reduce water consumption. A mixed-method approach was deployed during the research, using surveys, interviews, and tests to detect the effectiveness of the device and system. The findings revealed the true potential of AquaAlert, focusing on sustainability and promoting the United Nation's Sustainable Development Goals (SDGs) related to clean water and sustainable cities. The paper will include the user-centered design approach, development process, and research methodology implemented to promote responsible water usage.

Keywords: Social Design · Information Communication Technology(ICT) · Sustainable Development Goals · Sustainability · Behavioral Design

1 Introduction

Information and Communication Technology (ICT) has been going through modern advancements that has brought a revolutionary change to how we access information and networks. Social design allows the development of goods and services that value societal improvement. By incorporating social design with ICT for development and deployment, we can bring out technologically advanced solutions and promote sustainable practices for public well-being. Water's overconsumption, and scarcity is a pressing issue that needs to be addressed. This research paper will focus on the integration of social design with ICT. We will present our findings from our product AquaAlert. AquaAlert is a smart water management system that provide real-time monitoring and feedback to users about their water usage. We have leveraged the principles of social design, that

N. Rangaswamy et al. (Eds.): IndiaHCI 2024, CCIS 2338, pp. 244–256, 2025.
https://doi.org/10.1007/978-3-031-80832-6_17

are supported by advanced machine learning algorithms. We will concentrate on how social design principles integrated with ICT came into use while developing AquaAlert and how this product promotes sustainable water practices. We will further showcase how technology and user-centric design came together to facilitate social change.

2 Literature Review

Our study expands on these frameworks by integrating ICT into social design to address water conservation, a key area for achieving global sustainability targets.

2.1 Social Design Definition

Social Design is aimed to address societal challenges by integrating design practices. It emphasizes collaboration and sustainability by focusing on creating positive social impacts through designs.

2.2 Sustainability in Social Design

Social Innovation plays an important role in sustaining and fostering social cohesion. Projects like the Design for Social Innovation and Sustainability (DESIS) network, depict how social design can help build communities by addressing local needs and leveraging community assets. One of the five components of Social Design is resilience-driven design activities. They aim to instigate or catalyze systemic change directed at a better long-term future for all, focusing more on creating sustainable future systems and practices [1, 2].

2.3 Methodologies in Social Design

Multiple studies depict the effectiveness of participatory design works. It shows how users interact with the design and co-design process and the role of stakeholders in decision-making to foster impactful sustainable practices. The Design for Social Innovation and Sustainability (DESIS) network reveals the usefulness of community-based approaches, leading to successful sustainability outcomes. Design activism leverages design as a tool for social change, often addressing systemic issues and advocating for social justice. Markussen's framework for disruptive aesthetics highlights the potential of design interventions to disrupt existing power structures and promote social equity [3, 4].

2.4 ICT Integration in Environmental Sustainability

Introduction to Design in ICT. The nexus between Information and Communication Technology (ICT) and sustainability has emerged as a critical area of research, aiming to harness the potential of ICT to foster sustainable development while mitigating its environmental impact [5].ICT enables advanced modeling, simulation, and decision support tools, which are essential for creating sustainable development scenarios and strategies. ICT facilitates the replacement of physical resources with digital alternatives, significantly reducing environmental impact. Sustainable HCI focuses on designing technology that encourages sustainable behavior among users through feedback mechanisms and behavioral nudges [5].

Role of ICT in Environmental Monitoring

Sensor Networks and IoT. Internet of Things (IoT) technologies have started to impact society as a whole and have become a key enabler for sustainable development. IoT is emerging as a powerful enabler in many application domains, such as water and energy management. IoT can help achieve the aim of the Paris Agreement and the targets in the UN Sustainable Development Goals (SDGs) (Salam, 2019; IoT Forum2017). IoT and connected devices were considered to be the major drivers of change (Laine, 2014). IoT assumes the combination of three main "elements: web-based (middleware), things-based (e.g. sensors), and semantic-based (knowledge). The use of IoT as part of modern-day urban development is understood in terms of creating engineered systems that act as enablers of sustainability by ensuring active protection of the natural and environmental systems (Council, 2013) [6].

Real-time Monitoring Systems. Traditional approaches to energy management are being replaced by sophisticated, real-time monitoring systems that provide a granular understanding of energy usage patterns [7]. Smart sensors, including but not limited to smart meters, smart plugs, and IoT-enabled devices, are instrumental in capturing real-time information [8]. These sensors can measure electricity, gas, and water consumption [9].

AI and Machine-Learning. In the smart cities concept, ICT is playing a vital role in policy design, decision, implementation, and ultimately productive services [10]. Advanced analytics techniques, including machine learning algorithms, statistical models, and pattern recognition, enable the identification of trends and anomalies in energy consumption. Visualization tools such as dashboards and interactive graphs provide stakeholders with an intuitive understanding of complex data, facilitating informed decision-making [11].

Persuasive Technology. The idea is that any intended behavior change can be classified according to one (or more) of the positions of the matrix. One of the applications of Fogg's Behaviour Grid can be combined with environmentally related behaviors. They included product-related and general lifestyle changes [12]. With AquaAlert we have initiate sustainability every day, by creating an active model that motivates the audience to bring in this behavioral change without hampering their present lifestyle.

Ambient Awareness. Ambient intelligence (Artificial Intelligence and Machine Learning (AI-ML)) is a multidisciplinary paradigm based on the Invisible Computer and Ubiquitous Computing. AI-ML is a user-centric paradigm [13]. Ambient awareness systems inform users about the environmental impact of their actions, fostering greater responsibility [5]. The fundamental concepts of Artificial Intelligence and Machine Learning (AI-ML) include - User-oriented design, Privacy preservation, Personalization, and Social Intelligence AmI has the characteristics of a smart environment, and it has an allocentric view. It needs location maintenance, and it is based on information availability. A device consisting of sensors will produce readily available data. This data may even be available in real time to generate triggers [13].

3 AquaAlert: Introduction

Information and communication technology (ICT), as discussed in various sections of this research can address issues like climate change, sustainable development, and water consumption. ICT allows real-time monitoring and communication, efficiency, and providing essential resource management. ICT for sustainability makes data-driven decisions easier, encouraging resource efficiency and waste reduction. We considered using the recent prevalence of water emergencies as evidence to highlight the social design and information and communication technology (ICT) integration, with a particular emphasis on a smart water management system. Our hypothesis for the case study was that if we narrowed it down to one application of integration of social design and ICT, we could apply a similar analogy to other use cases. AquaAlert is a prime example of one such problem in the category of environment and sustainability. AquaAlert is a study and a product with hardware devices, mobile applications, and machine learning modules to track water usage. This section will enunciate the problem that India faces with water scarcity. Further, a proposed solution will be explained, a device that the authors developed as their input towards a sustainable future.

3.1 Problem

The goal of AquaAlert was to address the problem of water waste from leaks, which cost developing countries like India 45 million liters of water every day. 33% of people in India keep the tap open even without work while bathing and brushing. Water wastage estimates that every day 4,84,20,000 crore cubic meters i.e. 48.42 billion one-liter bottles of water are wasted. An average person needs 150 litres of water daily for hygiene, cooking, drinking, and other activities. Only 5 liters per day are used for cooking and drinking, accounting for about 3% of the total requirement. More than 45 liters of water per capita per day is wasted. Major sources of wastage include not turning off taps while brushing or shaving, leakages, and using fresh water for washing vehicles. A leaking faucet wastes 1 liter of water per day. Flushing the toilet wastes nearly 25 liters of water. Every third person in India leaves the tap running, wasting five liters of water a minute, while a shower wastes 10 liters per minute. 163 million Indians have no access to clean drinking water. 21% of diseases are linked to unsafe drinking water. Water conditions by 2030 can be estimated as:

(1) 40% of Indians will not have access to drinking water

(2) 84% of rural households do not have access to piped water
(3) 88% of rural households lack access to drinking water. Water demand will double by 2030. This will lead to severe water shortages.600 million Indians live in areas of extreme water stress. If water leaks can be fixed, starting with everyday unnoticed leaks in households, people can be saved from water scarcity [14].

3.2 Solution

AquaAlert is a combination of hardware and software. The hardware (AquaAlert device, consisting of sensors and detectors) is installed in the main water supply of a household. It calculates the amount of water flowing throughout the day in a user's home. The software part of AquaAlert is an application installed in the user's mobile phone (or any other smart-remote device). Using AquaAlert, one can find their daily, weekly, and monthly water consumption. The machine learning algorithm, Principal Component Analysis (PCA) is used to detect leaks or out-of-normal water usage. The hardware device ensures easy installation and integration with the mobile application through Wi-Fi modules. The user interface of AquaAlert is designed for any viewer to understand and get alerts based on their everyday water usage. One can separately check leaks in particular areas, like the kitchen, garden, and washroom, to stop using water, if possible at that instant. When the leakage is detected, a notification is sent to the user's mobile phone. AquaAlert can help customers save up to 20% on water usage and expenses. The idea behind AquaAlert is to bring behavioral change among people, build consciousness about the environment, and initiate triggers for the same. United Nations Sustainable Development Goals 6, 9, 11, and 12 constitute the impact of AquaAlert.

3.3 Machine Learning Integration

We have used Hugging Face transformers for initial deployment. We are working on a custom-built model for fine-tuned leak detection and water usage pattern recognition. The model monitors water flow rates over time. If an unusual pattern (e.g., a sudden spike or continuous flow) is detected that deviates from normal behavior, it classifies it as a potential leak. There will be an implementation of continuous learning by periodically retraining the model with new data, handling concept drift/data drift improving its accuracy and adaptability to different usage patterns.

ML Concept Overview

Key Components. Data Collection: Water flow data collected from sensors at the main water supply. → Preprocessing: Time-series analysis, data cleaning, and feature extraction (e.g., flow rate changes). → Modeling: Using LSTM for pattern recognition and AutoEncoders for anomaly detection. → Deployment: Containerized with Docker and exposed via Flask API, integrated into the overall system.

ML Architecture Blueprint

Data Flow. Sensors → Raw Data (Flow Rate, Timestamps) → Preprocessing Pipeline → ML Model (LSTM + AutoEncoder) → Real-time Anomaly Detection → Notifications to User

Machine Learning Pipeline. Data Input: Streaming data from hardware sensors.→ Data Preprocessing: Handle missing data, normalize, and create time-series batches.→ Model: LSTM for usage prediction and AutoEncoder for anomaly detection.→ Output: Anomaly detected (Leakage) or Normal Usage 1.

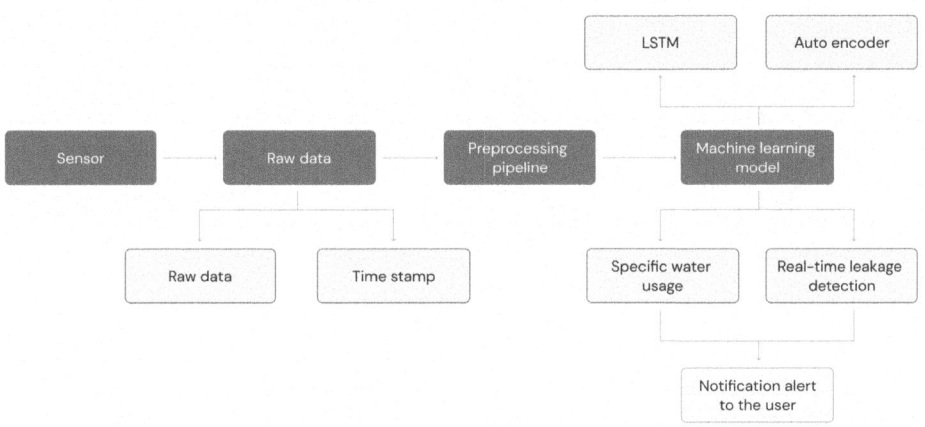

Fig. 1. Data Flow Diagram of AquaAlert

4   Research Methodology

Our study was a combination of approaches, where we combined quantitative surveys with qualitative interviews to examine if AquaAlert is effective in elevating sustainability.

Survey Sampling Techniques. We designed the survey to capture water usage behaviors and attitudes toward the adoption of technology across different demographic groups. We used random sampling to achieve diversity among the 173 participants. The survey included questions on: 1. Daily water usage 2. Water wastage awareness 3. Comfortability with technology 4. Other socio-economic factors All the questions were pre-tested on a sample group to test questions and their relevance to the study. We collected the data through online and paper-based surveys to maximize reach and ensure inclusivity. Further, we analyzed the survey data to create statistics and find out general patterns for examining the correlation between demographics and user behavior.

Demographic Insights

Age and Water Consumption Behavior. Most respondents are 18–25 years old, primarily students, suggesting that educational institutions could be a significant target for water conservation initiatives.

Gender and Awareness. The survey has more male respondents than female. Understanding if there is any gender-specific behavior toward water usage could help tailor educational content or promotional strategies.

Household Water Usage Patterns. Households with 3–4 individuals are the most common. This could imply a standard family size in the surveyed areas, for estimating average water needs and designing appropriately sized water-saving systems.

Water Consumption Awareness. Households reporting more than 300 Liters (15 Buckets) of daily consumption might indicate either a higher number of residents or less efficient water usage practices. Tailored solutions or educational campaigns could focus on these high-usage households to maximize water savings.

Economic Insights

Willingness to Invest. Most respondents are willing to invest less than 1,000 Rupees in a water monitoring system, suggesting that cost-effective solutions might have higher adoption rates. A smaller segment is willing to invest more (2,500 Rupees - 5,000 Rupees), indicating a market for premium features or advanced systems.

Behavioural Insights

Concern and Interest Correlation. Respondents who are "very concerned" about water saving are likely to invest in a monitoring system and use its features effectively. Tailored communication highlighting the benefits of water-saving solutions could convert those who are "somewhat concerned" to more active participants in conservation efforts.

Feature Preferences. Real-time monitoring and daily reports are highly desired features, indicating that respondents want immediate feedback and actionable insights. Rewards for saving water can be an effective motivational tool, suggesting that gamification elements might increase user engagement.

Alert Preferences. The preference for mobile app alerts shows a tech-savvy respondent base comfortable with digital solutions. Offering multiple alert methods (In-App Notifications, SMS, Email) ensures inclusivity, catering to those who might not be as tech-oriented.

5   Survey Findings

The survey, conducted for 173 people, disclosed the information that the major demographic of survey-takers aged 18–25 were a part of small-medium-sized households. The water consumption habits of every participant varied. However, most respondents expressed their concern about water wastage. The participant's primary water conservation practices included manual and plumber checks (Table 1).

5.1   Data Overview

Table 1. Survey Responses Breakdown

Category	Responses
Total Responses: 173	
Age Breakdown	
18–25	152 respondents
25–34	8 respondents
34–45	8 respondents
45+	5 respondents
Gender Breakdown	
Male	123 respondents
Female	49 respondents
Prefer not to say	1 respondent
Profession Breakdown	
Students	144 respondents
Working Professionals	18 respondents
Others (Business Owners, Housewife, Freelance, Retired, etc.)	11 respondents
Household Size Breakdown	
1–2 individuals	11 households
3–4 individuals	106 households
5–6 individuals	40 households
More than 6 individuals	16 households
Water Consumption Breakdown	
Less than 100 liters daily	31 households
100–200 liters daily	66 households
200–300 liters daily	31 households
More than 300 liters daily	22 households
Don't know	23 households

5.2 Data Outcome

After closing the survey and analysing the insights, we were able to achieve an outcome on what to include in our study and product. We can target the young adult audience with small households. If customers are made aware of their water bills and the usefulness of monitoring their daily water usage, we can empower them to make better, informed decisions.

6 Data Analysis

The data revealed several important insights into water usage behavior and the potential effectiveness of AquaAlert. Younger respondents (aged 18–25) demonstrated a greater willingness to adopt new technologies for water management, suggesting that educational institutions could be key partners in promoting AquaAlert. Meanwhile, older demographics were less inclined to change their habits or adopt new technology, possibly due to concerns about privacy or unfamiliarity with digital tools. Households with high water consumption were found to be more resistant to adopting AquaAlert, indicating that these users might perceive the technology as an inconvenience or unnecessary expense. This resistance suggests a need for targeted communication strategies emphasizing the cost-saving benefits of AquaAlert and its ease of use. The analysis also identified gender differences: female respondents, particularly those managing household chores, showed higher concern for water wastage and were more supportive of technological solutions. This finding suggests an opportunity for gender-targeted marketing campaigns to increase AquaAlert's adoption rates Fig. 2.

7 Discussion and Findings

The findings reiterate the role of ICT in promoting sustainability through a user-centric design. Our study also demonstrates that real-time data and feedback, when sent to the user, can bring social and behavioral change, resulting in lower water consumption. The study aligns with other theories of behavioral change, including Fogg's Behavior Model, suggesting behavior influencing through motivation, ability, and triggers (Lockton, 2012). This study additionally revealed challenges that AquaAlert may face, including resistance from high-consumption households due to privacy and other reasons. While ICT can incorporate change, we need to consider the socio-cultural factors that impact the adoption of a new technology.

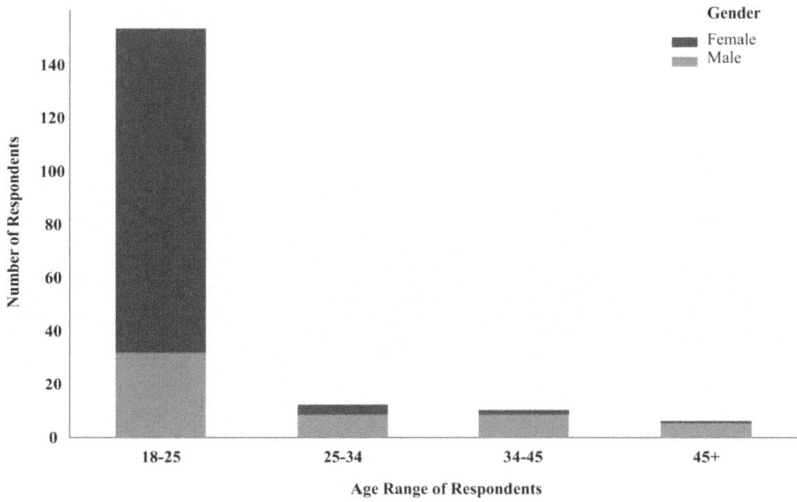

Fig. 2. Age and gender breakdown chart: Shows the distribution of respondents by age and gender. This bar chart shows the distribution of respondents by age group and gender. The majority of respondents are young (18–25) and predominantly male. This demographic is the most engaged with water conservation efforts.

8   Challenges

Privacy can be seen as a protection of basic rights, including the right to private space. The privacy of one's home is a classic example of a private space that is related to one's own identity [16]. Replicating a social design product like AquaAlert on a large scale and ensuring its installation and working can become challenging. The purpose of saving water comes into play only after the users are aware of the implications and allow themselves to get triggered for behavioral change. It is unusual for a provider to bill customers for ICT services with accurate accounting for hardware utilization and resulting energy use. ICT services are often cross-subsidized, which may create misdirected incentives [17].There were three main clusters in perceived ease of use for my product or practice. The first relates to physical effort, while the second relates to mental effort. The third is how easy a system is to learn [18]. These clusters may affect AquaAlert's attempt to action Figs. 3 and 4.

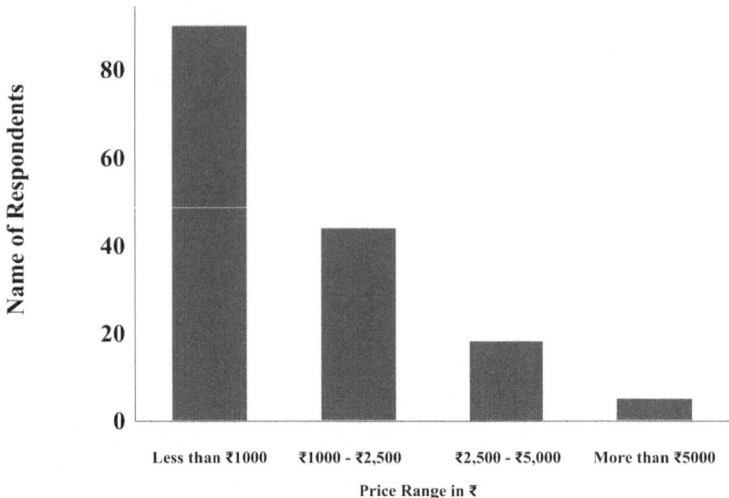

Fig. 3. Investment willingness chart: Depicts the range of investment respondents are willing to make for a water monitoring system. Depicts the range of investment respondents are willing to make for a water monitoring system. This bar chart shows the willingness of respondents to invest in a water monitoring system. Most respondents prefer affordable solutions, with the majority willing to invest less than 1,000.

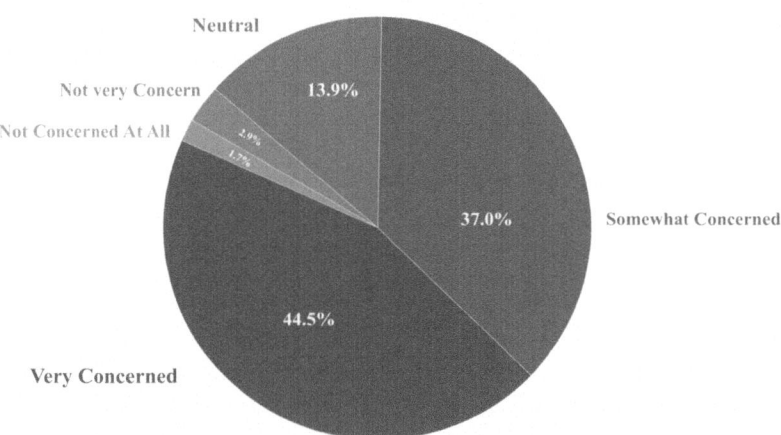

Fig. 4. Concern levels about water saving pie chart: Illustrates the levels of concern about water saving among respondents. This pie chart displays the levels of concern about water saving among respondents. A significant majority are "Very concerned" or "Somewhat concerned," indicating strong interest in water conservation.

9   Conclusion

This study demonstrates the potential of integrating social design with ICT to address sustainability challenges like water scarcity. AquaAlert is shown to be an effective tool for promoting water conservation by providing real-time monitoring, alerts, and user engagement features that encourage behavioral change. The survey data reveal a strong interest in such solutions, particularly among youngsters, tech-savvy demographics, and underscore the importance of affordability and user-centered design. To maximize its impact, AquaAlert should continue to focus on these core features while addressing potential barriers to adoption, such as privacy concerns and resistance from older users. Future work should explore these challenges and consider developing alternative versions of AquaAlert that maintain core functionalities but reduce perceived risks. Additionally, the principles behind AquaAlert could be extended to other sustainability domains, offering a versatile framework for ICT-driven social design solutions.

References

1. Chen, D.-S., Cheng, L.-L., Hummels, C., Koskinen, I.: Social design: an introduction. Int. J. Des. **10**(1), 1–5 (2016)
2. Tromp, N., Vial, S.: Five components of social design: a unified framework to support research and practice. Des. J. **26**(2), 210–228 (2022)
3. "Navigating care in social design: a provisional model" E Knutz, T Markussen, T Lenskjold 2019●dl.designresearchsociety.org
4. Markussen, T.: The disruptive aesthetics of design activism: enacting design between art and politics. Des. Issues **29**(1), 38–50 (2013)
5. Hilty, Lorenz M.., Aebischer, Bernard (eds.): ICT Innovations for Sustainability. Springer International Publishing, Cham (2015)
6. Rosca, M.I., Nicolae, C., Sanda, E., Madan, A.: Internet of Things (IoT) and Sustainability. In: R. Pamfilie, V. Dinu, L. Tachiciu, D. Plesea, C. Vasiliu eds. 2021. 7th BASIQ International Conference on New Trends in Sustainable Business and Consumption. Foggia, Italy, 3-5 June 2021 (2021)
7. Abubakar, I.., Khalid, S..N.., Mustafa, M..W.., Shareef, Hussain, Mustapha, M..: Application of load monitoring in appliances' energy management – a review. Renew. Sustain. Energy Rev. **67**, 235–245 (2017). https://doi.org/10.1016/j.rser.2016.09.064
8. Real-time energy monitoring systems: Technological applications in Canada, USA, and Africa, by Ahmad Hamdan, Sedat Sonko, Adefunke Fabuyide, Cosmas Dominic Daudu, and Emmanuel Augustine Etukudoh
9. Liang and Shah, 2023
10. Applications of Artificial Intelligence and Machine Learning in Smart Cities, by Zaib Ullah, Fadi Al-Turjman, Leonardo Mostarda, Roberto Gagliardi
11. Menukhin, O.: "Large-scale Visualisations in Support of Strategic Decisions" (2022)
12. Lockton, D.:'Persuasive technology and digital design for behaviour change', working paper (2012). http://danlockton.co.uk
13. Ambient Intelligence as One of the Key ICT Factors for Energy Efficiency in Building by Antun Kerner , Dina Simunic and Ramjee Prasad

14. 49-billion-liters-of-water-is-wasted-daily-in-the-country-due-to-carelessness neerain.com/49-billion-liters-of-water-is-wasted-daily-in-the-country-due-to care-lessness. Accessed 31 July 2024
15. Sensitivity analysis of water wastage in Indian households. https://www.sciencedirect.com/science/article/abs/pii/S2214785322066585. Accessed 31 July 2024
16. Ethics and Privacy of Communications in the E-Polis by Ari-Veikko Anttiroiko, gordana Dogic Crnkovic, Virginia Horniak
17. The Five Most Neglected Issues in "Green IT" by Lorenz M. Hilty and Wolfgang-Lohmann
18. Perceived Ease of Use, and User Acceptance of Information Technology Author(s): Fred D. Davis Source: MIS Quarterly,Vol. 13, No. 3 (Sep., 1989), pp. 319–340
19. The 17 Goals — Sustainable Development. https://sdgs.un.org/goals. Accessed 31 July 2024
20. Manzini, E.: Design. An Introduction to Design for Social Innovation, When Everybody Designs (2015)
21. Thorpe, A., Gamman, L.: Design with society: why socially responsive design is good enough. CoDesign **7**(3–4), 217–230 (2011)

Posters and Demos

ARoma: Augmented Reality Olfactory Menu Application

Aarav Balachandran$^{(\boxtimes)}$, Kritika Gupta, Prajna Vohra, and Anmol Srivastava

Indraprastha Institute of Information Technology Delhi (IIIT Delhi), Delhi, India
aarav21302@iiitd.ac.in

Abstract. This study aims to explore the integration of Augmented Reality (AR) and olfactory technology to enhance dining experience in restaurants. We present ARoma, an innovative AR olfactory menu application for Indian cuisine which provides users with 3D visualisation of dishes, detailed ingredient and nutritional information, and historical context, as well as an olfaction device to deliver the aroma of the dishes. Our research compares the traditional menu experience with the AR menu and ARoma, aiming to understand how these technologies affect customers' perceptions of food quality, dining enjoyment, and immersion. Our user study involved a sample size of 30 participants, divided into two groups. Group A compared traditional menu experiences with AR menus, while Group B experienced traditional menus followed by ARoma. Using this control group study and mixed-method approach, including quantitative surveys and qualitative interviews, we found that AR menus significantly enhance the dining experience by providing detailed and engaging information. Our findings suggest that AR and olfactory technology can significantly improve customer satisfaction and engagement in the food industry.

Keywords: Augmented Reality · Olfaction · AR-Menu · Dining Experience · Olfactory devices · Scent Dispersion

1 Introduction

1.1 Augmented Reality in the Food Industry

Augmented Reality (AR) revolutionizes how we interact with the world around us, seamlessly integrating digital elements into our physical environment. It enhances our perception and interaction with reality by overlaying computer-generated content onto real-world objects [10]. In technical terms, AR is defined as a real-time view of the physical world environment that has been enhanced by adding virtually generated information. By superimposing virtual objects upon the real world in real-time, AR improves the user's perception of the real world [12]. AR technology has applications across various industries, transforming how businesses operate and interact with customers. In the food industry context, AR holds a strong potential by creating digital menus that allow customers to

N. Rangaswamy et al. (Eds.): IndiaHCI 2024, CCIS 2338, pp. 259–276, 2025.
https://doi.org/10.1007/978-3-031-80832-6_18

visualize dishes in 3D before ordering, receive detailed ingredient information, and enjoy interactive, immersive dining experiences that combine the physical and digital worlds [3, 22].

Traditional menus often fall short of conveying the essence of dishes, relying on limited textual descriptions or static images. This can lead to misunderstandings and unmet expectations among customers. Customers may struggle to visualize the actual portion size of a dish, which can result in either over-ordering or under-ordering. Static images might fail to effectively communicate the texture, colour and presentation of a dish. Moreover, essential details about the dishes' ingredients, potential allergens and nutritional information are often missed out in restaurant menus due to their limited scope [13, 16, 27] for providing detailed and extensive information.

AR-based food menus offer a transformative approach to tackle these shortcomings of traditional menus. Marker-based AR, or recognition-based AR, functions by identifying distinct patterns or user-defined images to trigger augmentation. These markers, whether on paper or physical artifacts, are swiftly recognized and analyzed by cameras [31]. By utilizing marker-based menus, users can unlock interactive, three-dimensional representations of menu items simply by scanning them with their smartphones. This offers customers with an immersive dining experience with realistic and informative depictions of dishes, including details like ingredients, nutritional content, and even pricing [4]. With the help of realistic 3D visualisations, customers can correctly judge the portion size of the dishes as well as get accurate information about their presentations. Extra information regarding the dishes' ingredients and nutritional values can also be more easily incorporated in an AR based smartphone application with the help of buttons and drop-downs. AR menus also transcend language barriers, as food items are visually represented as 3D models, making them universally understandable. This not only aids in decision-making but also fosters trust and loyalty among customers.

1.2   Olfactory Approach as an Extension to AR

Conventional AR systems tend to work on only two significant senses: visual and auditory. Today, AR is not only limited to visual and auditory stimuli but can also be extended to different senses by incorporating haptic and olfactory elements. Multi-sensory media, unlike traditional AR systems, focuses on providing fully immersive interactions with the user, thus improving user experience [26].

While AR enhances visual and interactive aspects of dining, the potential of olfaction, or the sense of smell, remains largely untapped in virtual experiences. Olfaction holds a unique power to evoke emotions and memories, enriching immersive environments [5, 18, 20]. Combining AR with olfaction can create genuinely immersive dining experiences where users visualise and smell virtual representations of dishes. This integration of sensory stimuli elevates dining to a multi-sensory journey, enhancing enjoyment and engagement [20].

1.3   Introducing ARoma: An AR Olfactory Menu Application

In this experimental study, we present ARoma, an innovative augmented reality olfaction menu application designed specifically for Indian cuisine. ARoma aims to enhance the dining experience by providing 3D visualizations of dishes along with detailed ingredient and nutritional information. This information is crucial for individuals with dietary restrictions, including those with specific religious dietary beliefs, especially in a diverse country like India. Additionally, the application includes the historical background of each dish, making the dining experience not only more immersive but also educational and culturally enriching. This feature is particularly beneficial for tourists, offering them a deeper understanding and appreciation of Indian culinary traditions. To further augment the immersive experience, we have developed and integrated an olfactory device with ARoma. This device allows users to experience the aromas of the dishes, adding a powerful sensory dimension to the dining experience. By combining visual, informational, and olfactory elements, ARoma aims to create a holistic and engaging dining experience for restaurant customers.

The goal of this project is to leverage AR and olfactory technology to contribute to social good, particularly in the context of Human Computer Interaction (HCI). By making dining experiences more informative, and enjoyable, we hope to increase immersiveness, enhance cultural appreciation, and improve overall customer satisfaction in the food industry. The research questions that we aim to address through our study are as follows:

- **RQ1-** How does the AR experience provided by ARoma affect customers' perceptions of food quality and dining enjoyment compared to traditional menus?
- **RQ2-** How does the multi-sensory experience provided by ARoma affect customers' perceptions of food quality and dining enjoyment compared to traditional menus?

By addressing these research questions, we aim to provide insights into the effectiveness of ARoma in creating a more immersive and satisfying dining experience for customers. Our study will explore the potential of AR and olfactory technology to transform traditional dining. Ultimately, we hope that our findings will contribute to the broader field of HCI by demonstrating how multi-sensory technologies can be used to improve user experiences and promote social good in diverse cultural contexts.

2   Related Work

2.1   AR Menu

AR technology has emerged as a promising solution as it combines the real-world environment with computer-generated content, offering an interactive and immersive experience for diners by enhancing the dining experience. Early applications of AR in restaurant settings focused primarily on menu translation and basic 3D visualization [29]. For instance, a study had a mobile application that could translate Chinese menus into English and display 3D models of food items. While innovative, this approach was limited to a single language and could only render a few 3D models simultaneously [7]. As the technology evolved, researchers began exploring more comprehensive restaurant AR applications. In parallel developments, a digital food menu application using AR technology used unique stickers bearing the restaurant's name and logo as image targets to trigger the display of 3D food models [24]. This allowed for efficient recognition and tracking of restaurant-specific markers. They also proposed a system with features like real-time tagging, an interactive menu, and a food identifier. Their application allowed users to view 3D models of dishes by scanning a restaurant logo or marker, providing additional information such as prices, ingredients, ratings, and recipe videos. However, this system was still confined to a single restaurant's menu items. More recently, another research study developed an AR-based android application that uses QR codes as markers to display 3D food models from restaurant menus [4]. This offers greater flexibility in terms of the number of dishes that can be augmented, as QR codes can store more data than traditional fiducial markers [31]. Their system allows customers to visualize dishes in 3D along with price, ingredient, nutritional, and calorie information. The authors conducted a user experience evaluation, which showed positive results for criteria such as attractiveness, efficiency, and interactivity. A research study examined the potential of AR-integrated menus to create healthier dining experiences. Their research highlighted the growing concern for healthy eating habits among consumers, both at home and when dining out. They proposed that AR technology could be used to provide detailed nutritional information and health-related data directly on the menu, helping diners make more informed choices [8,9]. This approach not only caters to the increasing health consciousness of consumers but also positions restaurants to play a role in addressing public health concerns such as obesity and diabetes.

2.2 Integration of AR with Emerging Technologies

The integration of AR with other technologies has opened up new possibilities for enhancing the dining experience. For instance, a study developed "Menu Guide," an AR smartphone application that combines optical character recognition (OCR), sentiment analysis, and AR technology [25]. Their system scans traditional paper menus using OCR, performs sentiment analysis on customer reviews, and then projects ratings for each dish using AR. This innovative approach not only enhances the customer experience by providing instant feedback on menu items but also offers valuable insights to restaurateurs about their most popular and least preferred dishes. As these technologies continue to evolve, there is a growing need to understand user acceptance and adoption. Based on this, a study applied the Unified Theory of Acceptance and Use of Technology (UTAUT) model to evaluate user acceptance of AR menu systems [9]. Their findings indicated that Performance Expectancy was the strongest determinant of user acceptance, suggesting that the perceived usefulness of AR menus in enhancing the dining experience is crucial for their widespread adoption. While AR menu systems have been developed for various cuisines and dining experiences, there is a notable lack of focus on Indian cuisine. This gap is significant given the complexity and diversity of Indian food. AR menus designed for Indian restaurants could offer unique benefits, such as ingredient breakdowns and region-specific information [15,21]. This will allow diners to interact with each component and learn about its origin and flavour profile. This could help demystify the vast array of Indian dishes for unfamiliar diners, showcasing the intricate blends, cooking methods, and regional variations that make Indian cuisine rich and diverse.

2.3   Combining AR and Olfactory Devices

The integration of olfactory systems in HCI has seen significant advancements, with various innovative approaches aimed at enhancing user experiences through the incorporation of smell. Our research builds upon these by combining AR and olfaction within the context of restaurant menus. While previous systems have focused on general olfactory interactions, wearable technologies, or isolated scent delivery mechanisms [5,6,11,17,23,30,33], our study specifically targets the dining experience in restaurants. We aim to develop an AR olfactory menu application, ARoma, that integrates visual AR elements with advanced olfactory technology to create a comprehensive and immersive dining experience. This combines visual, informational, and olfactory elements to enhance customer engagement and satisfaction in restaurant settings. Unlike systems primarily focusing on scent diffusion or wearable technology, ARoma will leverage AR to provide a visual context for the olfactory experience. Furthermore, while generalized applications offer broad control over scent emission, our research narrows the focus to the specific needs and opportunities within the dining sector. By synthesizing the lessons learned from these diverse olfactory systems and applying them to the unique challenges of restaurant menus, we aim to create a novel, multi-sensory experience that enhances the dining process [14]. This integration of AR and olfaction in a practical, real-world context represents a significant step forward in applying olfactory HCI systems. A similar approach was employed in a study incorporating an advanced olfactory display system to enhance the sensory experience [19]. This system utilizes techniques to deliver precise and controlled scent emissions. The core of the olfactory display is based on a capillary arrangement and drive circuit, this allows for the controlled release of aromas corresponding to selected menu items. This system employs a heat-based approach for scent dispersion, chosen for its simplicity and cost-effectiveness. Temperature-controlled phase transitions in polymers regulate the release of essential oils and other aromatic compounds. The olfactory display is designed to be compact and easily integrated into the dining table setup, with wireless Bluetooth connectivity allowing seamless communication with the Virtual Food Menu (VFM) application [19]. This sophisticated olfactory system enables the creation of controlled bursts of scents with varying intensities, providing users with a nuanced and immersive aromatic experience that complements the visual AR elements of the virtual menu.

3   Design Process

The design process for ARoma involved several steps. Initially, we designed a mobile based AR menu application incorporating integral design features such as 3D visualizations and information overlays. This was followed by the creation of the prototype of an olfactory device allowing customers to experience the aromas of the AR menu dishes. Finally, to integrate the olfactory device with the AR menu, we switched from the mobile application to a kiosk-style setup for ARoma.

3.1   AR Menu Application

The AR menu application was designed to offer users an engaging and informative restaurant dining experience to customers. The menu leverages AR to present users with interactive 3D visualizations of various food items in the menu, along with displaying detailed information about the ingredients and nutritional value of each dish. The application also delves into the cultural history behind it. This immersive approach aims to enhance customer engagement and facilitate informed decision-making. Our prototype for the AR menu consisted of three dishes of Indian cuisine namely Samosa, Dal Makhni and Gulab Jamun (refer Fig. 1).

Fig. 1. Menu cards which act as AR markers

Design Features: The key design features of the interactive AR menu application include the 3-dimensional representation of food items and the digital informative overlays highlighting ingredients, nutritional information and cultural significance of the dishes.

The 3D assets for the food items were sourced from Sketchfab [28]. These 3D assets were superimposed on the respective dish menu cards, with each menu card displaying the corresponding dish in the AR menu (refer Fig. 2). By utilizing these assets, we could accurately represent a diverse variety of dishes in our AR menu prototype. This aspect of virtual plating adds a new dimension to the dining experience, enabling users to engage with the menu more tangibly and interactively. The 3D representations of the dishes provide customers with accurate information about the size, colour, texture and presentation of the actual dishes. Moreover, the 3D assets in the AR menu were designed to rotate, allowing users to view the dish from all angles and see it in its entirety. This immersive feature helps customers make more informed decisions and feel a deeper connection to the cuisine.

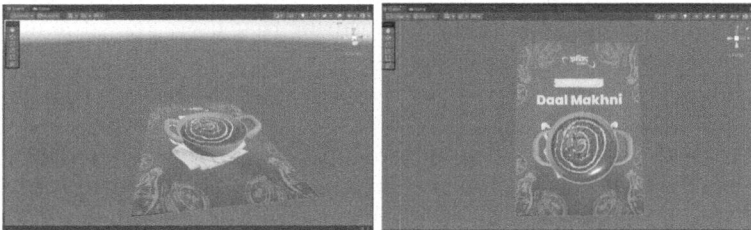

Fig. 2. 3D visualisation of Dal Makhni in ARoma

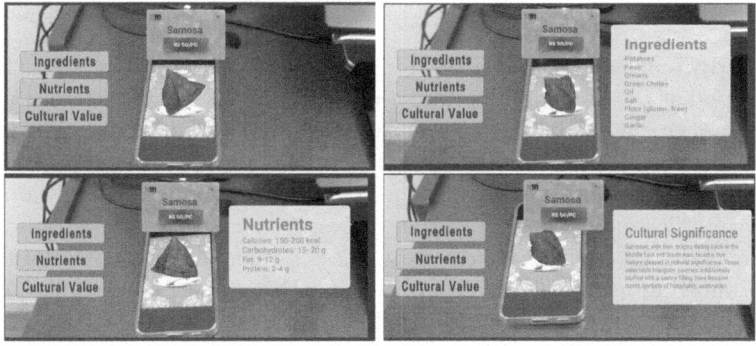

Fig. 3. Samosa in ARoma with buttons for ingredients, nutrients and cultural value

Further, including interactive and informative digital overlays within the AR menu prototype serves multiple purposes, each contributing to a richer and more engaging dining experience. The application displays these overlays using different buttons. The AR interface displays the name of the food item along with its price. The overlays offer insights into the ingredients, nutritional value and cultural value of the food dish. Our AR menu prototype prominently displays a label indicating whether each dish is vegetarian or non-vegetarian. A spice level indicator is also included to consider individuals with different levels of spice tolerance (ref Fig. 3).

Including the list of ingredients in the dishes on the menu was crucial for several reasons. Providing detailed information about the ingredients ensures that users can make informed choices about ordering food items that align with their dietary needs and preferences. This feature also acknowledges and respects religious nutritional restrictions, ensuring that users with specific religious beliefs can navigate the menu in adherence to their religious dietary practices. Additionally, this is particularly helpful for those who have allergies to specific food items or ingredients, as they can conveniently identify and avoid potential allergens. The dish's nutritional value includes calories, carbohydrates, fat, and protein. Providing this information empowers users to make healthier choices and promotes transparency and accountability, ensuring that users know the nutritional content of their chosen dishes. When users are made fully aware of what they are consuming, it enhances their dining experience by reducing uncertainty and fostering confidence in their eating choices.

The AR menu also displays the cultural importance of the food items. Exploring the historical background of menu items adds depth and context to the dining experience. It allows users to appreciate different dishes' cultural significance and heritage. This enhances the dining experience by fostering a deeper connection to the cuisine and its origins. This section talks explicitly about the dish's origin, as many dishes have deep rooted ties to specific regions, each with its culinary traditions and flavours. By highlighting the regional significance of menu items, users gain insights into the diverse culinary landscape.

Mobile Application (Prototype 1): The initial prototype of the AR menu was developed as a mobile application, aiming to provide a personal and portable dining enhancement tool. The mobile app enabled users to interact with 3D models of food items and access detailed information overlays through their smartphones. The user interface featured intuitive buttons for revealing dish names, prices, ingredients, nutritional values, and cultural backgrounds. This initial prototype focused on creating an engaging and informative dining experience by allowing users to visualize and learn about their food choices directly from their mobile devices, promoting informed decision-making and enhancing overall satisfaction.

Kiosk Application (Prototype 2): After the mobile application's initial testing phase, we identified the potential to further enhance the dining experience by integrating an olfaction device, which was not feasible with the mobile application due to technical and logistical constraints. To achieve this, we transitioned to developing a kiosk-like application. This stationary setup allowed us to integrate the olfaction device with the AR menu, enabling users to experience the aroma of the dishes along with the visual and informational AR features.

The kiosk application retained all the interactive features of the mobile prototype, with additional sensory engagement through the olfaction device. This setup provided a more immersive and holistic dining experience, where users could see, learn about, and even experience the aroma of the dishes before ordering. The larger interface of the kiosk also allowed for a more detailed and user-friendly interaction, catering to a broader audience in a restaurant setting. An important use case for this kiosk setup could be its deployment in restaurants as a fun and engaging element for customers. Such a setup not only enhances the dining experience but also serves as a unique attraction, drawing in customers interested in a novel way to explore the menu. Such a setup can distinguish restaurants from their competitors, potentially increasing customer satisfaction.

By iterating from a mobile application to a kiosk application, we aimed to maximize the potential of AR technology in enhancing the dining experience to increase user satisfaction and engagement.

Technical Implementation. The AR menu application was developed using the Unity game engine [32], with the Vuforia SDK [2] enabling marker-based AR functionality of ARoma. For the mobile prototype, users could interact with 3D models and information overlays on their smartphones, designed using Figma [1]. In transitioning to the kiosk version, we integrated additional hardware, such as a screen display and an olfaction device, to enhance sensory engagement. This required synchronizing visual and olfactory outputs to maintain an intuitive interface while expanding the immersive dining experience.

3.2 Olfaction Device

The prototype of the olfaction device was devised to bring the idea to life using a plastic container, cardboard, a motor, Arduino, and scents from various food items. The process involved enclosing a sample of the scent-spreading substance within a partitioned container with an open front and a perforated back (refer Fig. 4). This feature is activated based on the dish chosen by the user and released the corresponding scents to provide a multi-sensory dining experience. The idea stemmed from the understanding that food selection is not solely based on visual appeal, but also other sensory stimuli, significantly the aroma of the food item. [20]. The scent disposal mechanism in the prototype operates by having different sections for each dish's scent. We carefully selected fragrances that represent the Indian experience in some way. Each fragrance was meant to transport users to culturally significant moments. The scents are created using spices, essential oils, or ingredients that have distinctive smells specific to the dishes. Once the user views a dish on the AR menu, it triggers the Arduino to rotate the lid of the cylindrical olfaction device, positioning the corresponding section with the dish's scent in the open area. This allows users to experience the aroma of the dish.

4 Methodology

To investigate the impact of ARoma on customers' perceptions of food quality and dining enjoyment, we designed a controlled experiment involving two groups

Fig. 4. A basic prototype of the olfaction device consisting of ingredients of the AR menu dishes for the scents. The lid has a servo motor attached to trigger its rotation which is controlled using an Arduino.

of participants (refer Fig. 5). The study aimed to compare traditional menus, AR menus, and ARoma (AR menus with olfactory integration).

4.1 Participants

We floated a Google form across various social media platforms and community groups to recruit participants for our control group study. The form collected basic demographic information and asked if the individual would like to participate in the study. Individuals who volunteered by submitting the form were contacted and invited to participate. A total of 30 participants were recruited for the study out of which 17 were female and 13 were male. The participants were randomly divided into two groups of 15 each, ensuring that both groups had a diverse representation of participants in terms of age and gender. All participants had prior experience dining in restaurants but had varied familiarity with AR technology.

4.2 Control Group Study

The study was conducted in a controlled environment simulating a restaurant setting. The two groups experienced different conditions to draw comparisons between traditional menus, AR menus and ARoma.

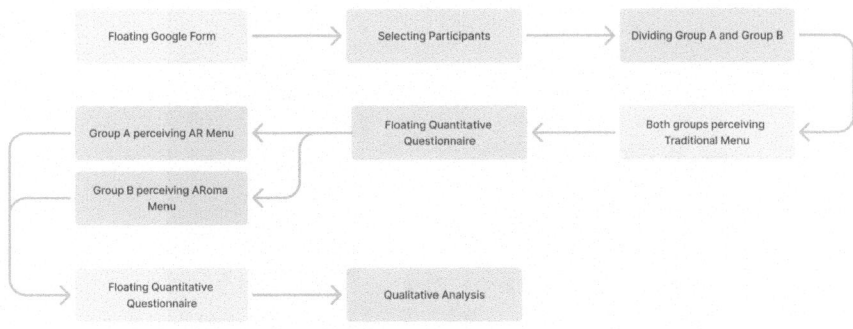

Fig. 5. Flow Diagram of the User Study

Group A: Participants in Group A were first presented with the traditional menu consisting of Indian cuisine dishes. They were given sufficient time to review the menu and make their perceptions based on the textual descriptions and static images provided. Once they completed this task, participants were asked to fill out the quantitative questionnaire (refer Table 1) assessing their experiences with the traditional menu. Next, the participants were introduced to the AR menu mobile application. They were guided on how to use the AR application to view the 3D representations of the dishes and explore the additional information about each dish (ref Fig. 6). After reviewing the AR menu, participants were asked to fill out the same quantitative questionnaire regarding their experiences with the AR menu. Finally, qualitative interviews were conducted to gather in-depth feedback and insights into their experiences with both menu types.

Group B: Participants in Group B followed a similar procedure with the addition of olfactory enhancement in ARoma. Initially, they were presented with the traditional menu and given time to review and evaluate it. They filled out the quantitative questionnaire assessing their experiences with the traditional menu once they were done. Next, participants were introduced to the ARoma setup. They were instructed on using ARoma to visualize the dishes in 3D, access detailed information, and experience the olfactory device that emitted the corresponding scents of the dishes. After interacting with ARoma, participants were asked to fill out the same quantitative questionnaire about their experiences ARoma. Finally, qualitative interviews were conducted to delve deeper into their experiences and gather detailed feedback on the impact of the multisensory experience.

Fig. 6. AR Menu user study with a participant

Table 1. Quantitative Interview Questions and Rating Scale

S.No	Interview Questions	Scale (1 to 10)
1	How would you rate the visual appeal of the menu?	1 (Very Poor) to 10 (Excellent)
2	How easy was it to understand the dish descriptions on the menu?	1 (Very Difficult) to 10 (Very Easy)
3	How satisfied are you with the amount of information provided about the dishes (ingredients, nutritional content etc.) on the menu?	1 (Very Unsatisfied) to 10 (Very Satisfied)
4	How well do you think the menu conveys the portion size of the dishes?	1 (Very Poorly) to 10 (Very Well)
5	How well does the menu convey to you the texture, colour and presentation of the dishes?	1 (Very Poorly) to 10 (Very Well)
6	How would you rate your overall dining enjoyment, immersivity, and engagement with the menu?	1(Very Poor) to 10 (Very enjoyable, immersive and engaging)

5   Results

5.1   Quantitative Results

The quantitative analysis of the study was done using a likert scale based questionnaire (refer Table 1). The quantitative analysis reveals a significant difference in their perceptions and satisfaction between traditional menus, AR menus and ARoma. In Group A, where participants were exposed to both traditional and AR menus, the average score for the traditional menu was 5.72, while the AR menu received a significantly higher average score of 8.2 (refer Table 2). This indicates a notable improvement in the overall dining experience when using AR. Similarly, in Group B, which compared traditional menus with ARoma, the traditional menu received an average score of 5.82, whereas ARoma achieved an even higher average score of 8.97 (refer Table 3). These results suggest that the AR and ARoma menus significantly enhance participants' perceptions of food quality, ease of understanding dish descriptions, satisfaction with the information provided, and the overall dining experience, including visual appeal, engagement, and immersivity.

Table 2. Quantitative Results Average Score out of 10: Group A

	Traditional Menu	AR Menu
Score	5.72	8.2

Table 3. Quantitative Results Average Score out of 10: Group B

	Traditional Menu	ARoma
Score	5.82	8.97

5.2 Qualitative Results

The participants were interviewed after experiencing both the traditional menu and the AR menu (Group A), or the traditional menu and ARoma (Group B). The interviews were recorded and transcribed for a detailed content analysis. The interview transcripts were coded to identify recurring themes related to immersivity, engagement, decision-making, and the role of olfaction. The themes identified were Visual Appeal and Engagement, Information Richness, Immersivity, Role of Olfaction and Overall Enjoyment and Satisfaction.

Visual Appeal and Engagement: Participant 1 from Group A noted, "The traditional menu was just text and a few pictures. It wasn't very engaging. I couldn't really imagine what the dish would look like or how much food there would be." In contrast, Participant 2, also from Group A, remarked, "The AR menu was amazing! The 3D images made the dishes look so real. I spent more time looking at the menu because it was so interactive." This sentiment was echoed by Participant 16 from Group B, who stated, "The addition of smell made it even more engaging. It was like I could almost taste the food just by smelling it."

Information Richness: Participants frequently mentioned the limited information available in traditional menus. Participant 4 from Group A said, "The traditional menu didn't give much information about the dish's ingredients. I didn't learn anything about the history or cultural significance of the dishes." However, Participant 5, who used the AR menu, commented, "The AR menu provided so much more information, like the ingredients and nutritional facts. I loved learning about the history of the dishes. It made the dining experience richer." Similarly, Participant 18 from Group B, who used ARoma, noted, "With ARoma, I got all the details plus the smell. It was a complete sensory experience."

Immersivity: Participant 7 from Group A described the traditional menu as "just functional. It didn't add to the dining experience." They further mentioned, "It was just reading and choosing. Nothing immersive about it." Conversely, Participant 8 from Group A stated, "The AR menu made me feel more connected to the food. Seeing the dishes in 3D was like a preview of the meal." This was further enhanced in Group B, as Participant 20 highlighted, "ARoma was something else. The smells combined with the visuals made it feel like the dish was right in front of me, even before I ordered it."

Multi-sensory Experience: Participant 10 from Group A noted, "The AR menu was great for visualizing the food, but I think adding smell would take it to the next level." This addition was particularly appreciated by Group B participants. Participant 22 remarked, "The olfactory element was incredible. It triggered memories and made me more excited about the food." Participant 25 added, "The smell made it feel so real. It wasn't just about seeing the food; it was about experiencing it even before it arrived."

Overall Satisfaction: Participant 13 from Group A summed up their experience by saying, "The AR menu definitely made the dining experience better. I felt more informed and engaged." Group B participants expressed even higher satisfaction. Participant 28 commented, "ARoma was a game-changer. The combination of visuals and smells made dining so much more enjoyable. It was immersive and informative, and I felt more connected to the dishes."

The qualitative analysis indicates that both AR and ARoma significantly enhance the dining experience by providing more detailed information, increasing engagement, and creating a more immersive and multi-sensory environment. The olfactory element in ARoma, in particular, played a significant role in enhancing the overall immersivity and enjoyment of the dining experience.

6   Discussion and Future Work

6.1   Interpreting the Impact of AR Menu on Customer Perceptions

Our first research question (RQ1) aimed to understand how the experience provided by our AR menu affects customers' perceptions of food quality and dining enjoyment compared to traditional menus. The quantitative results clearly demonstrate a significant preference for AR menus over traditional ones, with Group A participants rating AR menus considerably higher (8.2) than traditional menus (5.72).

This substantial difference in ratings suggests that AR technology fundamentally alters how customers interact with menu information. The higher scores likely reflect enhanced engagement with the menu content, leading to improved perceptions of food quality and increased anticipation for the meal. AR menu's ability to present dishes in a more vivid and interactive manner appears to create a more compelling and enjoyable menu-browsing experience. The qualitative data further illuminates why AR menus were preferred. Participants consistently reported that AR menus provided a more comprehensive understanding of dishes, their ingredients, and nutrients, allowing them to make more informed decisions. Moreover, including cultural context and historical significance of dishes added depth to the dining experience, connecting customers to the culinary heritage behind each meal. This enriched information not only educated diners but also enhanced their appreciation for the food's cultural roots. The increased information availability, encompassing nutritional facts and cultural narratives, seems to boost confidence in food choices and create a more meaningful dining context, potentially leading to higher satisfaction with the overall dining experience.

6.2   Evaluating the Multi-sensory Experience of ARoma

Our second research question (RQ2) explored how the multi-sensory experience provided by ARoma affects customers' perceptions compared to traditional menus. Adding olfactory stimuli to the AR experience further amplified the positive effects observed with visual AR alone, as evidenced by the even higher ratings for ARoma (8.97) compared to traditional menus (5.82) in Group B.

This marked improvement suggests combining visual and olfactory stimuli creates a synergistic effect, enhancing the overall perception of food quality and dining enjoyment. The multi-sensory preview provided by ARoma seems to create a more immersive and realistic representation of dishes, potentially leading to heightened expectations and enjoyment of the actual meal. The qualitative data reveals that the olfactory component adds depth to the dining experience by engaging emotions and memories. This emotional engagement appears to create a more profound connection to the food, potentially influencing not just immediate perceptions but also long-term memories of the dining experience. Furthermore, the increased excitement reported by participants using ARoma indicates that the multi-sensory preview builds anticipation for the meal. This heightened anticipation could contribute to a more positive overall dining experience as customers enter the meal with elevated expectations.

6.3   Future Implications

Moving forward, our development will focus primarily on refining the olfactory delivery mechanisms of ARoma. We plan to expand the application's content to include a broader spectrum of cuisines and dietary preferences, making ARoma more inclusive and adaptable to diverse user needs. Another potential enhancement involves adapting the prototype to a more sophisticated scent dispersal system. This would be possible by exploring specific diffusion techniques to release and absorb the smell. This would help in reducing the amount of smell that is released [33]. Additionally, integrating an ultrasonic sensor to detect user presence would activate the device, ensuring the scent reaches the user precisely when needed. This setup would allow for controlled and efficient scent dispersal, providing a more immersive and engaging dining experience.

7   Conclusion

The clear preference for AR menus and ARoma over traditional menus observed in this study has significant implications for the restaurant industry and dining experiences. These technologies have the potential to enhance customer engagement, improve decision-making, and create more memorable dining experiences. By providing rich visual and olfactory information, ARoma could lead to increased customer satisfaction and potentially influence dining habits and food appreciation on a broader scale. ARoma not only enhances the dining experience but also contributes to social good by promoting inclusivity, health consciousness, and cultural appreciation. As these technologies continue to develop, they may reshape the landscape of the restaurant industry and our relationship with culinary experiences.

References

1. Figma (2024). https://www.figma.com. Accessed 20 July 2024
2. Home — engine developer portal (2024). https://developer.vuforia.com/. Accessed 2 July 2024
3. Ahn, S., Santosa, S., Parent, M., Wigdor, D., Grossman, T., Giordano, M.: Stickypie: A gaze-based, scale-invariant marking menu optimized for ar/vr. In: Proceedings of the 2021 CHI Conference on Human Factors in Computing Systems, pp. 1–16 (2021)
4. Amin, S.N., Shivakumara, P., Jun, T.X., Chong, K.Y., Zan, D.L.L., Rahavendra, R.: An augmented reality-based approach for designing interactive food menu of restaurant using android. In: Artificial Intelligence and Applications. vol. 1, pp. 26–34 (2023)
5. Amores, J., Maes, P.: Essence: Olfactory interfaces for unconscious influence of mood and cognitive performance. In: Proceedings of the 2017 CHI Conference on Human Factors in Computing Systems, pp. 28–34 (2017)
6. Amores Fernandez, J.: Olfactory interfaces: toward implicit human-computer interaction across the consciousness continuum. Ph.D. thesis, Massachusetts Institute of Technology (2020)
7. Arioputra, D., Lin, C.H.: Mobile augmented reality as a chinese menu translator. In: 2015 IEEE International Conference on Consumer Electronics-Taiwan, pp. 7–8. IEEE (2015)
8. Balasubramanian, K., Konar, R.: Moving forward with augmented reality menu: changes in food consumption behaviour patterns (2022)
9. Balasubramanian, K., Kunasekaran, P., Konar, R., Sakkthivel, A.M.: Integration of augmented reality (ar) and virtual reality (vr) as marketing communications channels in the hospitality and tourism service sector. In: Adeola, O., E. Hinson, R., Sakkthivel, A.M. (eds.) Marketing Communications and Brand Development in Emerging Markets Volume II: Insights for a Changing World, pp. 55–79. Springer International Publishing, Cham (2022). https://doi.org/10.1007/978-3-030-95581-6_3

10. Batat, W.: How augmented reality (ar) is transforming the restaurant sector: Investigating the impact of "le petit chef" on customers' dining experiences. Technol. Forecast. Soc. Chang. **172**, 121013 (2021)
11. Brooks, J., Lopes, P.: Smell & paste: Low-fidelity prototyping for olfactory experiences. In: Proceedings of the 2023 CHI Conference on Human Factors in Computing Systems, pp. 1–16 (2023)
12. Carmigniani, J., Furht, B., Anisetti, M., Ceravolo, P., Damiani, E., Ivkovic, M.: Augmented reality technologies, systems and applications. Multimedia Tools Appl. **51**, 341–377 (2011)
13. Filimonau, V., Krivcova, M.: Restaurant menu design and more responsible consumer food choice: an exploratory study of managerial perceptions. J. Clean. Prod. **143**, 516–527 (2017)
14. Fiore, A.M., Yah, X., Yoh, E.: Effects of a product display and environmental fragrancing on approach responses and pleasurable experiences. Psychol. Market. **17**(1), 27–54 (2000)
15. Jain, A., Bagler, G.: Culinary evolution models for Indian cuisines. Phys. A **503**, 170–176 (2018)
16. Kuo, F.F., Li, C.T., Shan, M.K., Lee, S.Y.: Intelligent menu planning: Recommending set of recipes by ingredients. In: Proceedings of the ACM Multimedia 2012 Workshop on Multimedia for Cooking and Eating Activities, pp. 1–6 (2012)
17. Lei, Y., Lu, Q., Xu, Y.: O&o: A diy toolkit for designing and rapid prototyping olfactory interfaces. In: Proceedings of the 2022 CHI Conference on Human Factors in Computing Systems, pp. 1–21 (2022)
18. Maggioni, E., Cobden, R., Dmitrenko, D., Hornbæk, K., Obrist, M.: Smell space: mapping out the olfactory design space for novel interactions. ACM Trans. Comput.-Human Interact. (TOCHI) **27**(5), 1–26 (2020)
19. Magrey, B.S., Chauhan, A., Ramneet: Enhancing dining experiences: Virtual food menu with aroma dispenser integration. In: 2023 Global Conference on Information Technologies and Communications (GCITC), pp. 1–5 (2023). https://doi.org/10.1109/GCITC60406.2023.10426287
20. Miotto, L.: Using scents to connect to intangible heritage: Engaging the visitor olfactory dimension: Three museum exhibition case studies. In: 2016 22nd International Conference on Virtual System & Multimedia (VSMM), pp. 1–5. IEEE (2016)
21. Nanjangud, A., Reddy, M.: The test of taste': New media and the 'progressive Indian foodscape. J. Creat. Commun. **15**(2), 177–193 (2020)
22. Nazmi, N.A.M., Rizhan, W., Rahim, N.: Developing and evaluating ar for food ordering system based on technological acceptance evaluation approach: a case study of restaurant's menu item selection. Int. J. Eng. Trends Technol. **70**(5), 1–8 (2022)
23. Niedenthal, S., Fredborg, W., Lundén, P., Ehrndal, M., Olofsson, J.K.: A graspable olfactory display for virtual reality. Int. J. Hum Comput Stud. **169**, 102928 (2023)
24. Rane, P., Usmani, A.: Digital food menu application for restaurants based on augmented reality. Int. Res. J. Eng. Technol. **8**(3), 2651–2654 (2021)
25. Reddy, A.D., Nath, A.K., Aditya, T., Kumar, A., Sebastian, A.: Menu guide: An ar application for smartphones. Int. Res. J. Comput. Sci. (IRJCS) **6**(06) (2019)
26. Rodrigues, J.M., Ramos, C.M., Pereira, J.A., Sardo, J.D., Cardoso, P.J.: Mobile five senses augmented reality system: technology acceptance study. IEEE Access **7**, 163022–163033 (2019)
27. Rule, A.F.: Food labeling; nutrition labeling of standard menu items in restaurants and similar retail food establishments (2014)

28. Sketchfab: Sketchfab. https://sketchfab.com/. Accessed 20 July 2024 (2023)
29. TEJ, M.B., Bellam, K.: Augmented reality restaurant menu. Int. J. Comput. Sci. Eng. Inform. Technol. Res. **12**(1), 29–40 (2022)
30. Tomasi, D.: Olfactory virtual reality (ovr) for wellbeing and reduction of stress, anxiety and pain (2021)
31. Uma, R., Sirisha, U., Varshaa, V.: Marker based augmented reality food menu. In: 2022 1st International Conference on Computational Science and Technology (ICCST), pp. 967–971. IEEE (2022)
32. Unity Technologies: Unity (2023). https://www.unity.com. Accessed 20 July 2024
33. Wang, Y., Cui, Z., Gong, H., Chen, T.: Olfackit: A toolkit for integrating atomization-based olfactory interfaces into daily scenarios. Int. J. Human–Comput. Interact. 1–20 (2023)

Asynchronously or Synchronously?: Key Insights of Doing Co-Design of Technology with a Vulnerable Population Online

Juan F. Maestre[1]([✉]) and Patrick C. Shih[2]

[1] Department of Computer Science, Swansea University, Wales, UK
`j.f.maestreavila@swansea.ac.uk`
[2] Luddy School of Informatics, Computing, and Engineering, Indiana University, Bloomington, USA

Abstract. Co-design is a collaborative and participatory design (PD) method frequently used in face-to-face settings. However, in-person studies can be difficult or even impossible to conduct in certain situations due to different constraints. Thus, an increasing line of work has been relying on methods that allow researchers to conduct PD studies remotely. In this paper, we cover findings of a case study with 25 participants being part of asynchronous and synchronous remote co-design workshops. It was found that there are important differences between the two modalities regarding participation and engagement, activity design, as well as issues with privacy and confidentiality. We also provide methodological implications and actionable steps to conduct remote co-design studies both synchronously and asynchronously more effectively.

Keywords: Collaborative design · Co-design · Remote study · Asynchronous · Synchronous · Vulnerable populations · Online co-design

1 Introduction

Collaborative Design (Co-design) is a methodology that draws from Participatory Design (PD) [25] as well as user-centered design [1] principles. Technology design research studies using PD approaches like co-design are commonly conducted in in-person settings synchronously [3,26,29]. However, conducting collaborative research studies in person is not always feasible due to different constraints. For instance, one constraint could be that researchers and participants are located in different geographic locations [19]. Participants may also prefer to be part of a study anonymously in order to protect their identities [21,22]. In particular, the Covid-19 global pandemic set unprecedented barriers for collaborative in-person research with human subjects. Consequently, an increasing number of researchers have been conducting collaborative workshops remotely. More research is needed to explore the use of PD methods to conduct co-design studies in both asynchronous and synchronous modalities. Consequently, in this

N. Rangaswamy et al. (Eds.): IndiaHCI 2024, CCIS 2338, pp. 277–295, 2025.
https://doi.org/10.1007/978-3-031-80832-6_19

paper, we discuss key findings and methodological implications from on a comparison of a co-design study conducted both synchronously vs. asynchronously with people living with the Human Immunodeficiency Virus (HIV). We conducted a study to generate technology design concepts that could help people living with HIV cope with HIV-related stigma. We decided to work with this participant population due to prior work arguing about the importance of further assessing the use of remote methodologies to conduct PD-based research with this type of marginalized and vulnerable groups in both academic and industry settings [21].

1.1   Asynchronous and Synchronous Co-Design

Technology design researchers have been exploring how to conduct co-design studies in ways that are more flexible and less disruptive to study participants. For instance, Tudor and Radford-Davenport conducted a co-design study asynchronously in an in-person setting [27]. The researchers argued that they could still get feedback from study participants asynchronously via the use of a physical whiteboard located in a shared space used by participants where people could stick post-it notes on design concepts or ideas whenever they could get to the physical space. Findings from this study suggest that asynchronous participation could still lead to getting more feedback from participants as well as promoting discussion among participants about the proposed designs even though they do not interact with one another in a co-located fashion. Similarly, Dillahunt et al., created physical booklets delivered to participants by regular mail. Participants could fill out the booklet activities with their answers and drawings of their design concept ideas wherever and whenever they wanted prior to a submission deadline. Once the asynchronous study activities had been completed, the study participants sent their booklet back to the researchers successfully [5]. Yet, this type of asynchronous deployment of co-design study activities requires a great level of planning and logistical effort, physical infrastructure, materials, and time [6]. Consequently, researchers have been turning to fully online platforms to carry out remote co-design studies. In the following paragraphs, we explain the methods and tools most used for this purpose.

1.2   The Use of the ARC Method for Asynchronous Co-Design

An increasing number of technology design researchers have employed the Asynchronous Remote Communities (ARC) method [18] to conduct remote studies asynchronously. The most common platform used for ARC has been the social media platform Facebook. Typically, study participants are invited to a private Facebook group where they complete study activities on a weekly basis [18,22]. In particular, this method has helped researchers overcome barriers to access and recruitment of hard-to-reach populations [22]. Scholars in computing have been using ARC in order to work with groups of people who are difficult to recruit due to their stigmatized identity (e.g., members of the LGBTQ+ community [15,28]) as well as study participants who have experienced another type of stigmatizing experience like miscarriage (e.g., [11]). Maestre et al., reported that the ARC method proved to be successful when conducting research remotely with people living with HIV to co-design personalized technology with and for them [21,22].

Table 1. Co-design activity descriptions (source: [20])

Stage Activity	Description	Synchronous	Asynchronous
Stage 1 A1: Introductions	Brief introductions by participants and researchers.	Session 1	Week 1
Stage 1 A2: Letters from the future	Participants write and/or draw technology concepts that could help people living with HIV to cope with stigma.	Session 1	Week 2
Stage 1 A3: Organization of ideas	Participants organize and discuss ideas from A2.	Session 1	Week 3
Stage 1 A4: Technology concept generation	Discussion of ideas and generation of a technology concept based on activities A2 and A3.	Session 1	Week 4
Stage 1 A5: Initial prototype concepts	Participants draw a technology concept based on results from activity A4.	Session 1	Week 5
Stage 1 A6: Session 1 debrief survey	Participants complete stage 1 debrief survey.	Session 1	Week 5
Stage 2 A7: What-if scenarios	Discussion of scenarios of technology concepts based on stage 1 outcomes. Participants can iterate on the technology concepts.	Session 2	Week 6
Stage 2 A8: Envisioning cards	Participants iterate on technology concepts based on envisioning cards prompts.	Session 2	Week 7
Stage 2 A9: Session 2 debrief survey	Participants complete stage 2 debrief survey.	Session 2	Week 7
Stage 3 A10: Final technology concept	Presentation of final technology design concept based on stage 2 outputs.	Session 3	Week 8
Stage 3 A11: Session 3 debrief survey	Participants complete stage 3 debrief survey.	Session 3	Week 9

2 Methodology and Procedure

As also explained in [20], the co-design study consisted of three stages where participants had to complete the activities listed in Table 1. The first stage consisted of a *Future Workshop* [10] for the generation of initial design concept ideas. We asked participants to imagine a utopian future where people living with HIV use technology to help them cope with HIV-related stigma in an effective way. We then asked participants to write a letter describing such futuristic technology (activity A2 in Table 1). Participants then filled out and added post-it notes with their ideas on a virtual board (Mural). The post-it notes could be organized by both researchers and participants and helped guide discussion among participants (activity A3 in Table 1). By the end of this stage, participants collaboratively drew a technology design concept that combined their individual ideas (activities A4 and A5 in Table 1). During the second stage, we showed participants a sketch of the co-created technology design concept created in stage one re-drawn by two UX designers. The re-drawn concept sketch was strictly based on the discussion and insights generated by participants in the first stage and also based on notes taken during the first stage as well as notes added to the virtual board. Participants iterated and provided more ideas on the initial technology design concept based on what-if scenarios visually presented as a storyboard that depicted the use of the co-designed concept generated in stage 1 (activity A7 on Table 1 and Fig. 1a).

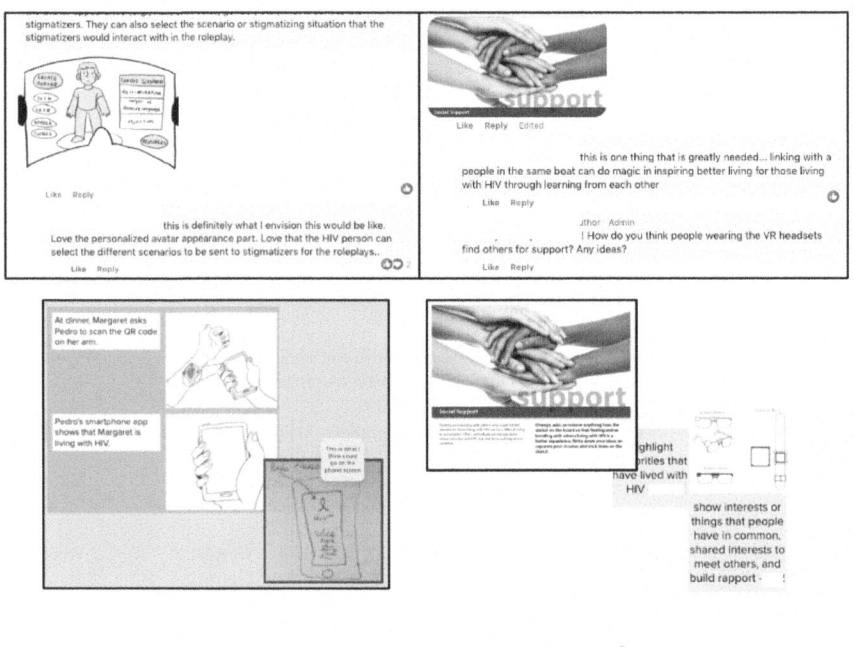

a   b

Fig. 1. Sample screenshots of the a) what-if scenario activity (A7), and b) envisioning cards activity (A8) on both Facebook (top) and Zoom (bottom)

During the second stage, we used envisioning cards [7,8] (activity A8 in Table 1 and Fig. 1b). Each envisioning card included a tension identified in [23] that people living with HIV experience when using key stigma coping strategies such as seeking support or self-disclosure of HIV status to others. The third and final stage consisted of a presentation of the final sketch of the co-created technology concept which included the iterated and additional ideas discussed during stage two. Participants engaged in discussion and provided feedback on the final sketch. At the end of each of the three stages, participants filled out an online debrief survey (activities A6, A9, A11 in Table 1) that asked participants about their experiences with the workshop activities.

The workshops were conducted both asynchronously and synchronously. The goal of conducting the study under these two modalities was two-fold. Firstly, it was important to maximize the chances for recruitment and participation as participants could choose their preferred mode of participation. Secondly, we wanted to identify, explore and discuss similarities and differences in the co-design process between these two very popular ways to do remote research synchronously and asynchronously in our field. For the synchronous modality, participants were asked to complete the corresponding session activities by joining a Zoom meeting and accessing a virtual board. We chose to use the video conference tool Zoom as it had been used successfully for similar remote synchronous research studies [2,9,16,17]. Each consecutive session of the study lasted 1 h and 30 min. Each session corresponded to each of the three stages explained above and were scheduled two weeks apart from each other. For the asynchronous modality, the study was conducted in a secret and private Facebook group. We used Facebook as this has been the platform commonly used for research studies conducted asynchronously using the ARC method [11,15,21,22,24,28]. Participants were asked to complete weekly activities during a period of nine weeks (see Table 1). Each activity prompt was published as a post on the social media group at the beginning of each week on Monday. We asked participants to complete each activity by Sunday. If a participant had not completed the activity by Friday, a private chat message was sent to the participants with a reminder. Participants completed activities via interacting with others (e.g., writing comments and uploading images) in the comments area of the corresponding activity post (see Fig. 1). They also used the virtual board for activities A3 and A4. All research procedures and materials were approved by the IRB department at Indiana University.

2.1   Recruitment

Participants were recruited from online support groups on social media. The online support groups were first identified via a search on Facebook using the keywords "HIV" and "support". We were allowed to recruit from nine groups. The recruitment ad posted in the group invited individuals older than 18 living with HIV to participate in a study which had the purpose to design interactive technology that could help people living with HIV cope with HIV-related stigma. The recruitment post also included a link to a pre-study online survey. The survey contained questions regarding prior experiences with stigma, use of coping strategies against stigma, as well as general demographic information. Survey respondents were invited to be part of a co-design study to be conducted remotely and in a group either on Facebook or Zoom, depending on their preference. Those interested to participate provided contact information to be invited to the study and consent. Survey respondents entered a drawing of two USD$25 Amazon gift cards. Participants that completed the co-design portion of the study were compensated with either a USD\$50 Amazon gift card (for those living in the U.S.), or a USD\$50 PayPal transfer for those residing abroad.

2.2 Participants

Forty six survey respondents out of a total of fifty nine pre-study survey respondents, indicated that they were interested in being part of the co-design study. Interested participants contacted the first author via email or phone and were guided through the study consent process. Twenty five participants (7 women and 18 men) of different race/ethnicity (16 White, 4 Black, 3 Asian, 2 Latino) completed the consent process and participated in the study. The average age was 49.5 (sd=12.9) years. Sixteen participants were from the US, two from the UK and the Philippines, respectively. There was one participant from each Indonesia, Thailand, South Africa, and Uganda. All participants self-reported that they could write and speak English fluently as well as having access to Internet and a smartphone. Participants were assigned randomly to a group in either the synchronous or asynchronous modality according to their participation modality preference. There were two groups of participants for each modality (two Facebook groups for the asynchronous modality: GFB1, GFB2; and two Zoom groups for the synchronous modality: ZG1, ZG2). All groups were composed of 5 to 7 participants.

2.3 Data Analysis

We performed a content analysis [12] of the study metadata regarding participation and engagement. Based on [19,22], participation was determined by the number of comments generated in the asynchronous modality and by turns taken to speak in the synchronous modality. Engagement was determined by activity completion and delays (i.e., number of days needed to complete the weekly activity in the asynchronous modality) [19]. We also investigated activity preferences and technology used by participants to join the study, which is data collected from the debrief surveys. We use descriptive statistics to show the results. The co-authors met remotely via Zoom regularly to do peer debriefing and verification of results [4,14]. The analysis of the actual contents and outcomes of the co-design workshops (e.g., features and functionality of the technology design concepts) is outside the scope of this paper and is explained and discussed in [20].

3 Findings

In this section, we present results from a meta-analysis of data generated by participants during the study. We report on levels of participation and engagement, activity completion and activity preferences contrasting between the synchronous (SM) and asynchronous (AM) modalities. Table 2 summarizes the key differences of key aspects between the two modalities.

3.1 Recruitment

Both modalities led to similar percentages in terms of participants demographic. Most participants were White (60% for the AM and 70% for the SM), men (70% for the SM and 73.3% for the AM) with an overall average age of about 50 years old for both modalities. They were also non-heterosexual (60% for both modalities), had a level of education above a high school diploma (87% for the AM and 90% for the SM). Nevertheless, as shown in Fig. 2, the AM led to more international (40% vs 20% in the SM) and Black participants (26.7% vs 0% in the AM). Overall, there were fewer participants unemployed in the SM (30% 6.7%) or living on disability in the SM (40% vs 26.7%).

3.2 Participation and Engagement

Participants generated an average of 275.25 (s=95.1) total number of comments across study activities in the AM modality. In the SM modality, participants took 445.5 (s=4.9) turns to speak in the synchronous modality. As shown in Fig. 3, the level of participation fluctuated more in the asynchronous in comparison to the synchronous counterpart. On average though, there was an upward trend in engagement throughout the study for the AM, with a pronounced increase in participation in stage 2 (Fig. 3b). In contrast, engagement in the SM remained high

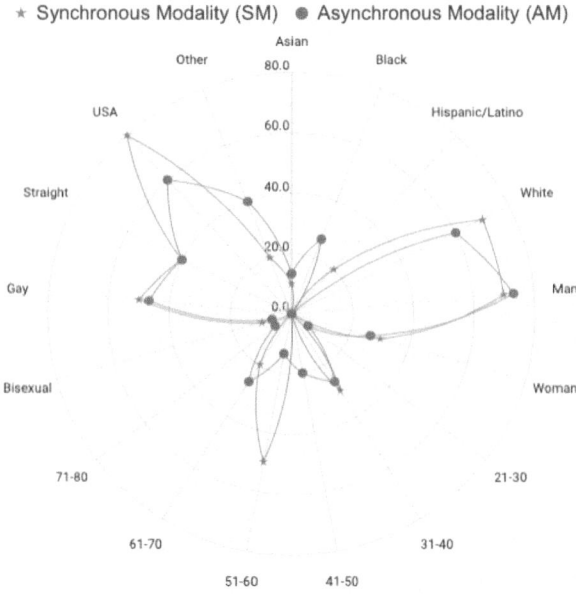

Fig. 2. Demographics for online recruitment for asynchronous (AM) and synchronous (SM) modalities

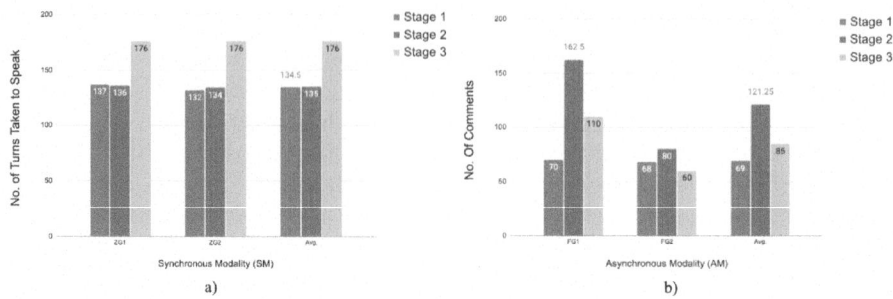

Fig. 3. Participation. Total number of (a) turns taken to speak in the synchronous (SM) and (b) number of comments generated in the asynchronous (AM) modality for each stage in the study

and constant during the entire duration of the study with a pronounced increase in level of participation towards the end of the study in session 3 (Fig. 3a). Additionally, participants in the synchronous modality interacted with more participants during the completion of an activity, whereas participants in the AM interacted with one or two other participants usually a couple of times during a single activity. Thus, participant-to-participant interaction was higher in the synchronous modality. Four participants (26.6%) dropped out in the AM whereas only one participant (10%) dropped out in the SM. One participant dropped out in week 3 in FG1. One participant dropped out of the study in week 2, 3, and 4, respectively in FG2. One participant dropped out after session 1 in ZG1. The reasons participants from the AM gave for leaving the study were that they were overwhelmed by the current pandemic situation (n=1) and lack of time to complete weekly activities (n=2). Two other participants (one from the AM and the other from the SM) did not provide a reason for leaving the study.

3.3 Activity Completion

As shown in Table 3, taking into account non-attendance of participants in the synchronous modality in the calculation, there was an average activity completion rate of 86.9% (s=7.8) and 78.2% (s=15.4) for the asynchronous and synchronous modalities, respectively. However, if we do not consider non-attendance of participants in the synchronous modality, rates of completion for the synchronous modality would actually be higher (93.9%, s=2.9) than the asynchronous modality (86.9%, s=7.8). In any case, the average activity completion per participant was 86.2% (s=8.8) and 77.1% (s=16.4) for the asynchronous and synchronous modalities, respectively. Thus, overall activity completion was higher in the asynchronous modality.

There was a higher completion of survey-based activities (A6, A9, A11) in the asynchronous modality (avg. of 87.8%) than in the synchronous modality (avg. of

Table 2. Key differences between the asynchronous (AM) and synchronous (SM) modalities

	Asynchronous (AM)	Synchronous (SM)
Recruitment		
Not living in the US (%)	40	20
Over $1000 USD monthly income (%)	80	60
Unemployed (%)	6.7	30
Living with a disability (%)	26.7	40
Participation & Engagement		
Dropout (#, %)	4 (26.7)	1 (10)
Avg. number of comments / turns to speak (avg. #, s)	275.25 (s=95.1)	445.5 (s=4.9)
Activity completion (avg. %, s)	86.9% (s=7.8)	78.2% (s=15.4)
Debrief online survey completion (avg. %)	87.8	68.3
Delay in overall activity completion	2.1 (1.2)	-
Delay in debrief online survey completion	1.4 (1.3)	2.7 (0)
Dropout feedback	More likely	Less likely
Activity 'backtracking'	Mainly done by participant	Facilitated by researcher
Different time zones	Very supportive	Not supportive
Technology to Join the Study		
desktop (#, %)	6 (40)	1 (10)
Laptop (#, %)	3 (2)	5 (50)
Smartphone (#, %)	5 (33.3)	-
Tablet (#, %)	-	3 (30)
Activity Preferences		
Most enjoyed activities	Letters from the Future (A2), organization of ideas (A3), and envisioning cards (A8).	Letters from the Future (A2), concept generation (A4), and final design concepts (A10).
Least enjoyed activities	Drawing (A5)	Drawing (A5)
Most difficult activities	Drawing (A5)	Drawing (A5)
Least difficult activities	What-if scenarios (A7)	Concept generation (A4), and debrief surveys (A6, A9, A11)
Facilitation & Moderation		
Discussion going off topic	Rare	Common
Researcher moderation skills	Low	High
Edition / revision of language	Possible	Not possible
Use of virtual board	Harder to teach to participants. Requires link to video tutorials and proactive clarification via DMs.	Easier to teach to participants.
Privacy and Confidentiality		
Participant identity	Use of fake social media profile	Use of pseudonym and possibility to turn video-camera off
Platform security	Use of secret/hidden social media groups	Use of individual links for password protected video-mediated sessions

Table 3. Activity completion. FG1 = number of participants who completed the activity in FG1. FG2 = number of participants who completed the activity in FG2. ZG1 = number of participants who completed the activity in ZG1. ZG2 = number of participants who completed the activity in ZG2. *One participant dropped out in week 3 in FG1. One participant dropped out of the study in week 2, 3, and 4, respectively for FG2. One participant dropped out after session 1 in ZG1

Activity	FG1 (#,%) n = 7*	FG2 (#,%) n = 8*	ZG1 (#,%) n = 5*	ZG2 (#,%) n = 5
A1 (intro)	7 (100%)	8 (100%)	5 (100%)	4 (80%)
A2 (letter)	7 (100%)	5 (71.4%)	5 (100%)	4 (80%)
A3 (org. ideas)	6 (100%)	5 (83.3%)	5 (100%)	4 (80%)
A4 (initial con.)	6 (100%)	3 (60%)	5 (100%)	4 (80%)
A5 (drawing)	4 (66.7%)	3 (60%)	4 (80%)	4 (80%)
A6 (d. survey)	4 (66.7%)	3 (60%)	5 (100%)	2 (40%)
A7 (what-if)	6 (100%)	4 (80%)	3 (75%)	3 (60%)
A8 (envision)	5 (83.3%)	4 (80%)	3 (75%)	3 (60%)
A9 (d. survey)	6 (100%)	5 (100%)	3 (75%)	3 (60%)
A10 (final con.)	6 (100%)	5 (100%)	4 (100%)	3 (60%)
A11 (d. survey)	6 (100%)	5 (100%)	3 (75%)	3 (60%)
Completion % avg. per group (%/s):	92.4% (13.7)	81.3% (16.9)	89.1% (12.6)	67.3% (13.5)
Completion % avg. per modality (%/s):	86.9% (7.8)		78.2% (15.4)	
Median:	6 (100%)	5 (83.3%)	4 (80%)	3 (60%)

68,3%). For other activities, the lowest rate of activity completion corresponded to activities A5 (initial drawing of technology concept) and A6 (first stage online debrief survey) in the asynchronous modality. The lowest rate of activity completion corresponded to activities A5 (initial drawing of technology concept) and A11 (third session online debrief survey) in the synchronous modality. The activities with the most delay were A2 (letter from the future) and A5 (initial drawing of technology concept) in the asynchronous modality; and activities A9 and A11 -which corresponded to the debrief surveys for the second and third sessions- in the synchronous modality. As shown in Table 4, there was an average delay of 2.1 (s=1.2) days to complete weekly activities in the asynchronous modality. Evidently, the highest delays occurred in activities that required the participant more than just writing a comment or speaking such as drawing a concept (A5), what-if scenarios (A7), or envisioning cards (A8). There was an average delay of 1.4 (s=1.3) and 2.7 (s=0) days of delay to complete online survey activities in the asynchronous and synchronous modalities, respectively. Thus, delays of survey-based activities were higher in the synchronous modality. The reasons for not completing activity completion in the synchronous modality were that participants did not attend a Zoom session and therefore did not complete the activities for that session and the corresponding debrief survey; or, when participants who did join a session did not fill out the debrief survey afterwards (there were only three occurrences of this during the entire study though). In

Table 4. Activity completion delay. D [FG1/FG2/ZG1/ZG2] = average of days to complete an activity in groups FG1, FG2, ZG1, and ZG2, respectively. *= for online survey activities only 9iolk9io0-=

Activity	DFG1 (avg,s) n=7	DFG2 (avg,s) n=8	DZG1 (avg,s) n=5*	DZG2 (avg,s) n=5*
A1 (intro)	1.6 (3.3)	1.3 (1.8)	-	-
A2 (letter)	3.4 (2.9)	6.2 (2.4)	-	-
A3 (org. ideas)	1 (0)	1.4 (0.5)	-	-
A4 (initial con.)	0.3 (0.8)	1.7 (1.5)	-	-
A5 (drawing)	2.3 (2.6)	5.0 (3.5)	-	-
A6 (d. survey)	0.5 (0.6)	1 (1)	2 (3.1)	2 (2.8)
A7 (what-if)	1.8 (2.7)	3.8 (3.9)	-	-
A8 (envision)	0.2 (0.4)	3.5 (2.6)	-	-
A9 (d. survey)	0 (0)	2.2 (2.6)	3.3 (2.6)	2.3 (3.2)
A10 (final con.)	1.5 (2)	3 (2.2)	-	-
A11 (d. survey)	1 (1.7)	3.8 (1.8)	2.7 (2.4)	3.7 (3.8)
Delay per group (avg/s):	1.2 (1)	3 (1.7)	2.7 (0.7)	2.7 (0.9)
Delay per modality (avg/s):	2.1 (1.2)		2.7 (0)	
Delay per group (avg/s)*:	0.5 (0.5)	2.3 (1.4)	2.7 (0.7)	2.7 (0.9)
Delay per modality (avg/s)*:	1.4 (1.3)		2.7 (0)	

this sense, in the synchronous modality there is an overall lower rate of activity completion per participant compared to the same rate of activity completion in the asynchronous modality.

3.4   Activity Preferences

Activity preference was determined by how difficult and by how much the participant enjoyed each of the study activities (based on guidelines in [19,22]). In each debrief survey (A6, A9, and A11), participants rated with a 4-point scale (1 = "Not at All", 4 = "Very Much") how much they enjoyed (xl) and how difficult (xd) they found each of the activities. On the one hand, the median for how much participants enjoyed activities throughout the study was 3.9 for the synchronous modality, and 3.4 for the asynchronous modality. On the other hand, the median for how difficult participants found activities throughout the study for the synchronous and asynchronous modality was 1.6 and 2.4, respectively. In the case of the synchronous modality (Fig. 4(a), aside from introductions, participants enjoyed the letters from the future activity (A2) (xl=3.9, xd=1.5) the most, as well as activities in which they could engage in discussion around technology concept generation (A4) (xl=4, xd=1.3) and final design concepts (A10) (xl=4, xd=2). In the asynchronous modality (Fig. 4(b), participants enjoyed the letters from the future activity (A2) the most (xl=3.7, xd=2.4), as well as the organization of ideas activity (A3) (xl=3.7, xd=2.2) and the activity with envisioning cards (A8) (xl=3.6, xd=2.4). The activity that participants enjoyed the least and found the most difficult to complete in both modalities was the drawing of technology concepts activity (A5) with scores of xl=3.5, xd=2.3 in the synchronous modality; and xl=2.9, xd=3.1 in the asynchronous modality.

In the synchronous modality, 13 responses to the question "what was the activity you enjoyed the most/the least, and why?" highlighted that participants enjoyed the most activities that promoted discussion of ideas amongst participants (A3, A4, A7, A8, A10). The reasons provided were that discussion of ideas allowed participants to discuss participants' ideas from various perspectives and come up with ideas that they had not thought of before. Additionally, activities which made use of elicitation artifacts (A7 and A8) were also mentioned (n=3) as enjoyable. Consequently, and as seen in Fig. 4(b), when asked about the least difficult activities throughout the study, there were seven mentions of activities where discussion of ideas took place as the least difficult to complete. In the asynchronous modality, activities which allowed them to exchange comments were rated as the most enjoyable. In particular, six responses were given to denote the Letters from the Future (A2) as the most enjoyable activity in the study (e.g., *"I enjoyed the letter from the future the most. We were able to communicate our visions and our dreams as HIV positive individuals."*). In addition, seven responses mentioned those activities which made use of elicitation artifacts (A7 and A8) as the most enjoyable (e.g., *"The storyboards discussion because we were able to give comments of the situation and there is an open forum on the design of our technology. I enjoyed reading what other participants had to say."*).

As shown in Fig. 4(b), when asked about the least difficult activities in the study, six participants referred to the letter from the future activity (A2) (e.g., *"The imagining living in a world without stigma because the words flowed easily. I know what I have been through in my life because of stigma so this task was easy."*). Four participants pointed out activities that used elicitation artifacts (A7, A8) and discussion of the final design concept (A10) as the least difficult (e.g., *"Replying to the design concepts with feedback and giving my opinion on the final design images. It was nice to see the technology visual and it was nice to read what the technology does. It just made it easier to give my opinions."*). In both modalities, however, the least enjoyable activity was the one that required participants to draw their ideas (A5). The main reasons were that they did not consider themselves to have sufficient skills to draw. Ultimately, trends in activity preference are rather similar for both modalities with overall higher values seen in the synchronous modality. Participants in the synchronous modality gave an overall higher score (median: 3.9) on the enjoyment scale and a lowest score (median: 1.6) on the difficulty scale, respectively. In comparison, in the asyn-

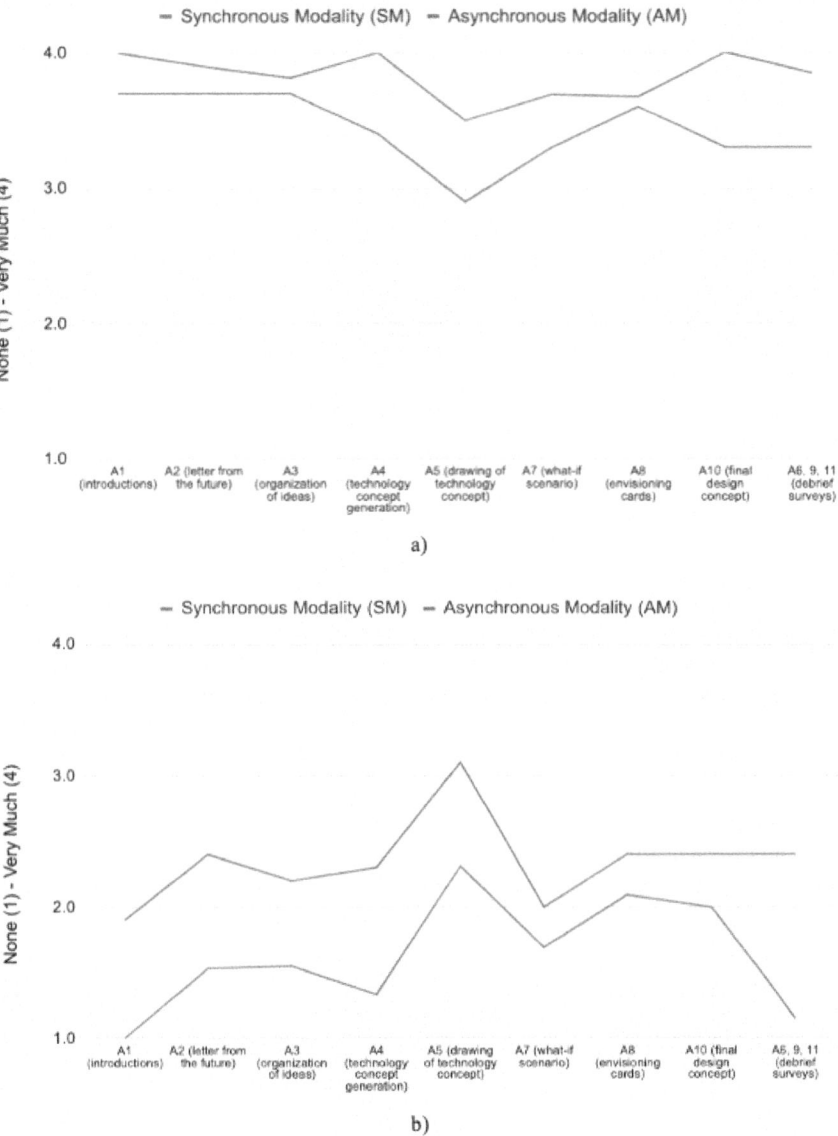

Fig. 4. Activity preferences. Enjoyment (a) and difficulty (b) in study activities in the asynchronous (AM) and synchronous (SM) modalities

chronous modality, the medians of 3.4 and 2.4 correspond to the scores given for activity enjoyment and difficulty, respectively.

3.5 Privacy and Confidentiality

In the asynchronous modality, only one participant self-reported having used a profile with fake information while participating in the study to further protect their identity. In the synchronous modality, participants had the option to turn their video cameras off and complete the session activities via audio only and send their activity-elicited artifacts back to the lead researcher's personal email if necessary. There was no participant turning their video camera off during the entire duration of the study though.

4 Discussion

Using a remote methodology allowed us to access and recruit a higher number of participants living with HIV than what has normally been the case for similar in-person co-design studies in our field. This aligns with findings reported by other researchers in the field working with the same or similar populations. For instance, Maestre et al., reported that the use of the ARC method in remote asynchronous studies led to higher number and greater variety of participants than similar prior in-person studies [21, 22]. Both the asynchronous and synchronous modalities led to similar demographics. Interestingly, the synchronous modality led to a higher percentage of participants with lower-income, or who were unemployed, as well as more participants who self-reported living with one or more disabilities. In addition, it was interesting to note that all participants who self-reported to be Black preferred to join the study under the asynchronous modality. In this sense, the synchronous and asynchronous modalities may lead to different ways of increasing diversity of participants. Based on our findings, an asynchronous modality via social media-based ARC was an effective way for recruiting international participants living in different time zones, while a synchronous modality via Zoom may lead to a higher number of people living with disabilities and lower incomes.

In the following paragraphs, we discuss the similarities and differences regarding key aspects between the asynchronous and synchronous modalities that, based on our findings, had the most impact on participation and engagement. These aspects are: participation level flexibility and activity design.

4.1 Participation Level Flexibility

Overall participation and engagement were high during the study in both modalities. The synchronous modality had the lowest participant dropout. Only one participant dropped out of the study in this modality, whereas four participants left the study in the asynchronous groups. Asynchronous remote studies tend to be longer in duration than their synchronous counterpart [19]. Research with asynchronous studies has shown that participants decrease their participation and engagement as the study duration increases though [19, 24]. For instance, MacLeod et al.'s findings showed that active participants started to drop out of the study after week 12 of the study. Research on remote learning spaces like Massive Open Online Courses (MOOCs) have also reported that asynchronous courses in these spaces have a higher dropout rate than their synchronous counterparts [30]. In this sense, researchers may be able to minimize dropouts via conducting remote co-design sessions synchronously instead. The fact that only one participant dropped out from the synchronous modality may have been due to the flexibility participants in this modality had to be able to miss one session and be able to join the rest of the sessions. In fact, participants who could not join the first Zoom session could easily catch up in the second session where the facilitator would explain -or show- the outcomes generated during the previous missed session. Consequently, it may be important to design activities in a way that it would still be easy for participants to recover from a missed co-design workshop session. Indeed, prior research using a remote asynchronous modality has suggested to design study activities that are not incremental - or that build upon the outcomes or completion of previous activities- so that participants can skip activities and still be able to continue being part of the study and avoid dropping out [18,24].

4.2 Activity Design

There was higher completion of activities in the asynchronous modality. However, there was an overall higher delay in completion of activities in this modality as well. Activities in the asynchronous modality could be completed by participants even when the weekly deadline for that activity had passed. This is something that could not be done by participants in the synchronous modality. Activities of a synchronous session could not be completed in a following session. Additionally, participants in a synchronous modality felt a bit disoriented upon joining a session after missing a previous one. Thus, for this modality, we had to be ready to prepare the session's material in such a way that we could show and remind to participants -especially to those who did not attend a previous session- the progress of the co-designed technological concept. This was accomplished by using the virtual board and an explicit explanation of the artifacts (e.g., co-created technology design sketches, scenarios, etc.) by the lead researcher acting as the moderator of the session. In the Facebook groups, participants could scroll the group's timeline back - or take a look at the virtual whiteboard - to read and see the contents of previous activities. Prior research with asynchronous groups has suggested to not design incremental or sequential activities so that participants who skipped activities do not lose motivation - or feel lost- when resuming their participation in the study [19,24].

Participants in the synchronous modality who did not complete the activities of the previous session could still provide feedback and be part of the discussion after looking at the collective progress made in the group regarding the design of the co-created technology. In the asynchronous modality, however, participants may need to dedicate more time, as well as employ more cognitive effort to complete activities. Participants had to go back and review what had been done by the group previously in order to keep up with the rest of the group (hence the higher delays in completion of activities in this modality). Ultimately, this situation may still impact overall levels of participation and engagement as well as dropout rates. In any case, regardless of type of activities and whether they ask for a more individualistic or collaborative participation, a study conducted asynchronously on a social media platform like Facebook seems to be a more suitable platform to support individual study activities or group activities that follow a stricter incremental sequence (incremental activities). In contrast, a synchronous modality may be less supportive of incremental activities to be completed individually across multiple sessions as participants would not be able to complete activities of missed sessions.

Finally, it was necessary for us to get familiarized with the language that participants used regarding living with HIV to avoid using terms that could be offensive or that could further stigmatize the participants (e.g., "infected with HIV", "people with AIDS", etc.) Unlike what the synchronous modality, in the asynchronous modality, we had more time to check and revise/edit our written language prior to submitting a post, chat message, or comment.

4.3   Matching Study Materials with Participants' Skills

we suggest caution when introducing co-design activities that require participants to use creative skills that participants may not feel comfortable using. Especcially in cases when the outcomes of their activities may be seen by the other participants in the group, which is typically the case in co-design workshops - in particular in an asynchronous modality where artifacts produced by participants are available to others more permanently-. For instance, potential participants could be asked about their preferences for creative activities (or skills/level of knowledge) in screening surveys before researchers pick participants that could express themselves in more creative ways. In fact, Ramirez et al., argues that it is important to match participant skills with participatory design workshop activities [13]. In addition, these types of creative tasks or activities could also be better communicated to participants during informed consent processes beforehand. In hindsight, it turned out to be a good decision to have a team of UX designers who depicted the co-designed tech concepts in visually-appealing sketches and scenarios based on participants' ideas and data collected from workshop activities. Participants indicated that they enjoyed activities where they could give feedback to a sketch or scenarios based on their ideas and input where they could see visually how their group ideas were coming together and taking shape.

5   Conclusion

Our study shows that it may be quite feasible to use online methods for recruitment and data collection when conducting remote collaborative design studies with vulnerable populations both synchronously and asynchronously. Overall participation and engagement was high in both modalities. The differences between modalities are marked by key aspects such as participation level flexibility, format of activities, facilitation, and issues regarding privacy. Regardless, co-design activities ought to be designed in a way that matches participants' skills and communication preferences. Additionally, researchers ought to be properly trained regarding participants' culture and use of language prior to conducting collaborative work with vulnerable groups. We exhort researchers using remote collaborative design methods to further apply and explore the insights and knowledge generated in this research study experience in order to continue improving the use of co-design in our field.

Acknowledgements. Many thanks to Dara Groves, Megan Furness, Oliver Allen, Kenneth Harper, Tiffany Veinot, Katie Siek, Kay Connelly, Lana Yarosh, and Adel Al-Dawood for their help and feedback during initial versions of the study and paper.

References

1. Abras, C., Maloney-Krichmar, D., Preece, J., et al.: User-centered design. Bainbridge, W. Encyclopedia of Human-Computer Interaction. Thousand Oaks: Sage Publications, vol. 37, no. 4, pp. 445–456 (2004)
2. Archibald, M.M., Ambagtsheer, R.C., Casey, M.G., Lawless, M.: Using zoom videoconferencing for qualitative data collection: perceptions and experiences of researchers and participants. Int. J. Qual. Methods **18**, 1609406919874596 (2019)
3. Bonsignore, E., et al.: Traversing transmedia together: co-designing an educational alternate reality game for teens, with teens. In: Proceedings of the The 15th International Conference on Interaction Design and Children, pp. 11–24 (2016)
4. Brewer, J.: Qualitative-quantitative research methodology: exploring the interactive continuum. Contemp. Sociol. **28**(2), 245 (1999)
5. Dillahunt, T.R., et al.: Trust, reciprocity, and the role of timebanks as intermediaries: design implications for addressing healthcare transportation barriers. In: CHI Conference on Human Factors in Computing Systems, pp. 1–22 (2022)
6. Fails, J.A., Kumar Ratakonda, D., Koren, N., Elsayed-Ali, S., Bonsignore, E., Yip, J.: Pushing boundaries of co-design by going online: lessons learned and reflections from three perspectives. Int. J. Child-Comput. Interact. **33**, 100476 (2022)
7. Friedman, B., Hendry, D.G.: Value Sensitive Design: Shaping Technology with Moral Imagination. MIT Press (2019)
8. Friedman, B., Kahn, P., Borning, A.: Value sensitive design: theory and methods, Technical report, University of Washington, vol. 2 , p. 12 (2002)
9. Harrington, C., Dillahunt, T.R.: Eliciting tech futures among black young adults: a case study of remote speculative co-design. In: Proceedings of the 2021 CHI Conference on Human Factors in Computing Systems, pp. 1–15 (2021)
10. Jungk, R., Müllert, N.: Future workshops: how to create desirable futures. Institution for Social Inventions (1987)
11. Kresnye, K.C., Maestre, J.F., Jelen, B., Alqassim, M.Y., Wolters, M.K., Siek, K.A.: Lessons learned from research via private social media groups. In: Extended Abstracts of the 2019 CHI Conference on Human Factors in Computing Systems, pp. 1–8 (2019)
12. Krippendorff, K.: Content Analysis: An Introduction to its Methodology. Sage Publications (2018)

13. Laura Ramírez Galleguillos, M., Coşkun, A.: How do I matter? A review of the participatory design practice with less privileged participants. In: Proceedings of the 16th Participatory Design Conference 2020-Participation (s) Otherwise-Volume 1, pp. 137–147 (2020)
14. Lewis, S.: Qualitative inquiry and research design: choosing among five approaches. Health Promot. Pract. **16**(4), 473–475 (2015)
15. Liang, C.A., et al.: Designing an online sex education resource for gender-diverse youth. In: Proceedings of the Interaction Design and Children Conference, pp. 108–120 (2020)
16. Lobe, B., Morgan, D., Hoffman, K.A.: Qualitative data collection in an era of social distancing. Int. J. Qual. Methods **19**, 1609406920937875 (2020)
17. Lobe, B., Morgan, D.L.: Assessing the effectiveness of video-based interviewing: a systematic comparison of video-conferencing based dyadic interviews and focus groups. Int. J. Soc. Res. Methodol. **24**(3), 301–312 (2021)
18. MacLeod, H., Jelen, B., Prabhakar, A., Oehlberg, L., Siek, K., Connelly, K.: A guide to using asynchronous remote communities (ARC) for researching distributed populations. EAI Endorsed Trans. Pervasive Health Technol. **3**(11), e4–e4 (2017)
19. MacLeod, H., Jelen, B., Prabhakar, A., Oehlberg, L., Siek, K.A., Connelly, K.: Asynchronous remote communities (ARC) for researching distributed populations. In: PervasiveHealth, pp. 1–8 (2016)
20. Maestre, J.F., Groves, D.V., Furness, M., Shih, P.C.: It's like with the pregnancy tests: co-design of speculative technology for public HIV-related stigma and its implications for social media. In: Proceedings of the 2023 CHI Conference on Human Factors in Computing Systems. CHI '23, Association for Computing Machinery, New York, NY, USA (2023). https://doi.org/10.1145/3544548.3581033
21. Maestre, J.F., Kresnye, K.C., Dunbar, J.C., Connelly, C.L., Siek, K.A., Shih, P.C.: Conducting HCI research with people living with HIV remotely: lessons learned and best practices. In: Extended Abstracts of the 2020 CHI Conference on Human Factors in Computing Systems. pp. 1–8 (2020)
22. Maestre, J.F., et al.: Defining through expansion: conducting asynchronous remote communities (ARC) research with stigmatized groups. In: Proceedings of the 2018 CHI Conference on Human Factors in Computing Systems, pp. 1–13 (2018)
23. Maestre, J.F., Zdziarska, P., Min, A., Baglione, A.N., Chung, C.F., Shih, P.C.: Not another medication adherence app: critical reflections on addressing public HIV-related stigma through design. Proc. ACM Hum. Comput. Interact. **4**(CSCW3), 1–28 (2021)
24. Prabhakar, A.S., et al.: Investigating the suitability of the asynchronous, remote, community-based method for pregnant and new mothers. In: Proceedings of the 2017 CHI Conference on Human Factors in Computing Systems, pp. 4924–4934 (2017)
25. Spinuzzi, C.: The methodology of participatory design. Tech. Commun. **52**(2), 163–174 (2005)
26. To, A., Carey, H., Kaufman, G., Hammer, J.: Reducing uncertainty and offering comfort: designing technology for coping with interpersonal racism. In: Proceedings of the 2021 CHI Conference on Human Factors in Computing Systems, pp. 1–17 (2021)
27. Tudor, L., Radford-Davenport, J.: Asynchronous collaborative design. In: CHI'05 Extended Abstracts on Human Factors in Computing Systems, pp. 1837–1840 (2005)

28. Walker, A.M., DeVito, M.A.: More gay fits in better: intracommunity power dynamics and harms in online LGBTQ+ spaces. In: Proceedings of the 2020 CHI Conference on Human Factors in Computing Systems, pp. 1–15 (2020)
29. Walsh, G., et al.: Layered elaboration: a new technique for co-design with children. In: Proceedings of the SIGCHI Conference on Human Factors in Computing Systems, pp. 1237–1240 (2010)
30. Zheng, S., Rosson, M.B., Shih, P.C., Carroll, J.M.: Understanding student motivation, behaviors and perceptions in MOOCs. In: Proceedings of the 18th ACM Conference on Computer Supported Cooperative Work & Social Computing, pp. 1882–1895 (2015)

Camera-Based ASL Alphabet Recognition Using Hand Landmark Features

Anwesha Chakravarty$^{(\boxtimes)}$ and Ayesha Choudhary

Jawaharlal Nehru University, New Delhi 110067, India
anwesh45_scs@jnu.ac.in, ayeshac@mail.jnu.ac.in

Abstract. Sign language is the fundamental mode of communication for people with hearing and speaking disabilities worldwide. The goal of automating sign language understanding is to establish inclusive visual communication to facilitate conversations between sign language users and the wider community. This paper deals with the problem of understanding ASL alphabet gestures and proposes a two-stage deep learning and computer vision-based framework for ASL alphabet recognition and classification into 26 distinct classes. Existing systems struggle with variations in signer appearance, complex backgrounds and limited high-quality data. The proposed method attempts to address these challenges by experimenting with features and classification techniques and uses a learning-based automatic annotation method for labelling data. This work contributes to the ongoing effort of building automated camera-based systems for inclusive communication that can potentially revolutionize visual communication.

Keywords: Sign Language Recognition · ASL · Keypoint Extraction

1 Introduction

Sign languages are visual languages used by individuals with hearing and speech disabilities to interact with others via hand gestures. Sign language recognition systems utilize advanced technologies to capture the visual components of sign language and use algorithms to analyze those and accurately understand and interpret sign language into spoken or written text. In this paper, we explore computer vision techniques and machine learning methods to understand American Sign Language (ASL) alphabets from hand gestures and build an automatic ASL alphabet recognition system to interpret fingerspelling. Fingerspelling in ASL involves each letter of a word being signed individually to form a sequence of hand shapes. Fingerspelling recognition requires the detection of each alphabet sign from a continuous sequence of signs and classify them as per the correct class.

Fingerspelling in sign language is critical for effective communication, particularly for communicating proper nouns such as names of people and places, acronyms, technical terms, and other entities without a standard sign. It can

N. Rangaswamy et al. (Eds.): IndiaHCI 2024, CCIS 2338, pp. 296–310, 2025.
https://doi.org/10.1007/978-3-031-80832-6_20

also be used to emphasize a particular word, clarify meaning, or introduce new vocabulary. Additionally, it is employed to bridge communication gaps, allowing signers to spell out words that may not be understood or recognized by the recipient. This adaptability makes the ASL alphabet a versatile tool within the language. Fingerspelling constitutes about 12 to 35% of ASL, as per the comprehensive study on ASL alphabets by Padden [1]. Accurate fingerspelling recognition is a very important task and can significantly improve the usability of sign language recognition systems, making them more comprehensive and reliable.

Sign languages have complex visual structures that can be difficult for computers to accurately recognize. A camera-based sign language recognition system has to overcome various challenges related to occlusion, variability in terms of illumination, complex and cluttered backgrounds, differences in hand shape and hand flexibility, and diverse appearances of signers, including different skin tones and facial features. In deep learning-based methods, the biggest challenge is to find large, diverse, annotated datasets to train neural networks. The challenge of fingerspelling recognition is significantly more complex than typical image classification problems due to the larger set of possibilities it must handle and the broader spectrum of classes. This expanded class set inherently increases the probability of misclassification.

To tackle the problem of ASL alphabet recognition, this study explores the various challenges involved in fingerspelling recognition and describes the dataset chosen, highlighting an automatic annotation method effective for annotating large datasets. Then, it experiments with the selection of appropriate features for training different machine learning models and evaluates their performance in classifying hand gestures into 26 distinct alphabet classes.

This paper has been divided into six sections. Section 2 provides a brief insight into the existing literature in this area. Section 3 describes the ASL alphabet gestures, the dataset chosen for this study, and an efficient method of data annotation. Section 4 delves into the main methodology, starting with various approaches based on Convolution Neural Network (CNN) architectures and their limitations, leading to the need for landmark extraction, the selection of features and the proposed framework. Section 5 analyses the results of the experimentation. The final section concludes the study and draws inferences for future work.

2   Related Work

CNNs have been conventionally used as a powerful tool for object detection problems in recent years of research, including in sign language understanding. On a range of benchmarks, it has been demonstrated that CNNs perform better than conventional machine learning techniques. Kothadiya [6], Wadhawan [7] and Abiyev [8] have proposed CNN-based approaches for static and isolated sign language recognition for fingerspelling that achieve excellent accuracies of over 97%. Kang [9] utilizes CNNs from depth maps of images. The authors claim to have attained a near-perfect accuracy of 99.99%, while for new signers, the accuracy ranges from 83.58% to 85.49%. The findings underscore the significance of including data from diverse subjects during the training process. Phothiwetchaku [10] has suggested a two-tiered method for recognizing Thai alphabets, concentrating on 25 fundamental motions that can be used to form any letter in Thai. The study by Khan [11] focuses on the Irish Sign Language hand shape dataset by streamlining feature extraction methodologies and utilizing Motion History Images (MHIs) to monitor sign language motions.

Hand gesture recognition has emerged as a vital field in computer vision with a wide range of applications, often outperforming traditional CNN methods and known for their fast model training. It can allow natural and intuitive human-computer interaction by enabling users to interact with machines using hand gestures. Oudah [12] has surveyed hand gesture recognition techniques, highlighting their applications and limitations. The survey focuses on computer vision methods, providing a comprehensive overview of the existing hand gesture recognition systems.

Li [13] has proposed a promising approach for hand gesture recognition by leveraging the strengths of CNNs for automatic feature extraction and SVMs for robust classification. Lyu [14] explores using a CNN with hand landmark detection for static gesture recognition to improve the accuracy of static gesture recognition using a collected dataset of 5,800 static gesture images from 4 people. Dang [15] proposes a static hand gesture recognition system comprising a feature extraction module that uses MMDetection to detect hand-bounding boxes for hand image data or body-bounding boxes for full-body image data, and the CNN-based model HRNet. Fowley [16] investigates the use of synthetic images to augment a dataset of fingerspelling signs and assesses whether this approach can reliably enhance the performance of gesture recognition. A key component of the methodology is the use of skeletal data, represented by skeletal wireframe images. The review of the existing literature in Sign Language Recognition suggests that the use of skeletal information or keypoints can offer significant advantages that enhance both the accuracy and efficiency of gesture recognition systems. By focusing on capturing key points such as hand joints or body landmarks, these methods provide a streamlined representation of sign language gestures. It also highlights the advantages of using large synthetic image datasets, and lightweight machine learning models for faster training and better performance. Despite the promising advancements in this field, there remains a need for further research to develop a reliable camera-based system for accurate detection and classification of sign hand gestures.

3   Background and Data Preparation

3.1   The ASL Alphabet

Alphabets in ASL are represented using 26 distinct static hand gestures or handshapes corresponding to each alphabet in English. Each letter of the ASL alphabet corresponds to a specific hand configuration, creating a visual representation of the English letters. Some gestures have arbitrary shapes, whereas many of these, like 'C', 'd', 'L', and 'O', resemble the shape of the corresponding English letter. The gestures representing the ASL alphabet are shown in Fig. 1. These handshapes enable signers to spell out words letter by letter.

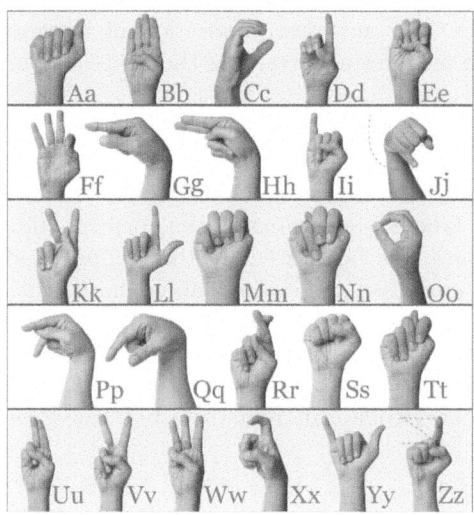

Fig. 1. Hand gestures representing the ASL alphabet.

The hand shapes used to represent the ASL alphabet are designed to be distinct, ensuring that each letter can be accurately identified. However, many letters have similar hand shapes but with slight variations in finger positioning that require careful differentiation. In ASL, the manual alphabet is often used in isolation to spell out individual letters or integrate them into the flow of a conversation. The isolated signs can be captured as static images in datasets for the purpose of training deep learning and computer vision-based recognition systems aimed at translating ASL into written or spoken language.

3.2 Dataset

The Synthetic ASL Alphabet [2] is a publicly available dataset of ASL alphabets. It is approximately 7 GB in size comprising 27,000 images depicting the complete alphabet. Lexset's Seahaven platform, a tool specializing in synthetic image generation, was utilized to create these images. Each image has a resolution of 512×512 pixels. The dataset offers a balanced split, providing 1,000 images for each alphabet sign and an additional 1,000 background images. The dataset exhibits high variability in terms of complex backgrounds, varying illumination conditions, and a range of signer skin tones, signs captured from diverse angles and orientations. The substantial size and inherent variability of the Synthetic

ASL Alphabet dataset make it an ideal choice for training deep learning models in automatic fingerspelling detection tasks.

Raw image data lacks the inherent context that is necessary for training supervised learning models. Accurate localization and annotation of objects according to appropriate classes serve as the critical foundation for training, providing information about the content in the image and helping to differentiate between objects. The accurate annotation of instances in the images is critical for extracting features and training the deep learning model.

3.3 Auto-annotation

In each image, the area containing the hand gestures of signs is marked using bounding boxes and labelled according to the corresponding sign. The manual bounding box annotation is facilitated by the computer vision tool Roboflow [3]. A label text file comprising the class label, the height and breadth of the bounding box, and the coordinates of the bounding box area's centre has been prepared in accordance with each sample image file. However, manual annotation of large image datasets is a tedious and time-consuming process and requires multiple expert signers. Hence, this remains a bottleneck in tasks like sign language recognition.

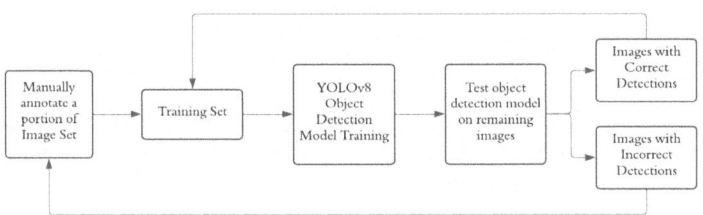

Fig. 2. The auto-annotation pipeline.

To address this problem, we use an automated annotation method that utilizes deep learning approaches of iterative refinement and active learning based on the model's performance, to efficiently annotate the Synthetic ASL Alphabet dataset containing 1,000 images per class. In this approach, a small subset of images from each class is manually annotated. An object detection model, YOLOv8 in this case, is trained on the labelled images, and upon training, the model detects signs in the remaining unannotated images. Detections with high confidence scores that are likely to be correct are added back to the training set. This process of training, testing, and refining the model continues until a desired number of images per class is correctly annotated. This iterative process continued until a satisfactory number of images were annotated per class. Ultimately, any remaining unannotated or incorrectly detected images are manually annotated. A similar technique to train the object detector iteratively on small batches of tagged images has been proposed previously by Adhikari [4]. They have concluded from experimenting with three datasets that this method can reduce the amount of manual annotation effort by up to 75%. The automatically annotated images are manually verified to allow no error in creating the ground truth for model training.

4   Methodology

4.1   CNN-Based Approaches

Because of their ability to automatically learn relevant features from image data by capturing the spatial relationships between pixels, Convolution Neural Networks have evolved as a powerful technique for object detection and image classification problems. For ASL fingerspelling recognition, CNNs can be trained on large datasets and are expected to extract features, identify the specific finger configurations that represent each alphabet, and ultimately classify the hand posture as per the correct fingerspelled alphabet class.

Training Traditional CNN Models. The annotated and pre-processed alphabet dataset of 27000 images is used to train two separate CNN models EfficientNet and YOLOv8 for alphabet detection and classification. Both the models were trained for 100 epochs until they reached optimal performance. Their performance has been evaluated using various metrics. The evaluation process includes testing the model on both seen and previously unseen ASL alphabet images and video frames.

Both models achieve exceptional accuracy for each class during training, indicating its potential for high performance in controlled settings. However, when tested on unknown video sequences in different settings, it often fails to recognize the exact alphabet sign, indicating the problem of overfitting on training data. This discrepancy highlights the challenges posed by the variability and intricate nature of the 26 distinct classes of gestures. This gives rise to the need for further experimentation and enhanced training methodologies to improve the detection of ASL alphabet signs.

Limitations. Applying CNNs directly on images for ASL fingerspelling recognition, despite their wide usage, presents several limitations. One major challenge is the reliance on large, well-annotated datasets for training, which can be expensive and time-consuming to create. A significant limitation is the tendency of CNNs to overfit when the dataset is not sufficiently diverse, resulting in a model with good training data performance but poor performance on unknown data. Given the high dimensionality and complexity of image data, CNNs can easily memorize training samples rather than learning generalizable features.

Moreover, it is challenging for CNNs to optimize for inter-class differences and intra-class similarities when the images share many common features, with only small changes in finger positions distinguishing each class. These subtle variations make it challenging for models to accurately separate classes while maintaining consistency within the same class, further complicating the training process. This is especially relevant for fingerspelling detection because each image sample contains a hand similar in overall appearance, while the difference lies in a finger position or orientation. This requires the model to be exceptionally precise in feature extraction and pattern recognition.

Additionally, CNNs can struggle with complex backgrounds, occlusion or overlapping fingers, as they primarily focus on local features within the image. Although the challenges related to variability in terms of hand size and colour are addressed, different handshapes of the signer, the angles between fingers, hand orientation and different styles of signing are difficult to capture. These subtle underlying details need to be perceived by the model to recognise gestures that belong to the same or different classes. It is a major challenge for CNNs to decipher these intricate patterns from entire hand gesture images that are fed to the network for training.

4.2   Hand Landmark Extraction

In sign language recognition, particularly for fingerspelling tasks involving the alphabet, keypoint extraction or landmark detection can prove to be a powerful approach. This method focuses on identifying and extracting the critical locations of the fingertips and key joints within a hand image. These keypoints, often referred to as landmarks, act like a skeletal representation of the hand posture. By analyzing the relative positions and spatial relationships between these landmarks in a particular image, the system can decipher the specific orientation of the hand in that image and, hence, the class of the sign being fingerspelled.

The advantages of using keypoint extraction include the reduction in complexity of the data by focusing on a smaller set of informative points instead of the entire image. Secondly, landmark detection offers robustness to variations. By focusing solely on the hand's skeletal structure extracted from images, this method eradicates the issues caused by variations in hand shape, signer appearance, signing style, backgrounds, etc. As long as the landmarks are accurately identified, the SLR system uses the relative position of landmarks and spatial relationships between them to interpret the hand posture effectively. Additionally, keypoint data can be used to extract landmark coordinates resulting in faster training of machine learning models and neural networks.

MediaPipe Hand Landmark Detection. The MediaPipe Hand Landmarker [5] enables the detection of hand landmarks in an image. It uses a machine learning model to generate the position of 21 hand landmarks in terms of world and image coordinates and the left- or right-handedness of identified hands. It can operate on either static data or a continuous stream. The hand landmarker uses a model bundle that consists of a palm detection model and a hand landmarks detection model. The hands are located using the palm detection model, which has an average precision of 95.7%. On the cropped hand image defined by the palm detection model, the hand landmark detection model locates particular hand landmarks. Within the identified hand regions, it accurately locates the keypoints of 21 3D hand-knuckle coordinates. The x and y coordinates are located, considering the top-leftmost point as the origin. The z coordinate is taken from the depth maps of images. The MediaPipe model has been trained on approximately 30,000 hand images from various backgrounds.

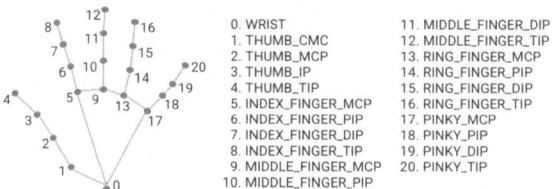

Fig. 3. The 21 hand landmark points in a palm as defined by MediaPipe.

Figure 3 shows the 21 demarcated hand landmark points as defined by MediaPipe. The hand landmark model bundle finds the keypoints of the 21 handknuckle coordinates within the identified hand areas after first localizing the hand over the entire image. The detected coordinates of these keypoints are then used to obtain features for training models.

In the ASL alphabet dataset images, hands are first localized within bounding boxes, and the detected regions are cropped. Next, MediaPipe is used to mark the 21 keypoints in each cropped hand image, and their (x, y, z) coordinates are extracted. Following the landmark extraction, the skeletal data is used to create suitable features for identifying and classifying alphabet gestures.

4.3   Hand Landmark Feature Selection

In gesture recognition tasks using hand landmark data, the features derived from the detected hand landmarks capture the spatial information of the hand and its pose, which is crucial for the model to understand the hand configuration and differentiate between various gestures. It is important for the model to understand the relative positions between different landmarks in order to understand the hand's overall structure. Features like the position and distance between the wrist and fingertips or between adjacent finger joints provide information about finger bending and hand orientation. Features like the bounding box dimensions of the hand or the distance between specific landmarks can provide information about hand size and shape, which can be helpful in differentiating certain gestures. Selecting the most relevant features can significantly improve the model's ability to learn the underlying patterns in hand pose data.

While all 21 hand landmarks provide valuable information, the coordinates of the five fingertips and their Euclidean distances from the wrist hold the most significance in differentiating hand signs. These features directly capture the hand's end effector points or fingertips and their relative positions to the base point, the wrist, which is crucial for defining the hand shape during sign language formation.

The initial feature set for training the models comprised the Euclidean distances between each of the five fingertips and the wrist. While these features provided some information, their performance indicated room for improvement. Consequently, the feature set was expanded to 21 features. This expanded set included the five Euclidean distances, which maintained their role in capturing the relative positions of fingertips to the wrist. Fifteen keypoint coordinates, the x, y and z values for each of the five fingertips were incorporated. These coordinates provide more precise spatial information about the location of each keypoint relative to the top-left corner of the cropped image, defined as the origin. The bounding box aspect ratio has also been added as a feature. This is calculated as the width divided by the length of the detected bounding box, which captures information about the overall hand shape associated with the sign gesture. This final set of 21 features offered a more comprehensive representation of the hand pose and was used to train the models for alphabet sign classification.

4.4   Proposed Alphabet Recognition Framework

Figure 4 demonstrates the pipeline of the proposed methodology for alphabet recognition utilizing hand landmarks. The first step is to detect and localise hand gestures from the original image using the YOLOv8 object detection model. Next, the hand region enclosed within the bounding box is extracted, and MediaPipe is used to detect the position of the 21 landmarks in the cropped hand image. The extracted (x, y, z) coordinates of the 21 keypoints are then utilized for feature selection. Machine learning models are then trained on these features for the classification of alphabet signs.

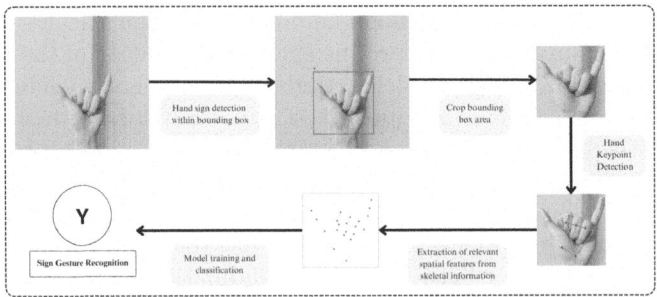

Fig. 4. Pipeline of the proposed landmark-based gesture recognition framework for ASL fingerspelling detection. Each step involved in the workflow is demonstrated using a sample image of the alphabet sign 'Y'.

While YOLOv8 demonstrates accurate hand detection in the experiments, its application for hand sign classification, specifically for alphabets, falls short due to the inherent intricacies and number of classes involved. Following the hand detection stage, the identified hand region within the bounding box is cropped, extracted and used by MediaPipe for landmark detection. The coordinates of these 21 keypoints, representing critical points on the fingers, palm, and wrist, are extracted and stored in CSV files. Relevant features are extracted from the landmark data, and finally, machine learning models are trained on the extracted features to recognize different hand gestures. Three popular algorithms are employed for this task: SVM, XGBoost and Random Forest. Both algorithms excel at classification problems, and the trained models are able to analyze unseen hand images, extract features, and classify the alphabet hand gestures based on the learned patterns. The evaluation results of the trained model are elaborated and analyzed in Sect. 5.

5   Experimentation Results and Analysis

Initially, two CNN models, EfficientNet and YOLOv8, were directly trained on the gesture image data for alphabet sign detection and classification. A high training accuracy and a steadily decreasing loss function indicate learning on the dataset, but its failure to distinguish signs that are similar in appearance from previously unseen frames indicates the need for better methods. YOLOv8 demonstrated its capability of accurate hand detection, but more methods were explored for classifying the detected hand gestures.

After bounding box detection of the hand gestures, the cropped regions are used to extract landmark points using MediaPipe, followed by the selection of appropriate features, which are finally fed into three separate classifiers for alphabet gesture recognition. An initial set of five features is used to train the classifiers. The initial evaluation revealed that the Random Forest classifier achieved an overall accuracy of 82%, while XGBoost and SVM classifiers attained 81% and 84% accuracy, respectively. Certain alphabet signs, particularly 'Q', 'D', 'Z', 'G', and 'P', exhibited lower performance with F1-scores below 0.65. These results suggested that the model struggled to distinguish between these specific hand gestures. An important observation from the initial evaluation was the variation in performance across different alphabet signs. Some signs have lower accuracies, while others exhibited higher accuracies. Specifically, signs 'B', 'F', 'Y', 'C', 'I', 'L', and 'W' stood out with F1-scores exceeding 0.90, indicating excellent performance in these classifications. The features used for training and tabular results are elaborated in the Appendix.

Then, the feature set is increased to 21 features, containing the (x, y, z) coordinates of the five fingertips, which are the most significant keypoints, and the aspect ratio of the bounding box that gives information about the hand shape. This final feature set is again used to train the three classifiers. At first, the hand region is detected within bounding boxes by YOLOv8. Hand landmark points are identified in the cropped hand region. After feature selection, the features are fed into classifiers for the accurate identification of alphabet classes.

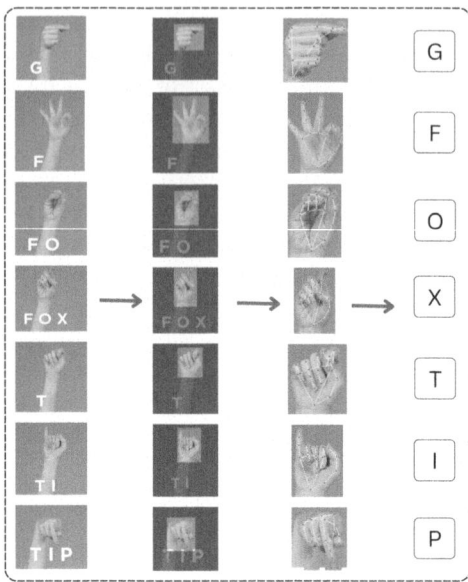

Fig. 5. Alphabet recognition results of the proposed framework. First, the hand region is detected within bounding boxes by YOLOv8, and then MediaPipe detects keypoints in the cropped region, from which the features are fed to machine learning-based classifiers for the accurate identification of alphabet classes.

The improvement in the feature set is directly reflected in the quantitative results obtained after training and evaluating the classification models. A significant improvement in the metric values for each alphabet class and the overall model accuracies is noted. The Random Forest and XGBoost classifiers both achieve overall accuracies of 98%, and the SVM classifier achieves an accuracy of 99%. This indicates that the inclusion of the coordinate values of significant keypoints adds structural information and improves the understanding of the hand orientation.

The performance of YOLOv8 suggests that its strength lies in hand detection but not necessarily the classification of specific signs within the detected hand region, in spite of the high detection accuracies. To address this problem, a two-stage approach is considered for improved ASL fingerspelling recognition. Combining YOLOv8 with another model that excels at hand pose classification leverages the strengths of both approaches for more robust recognition. This gives rise to the need for hand landmark extraction. By refining the features extracted from the hand keypoints, the combined framework better differentiates between similar signs based on subtle variations in hand orientation or finger positioning.

6   Conclusion

This paper highlights the potential of machine learning and deep learning methods to close the communication gap between those who communicate using sign language and others who do not. Accurate ASL fingerspelling detection in diverse and previously unseen settings enables a robust understanding of fingerspelled letters, which are often used to express uncommon words or terms in ASL.

The proposed two-step approach leverages YOLOv8's strength for hand localization and facilitates the identification of the hand region within bounding boxes in unseen video frames. However, for classification, separate models specifically trained for ASL sign recognition receive the cropped hand image extracted from the YOLOv8 bounding box as input and give the correctly classified alphabet class as output. The importance of hand landmark extraction over using the entire image is highlighted throughout the paper. In the given task of classifying 26 different classes based on extracted landmark features, the machine learning models Random Forest, XGBoost and SVM were chosen, which yielded high performance in the classification task.

There are immense opportunities for improvement with the availability of larger and more diverse sign language datasets. Future efforts will extend towards expanding the system's vocabulary to encompass a broader range of ASL signs including numbers, words, phrases and so on, and the recognition of dynamic signs. The broad goal is to develop a comprehensive ASL recognition system that differentiates and identifies each element of ASL from real-time ASL data.

Appendix

The detailed tabular ASL alphabet classification results are included in this section.

While all 21 hand landmarks provide valuable information, their importance varies for sign distinction. The coordinates of the five fingertips and their Euclidean distances from the wrist hold the most significance in differentiating hand signs. The initial 5-feature set uses these as features to directly capture the hand's end effector points or fingertips and their relative positions to the base point, the wrist for defining the hand shape during sign language formation, the results of which are given in Table 1.

Table 1. A comparison of the quantitative results of alphabet classification by the three classifiers: Random Forest, XGBoost, and SVM using the initial 5-feature set.

Alphabet	Random Forest			XGBoost			SVM		
	Precision	Recall	F1-Score	Precision	Recall	F1-Score	Precision	Recall	F1-Score
A	0.90	0.92	0.91	0.91	0.91	0.91	0.93	0.93	0.93
B	0.99	0.95	0.97	0.98	0.95	0.97	0.99	0.97	0.98
C	0.94	0.94	0.94	0.92	0.95	0.94	0.95	0.97	0.96
D	0.55	0.51	0.53	0.52	0.55	0.54	0.69	0.53	0.60
E	0.71	0.91	0.80	0.73	0.91	0.81	0.72	0.94	0.82
F	0.99	0.98	0.98	0.97	0.98	0.98	0.99	0.97	0.98
G	0.61	0.66	0.64	0.53	0.60	0.57	0.58	0.69	0.63
H	0.82	0.81	0.82	0.78	0.73	0.76	0.85	0.80	0.82
I	0.93	0.88	0.91	0.93	0.89	0.91	0.92	0.90	0.91
J	0.81	0.75	0.78	0.77	0.73	0.75	0.82	0.76	0.79
K	0.88	0.76	0.81	0.89	0.77	0.82	0.90	0.81	0.86
L	0.91	0.89	0.90	0.89	0.89	0.89	0.89	0.89	0.89
M	0.86	0.87	0.86	0.90	0.87	0.88	0.91	0.86	0.88
N	0.90	0.90	0.90	0.90	0.90	0.90	0.94	0.91	0.93
O	0.85	0.88	0.86	0.85	0.87	0.86	0.85	0.89	0.87
P	0.65	0.60	0.62	0.66	0.61	0.63	0.72	0.65	0.69
Q	0.43	0.37	0.40	0.49	0.46	0.47	0.45	0.44	0.45
R	0.87	0.88	0.88	0.88	0.87	0.88	0.89	0.93	0.91
S	0.79	0.88	0.83	0.84	0.84	0.84	0.81	0.88	0.84
T	0.81	0.89	0.85	0.81	0.90	0.85	0.83	0.89	0.86
U	0.83	0.75	0.79	0.80	0.72	0.76	0.88	0.79	0.83
V	0.82	0.91	0.86	0.78	0.89	0.83	0.79	0.88	0.83
W	0.91	0.92	0.92	0.92	0.84	0.88	0.91	0.91	0.91
X	0.70	0.71	0.71	0.71	0.68	0.69	0.71	0.76	0.73
Y	0.99	0.92	0.96	0.98	0.95	0.96	0.98	0.93	0.95
Z	0.66	0.56	0.60	0.67	0.59	0.63	0.81	0.56	0.66
Accuracy	0.82			0.81			0.84		

Consequently, the feature set was expanded to 21 features, which included the five Euclidean distances and fifteen keypoint coordinates: the x, y and z values for each of the five fingertips incorporated for gaining more precise spatial information about the location of each keypoint relative to the top-left corner of the cropped image, defined as the origin. The bounding box aspect ratio was also included to capture information about the overall hand shape associated with the sign gesture. This final set of 21 features offered a more comprehensive representation of the hand pose and the final results are given in Table 2.

Table 2. A comparison of the quantitative results of alphabet classification by the three classifiers: Random Forest, XGBoost, and SVM using the 21-feature set.

Alphabet	Random Forest			XGBoost			SVM		
	Precision	Recall	F1-Score	Precision	Recall	F1-Score	Precision	Recall	F1-Score
A	0.98	0.98	0.98	0.98	0.99	0.99	1.00	1.00	1.00
B	0.99	0.98	0.99	0.99	0.99	0.99	0.99	0.99	0.99
C	1.00	1.00	1.00	0.99	1.00	1.00	1.00	1.00	1.00
D	0.94	0.98	0.96	0.96	0.97	0.96	0.95	0.97	0.96
E	1.00	0.99	0.99	0.99	0.98	0.99	0.99	1.00	1.00
F	1.00	1.00	1.00	1.00	0.99	1.00	1.00	1.00	1.00
G	0.96	0.99	0.98	0.97	0.99	0.98	0.97	0.99	0.98
H	1.00	0.98	0.99	0.99	0.98	0.99	0.99	0.99	0.99
I	1.00	0.99	1.00	0.99	0.99	0.99	1.00	1.00	1.00
J	0.99	0.97	0.98	0.97	0.96	0.97	0.99	0.99	0.99
K	0.97	0.94	0.96	0.98	0.96	0.97	0.98	0.97	0.98
L	1.00	0.99	0.99	1.00	0.98	0.99	1.00	1.00	1.00
M	0.97	0.94	0.95	0.96	0.92	0.94	0.96	0.95	0.96
N	0.99	0.99	0.99	0.98	0.98	0.98	0.98	0.98	0.98
O	0.98	1.00	0.99	0.98	1.00	0.99	0.99	1.00	1.00
P	0.99	0.99	0.99	0.98	0.97	0.97	0.99	0.98	0.99
Q	0.98	0.98	0.98	0.99	0.97	0.98	1.00	0.97	0.99
R	0.96	0.99	0.98	0.97	0.99	0.98	0.98	1.00	0.99
S	0.96	0.99	0.97	0.97	0.99	0.98	1.00	1.00	1.00
T	0.96	0.99	0.97	0.96	0.99	0.98	0.96	0.99	0.98
U	0.99	0.96	0.97	0.99	0.96	0.98	0.99	0.95	0.97
V	0.97	0.98	0.98	0.99	0.98	0.99	0.98	0.99	0.99
W	0.97	0.95	0.96	0.98	0.98	0.98	0.98	0.96	0.97
X	0.99	0.97	0.98	0.99	0.98	0.98	0.98	0.98	0.98
Y	0.98	0.99	0.98	0.98	0.99	0.99	0.99	1.00	1.00
Z	1.00	0.96	0.98	0.95	0.99	0.97	0.99	0.99	0.99
Accuracy	0.98			0.98			0.99		

References

1. Padden, C.A., Gunsauls, D.C.: How the alphabet came to be used in a sign language. Sign Lang. Stud. **4**(1), 10–33. Gallaudet University Press (2003). https://doi.org/10.1353/sls.2003.0026
2. Lexset Synthetic ASL Alphabets. https://www.kaggle.com/datasets/lexset/synthetic-asl-alphabets. 22 Sept 2024
3. Roboflow. https://app.roboflow.com. 22 Sept 2024

4. Adhikari, B., Huttunen, H.: Iterative bounding box annotation for object detection. In:2020 25th International Conference on Pattern Recognition (ICPR), pp. 4040–4046. IEEE (2021). https://doi.org/10.1109/ICPR48806.2021.9412956

5. MediaPipe Hand Landmarker. https://ai.google.dev/edge/mediapipe/solutions/vision/hand_landmarker. 22 Sept 2024

6. Kothadiya, D., Bhatt, C., Sapariya, K., Patel, K., Gil-González, A.B., Corchado, J.M.: Deepsign: Sign language detection and recognition using deep learning. Electronics **11**(11), 1780 . MDPI (2022). https://doi.org/10.3390/electronics11111780

7. Wadhawan, A., Kumar, P.: Deep learning-based sign language recognition system for static signs. Neural Comput. Appl. **32**(12), 7957–7968 (2020). https://doi.org/10.1007/s00521-019-04691-y

8. Abiyev, R.H., Arslan, M., Idoko, J.B.: Sign language translation using deep convolutional neural networks. KSII Transact. Internet Inform. Syst. **14**(2) (2020). https://doi.org/10.3837/tiis.2020.02.009

9. Kang, B., Tripathi, S., Nguyen, T.Q.: Real-time sign language fingerspelling recognition using convolutional neural networks from depth map. In: 2015 3rd IAPR Asian Conference on Pattern Recognition (ACPR), pp. 136–140. IEEE (2015). https://doi.org/10.1109/ACPR.2015.7486481

10. Phothiwetchakun, W., Rakthanmanon, T.: Thai fingerspelling recognition using hand landmark clustering. In: 2021 25th International Computer Science and Engineering Conference (ICSEC), pp. 256–261. IEEE (2021). https://doi.org/10.1109/ICSEC53205.2021.9684663

11. Khan, H.M.S., Murtagh, I., McLoughlin, S.D.: Investigating motion history images and convolutional neural networks for isolated Irish sign language fingerspelling recognition. In: Proceedings of the LREC-COLING 2024 11th Workshop on the Representation and Processing of Sign Languages: Evaluation of Sign Language Resources, pp. 140–146 (2024)

12. Oudah, M., Al-Naji, A., Chahl, J.: Hand gesture recognition based on computer vision: a review of techniques. J. Imag. **6**(8), 73 (2020). https://doi.org/10.3390/jimaging6080073

13. Li, G., Tang, H., Sun, Y., et al.: Hand gesture recognition based on convolution neural network. Clust. Comput. **22**(Suppl 2), 2719–2729 (2019). https://doi.org/10.1007/s10586-017-1435-x

14. Lyu, L., Wang, D., Zhang, S., Zhao, Y., Zhou, S.: Static gesture recognition using CNN with hand landmark detection. In: Proceedings of the SPIE 12348, 2nd International Conference on Artificial Intelligence, Automation, and High-Performance Computing (AIAHPC 2022), p. 123480I. SPIE (2022). https://doi.org/10.1117/12.2641815

15. Dang, T.L., Tran, S.D., Nguyen, T.H., Kim, S., Monet, N.: An improved hand gesture recognition system using keypoints and hand bounding boxes. Array **16**, 100251. Elsevier (2022). https://doi.org/10.1016/j.array.2022.100251

16. Fowley, F., Ventresque, A.: Sign language fingerspelling recognition using synthetic data. In: Proceedings of the AICS, pp. 84–95 (2021)

Eyecare for All, a Service Design Approach

Kumaresh Chinnaswamy$^{(\boxtimes)}$ ⓘ, Manjusha Nair ⓘ, and Manoj Neelakanthan ⓘ

Infosys Limited, Plot No, 44, Hosur Rd, Konappana Agrahara, Electronic City, Bengaluru, Karnataka 560100, India
`{kumaresh_c01,Manjusha_Nair,manoj_neelakanthan}@infosys.com`

Abstract. This paper investigates the critical issue of limited eyecare accessibility in India, a significant concern where 80% of blindness and vision impairments are preventable with early detection and treatment. It presents a comprehensive solution to the dire need for improved eyecare accessibility, particularly in rural regions where the prevalence of preventable blindness and vision impairments remains high. The core of this innovative approach combines a service model dedicated to expanding eyecare access and affordability with a sophisticated mobile application designed for preliminary eye condition screenings. The combined solution addresses the critical challenges of early detection and treatment by enabling users to conduct self-assessments for common vision disabilities such as cataracts, uncorrected refractive errors, and front-eye diseases remotely. The mobile app, an integral part of the service model, features a clinically mimicked vision test, a triage system to assess treatment urgency, and the capability for capturing detailed eye images. Aimed at empowering individuals regardless of their geographical or financial constraints, the paper details the development, usability enhancements, and the transformative potential of this service model and app to bridge the eyecare accessibility gap. Additionally, it outlines plans for further implementation and assessment, emphasizing a system thinking approach and close collaboration with stakeholders across the eyecare ecosystem to ensure scalability and impact. Through this pioneering combination of service design and digital tool, the initiative marks a significant leap towards reducing the burden of untreated eye conditions and advancing preventive eye health care in underserved communities.

Keywords: Preventive eyecare · Healthcare in India · Blindness prevention · Accessibility in rural areas · Service design · Mobile application

1 Introduction

80% of blindness or eye conditions in India are due to a lack of accessible eye care. The problem of access is more acute in rural areas. The aims of the project were directed towards solving for the problem of *access* and *affordability* in eyecare in India [1]. Evidently this calls for an ecosystem mindset and system thinking to make any kind of innovation successful. Some key pointers that we worked towards in the programme –

- **Complex systems**

  Understanding the complexity of the eyecare ecosystem in India and adopting a holistic approach.
- **Compliance**

  Work with regulators in achieving compliance in new processes.
- **Test, validate, repeat**

  Build robust clinical evidence in the real-world, to gain trust of regulatory bodies, doctors, caregivers, and patients themselves.
- **Scale**

  Integrate new ways of working, and technology with existing ones to successfully scale the innovation.

In the course of the programme, we realized that for any intervention to be purposeful, clinical expertise or technology solutions are secondary to a deep understanding of the ecosystem, working closely and early with stakeholders in influencing mindsets, and facilitating a continuous feedback loop. Success in this endeavor meant –

- Significant increase in rates of early detection and treatment, leading to a percentage decrease in preventable eye diseases
- Significant screening of eyecare conditions at the grassroots level, leading to purposeful referrals to the right stakeholders in the eyecare ecosystem
- Seamlessly tracking journey of eye health, from initial assessment to effective treatment

2   Background

One of the perspectives was the experience of tele-consultations at the center of excellence of a multi-tier ophthalmology hospital network in India during the coronavirus (COVID-19) lockdown [2]. The cross-sectional hospital-based study involved tele-consultations in the March-April 2020 interim. In a situation where 'demand exceeded supply' or more clearly where the number of eyecare seekers exceeded the number of eye care professionals, a protocol was established to determine the order of priority, a form of rationing which in medicine is referred to as 'triage'.

The findings of this study suggested that -

- a majority of patient queries were related to symptoms of redness/pain/watering/blurred vision; and the most common advice was related to medications used by the patients.
- three-fourths of calls were made by follow-up patients
- a small percentage of patients were asked to visit the emergency of the hospital for further assessment
- a significant portion of patients belonged to the subspeciality of cornea, front of the eye conditions, followed by the back of the eye i.e. retinal conditions

The study concluded that tracking of tele-consultations enabled a timely response during the lockdown period. It provided valuable insights into the possibility of managing patient follow-ups remotely in the future. Notably only one-fourth of the follow-up patients who called were females. This gap in access needs to be understood better.

Attempts at measuring how good one's vision is from a distance (known as visual acuity) in a tele-consultation setting have been explored by many, starting with identifying the appropriate test or app to be used [3, 4]. A prominent ophthalmology hospital network investigated if caregivers could measure the patient's visual acuity with a vision-testing app on a smartphone [5]. The study showed that with minimal training the app, known as the Peek Acuity app could be used by a lay person for home assessment. In the study the app was administered by a caregiver who was given training and orientation to use the app. It is to be noted that except for one patient, everyone had access to an android smartphone and internet to download the app. This shows that the vast majority of patients and caregivers have access to smartphones. It was observed that the measure of visual acuity obtained in the clinic and that measured by the caregiver, were comparable. On the other hand, caution is necessary, since a good reading of visual acuity does not necessarily indicate absence of an eye condition; regular in-person eye check-ups are still needed for overall eye health.

The need for an Electronic Medical Records (EMR) system was found to be indispensable as access to the right information about patient records is crucial for the right advice [1]. The lack of EMR leads to dependence on the patient providing reports to the consulting doctor via email or WhatsApp. This asynchronous advice dependent on the availability of reports contrasts with the real-time resolution of the patient query with the availability of electronic medical records. A good EMR system complements other technology interventions to adapt quickly to times and continue to deliver patient care services.

The solution also needed to be architected suitably to address the problem at a population scale. We built this solution in accordance with the National Health Stack strategy and approach in India, which aims to create a digital health technology ecosystem to improve efficiency and transparency in healthcare.

The National Health Stack, in India is a cloud-based collection of services designed to provide foundational components for health programs. It is a shared digital infrastructure accessible by both the public and private sectors. The stack includes various components

Fig. 1. The National Health Stack underlying the eyecare programme

such as health registries, analytics platform, and upskilling platform (see Fig. 1). It aims to bring convergence and faster go-to-market for health initiatives.

3   Process

Creating a healthcare solution, especially within the intricate weave of eyecare in India, demands a thoughtful and meticulous approach. Our journey towards devising a novel solution to enhance eyecare accessibility and affordability was both challenging and enlightening. It required us to traverse multiple phases of research, collaboration, and iteration.

The process followed was iterative, the objective being a process and a solution that is always learning and improving, as shown in Fig. 2.

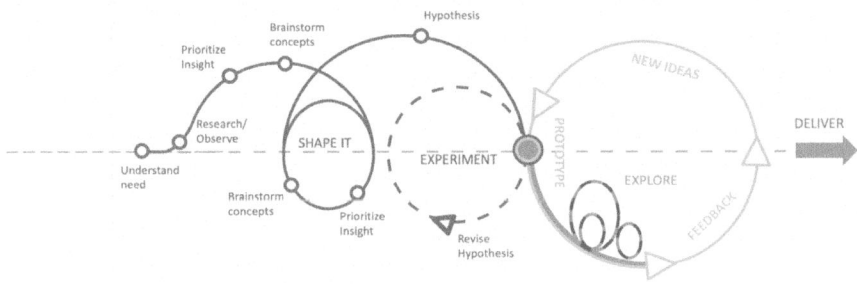

Fig. 2. The design process

Our healthcare and support workers, despite challenges, have created processes and methods that make it possible to bring eye care to the peripheries. Any solution we proposed needed to align with and nest within the existing healthcare ecosystem to leverage the inroads that they had made and the strength of existing networks.

Below, we lay out the core steps that formed the groundwork of our developmental process – steps that are fundamental to the creation of any impactful healthcare solution.

3.1   Studying Vision Assessments in the Clinic

Before we could design a solution, it was imperative that we understand how vision assessments work in the field. We undertook field trips to villages, interviewed and conducted workshops with doctors and other healthcare workers, and participated in ongoing assessments that were organized by the eye institute.

We noted that a typical assessment at the clinic consists of the following parts –

- a set of questions that are outwardly symptomatic and relate to the appearance of the eye, e.g., redness, swollen eyes, teary.

- questions that point to the patient's experience and are conventionally known as 'history-taking,' e.g., double vision, distortion, seeing flashes of light.
- a vision test using an eye chart as shown in Fig. 3
- examination by torchlight for external eye conditions that can be spotted

Fig. 3. Chart used for vision test

Given the diversity and literacy levels, communicating with patients in a language they can understand is a challenge in itself. Doctors and support staff need to be conversant in the local language. Importantly, a vision test relies on recognizing shapes and letters – typically demanding a basic level of literacy. In rural areas though, this barrier to taking the test is removed by replacing letters with shapes – shapes that are contextual, such as bangles. This frees the test from the constraint of the patient being literate. The example shown above is referred to as the 'Tumbling E' method, where a graphic is used in lieu of alphabets.

3.2 Competitive Analysis of Vision Testing Apps

Vision testing is central to the assessment of a patient's eye health, both for follow-ups and new patients. While there are many online tools available, there was a study conducted to validate them with standard clinical methods. Validation is defined by how close the measured acuity values are to the existing standards clinical tests. An in-person study was conducted to validate two apps – SmartOptometry and Peek Acuity. The validation was specific to the particular type of vision testing. For near vision testing, the clinical test was validated with SmartOptometry app. For distance vision testing, the test was validated with Peek Acuity app.

An Android Tablet (800 × 1280, Honor mediaPad T3 10, Model AGS-L09, Android version 7.0) was used for the Apps. Calibration instructions for Peek Acuity were followed. A sticker was placed on the floor, to mark the test distance of 2 m for Peek Acuity. For near vision testing, a 40 cm thread was attached to the Tab, to measure the viewing distance, from the participant, just near the forehead without touching. The Tab was kept at 100% brightness level. As the test involved identifying the optotype direction, participants were encouraged to point with their hand to minimize verbal response. Based on the direction pointed, the examiner swiped the touch screen for the Apps. Minimum engagement was maintained with all participants and the testing time ranged from 7 to 15 min.

The results showed no significant difference between the Peek Acuity app and the clinical method in testing distance vision. However, a significant difference in results was observed in near vision between the SmartOptometry app and the clinical method.

Peek Acuity was developed for community eye care to be used by eye care professionals in testing and for school screenings. The app was used as a home testing tool administered by a caregiver who was given training and orientation to use the app. The demonstration video on how to use the app was found to be helpful to orient the patient and the caregiver. A majority of participants had to view the video again to be able to perform the test a week later. These videos needed to be made available in the local language. Feedback on the app was favorable with the majority of patients and caregivers indicating that the instructions were clear and easy to use. The app is particularly useful for follow up visits, post surgery for example. The study thus concluded that Peek Acuity can be used a home vision-testing tool by caregivers with proper orientation.

However, the SmartOptometry app for near vision testing was not comparable to the clinical method, though still clinically acceptable. Age was also found to influence the measurements significantly. A reason was the pixelation of the digital screen. Therefore, SmartOptometry correlated better with clinical tests when a patient's vision was poor, and not when it was actually good.

Another study comparing an iPhone app with a chart found the app to be overestimating visual acuity, particularly for those with poor vision. Better screen resolution and higher contrast of the display screen were seen as reasons for this.

Overall, the study concluded that it is feasible and reasonably accurate to use these apps for measuring distance and near vision. They have thus an important role to play in televisual testing. Majority of the participants used Android platform, both apps are available on Android and can be downloaded from the Google Play Store. Instructions for testing were clear, indicating that most patients who are familiar with their smart devices will be able to manage this step. Although these apps were originally designed for eyecare professionals, the study shows that non-clinical person can also assess their vision on their own.

Comparative Study of Peek Acuity and Smart Optometry. Peek Acuity and Smart Optometry are smartphone-based vision testing tools targeting different user bases. Peek Acuity focuses on accessibility in low-resource settings, while Smart Optometry caters to clinical professionals. Understanding their features can guide the design of SightConnect, enhancing its usability and effectiveness.

Overview of Peek Acuity. The Peek Acuity app is designed to cater to both medical institutions and the general public, offering a unique approach to measuring visual acuity. It employs a "tumbling E" format that delivers results in both Snellen and LogMAR units, ensuring versatility and reliability in assessments. The app is accessible for free to individual users, while offering paid options for medical professionals, striking a balance between wide accessibility and specialized utility. While the user interface is clear and simple, ensuring an intuitive experience for users, the app's design necessitates the presence of an attendant for accurate usage. Moreover, it requires manual intervention by a medical examiner to interpret results, underscoring the importance of professional oversight in its application. Peek Acuity is currently available on Android platforms and comes with illustrated instructions, although it lacks audio guidance, making it essential for users to have visual or external assistance for navigation and operation.

Strengths and limitations of the app: The Peek Acuity app is highly accurate and reliable across different settings, and its low cost makes it accessible for community screenings and early detection without collecting personal data, ensuring privacy. However, it requires manual handling and cannot fully automate the diagnosis process. Also, it necessitates the presence of an attendant during testing, which could affect its usability.

Overview of Smart Optometry. The Smart Optometry app is tailored for eye care professionals, featuring a comprehensive suite of vision tests, including assessments for color and contrast sensitivity. Engineered with a professional-grade interface, it is ideally suited for clinical settings. Unlike Peek Acuity, the app demands a more intricate setup, necessitating users to undergo training to fully leverage its capabilities.

Strengths and limitations of the app: This tool is precise and dependable for a range of optometric evaluations and is designed specifically for professional use, offering comprehensive diagnostic resources. However, its higher cost and complexity act as a barrier to its adoption for screenings aimed at the general public.

Conclusion. Evaluating these apps led us to the following conclusions:

- **Peek Acuity** is best suited for community and low-resource settings due to its low cost, simplicity, and reliable performance. It is also ideal for preliminary vision assessments.
- **Smart Optometry** provides detailed optometric tools tailored for clinical use. It offers a broader range of tests but is more expensive and complex.

Comparative Analysis. The Comparative Analysis Framework evaluates Peek Acuity, Smart Optometry, and SightConnect across key metrics including accuracy, reliability, user experience, time efficiency, cost, and accessibility (Table 1).

Insights for Designing SightConnect. We gathered several valuable insights that helped us while designing our own solution:

- **Accuracy and Automation**: Incorporate features that minimize manual intervention, enhancing the automation of results.
- **Enhanced User Experience**: Draw from Peek Acuity's simplicity and Smart Optometry's professional-grade interface to create a balance that suits both professionals and general users.

Table 1. Comparative Analysis Framework

Criteria	Peek Acuity	Smart Optometry	SightConnect
Target Audience	Medical institutions and general public	Eye care professionals	General public
Accuracy	Highly accurate, minimal deviation from traditional eye charts	Accurate across multiple tests, validated in clinical settings	Accurate for routine and urgent consults but needs improvements for early consults
Reliability	Reliable across low-resource and clinical environments	Reliable in professional use, requiring training for full efficacy	Reliability affected by outlier measurements in specific classifications
User Experience	Simple, intuitive, minimal training; requires an attendant	Professional interface; user training needed	Simple, Intuitive self test
Time Efficiency	Fast testing time (77 s), efficient for rapid screenings	Slightly longer due to comprehensive test range	Takes 3 min as the test is comprehensive
Cost	Free for individuals; paid options for corporate use	Higher cost, targeted at professional markets with subscription fees	Variable costs based on clinical integration
Accessibility	Highly accessible on Android, no personal data collected	Primarily for clinical use; less accessible for the general public	Highly accessible on Android and IOS and available in 13 regional languages

- **Accessibility and Scalability**: Ensure low cost and broad compatibility with various devices, focusing on accessibility similar to Peek Acuity.

Comparative Analysis of all Apps. We evaluated a total of 12 such online tools on various parameters. The comparison is shown in Table 2, Table 3, and Table 4.

Table 2. Evaluation of apps – set 1

Criteria	Grabi	Peek Acuity	Eye diagnosis	Eye exam
Target audience	Medical Inst. & Common public	Medical Inst. & Common public	Medical Inst. & Common public	Everyone
Onboarding	Mobile based OTP	Open	Open	Open
Diagnosis type	Preliminary assessment	Preliminary assessment	Preliminary assessment	Preliminary assessment

(continued)

Table 2. (*continued*)

Criteria	Grabi	Peek Acuity	Eye diagnosis	Eye exam
Eye test methods	Capture eye using mobile camera (Needs Grabi Device to mount mobile)	Basic vision test using Alphabets	Capture eye using mobile camera	Basic vision test using Alphabets
Disorders identifiable	Disorders and damages in anterior segment of eye	Vision Acuity	Disorders and damages in anterior segment of eye	Vision Acuity
Result generation	Manual intervention/Medical examiner	Manual intervention/Medical examiner	Manual intervention/Medical examiner	App generated
Illustrated instructions	Available	Available	Unavailable	Unavailable
Audio instructions	Unavailable	Unavailable	Unavailable	Unavailable
Unique features	NA	NA	NA	1. Reminders for periodic assessment 2. Vision score history
Monetization	Free to use	Free for Individuals, Paid for Corporates	Free only for 2 weeks	Reminders and Vision score history need pro plan
User Experience	Unclear onboarding instructions Confusing navigation bar	Clear, Simple, Usable	Outdated design (Older stock Android design) Organising images is complex	Clear, Simple, Usable
User ratings	3.7	3.7	3	3.8
Reviews	Incompatibility in some mobiles	Needs an attendant to use	Complex to use, understand and navigate	Very limited functions, Unreliable result
Personal info collected	Name, Address, Phone number, Photos, Videos	No	No	No
Platforms	iOS, Android	Android	Android, Windows	Android

Table 3. Evaluation of apps – set 2

	Eye patient	Eye shape	Eye test	Eye test Visual optometry (Eye Care App)
Target audience	Everyone	Everyone	Everyone	Everyone
Onboarding	Email, Socials	Open	Open	Open
Diagnosis type	Intermediary assessment	Simple eye shape finder	Intermediary assessment	Intermediary assessment
Eye test methods	1. Visual Acuity 2. Visual Field 3. Color Contrast 4. Color Vision 5. Amsler Grid 6. Duochrome Test 7. Astigmatism 8. Tumbling E 9. Landolt C 10. IOL Questionnaire	No tests	1. Visual Acuity 2. Color Vision 3. Amsler Grid 4. Duochrome Test 5. Astigmatism 6. Tumbling E 7. Landolt C 8. OKN Strip 9. Red Desaturation	1. Snellen Chart 2. Color blindness 3. Visual acuity 4. OKN 5. Astigmatism 6. Landolt C
Disorders identifiable	1. Visual Acuity 2. Issues within internal eye 3. Color blindness	Nothing	1. Visual Acuity 2. Issues within internal eye 3. Color blindness	1. Visual Acuity 2. Issues within internal eye 3. Color blindness
Result generation	App generated	App generated	App generated	App generated
Illustrated instructions	Available	Unavailable	Available	Available
Audio instructions	Unavailable	Unavailable	Unavailable	Unavailable

(continued)

Table 3. (*continued*)

	Eye patient	Eye shape	Eye test	Eye test Visual optometry (Eye Care App)
Unique features	1. Eye facts during app startup 2. Educational blogs, videos and articles 3. Appointment reminders 4. Medicine intake reminders 5. Games 6. Personal doctor contact card	NA	Games	1.Eye exercises 2. Eye games 3. Progress tracker
Monetization	In app advertisements Eye care products for sale (only US)	Free to use	50% of the tests are available only in paid version	In app advertisements
User Experience	Clear, Simple, Usable	Simple	Clear, Simple, Usable	Clear, Simple, Usable
User ratings	4.3	2.2	4	3.2
Reviews	Mostly positive	Inconsistent results	Mostly positive	Too many ads, Unreliable results
Personal info collected	Email, Location, Camera, Contacts, Storage	No	No	No
Platforms	Android, Web	Android	Android	Android

4   The Solution

The team undertook field trips to villages and participated in ongoing assessments that were organized by the eye institute. They had an opportunity to experience firsthand the living and working conditions of caregivers and beneficiaries of the eyecare programme. A service model that would underpin the programme, lending it scale and meeting the objectives outlined in the introduction evolved as a result of these experiences. The app that facilitates the model is free-to-use and available to all Indian citizens on mobile, making it easy for people from all walks of life to install and self-test their eyes from anywhere.

Table 4. Evaluation of apps – set 3

	Eye tests Clear vision	Eyecharts Visual acuity	Ocular Check Acuity exam	Zeiss
Target audience	Everyone	Everyone	Everyone	Everyone
Onboarding	Open	Open	Open	Open
Diagnosis type	Intermediary assessment	Preliminary assessment	Preliminary assessment	Preliminary assessment
Eye test methods	1. Visual Acuity 2. Color Vision 3. Amsler Grid 4. Duochrome Test 5. Astigmatism 6. Tumbling E 7. Landolt C 8. OKN Strip 9. Red Desaturation	Multiple unnamed tests available	1. Vision acuity 2. Snellen chart	1. Vision Acuity 2. Color Vision 3. Astigmatism
Disorders identifiable	1. Visual Acuity 2. Issues within internal eye 3. Color blindness	Visual acuity and other eye related issues	Visual acuity	1. Visual Acuity 2. Issues within internal eye 3. Color blindness
Result generation	App generated	App generated	App generated	App generated
Illustrated instructions	Available	Available	Unavailable	Available
Audio instructions	Unavailable	Unavailable	Unavailable	Unavailable
Unique features	Games	NA	Locate nearby clinics	Locate nearby experts
Monetization	In app advertisements	50% of the tests are available only in paid version	Free to use	Free to use
User Experience	Clear, Simple, Usable	Complex to understand and Navigate using Phones. Meant for TV	Simple	Clear, Simple, Usable
User ratings	3.8	3.7	Unrated in Playstore	NA
Reviews				

(continued)

Table 4. (*continued*)

	Eye tests Clear vision	Eyecharts Visual acuity	Ocular Check Acuity exam	Zeiss
Personal info collected	Device ID	No	No	No
Platforms	Android	Android Phones and TV	Android	Web

4.1 The Service Model and Its Actors

The model of service is pyramid-shaped, with a large number of foot soldiers forming the base and just one specialized center of excellence forming the apex of the pyramid. The layers in between are meant to progressively screen patients for common eye conditions, with only the rarest needing treatment at a hospital. As Fig. 4 below shows, the combination of volunteers (known as vision guardians), primary eyecare centers manned by staff with basic training (known as vision technicians), and secondary eyecare centers manned by a lean team of ophthalmologists – together, forms what is known as a Village Vision Complex. This complex is self-contained and capable of healing 80% of conditions that are reported. The remaining 20% are referred upwards to the specialty hospital also known as the Center of Excellence. The service model is thus designed to meet the objective of the programme –solving for the commonest of disabilities of the eye leading to blindness, at scale. Illustrated in Fig. 4 is the service model for eye care.

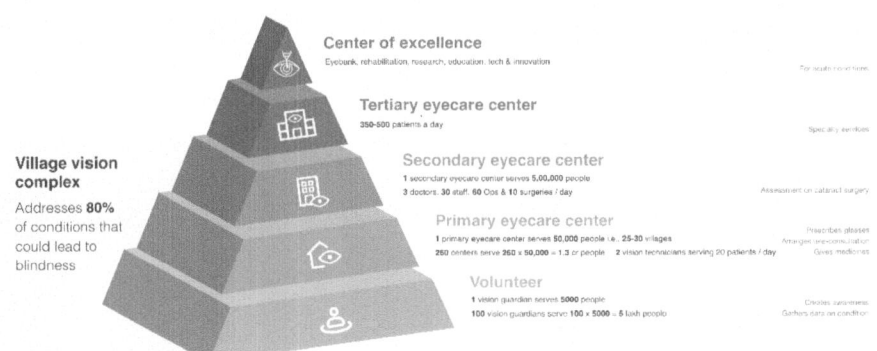

Fig. 4. Service model of eye care

4.2 The Mobile App

Given the high penetration of mobile phones, we proposed a mobile application, Sight-Connect, that would enable the team at the base of the pyramid, the volunteers in screening for conditions of the eye. The app that led to this proposal was further validated in field and clinical tests as described in the next section on Evaluation methods and findings (Sect. 5).

The design ensures that patients exit the triage as soon as the urgency level is determined. Following the tests, the app informs patients of their specific conditions and connects them with appropriate healthcare providers for further treatment and consultation.

The experience of the app was conceived in alignment to the process of vision testing in a clinic, as described in the section on Process (Sect. 3) and proceeded as follows -

Triage Test. Triage starts with a set of 20 questions with weightages assigned that help to prioritize the urgency of eye care needed. The outcomes are categorized into urgent cases, where the patient has to consult an ophthalmologist within 2 days, early cases where the consultation has to happen within 1 week, and routine which can be treated over a teleconsultation.

Tackling the Problem of Our Multilingual Population. Our population is vast, diverse, and speaks multiple languages. Hence it was important that the app be available to our target audience in their local language for maximum reach. We started with manually translating into Telugu, as shown in Fig. 5, to study user behavior when the triage was presented in their language.

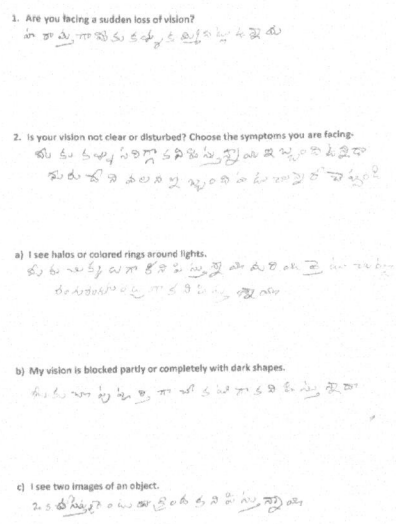

Fig. 5. Triage questions translated into Telugu

We then leveraged Bhashini, a National Language Technology Mission (NLTM) that provides language technology solutions to bridge the language and digital divide in India. By using specific tokenization and preprocessing methods to divide input text into tokens or subword units unique to each language, Bhashini aims to help Indian citizens translate content into different Indian languages and effectively communicate with others who do not know their language.

With the help of the Bhashini, we translated content into multiple Indian languages. Although a good start, the translated content was not directly usable in the triage. Our multilingual team then fine-tuned the translated content to match the sensibilities of the local users. Figure 6 shows the same triage question in multiple Indian languages.

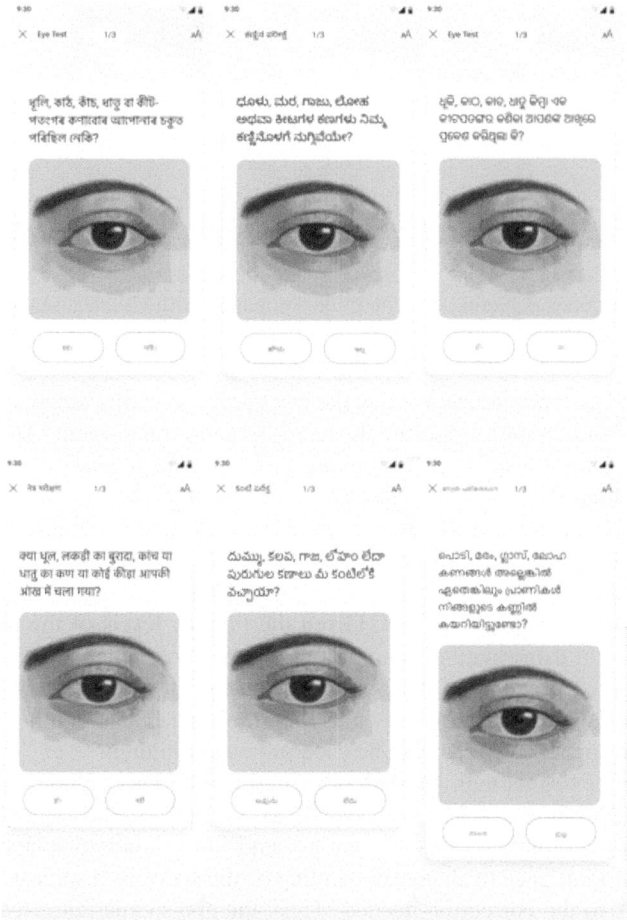

Fig. 6. Triage translated into multiple languages

Types of Questions. There are two question types, as shown in Fig. 7, through which the triage meets its objective –

a) a set of questions that are outwardly symptomatic and relate to the appearance of the eye, e.g., redness, swollen eyes, teary.

b) questions that point to the patient's experience and are conventionally known as 'history-taking,' e.g., double vision, distortion, seeing flashes of light.

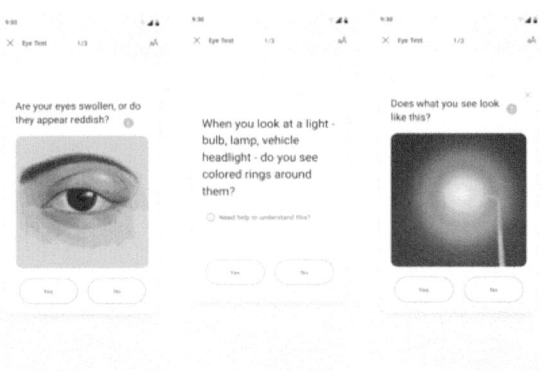

Fig. 7. Questions depicting eye condition, supported with visuals and voice input

Reading Test. The reading test mimics the eye chart test, helps identify difficulties in reading which is a common issue for those with vision impairment. The Tumbling E chart was used since it is more universal and avoids language barriers and can also be tried in young children.

This test is to detect uncorrected refractive errors or those that can be fixed by prescribing glasses. It also can detect potential cases of cataract. The app simulates the experience of a patient undergoing such a test in the hospital, but crucially, without the need for an expert to conduct the test. Given the literacy levels of the user group, we chose the method of using symbols and graphics instead of alphabets for testing vision. This is an accepted practice aligned with the process by which vision is measured, particularly in rural areas. This is known as the Tumbling E, and is more universal and avoids language barriers and can also be tried in young children.

The experience begins with lucid step-by-step instructions on how to take the test. Text is kept to a minimum, relying on visuals to convey the action intended. The user is encouraged to complete the test in one go, and the symbols displayed (instead of alphabets) are programmed to change depending on the previous response, progressively narrowing down to the correction needed. Thus, the app's experience leads to a result similar to the one obtained by a visit to an eye clinic.

The vision testing experience went through several iterations on testing with users. Beyond the problem of making the specific test comprehensible (e.g. show which direction this symbol is pointing to), users struggled to record their responses in the app. The synchronization between the two was arrived at through several iterations in the design. We considered the ergonomics of holding the phone at the required distance, interacting with it to give a response and lastly moving to the next in the sequence of tests. We arrived at an optimum design with the aim of enabling the user to do it herself without needing any help. Secondly, we found patients worrying about the 'correctness' of their response. In the spirit of accurate assessment, all responses were shown as-is without judgement; and the user was encouraged to complete the test with a transparent indication of progress and steps remaining. Screenshots in Fig. 8 below show key stages of the vision testing process.

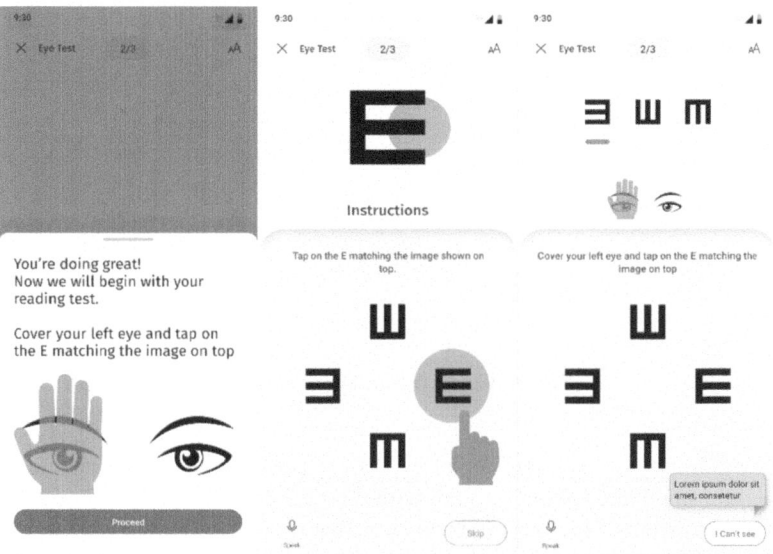

Fig. 8. Vision testing in the app using graphic representation of the letter 'E'

Visual Examination. Cataract – a condition that causes cloudiness in the lens of the eye and other conditions that manifest in the front of the eye are typically detected by a close examination of the eye in a clinic by an optometrist. The app facilitates this by a close-up photograph of the eye that a user can herself take (Fig. 9). The photograph is captured with a specialist program that helps patients take clinical-quality media.

Through a series of tests therefore, the app allows the user to identify if she has a problem. The results of this process were subjected to a clinical validation and the algorithm modified to bring the results closer to those observed by a doctor in the clinic. Through this correction, a fair degree of accuracy was achieved in the results generated by the app.

The next step towards treatment is informing and connecting the patient to the nearest eyecare provider. The app informs the patient on the seriousness of the eye condition and directs her to the eyecare provider nearest to her location.

4.3 Volunteer View and Actions

The volunteers (or vision guardians) play a key role in bridging the gap between the common man and quality expertise in eyecare. The app helps them in managing the

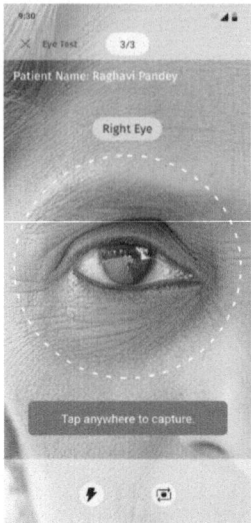

Fig. 9. Capturing the eye in close-up

eyecare programme as a key intermediary. They use it to plan and organize eye camps in the neighborhood and follow through with their duties.

One of the insights from our field trips was that (potential) patients were indifferent and skeptical about their health in general and eyecare in particular. This can be attributed to several reasons: fear of technology, apprehensions about cost, and a general air of nonchalance. The volunteer plays an important role in altering these perceptions and nudging the user into taking the test and following up. The app enhances volunteer productivity by providing reminders, updates, and notifications, as illustrated in Fig. 10, which displays the volunteer's view.

The app also allows them to mediate the assessments on behalf of the patient, and thus overcome some of the barriers mentioned above. To be more effective, they use a tablet that has both administrative and end-user features of the app.

5   Evaluation Methods and Findings

Evaluating and testing the solution was an important part of the process. We tackled this through User Experience evaluations and Clinical Validation.

5.1   User Experience Evaluation

We conducted four types of evaluations on the first version of the app to validate the app design.

Usability Test: The prototype's usability test revealed various insights among participants of different ages and reading levels. Here are the collated findings and insights drawn from the observations.

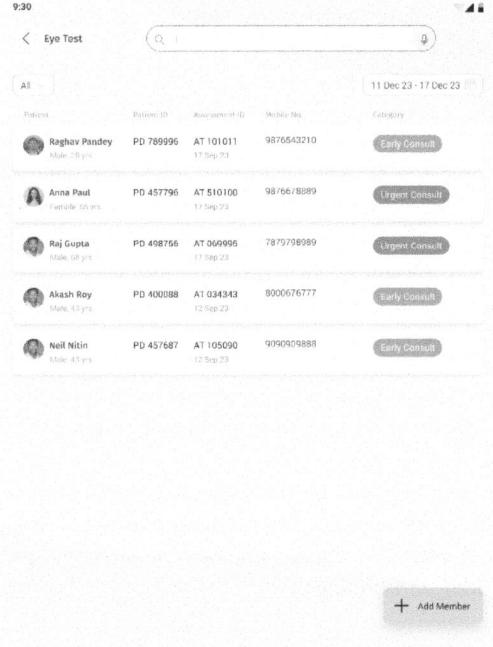

Fig. 10. View of volunteer's (or vision guardian) dashboard on a tablet version

a. Language and Comprehension Issues

- There was a notable variance in the ability to read and understand Kannada, with some participants unable to comprehend the instructions well. This was evident in both the reading of instructions and the understanding of specific terms within the test.

b. Navigational Challenges

- Participants encountered difficulties navigating the app, especially identifying actionable items like buttons for starting the test or proceeding to the next screen. This suggests that the app's user interface could be made more intuitive.
- Confusion arose from the design of instruction screens, with some users attempting to interact with non-interactive elements like instructional text.

c. Visual Design and Accessibility

- The small font size was problematic for participants, impacting their ability to read instructions comfortably.
- There was confusion over interactive elements, such as the letters for the eye test, which some participants didn't know how to use. Visual cues also were found to be ineffective for certain users.

- Participants missed seeing instructions, skipped or jumped to the next screen and then were confused about how to proceed.

d. Instructional Clarity

- Instructions for physical actions, such as holding the device at eye level, closing one eye at a time, and taking pictures of the eyes, were unclear to several users.
- Some instructions were misinterpreted or found to be ineffective, particularly those related to which eye should be closed during the test.

e. Assistance and Feedback

- A significant number of participants required external help to complete the test, highlighting the need for more self-explanatory and guided processes within the app.
- Feedback on the results page could have been clearer to users, with some finding the language difficult or needing help understanding the assessment outcome.
- The need for external assistance spanned across age groups but was more pronounced in older participants.

Role Plays: In the initial phase, we conducted role-plays to generate ideas to improve the experience. For this exercise, we chose some of our more empathetic coworkers to play roles of rural patients. We created personas with backstories and eye conditions that the participants were prepped with before we conducted the tests with them. Noted here are some of the observations from this exercise:

a. Patient/user finds the whole assessment long.
b. The questions, and tests are by themselves quickly completed – following the instructions and getting it right takes a lot of time.
c. The visual acuity test is hard to follow; simplify it further.
d. Eye scanning is neither easy nor accurate; a tool like Grabi will be useful to integrate.

UX Expert Review: Reviewing with a group of peer reviewers to identify problems on an early version gave us a lot of input to improve the user experience of the app. Here are some of the observations that we incorporated into the design:

e. Make the primary function of the app clear; set expectations right with the user.
f. There needs to be an option to exit as soon as an urgent or early consult condition is detected.
g. If the user can't see the symbol in the visual acuity test, there needs to be an option to exit or skip the test.
h. The results screen needs to be simpler and communicate the urgency of the condition.

These validations were carried out for both versions of the app to compare and track the improvement.

System Usability Score: A system usability score of 75% was obtained from 15 users (P1-P15), as shown in Table 5. The users were adults of ages between 33 and 74, at varying levels of mobile literacy–11 of whom had basic reading skills, and 4 required reading assistance to take the test.

Table 5. System Usability Test scores

	Q1	Q2	Q3	Q4	Q5	Q6	Q7	Q8	Q9	Q10	Total
P1	4	2	2	0	3	3	4	2	4	2	65
P2	4	3	4	4	3	3	2	3	4	2	80
P3	3	3	3	4	3	3	2	3	3	4	77.5
P4	4	4	4	0	4	4	4	4	4	4	90
P5	3	4	4	3	4	4	2	3	3	1	77.5
P6	2	4	4	1	4	4	4	4	4	4	87.5
P7	3	2	2	3	4	4	2	3	3	4	75
P8	2	2	1	1	3	4	2	2	1	3	52.5
P9	2	3	2	1	4	4	1	3	2	3	62.5
P10	3	1	2	1	3	4	2	2	2	2	55
P11	3	3	4	4	4	4	4	4	3	4	92.5
P12	3	3	3	4	3	3	2	3	3	4	77.5
P13	4	3	4	4	3	3	2	3	4	2	80
P14	3	4	4	3	4	4	2	3	3	4	85
P15	2	3	3	1	4	4	2	3	3	3	70
								Total SUS			**75**

5.2 Clinical Validation

A large validation study with 700 patients was carried out at the Eye hospital with an aim to evaluate the performance of the app in classifying consults into three urgency categories: routine (Class 1), early (Class 2), and urgent (Class 3), as compared to classifications made using the traditional hospital examination.

All of the patients were triaged using the app and then examined by a doctor in the traditional manner in the clinic. The clinical impression of the case as found in the hospital was then compared to the results of the app triage. The doctor's classification of Urgent, Early or Routine consult for each patient was compared to the app's recommendations, and findings were recorded.

The performance was evaluated using a confusion matrix and several key metrics, including precision, recall (sensitivity), f1-score, and support.

The analysis revealed that with the removal of outliers, visual acuity sensitivity accuracy could be improved by about 92% for Class 1, 58.5% for Class 2, and 72.4% for Class 3.

5.3 Changes Made to Improve Consult Accuracy

To enhance the model's learning capability, particularly for early consult categories, data augmentation, and resampling techniques were undertaken to ensure a balanced class distribution in the training set. Additional features were explored and current ones revised, which was crucial for their predictive power in distinguishing early consults. More complex models were adopted to better capture the nuances between different consult categories. Alternative evaluations were employed for more accurate performance measurement in imbalanced classes.

The weightage of the triage questions was then readjusted to align with doctors' clinical recommendations, making the app recommendations much more accurate. We believe that establishing a continuous monitoring and feedback system would facilitate iterative improvements over time.

6 Discussions

An SUS score of 75% combined with our validations and findings, revealed several things to us:

- Enhancing the visual design to make interactive elements more apparent and using larger fonts could improve usability.
- Revising the instructions and feedback to ensure clarity and simplicity might help users navigate the test more independently.
- Incorporating more intuitive guidance, such as animated demonstrations of physical actions required during the test, could reduce the need for external assistance.
- Tell them beforehand that the test has three parts. Alternatively, keep the first two sets going without any break, as they are both yes-and-no questions.
- Using voice/video instructions and feedback.
- Providing clearer, more detailed explanations of test outcomes could cater to a broader user base.
- Using AI to detect eye conditions can reduce the user's load.

We addressed these with a fresh approach and created a new version of the app.

The team believes that this needs to be an ongoing, iterative solution that keeps getting better the more it interacts with patients.

7 Future Plans

We have several ideas and plans to improve the app and service model and to ensure that its reach keeps growing. Our ultimate goal is to reach every last patient who needs quality eyecare but can't access it at present. Specifically, the goal of the programme is to achieve triage at the beginning stages for 80% of the population of India that is underserved today by the end of 2026.

- **New Functionalities:** Two main functionalities are on the anvil that will improve the effectiveness of the solution -

- **Distance Vision Test:** This test is traditionally done with an eye chart 6 m away from the patient. By introducing this test on the mobile app, we can enable the patient to do this on their own by getting someone to assist them. The vision guardian will also be able to use his digital tablet to conduct this test with the patients in the field.
- **Eye Bank Module:** The plan to add an eye bank module to work towards preventing corneal blindness is already underway. The team aims to leverage AI/ML to radically speed up the process of matching donors and recipients, making the work of doctors and support staff much simpler. The modified eye bank process is shown in Fig. 11.

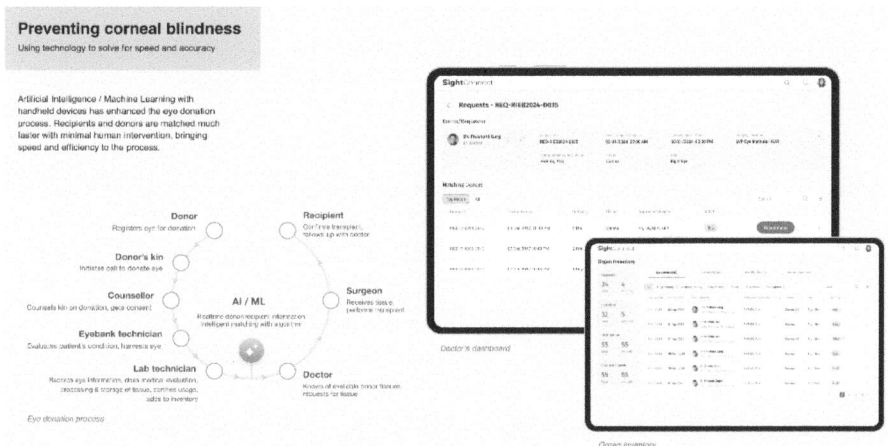

Fig. 11. AI/ML adds speed and accuracy to the eye bank process

- **Improving Diagnostic Algorithms:** In addition to expanding the app's capabilities to include more eye conditions, we are working on improving its diagnostic algorithms by reworking logic and adjusting weightage in the triage. At the core of SightConnect is a prediction engine that initially categorizes cases into Urgent, Early or Routine classes. These preliminary results undergo rigorous clinical validation, a critical step that ensures the accuracy of triage decisions and generates high-quality truth data.

Once the clinical validation data process yields sufficiently reliable results, the data is fed into an AI engine. This machine learning model analyzes the validated cases, along with their associated attributes and recommendations, to predict optimal hyperparameters for improved performance. These AI-generated suggestions are then passed back to the clinical validation layer, where they are integrated with live data from the SightConnect app and input from Vision Technicians. This iterative process creates a feedback loop that continuously refines the system's predictive capabilities. The machine learning model is regularly retrained, as indicated by the 'RE TRAIN X n times' component in the diagram. This ensures that SightConnect adapts to new patterns and evolving clinical insights over time. The ultimate output of this sophisticated system is a set of suggested weightages and classifications for new cases. These recommendations assist ophthalmology professionals in making informed triage decisions, potentially reducing wait times for critical cases and optimizing resource allocation in eyecare settings.

SightConnect's approach therefore represents an advancement in applying AI to ophthalmological triage (see Fig. 12). By combining predictions engine, clinical expertise, and machine learning, it offers a robust solution for enhancing the efficiency and accuracy of patient outcomes. These efforts have brought the overall accuracy up to 82% in the last trial. From a process point of view, we are striving to make the feedback loops shorter to bring more agility.

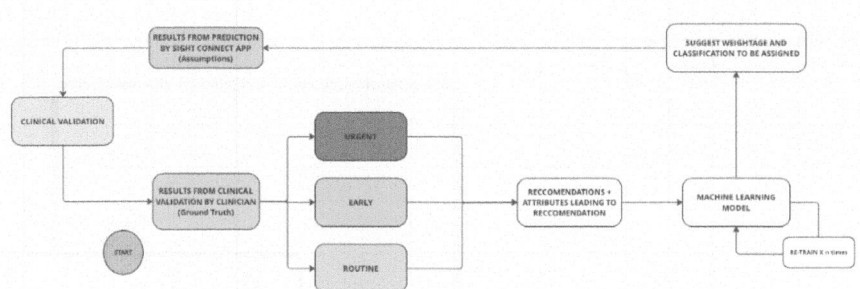

Fig. 12. AI-based feedback loop training the model

- **Voice Interaction:** In addition to the visual interface, we are also planning to add a voice interface that allows users to 'listen' to the screen and speak to record their input, which will significantly enhance the user experience and accuracy of the eye-testing app. This will improve accessibility through hands-free operation, and users with visual impairments can benefit from voice prompts and feedback. Such interaction can be more natural and reduce the cognitive load on the visually impaired users, making the app more inclusive, user-friendly, and accurate.
- **Scaling up the Service Model:** We are also exploring partnerships with more healthcare providers to facilitate seamless referrals for users requiring professional care. We are constantly striving to widen the reach of the app by approaching hospital networks, NGOs, and government bodies. Also, the platform encourages open innovation by enabling startups and other stakeholders to plug-in with their innovations and facilitate exchange of value between all players. We believe that continuous monitoring and evaluation will be crucial in refining the service model and ensuring its sustained impact on preventive eyecare.
- **App Communication Strategy**: We champion the app's accessible eye care through a comprehensive strategy employing mailers, brochures, social media posts, banners, and standees (for physical events). Our communication is focused on empowering rural communities, and so our diverse team created content in various Indian languages. This is an ongoing track wherein we also create content to reach out to and

connect with eye hospitals, NGO's and government bodies that we want to partner with.

- **Non-app Solutions:** During our expert reviews and discussions with stakeholders, including patients, doctors, technicians, and vision guardians, we gathered several ideas that didn't hinge on the mobile app as a medium. These are of great interest to us as they give us more channels through which to reach our target audience of rural patients. Some of these are –

  - **Kiosk for Eye Tests:** Considering that rural patients might not always be conducive to self-testing, this is a mobile kiosk that the patients can go to, to take the test, as visualized in Fig. 13. There will be vision guardian present to assist them, which removes the language barrier. The mobile kiosk will improve the solution's reach even in remote places.

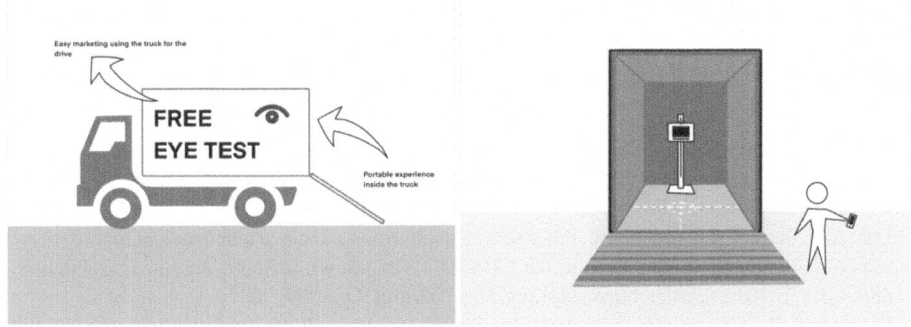

Fig. 13. Visualization of a mobile kiosk

- **Large Testing Screens:** These Android testing screens can be set up in Anganwadi's to test childrens' eyes.
- **Celebrity Voice Assistance:** Use voices of local celebrities (like regional actors, musicians, sports people), to make the app attractive to patients. This can be done using AI that can generate the celebrity voice using a sample voice. For example, this was done at a pan-India level by PhonePe with Amitabh Bachchan, and Cadbury, with Shahrukh Khan.

8   Conclusions

In conclusion, developing and implementing a service model with a mobile application for preventive eyecare represents a significant step forward in addressing the widespread issue of eye conditions in India, particularly in rural areas where access to healthcare is limited. By leveraging technology to facilitate early detection of common eye conditions such as cataracts, uncorrected refractive errors, and front-eye diseases, this application has the potential to reduce the prevalence of vision disabilities significantly. The app's triaging mechanism, vision testing protocol, and close-up eye examination feature are designed with the user's ease and accessibility in mind, ensuring that individuals can conduct preliminary screenings without the immediate need for professional intervention.

The collaborative efforts with a reputed eyecare institution have yielded an application that not only mimics the experience of an in-person eye examination but also provides a scalable solution to a problem that affects millions. The iterative design process, informed by user feedback, has resulted in an intuitive interface that accommodates users of varying literacy levels, further enhancing the app's reach and effectiveness.

The journey of developing this mobile application underscores the transformative potential of digital health solutions in democratizing access to healthcare services. It is a testament to the power of innovative technology in bridging the gap between underserved populations and the essential healthcare services they desperately need.

Disclosure of Interests. The authors have no competing interests to declare that are relevant to the content of this article.

References

1. Rani, P.K., et al.: Teleophthalmology at a primary and tertiary eye care network from India: environmental and economic impact. Eye **38**, 2203–2208 (2024). https://doi.org/10.1038/s41433-024-02934-4
2. Das, A.V., Rani, P.K., Vaddavalli, P.K.: Tele-consultations and electronic medical records driven remote patient care: responding to the COVID-19 lockdown in India. Indian J. Ophthalmol. **68**(6), 1007–1012 (2020). https://doi.org/10.4103/ijo.IJO_1089_20
3. Satgunam, P., Thakur, M., Sachdeva, V., Reddy, S., Rani, P.K.: Validation of visual acuity applications for teleophthalmology during COVID-19. Indian J. Ophthalmol. **69**(2), 385–390 (2021). https://doi.org/10.4103/ijo.IJO_2333_20
4. Rani, P.K., Das, A.V.: Setting up a primary eye care teleconsultation service. Community eye health **35**(114), 6–7 (2021)
5. Davara, N.D., et al.: Feasibility study for measuring patients' visual acuity at home by their caregivers. Indian J. Ophthalmol. **70**(6), 2125–2130 (2022). https://doi.org/10.4103/ijo.IJO_3085_21

Absent Networks: Finding Wellness Through Common Interests

Spiti Tiwari[1,2]([⊠]) [iD]

[1] Srishti Manipal Institute of Art, Design and Technology, Bengaluru, India
spititiwari96@gmail.com
[2] Manipal Academy of Higher Education, Manipal, India

Abstract. Cancer profoundly impacts both patients and their caregivers, often leading to social isolation and emotional distress. This study examines the complex challenges encountered by these groups, highlighting the scarcity of comprehensive support systems in India. By understanding the critical needs of patients and caregivers, the research identifies key opportunities for developing interventions aimed at creating a supportive community.

The proposed intervention leverages technology to create a network that connects individuals based on shared interests. Unlike traditional support systems that concentrate solely on medical care, this network is designed to provide emotional support and foster social interaction, enabling individuals to engage in activities and discussions unrelated to their illness.

This approach addresses social isolation by fostering connections grounded in common preferences, allowing patients and caregivers to rediscover aspects of their identities beyond cancer. Through this empathetic community, patients and caregivers can attain not only support but also a renewed sense of self and connection, thereby significantly enhancing their quality of life.

Keywords: Cancer · Caregivers · Social Isolation · Shared Interest · Rediscover Identity

1 Introduction

Chronic diseases, with treatments extending over several years, exert a profound psychological impact not only on patients but also on their families [1]. The period following diagnosis brings to light not just the patient's struggles but also the myriad challenges faced by their immediate family members, known as caregivers. The absence of centralized guidance and comprehensive support materials often forces families to resort to fragmented media sources and anecdotal advice, resulting in a trial-and-error approach to management. This lack of consistent information creates significant barriers, leading to social isolation and hindering both patients and their families from adopting a holistic healing approach aimed at improving quality of life.

Statistical data underscores the urgency of addressing these issues. Globally, about two in five cancer caregivers are diagnosed with depression, emphasizing the critical need for routine screening of depressive symptoms and the provision of psychosocial support [2]. The role of caregivers, often immediate family members, is fraught with high levels of depression, anxiety, and overwhelming burdens. As primary caretakers, they find their lives consumed by the disease. An Indian study highlights this strain: 70.22% of cancer caregivers experience mild-to-moderate burdens, while 21.38% face moderate-to-severe burdens. The levels of burden are notably associated with gender (male) and employment status (unemployment), although they do not significantly vary by marital status, education, caregiver age, or relationship to the patient [3].

The objective of this study is to gain a comprehensive understanding of the current support systems, and the multifaceted challenges faced by those affected by cancer, including both patients and caregivers. The research aims to identify the diverse hardships caregivers encounter and explore the forms of support most needed for optimizing holistic healing and relief.

The study revealed several key insights: patients and caregivers grapple with misinformation, seeking reliable guidance throughout the cancer journey. Shared experiences emerge as a primary source of support, often outweighing medical advice. Support groups are sought for various reasons, including motivation, a sense of belonging, hope, guidance, and distraction from their disease-dominated lives. However, financial constraints and language barriers significantly hinder participation in support groups, emphasizing the need for accessible and inclusive platforms.

These findings have led to the proposal of a design intervention that leverages technology to create a network designed to connect individuals affected by cancer based on their shared interests. This approach addresses the problem of social isolation by fostering connections grounded in common preferences, enabling patients and caregivers to rediscover aspects of their identities beyond cancer. Furthermore, the implementation of this intervention leverages existing structures, such as healthcare centers and NGOs, ensuring ease of access and integration into the current support landscape.

In essence, this intervention transcends conventional support systems by creating an empathetic and supportive community that not only aids in emotional recovery but also fosters personal growth and relational strength, thereby significantly improving the lived experiences of both patients and their caregivers.

2 Methodology

This study was conducted through a series of methodological steps aimed at identifying the challenges, needs, and current state of support systems available for cancer patients and their caregivers in India. The multi-phase approach of the study was divided into three parts:

Phase 1: Auto-ethnographic research was visualized through mind maps to identify key areas of concern and gaps in existing support systems.

Phase 2: Primary interviews were conducted to obtain diverse perspectives on the current support systems. These interviews included various stakeholders, such as cancer patients, caregivers, cancer survivors, cancer professionals, and individuals with no prior experience with cancer.

Phase 3: Due to the sensitive nature of these conversations, probing techniques were employed to uncover the participant's innate feelings and co-design solutions with cancer patients and their caregivers, thereby helping to understand their needs and expectations from support group systems.

An essential aspect of this research involved examining the context in both rural and urban settings in India.

The current study served as a pilot with 23 participants, aimed at identifying issues and developing a methodology for a larger study.

3   The Study

3.1   Phase 1: Initial Exploration and Identified Gaps

The research commenced with an auto-ethnographic exploration based on personal experience as a caregiver, visually depicted through a mind map. This approach provided an in-depth understanding of the practical challenges and emotional struggles faced in navigating support group networks. The key areas identified are as follows:

Necessity for Distinctive Care. The need for distinctive care based on the type and stage of cancer and the treatment offered. Patients experience side effects that require individualized care, which vary greatly from person to person.

Role of Immediate Family Members. Immediate family members often serve as unnoticed support providers without proper guidance, acting as the primary caretakers of the patient. This can lead to an overwhelming burden of palliative care, social, and emotional issues. The lack of understanding from people around them makes managing personal life difficult.

Prevalence of Misleading Information. The prevalence of misleading information on social media often diverts patients and their families from effective treatments, leading them to seek out religious or unproven methods for healing and cure [4].

Lack of Public Awareness and Existing Stigmas. The public's lack of awareness about cancer perpetuates existing stigmas and beliefs, which further affect community acceptance of those affected by the disease [5]. This often causes isolation for both patients and caregivers, as they tend to withdraw from the community to avoid the effort of explaining and communicating their condition.

Coping and Identification Issues. A lack of awareness about cancer can lead to coping issues in patients, making them reluctant to identify and associate themselves with the disease.

3.2   Comprehensive Insights into Cancer Support Systems

Primary interviews were conducted with a diverse range of stakeholders, including 4 cancer patients, 3 cancer survivors, 10 caregivers, 3 medical professionals, and 3 individuals without any direct experience with cancer. This multi-perspective approach provided validation and allowed for an in-depth analysis of the key factors identified earlier in the study.

These interviews also included residents of Chamba, Uttarakhand, conducted during a field trip to study the rural context. Immersive observation and direct interaction with residents facilitated a deeper understanding of the unique challenges and needs specific to rural areas, thereby enriching the data by incorporating rural perspectives into the analysis.

Major insights from the interviews extended the mind map and revealed how the concept of support varies across different societal strata. In impoverished or illiterate populations, the primary focus is on symptomatic relief, with social aspects often being secondary. Conversely, the educated class seeks both relief and an improvement in quality of life. The study found that cancer patients and their families tend to trust and rely more on information provided by others experiencing similar situations. Nearly all cancer patients, survivors, and caregivers reported feelings of isolation and expressed that cancer dominated their personal lives and identities.

Additionally, the diversity in India presents challenges such as linguistic barriers, accessibility, and affordability of resources, which hinder the establishment and effectiveness of support group networks (Fig. 1).

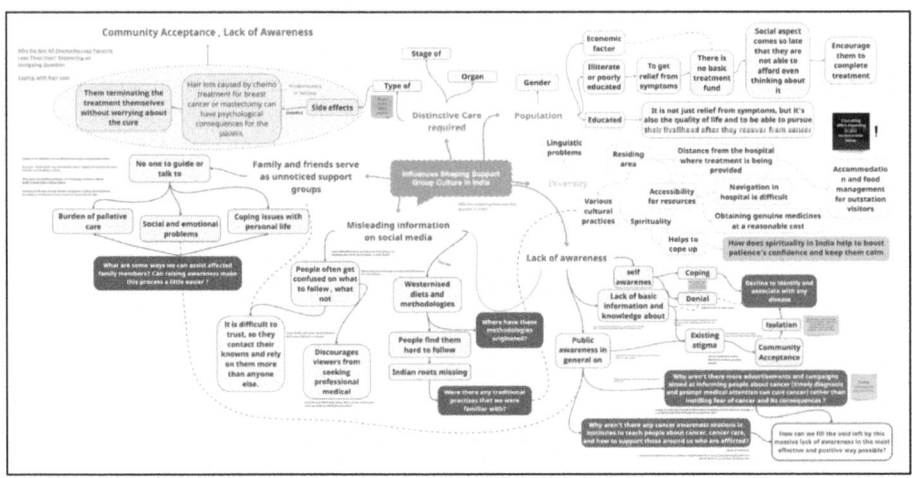

Fig. 1. A mind map to visually represent the information of phase 1 and phase 2 of the study.

This phase further branched out the mind map across each of the key factors, identifying interconnections and extending the understanding of the support needs within different contexts.

3.3   Phase 3: Probing Techniques as a Co-design Approach

During Phase 2 of the study, it was observed that the intensity of the interviews made it uncomfortable for interviewees to express themselves freely. To gain deeper insights into the specific needs and expectations of patients and their caregivers affected by cancer, a probing interview technique was adopted (Fig. 2).

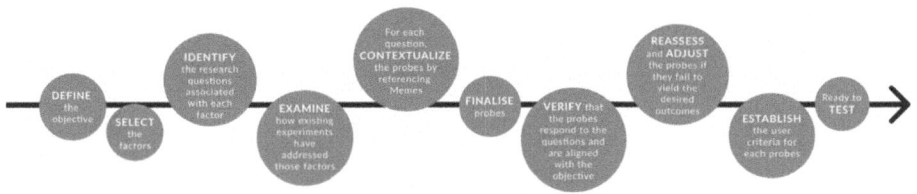

Fig. 2. A visual representation of design process for prompts (memes) utilized as probes.

Given the sensitive nature of the topic, memes were utilized as prompts to facilitate responses to each question. Memes, often used for humor, can also translate emotions or expressions in a lighter context.

This method not only encouraged interviewees to think more critically but also enabled them to share their views and thoughts more openly. This interactive technique proved effective in the co-design of the support concept in collaboration with the participants (Figs. 3 and 4).

Fig. 3. The probes used for interviews.

4   Design Intervention

The study revealed that patients and caregivers often lose aspects of their identities beyond their cancer diagnosis, leading to isolation and emotional distress. To address this, the concept of "Finding Wellness Through Shared Interests" was developed (Fig. 5).

				(Care-giver)	(Cancer Patient)

Caregiving felt more like a duty and responsibility

People hide cancer. Even though people have serious problems but don't tell.

Caregivers can help and guide each other.

If there is clarity people feel positive & boost them.

" I too want to help other patients by sharing my experience and inform them"

" Because we are dealing with it for first time everything we are doing is with google & from reading things here and there".

Impacted my academics and my career

There is no place where we can step aside and breathe freely without addressing cancer.

I was aware but not in depth. Got to know more with my mother's Condition.

People who were having their first chemo used to get help for patients who had 3rd or 4th.

My children gave me books on understanding Cancer and it helped me feel better.

They don't understand cancer and hence are unable to help or support the affected people.

I feel sometimes in support groups there needs to be family meet ups to share with each other.

Even though we researched but could not find the support group which is a good fit her.

"Professionally don't have anyone to consult with." (career wise).

Schools and institutions do not have any professional sessions related to cancer awareness.

"Should be a combination of expert led for proper guidance as information validation is required and outings so that we get change and can interact better"

People lose track of their hobbies and interests as they progress through life and struggle to recognise them.

THERE ARE Different OPINIONS on internet,I get confused.

Cancer patients feel free and open up more with fellow patients.

"Earlier I did not know who to talk , so I did not know how to deal with it"

Fig. 4. The key insights from cancer patients and caregivers derived from probing interviews.

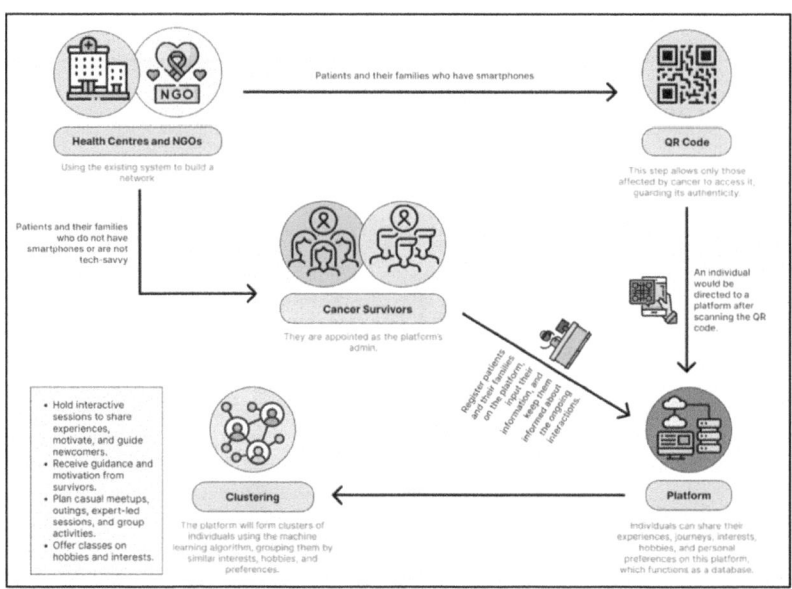

Fig. 5. Network diagram illustrating the concept of "Finding Wellness Through Shared Interests".

The conceptual framework proposes a network for individuals affected by cancer, structured as follows:

Integration with Existing Infrastructures. The proposed network integrates seamlessly with healthcare centers and NGOs, leveraging existing infrastructure to facilitate ease of access for patients and caregivers. This allows individuals to interact with NGOs during regular visits, streamlining connections and enhancing user accessibility.

Easy Registration via QR Codes. QR codes are strategically placed at healthcare centres and NGOs, enabling quick and secure registration for smartphone users. This ensures that access to the platform is exclusive to individuals affected by cancer, while also maintaining data privacy. It prevents external access to the network, safeguarding participants' information.

Support for Non-Tech-Savvy Users. In rural areas and for individuals not familiar with technology, cancer survivors are appointed to serve as platform administrators. They assist with user registration and provide updates, ensuring inclusivity even for those who lack access to mobile devices due to the digital divide.

Interest-Based Networking. Participants contribute information about their experiences, interests, hobbies, and preferences to form a comprehensive database. A machine learning algorithm clusters individuals with similar interests, fostering meaningful connections and introducing an element of surprise.

This algorithm considers factors like language, distance, and personal preferences to address the linguistic, cultural, and socio-economic diversity highlighted in the study.

Interactive and Supportive Activities

Interactive Sessions. Members can hold sessions to share, motivate, and guide newcomers.

Survivor Guidance. Users receive motivation and insights from cancer survivors.

Community Activities. The platform facilitates casual meetups, outings, expert-led sessions, and group activities.

Hobby Classes. Classes based on hobbies and interests offer personal growth and distraction from the illness.

Employment Opportunities for Survivors. Cancer survivors acting as platform admins provide employment opportunities and use their experiences to inspire and guide others.

The platform surpasses traditional support systems by emphasizing holistic healing and cultivating a sense of community. It addresses emotional, social, and psychological needs in addition to physical care. The design promotes sharing and interaction beyond the confines of the disease, aiding users in rediscovering their identities.

5 Summary and Future Scope

This study elucidated the profound impact of cancer on the lives of patients and their caregivers, underscoring the necessity for interventions that foster a supportive community. By focusing on understanding the distinct needs of both patients and caregivers, the research identified a crucial opportunity to alleviate social isolation by facilitating connections rooted in shared interests. The research culminated in the development of the concept "Finding Wellness Through Shared Interests," which aims to empower patients and caregivers to rediscover their identities and establish meaningful connections beyond the confines of their illness.

This research forms a foundational step in creating a comprehensive intervention. Future work will focus on refining this concept into a functional prototype. Since the current study serves as a pilot to identify challenges and lay the groundwork, the concept is in its nascent stages. The next phase will involve evaluating the prototype in real-world settings to determine its effectiveness in addressing the needs of cancer patients and caregivers. Feedback from individuals directly affected by cancer will be integral to refining the design and enhancing its impact.

The aim is to implement this initiative on a larger scale, thereby positively influencing the lives of numerous individuals impacted by this chronic disease.

Acknowledgments. I would like to express my sincere gratitude to all the participants who generously shared their experiences and insights for this research. Their willingness to participate was instrumental in ensuring the study's relevance and impact. I am also indebted to Srishti Manipal Institute of Art, Design and Technology for providing the necessary resources and support to conduct this research. Special thanks to Ms. Debjani Roy for her invaluable mentorship and guidance throughout this project. Her expertise and encouragement were invaluable in shaping the direction and outcomes of this study. Additionally, I am grateful to Ms. Aastha Chauhan for facilitating the field trip to Chamba, Uttarakhand, which provided invaluable firsthand insights into the challenges faced by individuals affected by cancer in rural areas.

Disclosure of Interests.   The author has no competing interests to declare that are relevant to the content of this study.

References

1. Unnikrishnan, B., et al.: Psychosocial burden among informal caregivers of adult cancer patients attending a tertiary care cancer center in coastal South India. SAGE Open **9**, 215824401987628 (2019). https://doi.org/10.1177/2158244019876287
2. Bedaso, A., Dejenu, G., Duko, B.: Depression among caregivers of cancer patients: updated systematic review and meta-analysis. Psychooncology **31**, 1809–1820 (2022). https://doi.org/10.1002/pon.6045
3. Mishra, S., Gulia, A., Satapathy, S., Gogia, A., Sharma, A., Bhatnagar, S.: Caregiver burden and quality of life among family caregivers of cancer patients on chemotherapy: a prospective observational study. Indian J. Palliat. Care **27**, 109 (2021). https://doi.org/10.4103/IJPC.IJPC_180_20
4. Johnson, S.B., et al.: Cancer misinformation and harmful information on Facebook and other social media: a brief report. JNCI J. Natl. Cancer Inst. **114**, 1036–1039 (2022). https://doi.org/10.1093/jnci/djab141
5. Squiers, L., et al.: Perceived, Experienced, and Internalized Cancer Stigma: Perspectives of Cancer Patients and Caregivers in India. RTI Press (2021). https://doi.org/10.3768/rtipress.2021.rr.0044.2104

Designing an Accessible Music Device for the Elderly: Enhancing Usability, Entertainment, and Well-Being

Akshay Desai[✉]

IDC School of Design, IIT-Bombay, Mumbai, India
akshaydessai@hotmail.com

Abstract. With the growth in technology, digital devices have largely replaced analogue devices. While this change is welcomed by many, the elderly users often struggle to adapt due to several reasons. This paper explores the possibility of designing a digital music device for elderly users in the Indian context. It examines the limitations, issues, and cultural aspects that affect their interaction with technology, and how these challenges can be addressed to create a more accessible and user-friendly device.

Keywords: Elderly · Accessible Design · Music player · NFC.

1 Introduction

India has a growing population of elderly, most of whom are not familiar with modern technology and prefer using older devices. This necessitates the development of innovative solutions to enhance their quality of life. One area where such innovation is particularly impactful is in the realm of digital entertainment, specifically through music players tailored to the needs and preferences of elderly users.

Music holds a special place in the lives of many elderly individuals. It is not only a source of entertainment but also a powerful tool for emotional and cognitive well-being.[3] Research has shown that music can help reduce stress, alleviate symptoms of depression, and improve memory and cognitive functions. For them, music often serves as a bridge to cherished memories and a source of daily comfort and joy. However, the technological advancements in music players have not always catered to the elderly demographic. Modern music players, with their complex interfaces, and dependence on digital literacy, can be daunting for them. These challenges are exacerbated by age-related issues such as declining vision, hearing, and motor skills, making it difficult for many to enjoy the benefits of digital music. Recognizing these challenges, this study focuses on designing a music player specifically for the elderly in India. The objective is to create a device that is not only easy to use but also culturally relevant. By addressing the specific needs and limitations of elderly users, this research aims

N. Rangaswamy et al. (Eds.): IndiaHCI 2024, CCIS 2338, pp. 345–352, 2025.
https://doi.org/10.1007/978-3-031-80832-6_23

to provide a practical solution that enhances their access to and enjoyment of music. This paper will explore the design process, user interface considerations, and the features that make the music player suitable for the elderly.

2   Background

India is home to a rapidly growing elderly population. According to the Census of India 2011, the population aged 60 and above is approximately 104 million, and this number is projected to rise significantly in the coming decades. [2] This demographic shift presents unique challenges and opportunities, particularly in enhancing the quality of life for the ageing population. One of the areas where innovation can make a substantial impact is in the realm of digital entertainment, specifically through music players designed with the elderly in mind.

Studies have shown that listening to music can improve mental health, reduce anxiety, alleviate symptoms of depression, and even aid in cognitive function. However, currently due to lack of digital literacy, the users do not have access to these resources and have to rely on the younger ones in the family for help regarding this. Elderly were less likely to troubleshoot issues and wait for family members to help them out. At the same time some users were afraid of burdening their children and other family members with technological needs. [3]

Despite the benefits, elderly individuals often face significant challenges using technology[4].

To address these challenges, NFC (Near Field Communication) technology presents a promising solution. NFC is a wireless communication method that allows devices to exchange data over short distances, typically a few centimeters. It requires minimal interaction, making it ideal for elderly users. By simply bringing an NFC-enabled card or tag close to the device, the desired music can be played without the need to navigate through menus or deal with complex controls.

NFC technology is already widely used in various applications, such as contactless payments and smart home devices, due to its ease of use and reliability. For the senior users, NFC can eliminate many of the barriers associated with traditional digital music players. The design of a music device incorporating NFC technology would enable older adults to access their favorite tunes with a simple, intuitive gesture, thus enhancing their quality of life.

3   Aim and Objective

This research aims to design a user-friendly music player tailored to the needs of elderly individuals in India. The study focuses on creating an intuitive interface, large and easily accessible controls, and features that cater specifically to the preferences and limitations of the elderly population. The ultimate goal is to enhance the accessibility and enjoyment of music for elderly users, thereby improving their overall well-being and quality of life.

4   Method

To better understand the situation that many elderly users face. Secondary research was conducted regarding how music affects culture and its impact on people, social life and their habits. The technology used to play music affects how people perceive music and a culture around it develops. Such as the transition from cassette, CDs to online music has impacted how people listen to music. Thus, the study was also to understand how a new music device would affect the life of elderly and those around them.

Participants for interviews were recruited via acquaintances, I considered users above the age of 60, those who used smartphones and were interested in listening to music on a daily basis. A total of 8 participants were interviewed. Three of the 8 participants lived in tier III cities while remaining five lived in a tier I city. The objective of the study was explained to them and pre-planned questions about current technology, hurdles faced and how they perceive themselves in this new digital world, were the topics where a general discussion was done. Most participants would fondly recollect days of using cassette tapes, radio and old TVs. The society had built an ecosystem around these products, buying and sharing these cassettes was a social experience that people looked forward to. Users were asked to carry out the task of connecting their smartphone to a Bluetooth speaker, pair it. And play a specific song from the music player.

How they interact with mobile phones was studied and issues with the current music player were better understood. Participants were asked to connect their smartphone to a Bluetooth speaker and play a song, their struggles were observed in carrying out this task. Observations and data points were later categorized as design problem, observation, user statements and design idea.

5   Findings

The research revealed several key insights:

Several elderly users struggle with text input via the qwerty keypad, and do not have the patience to learn it, this leads to a frustrating experience making them not use the device. Also, several users were not comfortable with text input in English and preferred regional languages, however text input via regional languages is also challenging. Most users use apps such as whatsapp and facebook in their phones and they surpass the need for text input via voice notes and forwarding received messages.

After the task of connecting smartphone to Bluetooth speaker and playing a song it was observed that they struggle in connecting smartphone to speaker, for several reasons; they do not have a correct conceptual model of how these devices work, how Bluetooth works and transfers data. The task of finding the available devices in Bluetooth settings is difficult for them for the same reason. Oftentimes, with the speakers available in the Indian market, the connecting process does not work as advertised and requires troubleshooting from the user, elderly users were unable to troubleshoot and resolve the issue and tend to ask for help from the younger ones in the family.

It is crucial to understand that times when elderly users manage to play music on smart devices, the experience is still be overwhelming. The interaction typically requires significant patience and cognitive effort, as they navigate through interfaces that may not be intuitive or user-friendly for them. This heightened mental load leads to frustration, ultimately detracting from the overall user experience. Consequently, this negative experience diminishes their willingness to engage with these devices in the future, potentially leading to a decline in their use of technology for similar tasks.

Users were asked to use voice recognition through Amazon Alexa and Google Assistant. The experience was a hit and a miss, at times it worked while other times it did not, this was especially the case with regional languages. They were unable understand the conceptual model of voice recognition and the delay in feedback and at times wrong interpretations left them frustrated. Several regional languages are currently not supported via voice search additionally, we observed that it was difficult for users to recollect the exact names of songs as in India the name of most songs is usually part of the lyrics. The overall experience leaves a lot to be desired.

A few users preferred playing songs on the radio and used their old cassette tapes as they found it to be familiar and convenient. They felt out of place with modern technology, as if it is "not meant for them" there is a certain fear of technology among the elderly making them reluctant to use modern technology, they do not understand it and find it intimidating to use. Contrasting to this, the users younger in age are curious and excited to try new gadgets, the fear of failing is non-existent as they are confident that they will be able to figure it out. This concludes that a familiar gadget to what elderly are used to, with a similar conceptual model will be easier to use.

The product should prioritize ease of use and align with the familiar conceptual models. Such a device should resemble the products they are accustomed to, ensuring a smoother transition and reducing the learning curve. Since the device is expected to be used on a daily basis, it should be as simple as "picking a book off the shelf." This approach aims to make the device accessible and user-friendly, minimizing cognitive load and enhancing the overall user experience.

Elderly users prefer products which provide tactile feedback[1] as it provides appropriate and understandable feedback. This also brings back familiarity a certain confidence in interacting with the product.

Elderly users often face challenges in learning new technologies due to age-related declines in cognitive and learning abilities. This demographic may find it difficult to adapt to new gadgets, requiring considerable perseverance and repeated practice to become proficient. Despite their efforts, they frequently encounter difficulties when troubleshooting issues as solving a problem requires one to understand how the technology works.

Further understanding of existing products (benchmarking) was done and a few users had the Saregama Caravan, which they preferred to use as they found it to be effortless and convenient. Caravan is a popular product in India and is often given as a gift by the youth to their elderly parents. This shows that there is a need for such a product and the people are willing to pay a premium for a better user experience. There are a few limitations with Caravan, it allows only preloaded songs to be played and does not provide the option to select individual tracks; users can only choose a predefined playlists. It has a mobile app and Bluetooth connectivity, but similar issues which are stated above will arise through it.

6 Designing a Solution

6.1 Design Exploration

The following possibilities to address this issue were explored:

To design a new UI (user interface) for phones such that users can easily navigate and search for a track, functions such as play, pause, skip should be easy and intuitive to use. However, this requires them to interact with the phone, issues regarding input of text still prevails and requires them to connect the phone to a speaker.

To design an independent digital device that can play music without the need for a smartphone. This process will be easier for them as they will not require to give a text input. However this approach will need an innovative way for the user to provide an input.

To design a user friendly method to connect a phone to a speaker, as the current method of connecting via Bluetooth is inconvenient for the elderly users. This however does not eliminate the issues regarding text input and navigation issues on the phone.

6.2 Finalizing a design

After considering the merits and demerits of each approach, it was determined that an independent digital device capable of playing music without relying on a smartphone best meets the users needs. This approach ensures that the user experience remains straightforward and similar to previously used products, minimizing the need for learning new methods.

The proposed solution comprises two components: a digital music device (speaker) connected to an online streaming service via Wi-Fi, and NFC cards. Each NFC card represents an album and typically contains an average of ten songs. To play the tracks associated with a specific NFC card, the user simply taps the card against the device. This action transfers the necessary data to the speaker, which then streams the selected songs. Users can skip tracks using the buttons on the device. Users would have the option to download songs from their preferred cards for offline listening, providing a dedicated download button will make it convenient (Fig. 1).

7 Evaluation

The users were asked to carry out two tasks: First, connect their smartphones to a Bluetooth speaker and play a specific song. Second, they were then introduced

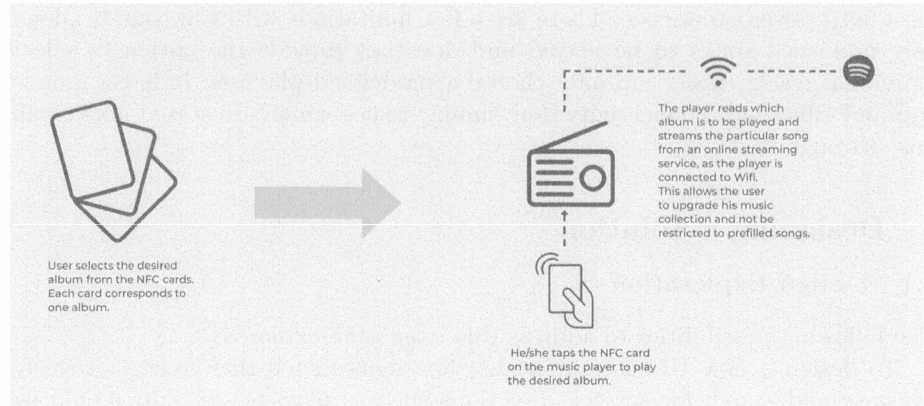

Fig. 1. Conceptual model of the device

to the NFC music player and its functionality. Users were asked to perform a simulated task by tapping a card on a speaker, while the interviewer played the song, simulating the product's operation. Users then completed the System Usability Scale (SUS) questionnaire for both systems: playing music via a smartphone with Bluetooth speaker and using the NFC music player. The SUS score for playing music through the smartphone and Bluetooth speaker was 36.7, while for the NFC music player, it was 80.5.

Additional issues were discovered while playing music through Bluetooth speakers such as: while turning on the Bluetooth speaker, most speakers require users to long-press the power button; however, users would either press it once or, when told to long-press, would continue holding the button even after the speaker had turned on. Speakers with a toggle switch for the power button did not have this issue. Once the speaker was powered on, users struggled to find the Bluetooth settings on their phones. After locating the settings and noticing the speaker's name on the screen, they often did not realize that they needed to tap on the speaker's name to connect it. Although these actions can be learned over time, it requires constant repetition and perseverance from the user. When the process did not work as expected, troubleshooting became a challenge, as users were unsure whether to restart the Bluetooth speaker or select 'forget speaker' from the settings and reconnect.

While explaining the NFC music player, users were given examples of touchless card payments and metro train cards. These examples instilled confidence and trust in the system, which is reflected in the SUS score. Users felt that compared to playing music via the smartphone, the NFC music player was an easier method. They did have concerns about managing multiple cards and keeping them safe. However, it was observed that even though smartphones provide access to virtually unlimited songs, many users struggled to search for and find specific songs. Several users relied on YouTube to play music and often chose the songs suggested on YouTube homepage, limiting their access to the full range of available music. In contrast, three of the five users felt that the NFC music player provided access to a larger music library than the smartphone.

The five users who participated in the evaluation were familiar with the 'Saregama Carvaan' and had used it previously. According to them, the ability to play music of their choice was an added advantage in this case. Two out of the five users asked if this was an existing product, as they would be interested in purchasing it. However, the sample size of five users is insufficient and requires further research to better understand the use case and identify any potential drawbacks. To gain deeper insights, providing users with a working prototype would be beneficial (Fig. 2).

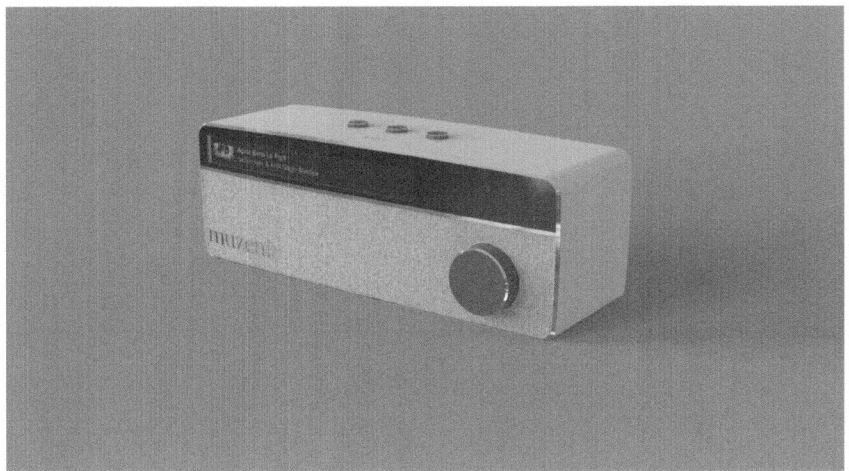

Fig. 2. Product render

8   Conclusion

The research helps us understand the need and importance for an accessible device for the elderly. It explores the current issues that the elderly have with technology, their perceptions and cultural aspects. Technology has the potential to address the needs of elderly users effectively, and provides ample design opportunities. It is crucial for technological solutions to be tailored to the requirements of this demographic rather than compelling users to adapt to "modern technology". The findings suggest that designing with a user-centered focus, considering the unique challenges and preferences of elderly individuals, will enhance usability and overall satisfaction.

References

1. Claypoole, V.L., Schroeder, B.L., Mishler, A.D.: Keeping in touch: tactile interface design for older users. Ergonomics Des. **24**(1), 18–24 (2016)
2. Dey, S., Nambiar, D., Lakshmi, J.K., Sheikh, K., Reddy, K.S.: Aging in Asia: Findings from New and Emerging Data Initiatives. National Academies Press, US (2012)
3. Diaz Abrahan, V., Shifres, F. and Justel, N.: Cognitive benefits from a musical activity in older adults. Front. Psychol. **10**, 652 (2019)
4. Renaud, K. and Van Biljon, J.: Predicting technology acceptance and adoption by the elderly: a qualitative study. In: 2008 annual research conference of the South African Institute of Computer Scientists and Information Technologist, vol. 338 (2008)

Artworks and Installations

Raising Awareness of the Significance of Awadhi Mother Tongue Among Young Adults via Exhibition Design

Apoorv Anurag$^{(\boxtimes)}$ and Swati Pal

IDC School of Design, Indian Institute of Technology, Bombay, India
apoorv3226@gmail.com

Abstract. Many mother tongues worldwide are facing a decline in usage and reputation [1], including Awadhi, spoken in Uttar Pradesh, India. Despite its rich literary heritage, Awadhi is often viewed as unsophisticated and inferior, partly due to a lack of awareness and limited use in education and employment [2]. UNESCO's World Atlas of Languages lists Awadhi as having a 'Potentially Vulnerable' language status situation [3]. This project aims to raise awareness about Awadhi through interactive exhibitions, which may eventually enhance perception about it. For this we are targeting young adults aged 17–25 years in schools and colleges in Uttar Pradesh's Awadh region. However, our project scope does not aim for them to start speaking Awadhi.

Keywords: Language Exhibition Design · Interactive Installations · Linguistic Prejudice

1 Introduction to Awadhi

1.1 Geography

Awadhi is an Indo-Aryan language, primarily spoken in the Awadh region of Uttar Pradesh, India by 38.5 Lakh speakers, according to the 2011 Census [4]. Its name originates from 'Ayodhya,' a district in Uttar Pradesh and the homeland of the Hindu deity Lord Rama. In addition to Awadhi, Uttar Pradesh is home to six other mother tongues: Kauravi, Braj, Kannauji, Bhojpuri, Bundeli, and Bagheli. These languages are mutually intelligible and easily understood by speakers of modern Hindi without special effort [5] (Figs. 1, 2 and 3).

© The Author(s), under exclusive license to Springer Nature Switzerland AG 2025
N. Rangaswamy et al. (Eds.): IndiaHCI 2024, CCIS 2338, pp. 355–362, 2025.
https://doi.org/10.1007/978-3-031-80832-6_24

Fig. 1. The three interactive installations designed for our Awadhi Exhibition.

Exemplar text in Awadhi Bhasha

अरे आपन भासा के बारे में का कही.. एतना प्रेम है बोली मा कि बताये नहीं सकित है। कुछ भी बोल देयो कोहु को, सब अच्छे लागत है।

English Translation:
Hey, what can I say about my language? I cannot express how much love is in this language. One can say anything to anyone, everything sounds good.

Fig. 2. Exemplar text in Awadhi [9].

1.2 Literary Significance of Awadhi

Renowned poets such as Tulsidas, with his 'Ram Charita Manas' and 'Hanuman Chalisa', and Malik Mohammad Jayasi, with his 'Padmavat,' have penned masterpieces in Awadhi. Additionally, the dohe (couplets) of Kabir Das and Rahim Das further enriched its literary heritage. These poets flourished during the Bhakti period (suitably termed as the Golden Period of Awadhi Literature) during the 14th to 17th Century and explored themes of love, sacrifice, and death [5].

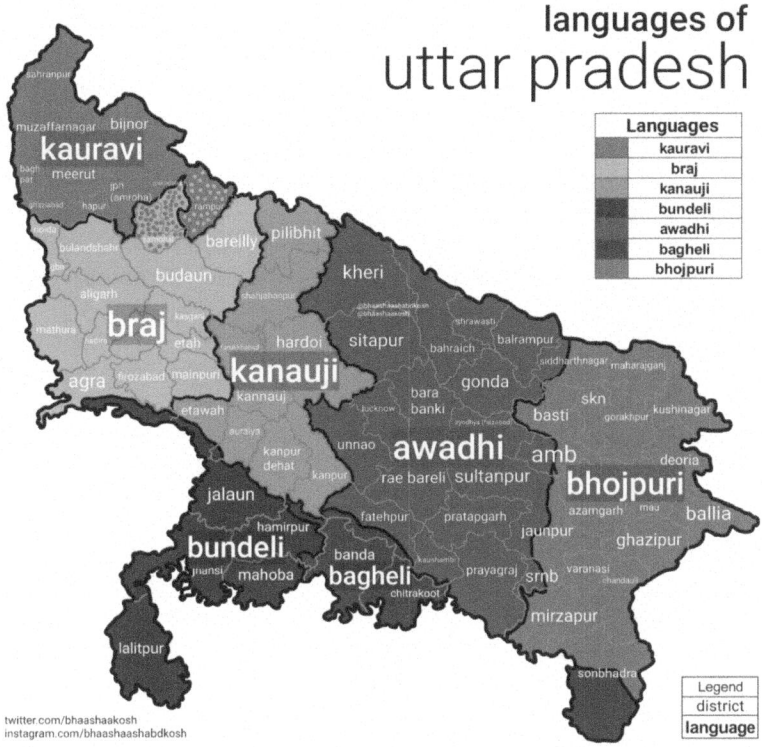

Fig. 3. The map shows the major seven mother tongues of Uttar Pradesh as per Grierson's Linguistic Survey of India [6–8]. Districts created in and after 2010 are not shown in this map.

2 Secondary Research Linguistic Prejudice and its Impact on Awadhi

Despite its rich literary heritage and sizable speaker base, Awadhi is often deemed an 'impure' dialect compared to Standard Hindi. Due to mutual intelligibility and negative perceptions, many young Awadhi speakers switch to Hindi, especially when moving to urban areas for better education or employment opportunities. With limited support from the educated community and limited literary backing, Awadhi remains primarily in rural areas. This shift diminishes Awadhi's linguistic status, contributing to its decline in passage across generations too [2,5].

3 Primary Research

To explore the perceived lack of prestige for Awadhi, we conducted 11 interviews with young educated adults from Awadh and spoke with the creator of an Awadhi promoting YouTube channel 'Awadhi Bani' [10]. The key insights were:

1. Widespread misconceptions about even the name of Awadhi (often calling it 'dehati' or confusing with Bhojpuri), unawareness about Awadhi literature, region, history, and differences from other mother tongues of the state.
2. Urban schools discourage the use of Awadhi, often banning it. In the curriculum, Awadhi is limited to a few poems and verses in NCERT Hindi textbooks, which can be a good starting point to know about its significance, but often ignored due to the already tight curriculum.
3. Awadhi remains predominantly an oral language, with decreasing literacy as fewer engaging works are published and its presence in mainstream media remains limited.
4. While most young adults recognized the importance of preserving their native language, some were unaware of their negative perceptions until prompted via interviews.
5. Many Awadhi speakers, who moved to different states, realize their diminished linguistic pride compared to other linguistic communities.

4   Ideation

Based on our research, we developed strategies to guide our ideation. They include creating engaging content for youth, fostering supportive school and college environments, addressing negative perceptions, and enhancing language skills post-awareness. To best implement these strategies, we have chosen to design an interactive exhibition for schools and colleges in the Awadh region. This approach targets students aged 17–25 and offers a fun, group-oriented learning experience about their native language without adding any academic pressure. This initiative complements the Indian government's efforts like 'Bharatiya Bhasha Utsav' [11], where technology innovations are being welcomed to play a pivotal role in promoting and teaching Indian mother tongues.

5   Exhibition Design Outcome

To raise awareness about the Awadhi-speaking region and its significance in Indian literature and music, we developed three distinct installations for the exhibition. Each installation highlights one of these key themes. Here are the final three installations:

5.1   Theme 1 Installation : Interactive Linguistic Floor Map

Our interactive 8 x 8.5 ft floor map aims to tell the audience about where Awadhi is spoken and how it differs from other mother tongues in Uttar Pradesh. The map displays various linguistic regions in different colours, with blurred boundaries to show the natural merging of languages (Fig. 4). To make the map interactive, we integrated piezo sensors underneath and utilized the Arduino system for tangible prototyping. Visitors can choose a sentence from a set of given

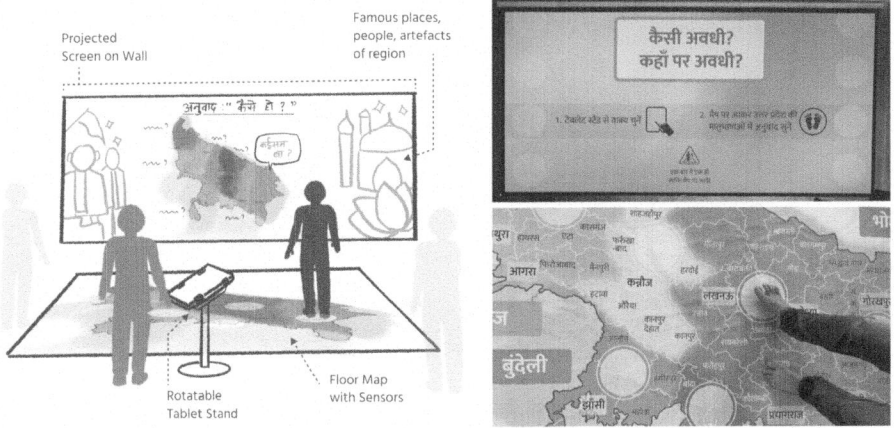

Fig. 4. The left image shows the components of the first installation. The right images display the default projector screen and a close-up of the floor map.

sentences on a tablet and step at designated white spots on different linguistic regions of the map to hear different translations. Sentences include conversational phrases and popular movie dialogues by Prayagraj-born Amitabh Bachchan to engage interest. The translations were collected from people living in each of the seven linguistic regions. A projected screen displays the translated texts and related regional images, enhancing the immersive experience. Although only one person can use the map at a time, its large size allows others nearby to view and engage in discussions.

5.2   Theme 2 Installation : Awadhi Poet Finding Activity

We aim to highlight Awadhi's rich literary heritage through an engaging treasure hunt activity featuring four eminent poets: Kabirdas, Jayasi, Tulsidas, and Rahimdas. The installation features two screens: a wall-mounted display and a touchscreen. Participants start by swiping to open the "Kavi ke Clue" book on the touchscreen, solving clue questions to discover golden diamonds representing each poet. Each discovery provides captivating information about the poet's life and works, on the wall-mounted display. Hints are available for tough clues, ensuring participants are not frustrated. If they answer a clue incorrectly, the poet is still revealed, and the information begins playing to save time and maintain engagement (Fig. 5).

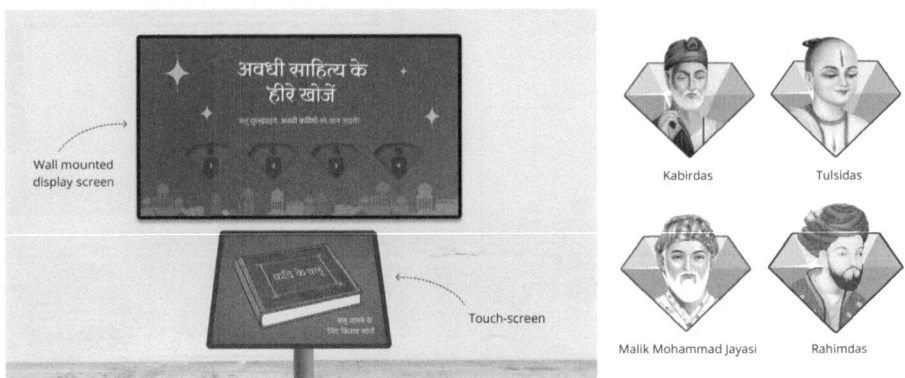

Fig. 5. Setup of the second installation with diamonds representing the four poets to be found.

5.3   Theme 3 Installation : Awadhi Picture Playlist Booth

Our objective is to showcase the current relevance of Awadhi in the Indian music industry and dispel misconceptions that it is only associated with cringe-worthy, 'massy' regional songs. In this exhibit, visitors can listen to popular Awadhi songs and create personalized picture playlists by tapping the heart icon to add songs. Once they have finalized their playlist, visitors can take a picture, which will be printed on a sheet featuring a QR code containing the playlist. The back of the sheet includes interesting facts about Awadhi and additional resources provided via another QR code. Additionally, we offer a section of surprise Awadhi songs that we have uniquely added. This engaging activity allows visitors to take home a personalized and informative souvenir (Fig. 6).

Fig. 6. The setup of the third installation and the participants' picture playlists.

6 Evaluation

We organized a small two-day Awadhi exhibit to evaluate the effectiveness and impact of our installations. The map installation was fully developed, while the other two were evaluated using the Wizard of Oz method due to technical constraints, such as the lack of coding time and immediate picture printing. However, pictures were distributed later. After a quick pilot test and addressing immediate issues, we conducted a full evaluation with 13 participants aged 20–26 years from Uttar Pradesh. We observed each of their interactions with the installations and assessed usability by asking questions after each activity. Issues like adding a pause/play feature for the poet's information were promptly addressed. To measure the overall impact, we used pre- and post-questionnaires to assess the overall impact on participants' awareness. Results revealed increased knowledge about Awadhi, with previously unaware participants recalling many details and acknowledging to be mindful of the negative perceptions of their mother tongue in the future. A subsequent exhibition at Design Degree Show at IDC School of Design, IIT Bombay received positive feedback, with attendees and people from Uttar Pradesh, including professors from IIT BHU, praising the project's importance in promoting state's mother tongues (Fig. 7).

Fig. 7. Images from the evaluation rounds, featuring participants interacting with each installation.

7 Conclusion

To raise awareness and shift negative perceptions of Awadhi, we designed a language exhibit for young adults, from Uttar Pradesh, featuring three interactive installations. Based on research-driven strategies, these installations emphasized upon Awadhi's usage, significance, and relevance. There have been multiple refinements and testing to come up with the final installations. Evaluation had shown participants had more awareness and a renewed appreciation for

Awadhi. Future plans include exhibiting these installations to educational institutions across Uttar Pradesh and exploring additional ideas to enhance them and disseminate awareness. This model can also be adapted to advocate for other regional languages.

References

1. Dash, R.: Revitalizing endangered languages in India, can public-private partnership (PPP) work?. In: Proceedings of the 2nd International Conference on Social Sciences in the 21st Century. Oxford, United Kingdom (2020)
2. Saksena, B.: Evolution of Awadhi (a Branch of Hindi), 2nd edn. Motilal Banarsidass Publications, India (1971)
3. UNESCO: Awadhi in India. https://en.wal.unesco.org/countries/india/languages/awadhi. Accessed 4 August 2024
4. Office of the Registrar General and Census Commissioner, India (ORGI): LANGUAGE (PAPER 1 OF 2018) CENSUS OF INDIA 2011. India (2018)
5. Suryaprasad, D.: Awadhi Bhasha aur Sahitya Sampada, 1st edn. Swadhyaya Publications, Lucknow, Uttar Pradesh, India (2006)
6. Grierson, G.A.: Linguistic Survey of India, vol. 9, Pt. 1 Indo-Aryan Family. Central Group. Specimens of Western Hindi and Pañjabi, p. xv. Superintendent Government Printing, India (1916)
7. Grierson,G.A.: Linguistic Survey of India, vol. 5, Pt. 2 Indo-Aryan Languages. Eastern Group. Specimens of the Bihari and Oriya Languages, p. xi. Superintendent Government Printing, India (1903)
8. Grierson, G.A.: Linguistic Survey of India, vol. 6 Indo-Aryan Family. Mediate Group. Specimens of the Eastern Hindī Language. Superintendent Government Printing, India (1904)
9. Quint Hindi: Boli to anmol hai, jo koi jane bol. https://hindi.thequint.com/voices/citizenq/bol-awadhi-language-precious. Accessed 4 August 2024
10. Awadhi Bani Youtube Channel. https://www.youtube.com/@AwadhiBani/featured Accessed 4 August 2024
11. Bhartiya Bhasha Samiti, Ministry of Education: Bhartiya Bhasha Diwas - A concept Note. India (2023)

Dreamcatcher a Real-Time Generative Art Studying Subconscious Imagery

Fabin Rasheed[1]([✉]) [iD], Matthew Waldman[2] [iD], and Prasad S. Onkar[3] [iD]

[1] Indian Institute of Technology Hyderabad, Sangareddy, Telangana, India
md24resch14001@iith.ac.in
[2] Keio University Graduate School of Media Design, Hiyoshi, Japan
waldman@keio.jp
[3] Indian Institute of Technology Hyderabad, Sangareddy, Telangana, India
psonkar@des.iith.ac.in

Abstract. The Dreamcatcher project explores subconscious imagery by integrating brainwave data with AI-generated imagery to create a 3D sculpture. The project explores the connections between dream imagery and waking life and investigates the concept of synchronicity, drawing on Jungian psychological theories. By documenting images perceived during hypnagogic states, the artwork examines the potential of dreams to reflect deeper psychological insights. The project serves as a non-clinical exploration of how technology can intersect with subconscious processes, contributing to broader discussions on the relationship between mind and technology.

Keywords: Generative art · Dreams · Subconscious

1 Introduction

The intersection of art and technology has always provided a fertile ground for innovation and new forms of expression. In recent years, this convergence has extended into the realm of the subconscious, where artists are exploring the depths of the human psyche through digital means. The "Dreamcatcher" is such an exploration, blending traditional dream interpretation frameworks with modern technology, including artificial intelligence (AI) and brain-computer interfaces. By transforming subconscious brainwave data into real-time generative art, the project creates a dynamic interaction between human cognition and digital interfaces. This interaction not only allows for a visual representation of dreams but also investigates the synchronicity between subconscious imagery and real-life events, offering a novel approach to psychological healing and artistic expression.

1.1 Theoretical Foundations: Exploring Dream Traditions and Jungian Psychology

The study of dreams has a long and varied history across different cultures and spiritual practices. In the West, Carl Jung's work on dreams has been

N. Rangaswamy et al. (Eds.): IndiaHCI 2024, CCIS 2338, pp. 363–369, 2025.
https://doi.org/10.1007/978-3-031-80832-6_25

particularly influential. Jung viewed dreams as a window into the unconscious mind, where symbols and archetypes reveal deeper truths about the individual's psyche. He believed that dreams serve a compensatory function, balancing the conscious mind's one-sidedness and providing insight into unresolved issues [4]. Central to Jung's theory is the concept of synchronicity, the idea that events are meaningfully related through their occurrence rather than causality. This concept resonates deeply with the Dreamcatcher project, which explores connections between subconscious images and real-world events [3]. The concept of synchronicity has also gained attention in recent psychological studies, particularly in how it might be understood through the lens of complex systems theory. For instance, Cambray discusses how synchronicity can be seen as an emergent property of self-organizing systems, where seemingly unrelated events are connected by a deeper, often unconscious, order [1].

Recording dreams immediately upon waking is essential for capturing fleeting memories, processing emotions, and stimulating creativity. Dreams often fade quickly due to rapid memory decay and interference from wakefulness, making prompt documentation crucial. Particularly when recorded as images, this practice helps reinforce details and inspires novel ideas. The Dreamcatcher project enhances this process by using AI models to convert verbal descriptions into visual representations, preserving the ephemeral nature of dreams for deeper analysis and problem-solving. This immediate capture supports both personal reflection and the development of lucid dreaming practices.

In Tibetan Buddhism, Dream Yoga is a practice aimed at achieving lucidity in dreams and using this awareness to explore the nature of reality. Tibetan Dream Yoga teaches that the dream state is as real as the waking state, and by becoming aware of dreams, practitioners can transcend the illusions of both states [11]. Sufi traditions emphasize the spiritual significance of dreams, viewing them as symbolic messages that provide insight and guidance for both personal and collective matters [9]. These practices have inspired the Dreamcatcher project in capturing subconscious imagery and exploring its waking-life relevance, and their application in psychological healing.

Moreover, Robert A. Johnson's contributions to Jungian dream interpretation have significantly informed the project, particularly in understanding how dreams can be linked to real-life events. His work explores how dreams reflect unconscious processes and how these symbolic messages can inform our waking lives, helping individuals uncover deeper meanings and connections between their inner experiences and external realities [2]. Studies by Zadra and Stickgold [12] have shown that dreams are closely linked to emotional regulation and memory processing, providing a scientific basis for the therapeutic potential of dream analysis. This aligns with the Dreamcatcher project's objective to use dream imagery for personal healing and understanding.

Although the larger investigation in the project involved both sleep as well as semi-sleep states, the Dreamcatcher project is rooted in the exploration of hypnagogia-a transitional state between wakefulness and sleep. This state has been historically used by artists like Salvador Dalí and inventors like Thomas Edison for creative inspiration. [5]

2 The Dreamcatcher Project

The Dreamcatcher project is an extension of the Numaverse [7] project, initiated in 2021, which aimed to"photograph" the subconscious and study its connections. The Dreamcatcher was conceived as a way to explore deeper states of consciousness through meditation, using brainwave readings and AI-generated images to create a generative 3D sculpture. (Fig. 1) The sculpture, designed in the form of a dreamcatcher, integrates real-time brainwave data with subconscious imagery, resulting in a dynamic and evolving piece of art that captures the essence of the dream state. The 3D form was selected to align with the artist's ongoing style of creating 3D sculptures, while also ensuring compatibility for future use in immersive media. The decision to shape it as a dreamcatcher was an intuitive one, emerging naturally from the exploration of subconscious imagery.

Fig. 1. The Dreamcatcher sculpture

In the Dreamcatcher project, the artist enters the hypnagogic state while wearing an EEG headset, which monitors brainwave activity. The brainwaves are then translated into data that influences the visual aspects of the dreamcatcher, such as the color and arrangement of its feathers. Concurrently, the artist uses AI to generate images based on the visualizations seen during the hypnagogic state, which are then incorporated into the sculpture. These generated images are studied for their connections to real-world events, synchronicities, and their potential role in psychological healing.

2.1   Creation Process and Technical Steps

The creation of the Dreamcatcher involves several technical steps that blend art, technology, and the subconscious. The process begins with the artist setting an intent before entering a meditative state. This intent is spoken into a set of headphones, and the speech is transmitted to the Numaverse Engine, a custom-built software on the artist's computer. As the artist enters the hypnagogic state, any images or visions that arise are described verbally and recorded through the headphones. These descriptions are then processed by the engine, which uses OpenAI's Whisper API [6] for voice-to-text conversion. (Fig. 2)

Once the spoken descriptions are converted into text, they are used as prompts for DALL-E, an AI model designed for image generation [8]. The images generated by DALL-E are based on a specific style defined by the artist and are integrated into the Dreamcatcher sculpture. The style is defined using a prompt-text which is prefixed to the image prompt. The sculpture is composed of two sections: the upper part, which holds the primary intent image, and the lower part, featuring feathers that are dynamically generated in real-time based on EEG data. The saturation and color of the feathers reflect the artist's mental state during the session, with more vibrant colors indicating a calmer state (as inferred from alpha and theta brainwave readings) and muted colors corresponding to a more alert state. (Fig. 2) The real-time 3D sculpture is built on the threeJS library [10] and the final artwork is a 3D model in the GLB format.

Fig. 2. Parts of the Dreamcatcher sculpture showing the intent image (left), feathers and dream-images attached to the feathers (right)

The combination of these elements results in a unique and personalized 3D sculpture that evolves with the artist's mental state and subconscious imagery. The Dreamcatcher thus serves as both a visual representation of the artist's inner world and a tool for exploring the connections between dreams and waking life.

2.2 Synchronicity Study and Real-Life Applications

A significant aspect of the Dreamcatcher project is its investigation into synchronicity-the meaningful coincidence of events that are not causally related. This study involved the artist creating Dreamcatcher sculptures with images related to seven individuals, selected based on their connection to the artist. During the sessions, the artist asked the subconscious for images related to each person, and the resulting images were integrated into the Dreamcatcher. These images were later shared with the individuals to explore any connections or synchronicities with their real-life experiences.

The results of this study were intriguing, revealing deep personal connections and, in some cases, elements of psychological healing. For example, one participant related an image of a metallic standee with a painting board and a plant to their early experiences in the art world, which had been pivotal in their personal and professional development. Another participant connected an image of a snow skating shoe to fond memories of ice skating with friends, highlighting the emotional resonance of the Dreamcatcher images. (Fig. 3)

Fig. 3. Examples of generated dream images

The study of synchronicity within the Dreamcatcher project not only demonstrates the potential of dreams to reflect personal experiences but also suggests that these connections can be harnessed for psychological healing. By visualizing and exploring subconscious imagery, individuals may gain insights into unresolved issues, leading to emotional clarity and catharsis. This aspect of the project underscores its relevance not only as an art form but also as a tool for therapeutic intervention.

2.3 Future Research and Direction

As the Dreamcatcher project evolves, several innovative directions have emerged that promise to expand its impact and relevance across various fields. One key area for future research is the development of personalized dream interpretation tools that leverage advanced AI and neural networks. By fine-tuning AI models with individual users' dreams and personal backgrounds, the project could enable more accurate and meaningful interpretations of dream imagery. This could lead to the creation of a 'dream dictionary' tailored to individual subconscious patterns, offering deeper insights into personal psychology and enhancing the therapeutic potential of dream analysis. Additionally, the project could expand beyond static images to include dynamic formats such as animations, videos, or interactive content, further enriching the personalized dream interpretation experience and providing more immersive ways to record and analyze dreams.

Another promising direction is the exploration of immersive virtual reality (VR) environments as a medium for dream visualization. By integrating VR technology, the project can offer users an immersive experience of their dreams, allowing them to "enter" and interact with their subconscious landscapes. This approach could revolutionize how we study and understand dreams, making the abstract and ephemeral nature of dreams more tangible and accessible. Future studies could explore how such immersive experiences might be used in therapeutic settings to help individuals process and resolve psychological traumas or to explore complex emotional states.

In addition, the exploration of collective dream analysis represents another intriguing direction for future research. By studying the dreams of multiple participants simultaneously, researchers could identify common symbols, themes, and archetypes that emerge within a group and to understand the collective unconscious better. This could lead to a better understanding of how collective experiences and shared cultural backgrounds influence dream content. Moreover, collective dream analysis could be used to explore how subconscious imagery reflects societal issues, collective anxieties, or cultural narratives, potentially providing insights into the shared human experience at a deeper psychological level.

3 Conclusion

The Dreamcatcher project stands at the intersection of art, technology, and psychology, offering a unique approach to exploring the subconscious. By drawing on traditions and psychology, the project situates itself within a rich history of dream interpretation while pushing the boundaries of what is possible through modern technology. The creation of the Dreamcatcher, with its blend of EEG data, AI-generated imagery, and real-time generative art, represents a novel effort in the field of digital art and psychological exploration.

Through its study of synchronicity and the application of AI in dream visualization, the Dreamcatcher project not only creates a visually appealing piece of art but also offers insights into the nature of the human mind. As AI continues to evolve, projects like Dreamcatcher could play an increasingly important role in both the art world and the study of psychology, paving the way for new forms of expression and understanding.

Acknowledgments. The authors would like to express their gratitude to Ann Marie Alanes, Ashna Sahir, Colborn Bell, Daim Al Yad, Fanny Lakoubay, George Boya, Hernan Ortiz, Indrani Mitra, Jatin Pathi, Mehak Jain, Morrow Collective, and Pablo R Fraile for their support and help on the project.

Disclosure of Interests. Among the three Dreamcatcher sculptures created so far, the NFT of the first one was acquired by Pablo R Fraile to the RFC collection. The second one is in the collection of Colborn Bell.

References

1. Cambray, J.: Synchronicity: nature and psyche in an interconnected universe, no. 15 in Carolyn and Ernest Fay series in analytical psychology, Texas A&M University Press, College Station, 1st edn. (2009)
2. Johnson, R.A.: Inner Work: Using Dreams and Active Imagination for Personal Growth. Harper & Row, San Francisco (1986)
3. Jung, C.G.: Synchronicity: an acausal connecting principle. no. 297 in Princeton/Bollingen paperbacks, Princeton University Press, Princeton, N.J., 1st princeton/bollingen paperback edn. (1973)
4. Jung, C.G.: The Archetypes and the Collective Unconscious. Routledge (2014). google-Books-ID: hmXfBQAAQBAJ
5. Lacaux, C., et al.: Sleep onset is a creative sweet spot. Sci. Adv. **7**(50), eabj5866 (2021). https://doi.org/10.1126/sciadv.abj5866, https://www.science.org/doi/full/10.1126/sciadv.abj5866, publisher: American Association for the Advancement of Science
6. Radford, A., Kim, J.W., Xu, T., Brockman, G., McLeavey, C., Sutskever, I.: Robust speech recognition via large-scale weak supervision (2022). https://doi.org/10.48550/arXiv.2212.04356, http://arxiv.org/abs/2212.04356, arXiv:2212.04356
7. Rasheed, F.: Numaverse (2022). https://nurecas.com/numaverse
8. Shi, Z., Zhou, X., Qiu, X., Zhu, X.: Improving image captioning with better use of captions (2020). https://doi.org/10.48550/arXiv.2006.11807, http://arxiv.org/abs/2006.11807, arXiv:2006.11807
9. Sufi Dreamwork (2019). https://goldensufi.org/sufi-dreamwork/
10. Three.js - JavaScript 3D Library. https://threejs.org/
11. Wangyal, T.: The Tibetan Yogas of Dream And Sleep. Shambhala Publications (1998). google-Books-ID: 1ttOEAAAQBAJ
12. Zadra, A., Stickgold, R.: When Brains Dream: Understanding the Science and Mystery of Our Dreaming Minds. W. W. Norton & Company (2021). google-Books-ID: ADPxDwAAQBAJ

Feeling Lonely-with 20 Others:
The Visualization of Loneliness Using Gen AI
and Digital Narratives

Anisha Mane(✉) iD

Sir JJ School of Art, Mumbai, India
anishamane590@gmail.com

Abstract. The average person goes through 400 emotional experiences every day. We often categorize them to understand our emotional spectrum better. However, this categorization creates stereotypes that can limit the scope of representation. Misdiagnosis of emotions based on such stereotypes can lead to misdiagnosis of the symptoms of more severe mental health issues. In this paper, we have explored possible solutions to such misrepresentations through the personalized creations of the visuals of the emotion of loneliness using Generative AI. This has been done in an attempt to include more holistic visuals of various emotions. A digital platform has also been created, allowing viewers to access the library of stories and AI-generated images of emotions collected during research, Personally created for each story. They can submit their own stories to the collection which will be transformed into AI Images. This participatory model not only democratizes the process of emotional visualization but also fosters a community of shared experiences. Ultimately, 'Emotional Windows' highlights the potential of AI and digital platforms to transform how we perceive and engage with mental health, paving the way for more personalized and meaningful interventions in the future.

Keywords: Artificial Intelligence · Psychology · Loneliness

1 Introduction

Human beings are highly emotional. The average person goes through 400 emotional experiences every day [1]. Humans often seek to categorize and understand emotions, but this process can lead to oversimplification and stereotyping. Emotions are complex and multifaceted, lacking a clear visual image, which makes it challenging to represent them fully. Consequently, any attempt to visualize emotions risks capturing only a single aspect rather than conveying the entire spectrum. For instance, grief is thought of as someone crying, but it can also be expressed through silence, isolation, or even a forced appearance of normalcy.

This paper studies the visual representations of the emotion of loneliness. The author has explored the use of Generative AI tools, to visualize stories of loneliness collected from participants during research. These visuals offer a glimpse into the unseen aspects of this emotion. This exploration culminates in the art installation "Emotional Windows,"

N. Rangaswamy et al. (Eds.): IndiaHCI 2024, CCIS 2338, pp. 370–377, 2025.
https://doi.org/10.1007/978-3-031-80832-6_26

where viewers can witness how others express their loneliness. The installation also invites participation, allowing viewers to share their own stories on a digital platform, contributing to a growing collective narrative.

2 Background

Humans have a remarkable ability to remember specific images in long-term memory, even those depicting everyday scenes and events [2]. The human brain processes images around 60,000 times faster than text, taking only 13 ms to process an image, with 90% of the information transmitted to the brain being visual [3]. This highlights the importance of visuals in our perception.

Similarly, in psychology, visuals play a role in forming our understanding of abstract concepts like emotions. We are highly influenced by the visuals available online and in mass media when forming our thoughts and stereotypes. The mass media are ideal vehicles for stereotyping, because they extend throughout society, and frequently serve as trend-setters, taste-makers, labelers, and the raw material for daily conversation [4].

To ensure an accurate representation of emotions in visuals, it is important to consider a holistic approach to how the emotion is present in various contexts. This is a difficult task since emotional experiences can vary for every single person. Generative AI is one medium that can create very specific images based on words and prompts. The integration of computers and AI with human behavior has been an increasingly growing field, and it has brought about significant advancements in the understanding of human behavior. One promising area of research has been the use of AI tools such as ChatGPT in social psychology research [5]. This paper attempts to explore the use of AI and other digital tools to create visual representations of the emotion of loneliness and present it as an art installation.

3 Method

3.1 Gathering Data

The author collected the top 5 image search results for the keyword "loneliness" from mainstream media platforms, which have widespread use and diverse content, providing a comprehensive view of how loneliness is visually represented online (Table 1).

Table 1. Sources of used data.

Type	Platform	No. of images taken
Search Engine	Google, Pinterest	5
Social Media	Instagram	5
Visual Library	Getty Images	5
Psychology Website	Psych today	5

Each image was analyzed for common patterns and characteristics. The images were coded on the basis of the number of people in the frame, the environment, and the overall mood conveyed by the image.

3.2 Unstructured Interviews

Here, personal experiences of loneliness were explored and compared with the online visual representations gathered in the previous step (Table 2).

Table 2. Participant details.

Participant Demographics	Details
Number of Participants	25
Gender	12 male, 13 female
Age Range	21–31 years
Geographical Location	tier 1 and 2 cities
Background	Varied professional Backgrounds
Location	In-person
Data collection	25–35 min sessions. Responses were recorded and transcribed for analysis

Interview Process. The author conducted unstructured, inductive interviews to gather in-depth personal narratives. An informal discussion was held with each participant based on the following question: "Recall a moment in your life when you felt the most lonely. Could you describe your mental state during that time?".

3.3 Generative AI

The key elements from each participant's story, such as descriptions of their emotional state, details about their environment, and any significant visual or sensory details were input into the AI platforms Nightcafe and Midjourney for further analysis. To identify these key elements, the researcher conducted a thorough analysis of the interview transcripts, focusing on recurring themes, significant emotional expressions, and specific descriptive details.

3.4 Comparative Analysis

A comparative analysis was conducted between the two datasets:
Dataset 1: The top 25 images collected from various media platforms.
Dataset 2: The 25 AI-generated images based on participants' personal stories.
The analysis focused on several key aspects such as the presence of others, emotional tone, and environmental context.

3.5 Installation

Structure. A board with 9 AI-generated images of loneliness mounted on a 3x3 table.

Mechanism. Each Image can be opened like a window to reveal the QR code on the inner pane. (Refer Fig. 1).

Participating. QR code opens a digital platform where viewers can read the 25 stories of loneliness collected during research and upload their own story via a form (refer Fig. 5).

Response. Stories uploaded to the digital platform by viewers will be converted into AI-generated images and added to the visual library.

Fig. 1. Prototype showcasing structure of Emotional Window's installation

4 Result

4.1 Analysis

Online Visual Representations of Loneliness
The initial data gathered from social platforms revealed that loneliness is predominantly depicted through images featuring a single individual. We saw that **82% of Images (17 out of 25)** portrayed a solitary figure, often in a melancholic or isolated setting. These images consistently utilized muted color palettes, shadowed environments, and physical isolation to convey the emotion of loneliness. The composition frequently centers on the lone individual, with the background blurred or minimal, drawing attention to their solitude. The solitary figure is often framed with ample negative space around them, highlighting their isolation (Fig. 2).

Participant Experiences from Unstructured Interviews
The unstructured interviews provided a stark contrast to the visual narratives found online. We saw that **80% of participants (20 out of 25)** reported feeling lonely even while in the company of others. These images showed the various social settings, such as home, school, public places, etc. where participants felt lonely. The images contained a varied number of people present in the scene, including friends, family, or total strangers.

Fig. 2. Top Image results on Google, Pinterest and Getty for the word 'loneliness'

Fig. 3. AI images generated through the data provided by participants about their experience with loneliness.

This showed how Loneliness as an emotion can occur in different settings, and not just in isolation (Fig. 3).

Comparative Analysis
Compared to the online images, the interview-based AI-generated visuals provided a more complex and varied portrayal of loneliness, emphasizing that the emotion can be experienced in both solitude and social environments. The comparative analysis between the two datasets (online images vs. AI-generated images) highlighted several key differences. The online images predominantly focused on physical solitude as a representation of loneliness, while the AI-generated images based on participant stories emphasized emotional isolation, regardless of physical surroundings (Fig. 4).

4.2   Installation

A few responses were recorded from participants who interacted with the installation prototype. Participants engaging with the "Emotional Windows" installation gained a deeper understanding of loneliness by exploring visuals created through generative AI. By interacting with the artwork, they reflected on the diverse emotions shared by others, fostering empathy and insight into the often hidden aspects of loneliness.

Additionally, the installation offers a participatory element where they contributed their own stories, which allowed them to see their emotions visually translated and connect them to a broader community through the digital platform. Participants reported that they felt heard and understood.

A sample prompt, created with keywords chosen from the participant's story and description is - "A 30-year-old male, sitting in his house on the sofa, surrounded by

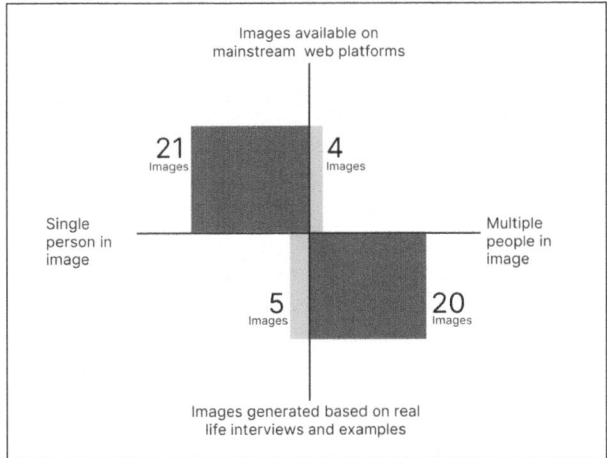

Fig. 4. Result of comparative analysis of 2 datasets

Fig. 5. Screens for the mobile interface of the installation

friends and family who are celebrating his birthday, feeling lonely on the inside, it is nighttime, and the room has one white ceiling light in the center."

5 Discussion

Research has always highlighted the dangers of misdiagnosing symptoms in mental health issues [6]. This is particularly dangerous in the case of loneliness, which is a key indicator of more serious conditions such as depression and PTSD [7]. By utilizing Generative AI, we have been able to create highly personalized visual representations that reflect the intimate and often unseen aspects of loneliness. This can help in eliminating stereotypes regarding loneliness and reducing misdiagnosis. These AI-generated images are not confined by conventional artistic limitations and can evoke emotions that resonate deeply with both the creators and the viewers.

The digital platform further extends the scope of this exploration by providing a space for continuous engagement and participation. This participatory model not only democratizes the process of emotional visualization but also fosters a community of shared experiences. The ability to access and interact with these visualizations online breaks down geographical barriers, making mental health discussions more accessible and inclusive. As AI technology continues to evolve, its application in mental health could lead to more sophisticated tools that help individuals better articulate and understand their emotional states.

6 Conclusion

The interactive nature of the installation, coupled with the digital platform, allows for an ongoing dialogue where participants can see their emotions brought to life and connect with others who share similar experiences.

The installation provides a safe space for individuals to express their feelings, fosters a sense of community, and encourages a deeper understanding of loneliness beyond superficial stereotypes. Ultimately, "Emotional Windows" highlights the potential of AI and digital platforms to transform how we perceive and engage with mental health, paving the way for more personalized and meaningful interventions in the future.

This installation aims to start a conversation around the possibilities of using AI in clinical settings and psychological processes to understand patients' emotions more visually. AI can also be a tool provided to participants for exploring and visualizing what they feel.

Digital platforms that present such visuals, similar to the one in this installation, can bring about a more inclusive narrative on internet platforms and reach out to a large number of people.

References

1. Bradberry, T., Antonakis, J.: Point/Counterpoint Is Emotional Intelligence a Good Measure of Leadership Ability? HR Magazine (2015)
2. Isola, Xiao, Torralba, and Oliva. What makes an image memorable? In: CVPR, pp. 145–152 (2011)
3. Hockley, W.E.: The picture superiority effect in associative recognition. Mem. Cognit. **36**, 1351–1359 (2008)

4. Mickiewicz, E., Browne, D., Firestone, C.: Television/Radio News and Minorities. The Aspen Institute and The Carter Center of Emory University (1994)

5. Salah, M., Al Halbusi, H., Abdelfattah, F.: May the force of text data analysis be with you: unleashing the power of generative AI for social psychology research. Comput. Hum. Behav. Artif. Hum. **1**(2) (2023)

6. Wakefield, J.C.: Misdiagnosing normality: Psychiatry's failure to address the problem of false positive diagnoses of mental disorder in a changing professional environment. J. Ment. Health **19**(4), 337–351 (2010)

7. Cacioppo, J.T., Hughes, M.E., Waite, L.J., Hawkley, L.C., Thisted, R.A.: Loneliness as a specific risk factor for depressive symptoms: cross-sectional and longitudinal analyses. Psychol. Aging **21**(1), 140–151 (2006)

Author Index

The manufacturer's authorised representative in the EU is Springer
Nature Customer Service Centre GmbH, Europaplatz 3, 69115 Heidelberg,
Germany. If you have any concerns regarding our products, please
contact ProductSafety@springernature.com

Printed and bound by CPI Group (UK) Ltd, Croydon, CR0 4YY
29/04/2026
02099544-0011